Hellenic Studies 30

PRACTITIONERS OF THE DIVINE

PRACTITIONERS OF THE DIVINE

GREEK PRIESTS AND RELIGIOUS OFFICIALS FROM HOMER TO HELIODORUS

EDITED BY

BEATE DIGNAS AND KAI TRAMPEDACH

CENTER FOR HELLENIC STUDIES
Trustees for Harvard University
Washington, DC
Distributed by Harvard University Press
Cambridge, Massachusetts, and London, England
2008

Practitioners of the Divine: Greek Priests and Religious Officials from Homer to Heliodorus
edited by Beate Dignas and Kai Trampedach
Copyright © 2008 Center for Hellenic Studies, Trustees for Harvard University
All Rights Reserved.
Published by Center for Hellenic Studies, Trustees for Harvard University, Washington, DC
Distributed by Harvard University Press, Cambridge, Massachusetts, and London, England
Production Editor: Ivy Livingston
Editorial Assistant: Emily Collinson
Cover Design and Illustration: Joni Godlove

LIBRARY OF CONGRESS CATALOGING-IN-PUBLICATION DATA

Practitioners of the divine : greek priests and religious officials from Homer to Heliodorus / edited by Beate Dignas and Kai Trampedach.
    p. cm. -- (Hellenic studies series ; 30)
Includes bibliographical references and index.
ISBN 978-0-674-02787-9
1. Greece--Religion. I. Dignas, Beate, 1968–. II. Trampedach, Kai. III. Title. IV. Series.

BL790.P73 2008
292.6'1--dc22

                                                    2008025657

Contents

Contents

Preface

From an idea to organize a symposium to welcoming participants and ultimately holding a book in our hands ... in our case, none of the steps in this process would have been possible without the Center for Hellenic Studies. When we were both junior fellows at the Center in the academic year 2001–2002, we soon found out that we shared a strong interest in Greek religion. Our *projects* for the research fellowship in Washington differed widely with regard to their themes, temporal scope, and source material. Both of us, however, were addressing the forms and dynamics of religious authority, and the frequent opportunity to exchange ideas became a challenge as well as an integral part of the research we conducted at the Center. It was not long before our casual daily conversations on aspects of our work sparked the idea of jointly organizing a conference. There was no doubt that *Greek priests* would be a topic that offered a multitude of opportunities.

While still agonizing over the practical aspects of our enterprise—not least the complex issue of joint funding by the University of Michigan and the Universität Konstanz—Greg Nagy, the director of the Center for Hellenic Studies and our host for the year, asked us if we wanted to hold the symposium there at the Center in Washington, DC. He was as serious as we were enthusiastic, and a year later the three of us together welcomed a group of fifteen scholars. The three-day international symposium, *Greek Priests from Homer to Julian*, took place from August 25–28, 2003. Prior to the meeting, the Center helped us establish a conference Web site, which enabled us to circulate all the papers promptly and facilitated communication between participants at all stages. Advance reading of all the contributions took place, and participants presented short summaries of their main arguments rather than full papers. Accordingly, there was ample time for discussion, and lively and fruitful discussions we had indeed. We would like to use this opportunity to once more thank all participants for their papers, ideas, and company. Special thanks go to Riet van Bremen, John Dillery, Jon Mikalson, and Anders Holm

Rasmussen, who participated in Washington but whose papers do not form part of this book.

The beautiful setting of 3100 Whitehaven Street, the generosity and considerate arrangements of our hosts Greg Nagy and Doug Frame, and the skills and kindness of the Center's librarians and administrative staff all contributed to the success of our symposium. Thank you!

All of us enjoyed the days in Washington tremendously, all of us learned a great deal and left even more convinced that our topic was an important and fascinating one. As we had envisaged, an ongoing exchange of ideas among participants has continued to take place beyond the meeting. While from the beginning we had intended to present the conference and its insights to a wider audience, we did not like the idea of "conference proceedings," but wanted to work instead toward a volume of essays that would *digest* and accentuate the common theme of the meeting. As editors we are grateful to all of the contributors for the willingness and good spirits with which they responded to our invitation to rethink and reshape their ideas. Not least, our warmest thanks go to Christian Seebacher, who skillfully and cheerfully helped the two of us deal with many aspects of editing the volume. Finally, we are indebted to Stephen Lake for translating two chapters, improving the English of translated contributions and for his vital support during the copyediting stage.

For reasons beyond our control, this final stage has taken much longer than anticipated, and neither we nor our contributors have been able to incorporate scholarship published after the date given below. Since then, works central to our topic have appeared, among other titles J.B. Connelly's *Portrait of a Priestess* (2007). We are, however, no less grateful to both Lenny Muellner and Ivy Livingston for their thorough technical and editorial support.

Albert Henrichs' essay *What Is a Greek Priest?* forms such an appropriate introduction to this volume that we have decided to present our own more general thoughts in the form of an epilogue. May the reader enjoy this book as much as we have enjoyed sharing in its genesis over the past three years.

Beate Dignas and Kai Trampedach
Oxford and Konstanz, November 2006

Abbreviations

AAA	*Archaiologika analekta ex Athenon*
AarchSyr	*Annales archéologiques de Syrie*
AASA	*Annali di archeologia e storia antica*
AD	*Antike Denkmäler*
AK	*Antike Kunst*
AKG	*Archiv für Kulturgeschichte*
AM	*Annales du Midi. Revue de la France méridionale*
AncW	*The Ancient World*
AntP	*Antike Plastik*
AR	*Archiv für Religionswissenschaft*
ArchClass	*Archeologia classica*
ASAA	*Annuario della Scuola archeologica di Atene e delle Missioni italiane in Oriente*
AvP	*Altertümer von Pergamon*
BABesch	*Bulletin antieke beschaving*
BCTH	*Bulletin archéologique du Comité des travaux historiques et scientifiques*
BICS	*Bulletin of the Institute of Classical Studies of the University of London*
CCG	*Cahiers du Centre Gustave-Glotz*
CE	*Chronique d'Égypte*
CEG	Hansen, P.A., ed. *Carmina epigraphica Graeca saeculorum VII-V a. Chr.* Berlin, 1983
CID	*Corpus des inscriptions de Delphes.* Paris, 1977–
Colby Q	*Colby Quarterly*
DGE	Schwyzer, E., ed. *Dialectorum Graecarum exempla epigraphica potiora.* Leipzig, 1923
F.Delphes	*Fouilles de Delphes.* Paris, 1902–
FiEphesos	Knibbe, D. *Forschungen in Ephesos IX/1/1. Der Staatsmarkt. Inschriften des Prytaneions.* Vienna, 1981
Gött.Gel.Anz.	*Göttingische Gelehrte Anzeigen*

Abbreviations

IAlexandreia Troas	Ricl, M., ed. *The Inscriptions of Alexandria Troas*. Bonn, 1997 (*IK* vol. 53)
IAmyzon	Robert, J., Robert, L., ed. *Fouilles d'Amyzon en Carie*. Paris, 1983
IApollonia	Cabanes, P., Ceka, N., eds. *Corpus des inscriptions grecques d'Illyrie et d'Épire I.2*. Athens and Paris, 1997
IAssos	Merkelbach, R., ed. *Die Inschriften von Assos*. Bonn, 1976 (*IK* vol. 4)
IBeroia	Gounaropoulou, L., Hatzopoulos, M.B., eds. Athens, 1998 Επιγραφες κατω Μακεδονιας (μεταξυ Βερμιου Ορους και του Αξιου Ποταμου). Τεχνος Α. Επιγραφες Βεροιας.
ICaesarea	Maritima Lehmann, C.M., Holum, K.G., eds. *The Greek and Latin Inscriptions of Caesarea Maritima*. Boston, 2000
IChios	*Die Inschriften von Chios*. In Graf, F. *Nordionische Kulte*. Rome, 1985:427–461
ICorinth	Meritt, B. D., ed. *Corinth VIII. 1, Greek Inscriptions 1896-1927*. Cambridge, MA, 1931; West, A.B., ed. *Corinth VIII. 2, Latin Inscriptions 1896-1926*. Cambridge, MA, 1931; Kent, J.H., ed. *Corinth VIII. 3, The Inscriptions 1926-1950*. Princeton, 1966
ICos	Paton, W. R., Hicks, E. L., eds. *The Inscriptions of Cos*. Oxford, 1891
ID	*L'Italia Dilettale*
IdCos	Segre, M., ed. *Iscrizioni di Cos*. Rome, 1993 (2 vols.)
IDidyma	Rehm, A., ed. *Didyma II*. Berlin, 1958
IEG	Sircar, D.Ch. *Indian Epigraphical Glossary*. Delhi, 1966
IEleusis	Clinton, K. *Eleusis: The Inscriptions on Stone*. Athens, 2005 (2 vols.)
IEphesos	Wankel, H., et al., eds. *Die Inschriften von Ephesos*. Bonn, 1979–1984 (9 vols.; *IK* vols. 11–17.4)
IErythrai	Engelmann, H., Merkelbach, R., eds. *Die Inschriften von Erythrai und Klazomenai*. Bonn, 1972–1973 (2 vols.; *IK* vols. 1, 2)
IHadrianoi	Schwertheim, E., ed. *Die Inschriften von Hadrianoi und Hadrianeia*. Bonn, 1987 (*IK* vol. 33)
IHeraclea Pontica	Jonnes, L., ed. *The Inscriptions of Heraclea Pontica*. Bonn, 1994 (*IK* vol. 47)
IHistriae	Pippidi, D.M., ed. *Inscriptiones Scythiae Minoris Graecae et Latinae, I, Inscriptiones Histriae et viciniae*. Bucharest, 1983
IK	*Die Inschriften griechischer Städte aus Kleinasien*. Bonn, 1972–
IKallatis	Avram, A., ed. *Inscriptiones Scythiae Minoris Graecae et Latinae, III, Callatis et territorium*. Bucharest and Paris, 1999

IKlaudioupolis	Becker-Bertau, F., ed. *Die Inschriften von Klaudiu Polis*. Bonn, 1986 (*IK* vol. 31)
IKnidos	Blümel, W., ed. *Die Inschriften von Knidos*. Bonn, 1992 (*IK* vol. 41)
IKyme	Engelmann, H., ed. *Die Inschriften von Kyme*. Bonn, 1976 (*IK* vol. 5)
ILabraunda	Crampa, J. *Labraunda. Swedish Excavations and Researches, III 1-2, The Greek Inscriptions*. Lund, 1969 and Stockholm, 1972
IMagnesia	Kern, O., ed. *Die Inschriften von Magnesia am Maeander*. Berlin, 1900
IMilet	Rehm, A., Hermann, P., eds. *Inschriften von Milet I*. Berlin, 1997; Herrmann, P., ed. *Inschriften von Milet II*. Berlin, 1998; Hermann, P., Günther, W., Ehrhardt, N., eds. *Inschriften von Milet III*. Berlin, 2006
IMylasa	Blümel, W., ed. *Die Inschriften von Mylasa*. Bonn, 1987 and 1988 (2 vols.; *IK* vols. 34, 35)
IPArk	Thür, G., Taeuber, H., eds. *Prozessrechtliche Inschriften der griechischen Poleis: Arkadien*. Vienna, 1994
IPergamon	Fränkel, M., ed. *Die Inschriften von Pergamon*. Berlin, 1890 (2 vols.)
IPerge	Şahin, S., ed. *Die Inschriften von Perge*. Bonn, 1999 and 2004 (2 vols.; *IK* vols. 54, 61)
IPortes	Bernand, A., ed. *Les portes du désert: Recueil des inscriptions grecques d'Antinooupolis, Tentyris, Koptos, Apollonopolis Parva et Apollonopolis Magna*. Paris, 1984
IPriene	Hiller von Gaertringen, F., ed. *Die Inschriften von Priene*. Berlin, 1906
IPrusa	Corsten, T., ed. *Die Inschriften von Prusa ad Olympum*. Bonn, 1991 and 1993 (2 vols.; *IK* vols. 39, 40)
IPrusias Hyp.	Ameling, W., ed. *Die Inschriften von Prusias ad Hypium*. Bonn, 1985 (*IK* vol. 27)
ISide	Nollé, J., ed. *Side im Altertum*. Bonn, 1993 and 2001 (2 vols.; *IK* vols. 43, 44)
ISmyrna	Petzl, G., ed. *Die Inschriften von Smyrna*. Bonn, 1982–1990 (3 vols.; *IK* vols. 23, 24.1, 24.2)
IStratonikeia	Şahin, M.Ç., ed. *Die Inschriften von Stratonikeia*. Bonn, 1981–1990 (3 vols.; *IK* vols. 21, 22.1, 22.2)
ITralleis	Poljakov, F. B., ed. *Die Inschriften von Tralleis und Nysa I*. Bonn, 1989 (*IK* vol. 36)
IvO	Dittenberger, W., Purgold, K., eds. *Die Inschriften von Olympia*. Berlin, 1896

Abbreviations

JEA	*The Journal of Egyptian Archaeology*
JRAI	*Journal of the Royal Anthropological Institute*
JS	*Journal des savantes*
LF	*Listy filologické*
LSAM	Sokolowski, F., ed. *Lois sacrées de l'Asie Mineure.* Paris, 1955
LSCG	Sokolowski, F., ed. *Lois sacrées des cités grecques.* Paris, 1969
LSS	Sokolowski, F., ed. *Lois sacrées des cités grecques, Supplément.* Paris, 1962
MIöG	*Mitteilungen des Instituts für österreichische Geschichtsforschung*
MonPiot	Fondation Eugène Piot, *Monuments et Mémoires publiés par l'Académie des Inscriptions et Belles-Lettres.* Paris
OA	*Oriens Antiquus*
OJA	*Oxford Journal of Archaeology*
OMS	Robert, L. *Opera Minora Selecta.* Amsterdam, 1969–1990
Pros.Ptol.	Peremans, W., et al., eds. *Prosopographia Ptolemaica.* Louvain, 1952
RA	*Revue archéologique*
RendLinc	*Atti dell'Accademia nazionale dei Lincei*
RFIC	*Rivista di filologia e d'istruzione classica*
RICIS	Bricault, L., ed. *Recueil des inscriptions concernant les cultes isaiques.* Paris, 2005
RPAA	*Atti della pontifica accademia romana di archeologia. Rendiconti*
SIRIS	*Studi e Ricerche della Scuola di Specializzazione in Archeologia di Matera*
ThesCRA	*Thesaurus Cultus et Rituum Antiquorum*

Introduction

What Is a Greek Priest?

Albert Henrichs

W HAT IS A GREEK PRIEST? It might seem redundant, if not preposterous, to raise such a question in a volume of essays devoted to this very topic. For more than two hundred years, students of antiquity and historians of Greek religion have been in the habit of designating some or even all Greek religious officials, functionaries, and agents of the divine indiscriminately as *priests*. The culprits include some of the most illustrious names in the modern study of Greek religion, from Nietzsche and Rohde to Wilamowitz and Walter Burkert. With rare exceptions, scholars have been all too comfortable in their tacit acceptance and use of this problematic term. As Mary Beard and John North pointed out fifteen years ago in their introduction to a collection of essays on the same subject, part of the problem lies in the fundamental discrepancy between the single word *priest* and its latter-day connotations of a personal religious vocation or sanctity and the wide range of cult-related public and private offices known from antiquity.[1] Despite their awareness of the problem, they did not abandon the controversial term and titled their book *Pagan Priests*, doubtless for lack of a more suitable modern substitute.

For similar reasons, the questionable designation is employed with varying degrees of discrimination in the majority of essays contained in this volume. This is hardly surprising in view of the fact that the term *priest*—like similar key words such as *religion, ritual, cult,* and *sacrifice*—is part and parcel of established scholarly parlance and of a conventional terminology that is more often than not derived from Latin and further compromised by two millennia of Christian usage. Indeed, *priest* and *prêtre* are ultimately derived from the

I am grateful to Beate Dignas and Sarah Nolan for various suggestions.
[1] Beard and North 1990:3 (no. 20 in the appendix below).

1

Greek *presbuteros* (elder) by way of the Latin *presbyter*.[2] But its Greek origin does not make *priest* a more authentic term. Its Greekness is deceptive because the underlying *presbuteros* is a quintessentially Christian designation that has no place in Greek religion, where age and reverence accorded to age carried less weight. In fact children and adolescents could hold religious office, including certain priesthoods.[3] In the first two centuries of Christianity, the semantics of *presbuteros* shifted gradually from the initial emphasis on biological age to one on rank and seniority within the evolving Church hierarchy. According to Lampe's *Patristic Lexicon*, *presbuteros* was used as a general honorific term for teachers, bishops, and "any respected member of the Church," and more technically "to denote a member of a particular ministerial order."[4] In its pristine form, Greek religion was distinctly less hierarchical. Outside Ptolemaic Egypt, for example, the title *arkhiereus* (chief priest) and similar designations for rank did not enjoy wide currency before the late Hellenistic and Roman imperial periods.[5] But age and hierarchy were not the only factors that separated pagan from Christian priests. To make matters worse, Christian presbyters were almost exclusively male; some texts explicitly exclude or marginalize women.[6] Such gender discrimination was alien to Greek religion, in which *hiere(i)ai*—conventionally rendered as *women priests*—were ubiquitous.[7] Against this background, it would be difficult to find significant common ground between the Christian notion of priesthood and pagan priests.

At first glance, the Romance derivations from the Latin *sacerdos*, as in French *sacerdoce* or Italian *sacerdote*, would seem to be slightly preferable, mainly because *sacerdos* appears to be etymologically analogous to *hiereus*, the principal Greek word for *priest*. As Fritz Graf puts it, "*ein hiereus ist einer, der mit hiera umgeht*."[8] It would be hard to argue with that definition from a linguistic point of view, but to describe a priest's activity as "to concern himself with

---

[2] More on the *Wortgeschichte* at Kluge 1975:565.

[3] Burkert 1985:98.

[4] Lampe 1961:1129–1131.

[5] See *DGE* 3.537–545; *LSJ* 251–253; and the index in Poland 1909 for pagan cult titles of this type. Lampe 1961:237–240 details similar titles in the Christian hierarchy.

[6] On the elusive evidence for women presbyters in early Christianity see Kramer 1992:178, 183–187.

[7] No comprehensive study of women priests in Greek paganism exists, but much pertinent information from a variety of sources can be found in Holderman 1913; Turner 1983; Kron 1996:139–182; Dillon 2002:73–106; and Cole 2004:122–136. On the variant spellings *hierea* (the older form) and *hiereia* see Threatte 1980:315, 317.

[8] Graf 1997:473 (app. no. 22). In the same vein Rudhardt 1958:291 ('*celui qui fait des hiera*') and Neumann 1998:342 ('*wer Heiliges treibt*'), among others.

hiera" raises more questions than it answers. What exactly are these *hiera*? The sacred is a vast territory, in Greek cult as in any other religion, and *hiera* can refer to a variety of things, from ritual implements to animal sacrifice. One of the most fundamental functions of the *hiereus/hiereia* is his or her role in sacrificial ritual.[9] This explains why some ancient and modern interpreters understand the *hiereus* primarily as a *sphageus* (slaughterer) or performer of animal sacrifice.[10] But as this volume abundantly demonstrates, Greek priests are more than mere *mageiroi* (butchers); they play important roles outside animal sacrifice.[11]

In the case of *sacerdos* and its modern derivatives, the etymological parallel with *hiereus* is deceptive. Like *priest* and *prêtre*, *sacerdos* and its Romance cognates too have Christian roots which intrude into modern discussions of Greek cult. As Jan Bremmer has shown in his analysis of the reception history of key words such as *religion* and *ritual*, each of these words has a complex "terminological genealogy," as he calls it, and their Christian ancestry translates into a host of tacit assumptions which it is nearly impossible to banish or to eradicate.[12] *Priest* definitely falls into this category of terms that should either be replaced by more suitable terminology in discussions of Greek religion or whose use should at least be closely scrutinized from the vantage point of a heightened self-awareness by those of us who continue to use them, as many doubtless will, for lack of more viable alternatives. I have searched the modern scholarship on Greek priests with little success for signs of such a critical awareness. One of the rare exceptions can be found in a dictionary entry on Greek and Roman priests by John North:

> Greek and Latin have several terms referring to these positions—
> *hiereis* and *sacerdotes* are only the most common; in English, "priest"
> is used as a generic term for all of them, but implies a potentially
> misleading unity of conception and an analogy with the roles of
> priesthood in later religions.[13]

---

[9] Gebauer 2002:471–478. The actual killing of the sacrificial animal and the handling of the *inner organs* (*splankhna*) were left to male sacrificers. While priestesses are widely attested, women performing sacrifice and slaughtering animals are the exception (Dillon 2001:245–246; Osborne 1993).

[10] Stengel 1910:1; Kern 1926:161 (app. no. 10); Gernet 1932:205–206 (app. no. 12).

[11] In purely sacrificial terms, however, the dividing line between the *hiereus* on the one hand and the *sphageus* or *mageiros* on the other is a fine one; see Berthiaume 1982 and van Straten 1995.

[12] Bremmer 1998.

[13] North 1996:1245. Similarly Dignas 2003:40: "Our term 'priest' does not translate into a single Greek word."

North has put his finger on what is arguably the most conspicuous short-coming of the term *priest* as applied to Greek cult. Derived from a monotheistic religion with an exclusively male and hierarchical clergy, the very concept of *priest* suggests a uniformity of identity and function that contrasts sharply with the inherent diversity of Greek religion.

The defining characteristic of Greek polytheism, or any polytheistic system for that matter, is its pluralism, both as a belief system and as an organized conglomerate of cults and rituals. A plurality of gods invites and requires a corresponding diversity of cults, rituals, and cult officials, and that diversity is reflected in the richness of the religious vocabulary. To lump the entire spectrum of major and minor functionaries, officeholders, and repre-sentatives of Greek religion together as *priests* amounts to a reductionism that is tantamount to Herodotus' approach to non-Greek religions. Constrained by his Greek heritage, Herodotus tends to see the religions and rituals of Persia, Egypt, and the Scythians through distinctly Greek eyes that make him virtu-ally blind to the idiosyncrasies and the fundamental otherness of the religious beliefs and practices of non-Greek cultures. His usual procedure is to define and describe non-Greek religions in terms of what they are *not* or do *not* do from a Greek point of view.[14] Herodotus' persistent *interpretatio Graeca* is analo-gous to a distinctive trend in the modern understanding of Greek priests. A widespread approach to the concept of Greek priests is the *via negativa* that defines them in terms of how the Greek evidence frustrates our Christianizing expectations of what priests and priesthoods should be.[15] For example, Ludwig Ziehen, one of the leading experts on Greek ritual in his time, insisted that the Greeks had "no priesthood in the proper sense of the word."[16] Walter Burkert prefaces his discussion of Greek priests with a negative definition of Greek religion that goes even further:

> Greek religion might almost be called a religion without priests: there is no priestly caste as a closed group with fixed tradition, education, initiation, and hierarchy, and even in the permanently established cults there is no *disciplina*, but only usage, *nomos*.[17]

It would seem absurd to characterize Greek religion with its omnipresence of priests as "a religion without priests," and of course, Burkert qualifies his

[14] Burkert 1990.
[15] Representative examples are app. nos. 1, 9, 10–11, 14, 16–17, and 26. On this issue, see now the judicious remarks of Pirenne-Delforge 2005:3.
[16] Ziehen 1913:1411.
[17] Burkert 1985:95.

deliberately paradoxical statement with the telling caveat "almost." He does not need to be reminded that the definitional standard that he applies to Greek religion—the notion of a "fixed tradition," of a "hierarchy," and of a consistent and invariable "*disciplina*" in doctrine and worship—imposes Christian categories on Greek religion and amounts to an *interpretatio Christiana* that is not essentially different from Herodotus' Greek reading of non-Greek religions. We ought to do better than that, and we can, as Burkert and others have shown, and as this volume confirms.[18]

No single term, whether *priest* or *sacerdos*, can do justice to the plethora of words that designate cult officials in Greek polytheism. There is strength in numbers, and that goes not only for the divinities themselves but also for the mortals who serve them. For the past two hundred years, there has been a broad consensus that *hiereus* is the most common Greek designation for the nearest pagan equivalent of the Christian priest. But what is it that differentiates a *hiereus* from a *hieropoios, hierothutēs, arētēr, theopropos*, or, most importantly, a *mantis*? It is significant that in the two essays on seers (*manteis*) in this volume, Michael Flower and Kai Trampedach each explicitly differentiates a *mantis* from a *hiereus*, a term treated by both as the Greek equivalent for *priest*. If I may play the *advocatus diaboli* for a moment, I wonder on which grounds these two instructive and indeed admirable essays on *manteis* were included in a volume on Greek priests if it is indeed true that the Greeks themselves differentiate between *hiereis* and *manteis* and if therefore seers should not be called priests. Protean and ambiguous, *priest* clearly means different things to different people. Like numerous scholars before them, both Flower and Trampedach use the term in a marked sense as a modern synonym of *hiereus*, whereas the title of this volume presupposes a broader, unmarked usage by equating *priests* with *practitioners of the divine* in general.

Let me illustrate the need for proper distinctions in these matters by two examples from my own immediate experience as an academic teacher as well as a scholar with a vested interest in Greek religion. One of the two courses I taught in the 2003 Harvard Summer School was called *Myth and Poetry in Greece and Rome*. Designed for a general audience, it required neither Greek nor Latin. Among the tragedies read was Sophocles' *Oedipus Tyrannus*, on which one of the students commented in an exam: "Oedipus in Sophokles refuses to listen to Teiresias, priest to Apollo." When I read this comment, I asked myself whether Teiresias could be aptly described as a priest or not. In the end I decided, reluctantly, that he was a seer and not a priest. The distinction between

---

[18] Burkert 1985:95–98; Sourvinou-Inwood 2000:38–42.

priests (*hiereis*) and seers (*manteis*) has often been drawn in modern scholarship, and rightly so.[19] The difference between the two is usually explained in terms of their ritual expertise, their professional status, and their mobility.[20] The importance of the *hiereus* was largely determined by the prestige of the divinity and cult he served; by contrast, the authority of the *mantis* depended entirely on the "reliability of his prophecies."[21] Priests were attached to particular sanctuaries; seers practiced their craft wherever their skills were needed—in different cities or demes, in public or in private, on the road, at sea, or on the battlefield.[22]

What exactly is the difference between a *mantis* and a *hiereus* in ritual terms, regardless of where their rituals take place? While both perform animal sacrifice, only a *mantis* possesses the ritual know-how that allows him to interpret the divine will from, among other things, the appearance and behavior of the inner organs of the sacrificial animal.[23] As a sacrificer of animals, a *mantis* must have been virtually indistinguishable from a *hiereus*, whereas most *hiereis* would have been hard put to do the work of a *mantis*. Is Teiresias not a priest because he was not attached to a particular temple or cult—even though some *manteis* were assigned to temples—or, if *priest* is equivalent to *hiereus* in this connection, is Teiresias more than a *hiereus* because he had technical skills that ordinary priests lacked? To put it differently, is the term *hiereus* ever applied to a *mantis* in the Greek record, and did it happen that the same person functioned as a *hiereus* as well as a *mantis*, either simultaneously or on separate ritual occasions? The priests colloquium from which these essays stem produced only partial answers to these questions.

My second example is more complex. In 1985 Richard Hamilton published an important article on the dramatic representation of various religious functionaries in five of Euripides' later plays. Titled "Euripidean Priests," it serves as a reminder that the portrayals of cult personnel in tragedy, epic, and other genres are literary constructs. He prefaced his own construct of Euripidean priests with the following disclaimer: "For lack of a better word I call them "priests," although Euripides uses no one term to refer to all of them."[24]

---

[19] See Flower and Trampedach in this volume. Cf. app. nos. 3; 11; 15; 21; 24; and 28.

[20] Expertise: app. nos. 15 and 28; status: no. 21; mobility: nos. 11 and 24.

[21] Harris 1995:27 (app. no. 21), discussed by Flower in this volume.

[22] Stengel 1920:54–66; Wachsmuth 1967:177–200; Burkert 1985:111–114; Flower in this volume.

[23] Stengel 1920:63 claims, without sufficient evidence, that experienced *hiereis* must have had some mantic skills which allowed them to interpret the *splankhna* as well as other sacrificial signs.

[24] Hamilton 1985:53.

Thanks to the author, I was given access to the article prior to its publication. In the spirit of "constructive disagreement,"[25] I queried the very concept of priests in Euripides in a letter to the author. I pointed out that Cassandra is a *prophētis*, Ion a *khrusophulax* and *tamias*, Theone a *thespōdos*, Dionysus in human disguise a *goēs epōdos*, and Iphigenia the only *hiereia* in that group; that all of these ritual functions are unrelated and not interchangeable; that modern students of Greek religion normally refer only to the *hiereis* as priests; and that the author was taking something for granted for which he ought to have made a case, regarding the alleged affinity between these various offices and their holders in Euripides. Not surprisingly, Hamilton did not reconsider his terminology or his approach, but acknowledged my concerns in a footnote in the published version.

Not much has changed in the twenty years since the publication of the "Euripidean Priests." The questionable term continues to be used indiscriminately in works on Greek religion, while my doubts about its appropriateness are stronger than ever. They were fully confirmed when I examined the scholarship on Greek priests for the past two hundred years and found that generations of scholars have reiterated the same preconceptions and stereotypes in their attempts to explain what Greek priests were or were not. A representative sample of scholarly opinion is collected in the appendix to this essay.[26] Starting with Karl Otfried Müller's *Prolegomena* (1825) and Christian August Lobeck's *Aglaophamus* (1829), there is a distinct tendency to define the essence of the Greek priests in ritual rather than social or economic terms and to emphasize their special knowledge. Müller associates them with prayer and sacrifice, a definition echoed time and again between 1829 and 2001 (app. nos. 1–2, 4, 7, 9, 30). Other scholars speak more generally of their ritual competence (app. nos. 13–14, 25, 26). Nobody will find fault with a definition that equates the function of the priest with the performance of ritual, but the fact remains that the vagueness of the term *priest* vitiates most modern discussions.

It is beyond doubt that the majority of animal sacrifices in ancient Greece were performed by *hiereis*. While some scholars regard the connection with sacrifice as the hallmark of the *hiereus* (app. nos. 10, 12), others emphasize that most if not all of his ritual functions, including his sacrificial duties, could be performed by any citizen regardless of whether he held a priesthood or not (app. nos. 1, 15, 29). Both sides have a point. In the words of Burkert, "sacrifice

---

[25] Hamilton 1985:73n62.
[26] The appendix was compiled with the assistance of Timothy Joseph. All emphases in the appendix are mine.

can be performed by anyone" and "anyone can become a priest,"[27] but a private citizen would not be recognized as a *hiereus* merely by performing sacrifice. It follows that the performance of sacrifice, though an essential *priestly* function, cannot be the principal criterion that defines a *hiereus*.

A more speculative definition makes the priest a "mediator" between the human and the divine sphere (app. nos. 3, 9, 12, 25, 27, 29), a notion presumably inspired by a passage in Plato (Plato *Symposium* 202d–203a). Since no personal or collective sanctity attached to the *hiereus*, the alleged "mediation" must have resided in the ritual function rather than the persona of the priest. In fact I would argue that especially in the case of animal sacrifice, it was the ritual performance itself rather than the performer that mediated between gods and mortals.

The most daring and elusive approach to the Greek concept of *priesthood* assumes "the identification of priest/god."[28] In Burkert, the same idea appears in a slightly mitigated form: "In a number of cases the priest seems almost to appear as a god."[29] As early as 1894 Erwin Rohde entertained the notion of the cultic "*Einigung von Mensch und Gott*" which he defined as a form of ecstasy.[30] In his student days Rohde had been a close friend of Friedrich Nietzsche, who pushed the Romantic construct of a union of god and mortal to its most implausible extreme: "On the main day of the festival the priest is the representative of his god and enters into a mystical union with him."[31] In the same lecture, Nietzsche insists that Greek priests were "originally" regarded "as a temporary incarnation of the divinity."[32] In *The Birth of Tragedy*, Nietzsche argues along similar lines that tragic heroes like Prometheus and Oedipus are incarnations and surrogates of the suffering god Dionysus.[33] This is fascinating stuff that boggles the mind and that is ultimately more German than Greek. Clearly there are better ways of trying to understand how the heroes of tragedy and the priests of actual cults relate to the divinities whom they worship.

Some of the questions I have raised are addressed in the colloquium papers, but others remain open because there are no obvious or easy answers. The word *priest* may well be too convenient to do without, but when applied

---

[27] Burkert 1985:95 (app. no. 15) and 98.

[28] Hamilton 1985:55 (app. no. 19).

[29] Burkert 1985:97 (app. no. 18). Several of Burkert's examples are identical with those adduced by Nietzsche 1875/76:462 (app. no. 6).

[30] Rohde 1894:333 (app. no. 8).

[31] Nietzsche 1875/76:462 (app. no. 6).

[32] Nietzsche 1875/76:464 (app. no. 7).

[33] Nietzsche 1872:67–71 (chapter 10). See Henrichs 2004:132–133; Henrichs 2005:454–455.

to things Greek it is demonstrably an anachronistic misnomer that needs to be queried and guarded against. In my view, it would be better for our understanding of the multifaceted complexity of Greek polytheism and of the distinctive specificity of its nomenclature if the misleading term could be banished altogether from the discussion. I do not expect to see the day when this happens. It is imperative, however, that we stay alert and that we remain mindful of the problematic nature of our conventional terminology. I hope that my remarks may encourage and facilitate this process.

Appendix

What Is a Greek Priest?
Some Representative Answers, 1825–2000

1. Müller 1825:249. "*Daß es aber in irgend einer Zeit einen eigentlichen Priesterstand, im Gegensatze von Laien, in Griechenland gegeben habe, halte ich für ganz unerweislich.* Der Gegensatz hätte sich doch ohne Zweifel in Handlungen zeigen müssen, die dem einen Stande zukamen, dem andern untersagt waren. Nun sind die Geschäfte der Priester in Griechenland: bisweilen eine kurze, einfache *Gebet*formel zu sprechen; mehr oder minder feierliche *Opfer* zu verrichten, wobei viel auf Gewandtheit und Genauigkeit der Verrichtung gesehn wurde; allerlei Cäremonien, z. B. der Blutsühne, die indeß in Athen die Epheten, keine eigentlichen Priester, hatten; Absingung von Hymnen, obgleich diese gewöhnlich Sache öffentlicher Chöre war; hie und da Weissagung. *Hierin ist Nichts, was die Priester von einem Laienstande trennte, da das Alles in allen Zeiten auch Nichtpriester verrichteten*; wie ja selbst das Weissageamt ein Jeder, sein Leben zu fristen, wie eine andre Kunst, treiben konnte."

2. Lobeck 1829:11. "Nullus est qui sacerdotibus plus quam vovendi, dedicandi, *precandi et sacrificandi scientiam* tribuat."

3. Hermann 1858:204. "Wenn der griechische Cultus seinem Begriffe nach ein Wechselverhältnis zwischen dem Menschen und der Gottheit darstellte, so bedurfte er zu seiner *Vermittelung* wesentlich zweier Menschenclassen [Priester und Seher], die zwar im weiteren Sinne auch unter gemeinschaftlichen Kategorien zusammengefasst werden, im eigentlichen Sprachgebrauche und der ganzen Sphäre ihrer beiderseitigen Wirksamkeit aber viel schärfer getrennt werden müssen, als man es in alter und neuer Zeit häufig findet."

4. Hermann 1858:214. "Worin die Geschäfte des Priesteramts bestanden, ... findet sich auch in den näheren Bezeichnungen ausgedrückt, welche namentlich die Dichtersprache *den Priestern als Betern und Opfere[r]n* beilegt."

5. Hermann 1858:215. "Manche Priester scheinen ausserdem bei festlichen Gelegenheiten in der typischen Tracht ihrer Gottheiten erschienen zu sein, wie es denn ohnehin im Wesen jener oben erwähnten mimetisch-symbolischen Aufführungen lag, *dass dabei der Priester die eigene Person der Gottheit darstellte*, ja selbst der Name der letzteren ging aus diesem Grunde mitunter auf den erstern über."

6. Nietzsche 1875–1876:462. "*Am Hauptfesttag ist der Priester der Repräsentant seines Gottes u. geht ein mystisches Eins-werden mit ihm ein.* Hier hat man vor allem an das Hauptfest zu denken, dh. das Jahresfest der Stiftung, wo die Geschichte der Entstehung dargestellt wird, *ist der Priester der Gott selbst.* Er hat die Kleidung seines Gottes an. So sah man zu Pellene die Priesterin der Athene mit Waffen und einem Helm auf dem Haupte, die Priesterin der Artemis Λαφρία zu Paträ fuhr auf einem mit Hirschen bespannten Wagen" (followed by many more examples).

7. Nietzsche 1875–1876:464. "*Aus allem ergiebt sich die ursprüngl. Auffassung des Priesters als einer zeitweiligen Inkarnation des Gottes ...* Jeder Priester ist das Mittel, die einmalige Geschichte des Gottes an jener Stelle zu verewigen, zu einer immer wieder geschehenden zu machen; es giebt im religiösen Leben kein Einmal. Man sieht, das *Opfern u. Beten* ist nicht die Hauptsache im Priesterthum, erst bei der späteren Verblassung des Verhältnisses: im Festjahr giebt es Tage, wo die urspr. Bedeutung deutlich hervortritt, andere Zeiten, wo sie zurücktritt. Der Priester ist ein Hauptgrund, weshalb die Götterbilder erst so spät sich entwickeln; eigentl. gehört zu ihm nur das Symbolon das Unterpfand, das er, als *zeitweiliger Gott*, selbst in Schutz nimmt: er vertritt, den Menschen gegenüber, die Anrechte des Gottes, in Opfergaben, in der Art der Verehrung."

8. Rohde 1894:332–333. "*Das deutlichste Beispiel der Einigung von Mensch und Gott bot in Delphi die Pythia, die wahrsagende Priesterin*, die alles Verborgene in Vergangenheit und Zukunft schaute, wenn der Gott sie ergriff. Apollo selbst nahm, eben in Delphi, wo er der Nachbar schwärmerischen Dionysoscultus geworden war, diese Keime der Mystik in seinen Schutz."

9. Stengel 1920:33. "*Aber ein eigentlicher Priesterstand hat in Griechenland nie existiert.* Es gab keinen Religionsunterricht, keine Predigt, und je mehr ängstlicher Aberglaube schwand, desto seltener bedurfte man eines *Vermittlers zwischen sich und der Gottheit ...* In homerischer Zeit spielen die Priester, wenn sie auch hohes Ansehn genießen, keine bedeutende Rolle. *Die Bezeichnungen* ἱερεύς *und* ἀρητήρ *zeigen, daß sie dem Gotte, dessen Heiligtum sie vorstehn, Opfertiere zu schlachten haben und Gebete zu sprechen*, im Auftrage der Stadt oder einzelner."

10. Kern 1926:161–162. "... wie sich aus dem *einen* Priester, der zunächst alles den Kult Betreffende besorgte und *den Namen* ἱερεύς *erhielt, weil das Schlachten der Opfertiere oft seine Hauptbeschäftigung war*, ein großes Personal entwickelte, wie wir es aus vielen Kulten kennen ... *Einen Priesterstand aber hat es in Griechenland nie gegeben*, so also auch keine Priesterschulen ... Auch von einem Priesterrecht oder gar einem Kirchenrecht kann nicht gesprochen werden."

11. Wilamowitz 1931:39–40. "Ganz so stand es mit den Priestern; *sie boten keine Lehre und beschränkten sich darauf, die feststehenden Formen ihrer Kultpraxis zu erfüllen und die Gläubigen zu derselben anzuhalten.* Sie werden irgendwelche Begründungen für die einzelnen Zeremonien angegeben haben, aber diese Ätiologien haben kaum einen Wert, jedenfalls keinen religiösen. Es gibt *Seher*, von den Göttern mit der Fähigkeit begabt, Vorzeichen zu deuten, die Götterworte zu verstehen, die Zukunft vorauszuschauen. Auch dies wird eine Kunst, die sich vererbt, und der Seher wird oft ein landfahrender, durch seine Kunst geschützter Mann wie die anderen fahrenden Künstler oder Handwerker."

12. Gernet 1932:205–206. "Religieusement qualifié, l'individu peut accomplir lui-même bien des opérations: il n'y a pas, entre laïcs et prêtres, une distinction absolue. Il n'y a pas de prêtre pour une bonne partie du culte: ni le culte domestique, ni le culte des morts n'en comportent ... Néanmoins, là où le prêtre apparaît, *c'est avec le sacrifice qu'il est le plus généralement en rapport.* Il joue, bien entendu, *un rôle d'intermédiaire*. Mais il est remarquable que ce rôle ne soit pas expressément réglé: il est difficile de dire quelle est la fonction propre du prêtre dans le sacrifice. *Le vocabulaire, qui apparente à* ἱερεύς *le verbe* ἱερεύω *(égorger une victime), ferait penser qu'elle est essentiellement de donner le coup mortel à l'animal sacrifié; mais ce n'est pas toujours le prêtre qui s'acquitte de ce soin, il peut seulement présider à l'immolation ...* Il est douteux que l'office caractéristique du prêtre soit l'objet d'une conception définie et *ne varietur*."

13. Nilsson 1967:54–55 ."Mit der Entwicklung der Religion zu einer höheren Stufe, auf der Götter und ihr Kult vorherrschend sind, *entwickelt sich der Zauberer zum Priester, bei dem* das Psychopathische zwar nicht ganz schwindet, aber zurückgedrängt wird und *das Wissen überwiegt.* Vor allem muss der Priester wissen, wie die Götter verehrt werden wollen, *er muss das Ritual kennen.* Der religiöse Konservatismus macht die Priester zu Hütern der Tradition; in gewissen Religionen haben sie das ganze Leben in die Bande des Ritualismus geschlagen. Anderseits bewahren und entwickeln sie das erworbene Wissen; aus ihnen werden die Schreiber genommen, sie regeln den

Kalender, damit die Feste der Götter an den richtigen Tagen begangen werden. *All dieses Wissen steht im Dienst der hergebrachten Religion.*"

14. Garland 1984:75–76. "The competence of the Greek priest extended no further than the enclosure wall of his sanctuary. He had *no religious authority* either elsewhere in Athens or in relation to any sacred ritual other than that which had to do with the particular god or goddess whom he individually served. His duties within his sanctuary were liturgical and administrative. *Liturgically it was his task to ensure that correct cultic procedure was at all times rigidly adhered to, particularly in regard to sacrifices.*"

15. Burkert 1985:95. "*Sacrifice can be performed by anyone* who is possessed of the desire and the means, including housewives and slaves. The tradition of rites and myths is easily learned through imitation and participation; much can even be acquired of *the specialist arts of the seer* simply through observation."

16. Burkert 1985:95. "To ensure that everything is done in proper order, a responsible official is required—the priest, *hiereus*, or the priestess, *hiereia*. *Priesthood is not a general status, but service for one specific god in one particular sanctuary. No one is a priest as such*, but the Priest of Apollo Pythios or the Priestess of Athena Polias; several priesthoods can, of course, be united in one person."

17. Burkert 1985:97. "In Greece the priesthood is *not a way of life*, but a part-time and honorary office; it may involve expense, but it brings *great prestige.*"

18. Burkert 1985:97. "*In a number of cases the priest seems almost to appear as a god.* In Thebes, the priest of Apollo Ismenios is a boy of noble family; at the Daphnephoria festival he follows behind the laurel pole, wearing a golden garland and a long festal robe and with his hair untied—the epitome of the youthful god with unshorn hair. At the Laphria festival in Patrai, the priestess of Artemis rides on a chariot drawn by deer; similarly, when the Hera priestess at Argos drives to the sanctuary on an ox-drawn cart, she is especially close to the cow-eyed goddess. At Pellene the priestess of Athena appears with helmet and shield, and in Athens the priestess of Athena wanders through the streets wearing the aegis. In mythology Iphigeneia is the victim, priestess, and double of Artemis."

19. Hamilton 1985:55. "What do we find when looking at the plays? We find that there is *a development toward the identification of priest and god*, specifically that the priest from one play to the next becomes closer to the god; that his vision of the god becomes purer; that he becomes more permanently allied

with the god; that he becomes more and more set apart; and that his religion becomes more subjective."

20. Beard and North1990:3. *"Two unargued assumptions underlie this general use of the term 'priest'.* First of all, it treats offices in many different periods and societies as if they were broadly equivalent; secondly it presupposes that these offices were specifically religious offices. But it is precisely these assumptions that need re-examination, if we are to gain any proper understanding of the nature of ancient priesthood ... The risk is that the unargued decision to translate any given title by the word 'priest' not only involves imposing our own categories, but also may obscure from us the distinctive nature of that official's role in his own society."

21. Harris 1995:27. "The Priest was one who performed sacrifices on behalf of a group of people who formed a religious association ... *Priests and priestesses derived their prestige from the importance of the cults they administered ...* The seer was very different from a priest. The seer did not inherit his position, nor was he appointed or elected to it. Instead he learned the skill of prophecy ... In contrast to the priest, ... *the seer owed his prestige to the success and reliability of his prophecies."*

22. Graf 1997:473. *"Priester sind Spezialisten für den Umgang mit dem Göttlichen, wie die geläufigste griechische Bezeichung nahelegt: ein* ἱερεύς *ist einer, der mit* ἱερά *umgeht* (wie der κεραμεύς mit κέραμα ,Töpfen'). Das Wort ist bereits in den mykenischen Linear B-Texten geläufig (ἱερεύς bzw. ἱέρεια ,Priester' und ,Priesterin') und bleibt von Homer ἱερεύς seit *Il.* 1,62; ἱέρεια seit 6,300) bis ans Ende der Antike die Normalbezeichung des Priesters."

23. Graf 1997:474. "Nur ausnahmsweise und meist spät *erscheinen Priester und Gottheit so eng verbunden*, dass der Priester in einer Prozession im Kostüm des Gottes erscheint. Frühes Beispiel ist vielleicht Phye bei der Rückkehr des Peisistratos (Hdt. 1.60)."

24. Graf 1997:475–476. *"Neben den Priestern stehen die Seher* (μάντεις)... Auch sie sind bereits bei Homer auf derselben Stufe wie der Priester belegt: Achill will den Grund für den Götterzorn, der die Pest im Lager verursacht hatte, von einem 'Priester, Seher oder Traumdeuter' erfahren (*Il.* 1,62f. μάντιν ... ἢ ἱερῆα, ἢ καὶ ὀνειροπόλον) *Priester und Seher unterscheiden sich vor allem durch die institutionelle Einbindung*: Priester sind an einzelne Poleis und ihre Heiligtümer gebunden, Manteis sind weniger institutionalisiert."

25. Neumann 1998:342. "Priester ist der für eine bestimmte Gruppe (Stamm, Familie oder Gemeinde) oder einen bestimmten Ort (Tempel oder dergleichen) als *Vermittler zur Gottheit* bestellte Kultfunktionär, der in der Regel

auch *heiliges Wissen* hütet (und lehrt) sowie Segen spendet. Sekundär können ihm auch administrative und judikative Aufgaben zukommen. Seine Autorität und Würde gründen im Charisma seines Amtes. Deshalb eignet ihm ein angemessener *(hoher) sozialer Status*, meist verbunden mit geistiger und politischer Macht."

26. Bremmer 1999a:7. "*Priests conducted larger rituals and supervised sanctuaries, but never developed into a class of their own because of the lack of an institutional framework.* Consequently, they were unable to monopolize access to the divine or develop esoteric systems, as happened with the Brahmans in India or the Druids among the Celts. On the whole, priesthoods had no great influence except for those of certain important sanctuaries, such as the Eumolpides and Kerykes in Eleusis and the Branchidai at Apollo's oracle at Didyma. *Despite their modest status, priests must have played an important role in the transmission of local rituals and myths*, and Hellanicus, one of the earliest historians, used priestesses of Hera in Argos as his most trustworthy chronological source."

27. Bremmer 1999a:28. "As *mediators between gods and worshippers*, priests distinguished themselves through their white or purple clothing, and on vases priestesses are often pictured with metal keys, some of which have been excavated; in fact, temples were usually closed to worshippers and only opened on fixed and festive days; it was the altar not the temple which was the real centre of the sanctuary."

28. Parker 1999:836. "*Manteis* (und *chrêsmologoi*) lebten als *rel(igiöse) Spezialisten* von der Religion, wie es ansonsten unüblich war."

29. Sourvinou-Inwood 2000:39–40. "*Not all sacrifices required a priest.* Private sacrifice, even in a sanctuary, could usually be performed by the private individual himself ... It appears that sacrifices for, and on behalf of, the *polis* are always performed by a priest ... *In his liturgical duties the priest was acting as a symbolic mediator between men and gods*; it was the *polis* who placed him in that symbolic position."

30. Gordon 2001:320. "Hauptaufgaben [der Priester] waren die Durchführung von *Opfern* ... unter Einschluß von *Gebeten* ... und die *Aufsicht über die Tempelanlagen* und -eigentümer."

Part One

PRIESTS AND RITUAL

1

Priests as Ritual Experts in the Greek World

Angelos Chaniotis

1. Who Needs Ritual Experts?

IN THE STUDY OF GREEK RITUALS more interest has been paid to the content, context, meaning, and function of rituals than to the persons who performed them—and I should add: for good reasons.[1] As F. Gschnitzer has shown,[2] when secular magistrates and priests conducted ritual activities such as oaths, curses, prayers, and sacrifices jointly, the priests conducted the religious services under the responsibility or on behalf of the political authority; although magistrates sometimes conducted religious activities without the assistance of priests, it was less common for public priests to perform rituals without the presence of secular authorities.

With the exception of priesthoods reserved for the members of particular families—which are in fact more numerous than one might imagine—it was within the realistic expectations of every Greek male of some means (and of quite a few women) that he might receive a priestly office through election, purchase, or lot. And one would also expect that any Greek would be in a position to sacrifice, make a libation, celebrate a wedding, pray to the gods, or organize a funeral.

The performance of rituals was doubtlessly one of the major duties of priests, in addition to the care of sanctuaries and their finances. A Delian decree, for example, concerning orderly behavior in the sanctuary of Apollo assigns the duty of performing an imprecation according to ancestral custom

---

[1] These reasons, all closely linked to the observation that priests were not *servants of the gods* as much as *representatives of their community,* are referred to throughout this volume.
[2] Gschnitzer 1989.

17

to the priests and priestesses (*SEG* 48.1037).[3] When priests or priestesses are honored, they are honored for their ritual activities. An honorary inscription for a priestess of Artemis in Ephesus presents a characteristic example: the priestess had performed the sacrifices and had distributed the sacrificial meat to the councils of the *boulē* and the *gerousia*, to the personnel of the sanctuary and to the victors at the Artemisia (Knibbe et al. 1993 no. 21. *SEG* 43.779); in Athens a priest was praised for offering the *eisiteteria* sacrifice to Zeus Soter and Athena Soteira for the council, that is, a sacrifice offered on the last day of the year before the new council took over its duties;[4] in the same city, a priestess of Aglaurus was praised for offering the sacrifices to Aglaurus, Ares, Helius, the Horae, Apollo, and the other gods on the festival *Eisiteteria* and for taking care of the orderly celebration of a *pannukhis*, a 'night-festival' (*SEG* 33.115).[5] Not every priest received an honorary decree, and this suggests that some of them were fulfilling their duties in a more successful manner than others; they were more generous, or more imaginative in the performance of the rituals, or interested in reviving rituals that had been neglected, or more interested in the staging of a festival. I will return to this point later.

Priests were certainly performers of rituals. But were they also ritual experts, that is, persons who had an expertise that surpassed that of the majority of their peers (of the citizens in public cults or of the fellow members of an association in private cults)? Did they engage themselves more actively than the majority of their equals in the performance, transmission, and shaping of rituals?

Given the usual modes of appointment of priests (election, lot, purchase), but also given the simple nature of most rituals, ritual experts were usually not needed. The existence of sometimes quite detailed cult regulations, as for example the cult regulation of Epidaurus concerning the daily service in the sanctuary of Asclepius, offered a novice in a priestly office the information he needed in order to fulfill his duties (*LSCG Suppl.* 25).

A cult regulation from Cos concerning the priesthood of an unknown deity, perhaps Artemis, defines the duties of the priestess (*ICos* ED 236).[6] Among other things, she should open the temples at sunrise on the days determined by religious custom (*hosion estin*), she should provide for the burning of incense, and she was to organize an *agermos* (collection of money for religious services) on the first of Artemisius. The opening of the temple and the *epithusis*

---

[3] Ca. 180–166 BC.
[4] Matthaiou 1992–1998.
[5] Ca. 245 BC.
[6] First century BC.

(burning of incense) did not require any further explanation; the days on which these ritual actions were to be performed were defined by custom and were probably recorded in a cult calendar; a large number of such cult calendars have been found on Cos.[7] If our priestess had questions concerning the ritual of *agermos*, there was a model which she could use: the *agermos* was to take place on the same conditions as those established for the cult of Artemis Pergaia. Cult regulations, both written and orally transmitted, provided for the norms to be followed by the persons who fulfilled cultic duties for a limited period of time. For several kinds of rituals, including sacrifices, a priest could rely on the assistance of a *hierothutēs* (sacrificial priest), a *mageiros* (butcher officiating in sacrifices), and a *kreonomos* (distributor of sacrificial meat).

But one who tries to find exceptions to the rule that priests are not ritual experts will not be disappointed. Mystery cults require secrecy and, consequently, ritual experts; magic rituals can be performed by any reader of a magical handbook, but nonetheless a specialist is most welcome;[8] with some instruction, a lot of practice, and even more imagination, most divinatory practices can be performed by anyone, but this did not make specialists of divination disappear;[9] and despite the fact that an increasing number of cult regulations provided instructions for purificatory rituals from the Archaic period onwards, still the figure of the specialized *kathartēs* (purifier) was quite common at least until the fourth century BC.[10] In most cases, expertise in rituals was not a requirement for the acquisition of a priesthood, but this does not mean that some priests were not ritual experts or did not become interested in rituals, their performance, their codification, their revival, or their reformation. Although in most cases we know nothing about the persons behind the writing down of sacred regulations, we may assume that they were usually holders of priesthoods. The rare and very vague references to the initiation (*teleisthai*) of priests also suggests that a priesthood required more than the willingness of a man or a woman to accept the expenses connected with this office.[11]

This paper attempts to identify the parameters that occasionally made a priest a ritual expert, both in Classical Greece and in the Hellenized East. The word *priest* is used in a more general sense, not as the translation of *hiereus* or *hiereia*, but as a designation of the personnel primarily responsible for a

[7] E.g. *LSCG* 151, 153, 165, 169.
[8] E.g. Dickie 1999; Frankfurter 2001.
[9] E.g. Georgoudi 1998.
[10] Parker 1993:207–234.
[11] Parker and Obbink 2000. SEG 50.766.

cult. I have not included in this survey references to the Egyptian cults practiced in the Hellenistic and Roman East, since their priests present a separate phenomenon.[12] I have, however, examined the cultic personnel of (sometimes only superficially) Hellenized cults in Asia Minor and the Near East.[13]

2. The Role of Generosity, Family Traditions, and Personal Piety

A first important factor can be seen in the individual attitude of the holder of a priesthood, involving the person's religiosity—which unfortunately can be neither defined nor observed with accuracy; the person's interest in the aesthetic aspects of ritual performance; or in a personal (or family) relation to a divinity or a cult.

A major (perhaps the most important) issue in the occupation of a priesthood was the possession of property and the willingness to spend money for the augmentation of the cult. Many priests and priestesses are honored not for their piety and the performance of rituals, but for their generosity. A Hellenistic honorary decree for a priestess of Demeter in Aenus underlines precisely the fact that she excelled in generosity during her term in office (*SEG* 36.654); Harpalus, priest of the *Theoi Euergetai* (Benefactor Gods) in Beroea, is praised for willingly accepting a priesthood which involved great expenses (*IBeroia* 2),[14] and in Hierocaesarea, the priestess of Artemis Stratoneike is honored not only for her piety, but also for her generous conduct during the festivals of the goddess (*SEG* 49.1567).[15] Gods often served as eponymous priests only because their sanctuaries provided the necessary funds, not the expertise; in Histria, for example, Zeus repeatedly served as eponymous priest of Apollo.[16] Priesthoods were auctioned to the person who offered the highest price, even to children, which are indeed sometimes attested as priests.[17] It is also for the requirement of money, and not primarily because of expertise, that many persons iterated a priesthood, accumulated offices, and sometimes served for life. Flavius Praxeas served in Philadelphia under the reign of Domitian as priest of five different cults for life.[18]

---

[12] But see Dignas on the cults of Sarapis in this volume.

[13] See also Gotter on *priestly dynasts* in Asia Minor in this volume.

[14] *Tēn megistēn kai pleiston deomenēn dapanēmaton hierosunēn eutharsos apedexato.*

[15] Second century AD. *eusebōs kai philodoxōs anastrapheisan en tais heortais.*

[16] E.g. *IHistriae* 222; *SEG* 50.683.

[17] See Parker and Obbink 2000 and Wiemer 2003. E.g. *SEG* 39.1069.

[18] See Weiss 1996.

Finally, it was not expertise, but the importance of the local sanctuary of Athena Lindia for the elite and its mentality that made the members of the Lindian aristocracy follow a priestly *cursus honorum* that brought them from the lower priesthoods of Poseidon Hippius, Apollo Pythius, and Dionysus or the office of *arkhierothutēs* (chief sacrificial priest), to the priesthood of Athena Lindia, and finally to the Rhodian eponymous priesthood of Helius.[19]

But even if expertise was not a requirement for the occupation of a priesthood it could be acquired by long service in the same sacred office—as in the case of a priestess of Athena, who held this office for sixty-four years (*CEG* 757)—or by the occupation of many priesthoods at the same time—as in the case of a lifelong priest of both Aphrodite and Isis Lochia in Beroea (*IBeroia* 20).

Family traditions could also contribute to the cultic expertise of the occupants of priestly offices. Besides the cultic activities of real or virtual family groups (tribes, *phratriai*, *genē*), the Greek communities acknowledged the priesthood of certain deities and the performance of specific cultic duties as the exclusive privilege of hereditary groups based on descent (*genē*). Functional names, such as the heralds (*kērukes*) or the ox-yokers (*bouzugai*) in Athens, indicate the specialization of hereditary groups in rituals.[20] The reorganization of the civic communities in the Archaic period, the writing down of law (including the registration of sacred regulations), and later the diffusion of democratic institutions affected to some extent the mode of appointment of the state's sacred officials and, consequently, the organization of cult. Although new religious magistracies were usually open to all citizens, the privileges of hereditary groups in traditional cults and rituals survived these changes. Also, traditional priesthoods were the exclusive privilege of certain families, and often remained so until the imperial period. Fourth-century inscriptions concerning the *genos* of the Salaminians (*IG* II² 1232, 1237; *LSCG* 19)[21] and the phratries of the Demotionidae in Athens (*LSS* 19)[22] and the Labyadae of Delphi (*CID* 1.9)[23] provide the fullest picture of the sacrificial calendars and the cultic activities of such real or virtual family groups. Their activities included the appointment of sacred officials, the administration of property, the performance of sacrifices, the participation in public cult (Salaminians), the performance of funerary rituals (Labyadae) and the observance of old rites of passage

---

[19] Lippolis 1988f:118–123. See also Dignas 2003.

[20] Parker 1996:56–66, 284–342.

[21] Taylor 1997; Lambert 1997 ead. 1999; Lohmann and Schäfer 2000.

[22] Hedrick 1990; Lambert 1994:96–141; Rhodes 1997.

[23] Sebillotte 1997.

for the children (Demotionidae). It is not certain whether membership in other early religious bodies with specific responsibilities in cult, such as the Milesian singers (*molpoi*) (*IMilet* 133), was originally based on heredity or on other criteria. Until the imperial period the evidence for priesthoods reserved to particular families (*dia genous*) abounds.[24] The existence of the adverb as appropriate for a priest (*hieroprepōs*), which describes the proper conduct of a priest in office, does not suggest ritual expertise, but it does show that the community associated with a religious office expectations that went beyond piety toward the gods. A priest who held the hereditary priesthood of Zeus Pigindenus in Caria is praised in a posthumous honorary decree not just for piety and justice but also for the fact that he had lived his life in a manner appropriate to a priest (*ezēkota hieroprepōs*; *SEG* 45.1515).

But even if a priesthood was not the privilege of a family, its wealth would often make its members occupy or even accumulate priesthoods. In Lagina we know, for example, of Heraclitus Eudemus Demetrius, member of a very important family, who served as priest of the *boulē* for life; his wife Tatarion Polynike Apphia was priestess of Artemis at Panamara for life; both of them volunteered to serve (*ex epangelias*) as priests of Hecate and fulfilled this service with piety and generosity; as a matter of fact, they waived their right on perquisites from sacrifices. In addition to the priesthood of *boulē*, Heraclitus also occupied that of Agrippa for life. Heraclitus and Tatarion handed down this engagement in the cultic life of their community to their children. The decree that honors them underlines the fact that their sons actively participated in the celebration of the mysteries of Dionysus, by performing the ritual cry (*iakhountas*) in all the mysteries (*ITralleis* 51, 88; *TAM* 5.2.931, 954, 966, 976; Şahin 1997 no. 10).[25]

The personal name is one of the forms of self-representation. Although we can hardly use names as evidence for the mentality and the attitude of their bearers, one may still notice that in some cases the name is related with the priestly occupation of a person. When a priest in Thyatira has the cognomen Sacerdotianus (*TAM* 5.2.979); when we see that a man with the theophoric name Dionys (an abbreviation of Dionysius) is a priest of Dionysus (*IG* X ii.i 248, Pelagonia); when a priestess in Beroea is known not only by her name Nike, but also by the *signum* the priestess (*tēn kai hieran*; *IBeroia* 312); when a priestess of Artemis in Callatis has a name (*Kathara* 'the Pure') that at least indirectly associates her with the cult of the virgin goddess and with

---

[24] E.g. *IG* XII iii 868; *IPerge* 241. Horsley 1992; Sanders 1993; Malay 1999 no. 55; Budin 2003.
[25] Cf. Parker 1991.

purity (*IKallatis* 68);[26] when Saitta, a priestess of Leucothea in Sinope, gives her son the name Dionysus (*SEG* 47.1692),[27] possibly an allusion to the myth that Dionysus had been raised by Leucothea—then in these cases we are probably dealing with persons who were more closely connected with the cult of the god whom they served. It is among such persons that one may most expect a strong interest in rituals.

Priestesses are usually represented in Archaic and Classical times as bearers of the temple key, that is, bearing an attribute that underlines their administrative duties.[28] Priests are represented with the sacrificial knife in their hands, an allusion to the ritual under their responsibility. But in several cases we may notice that priests wanted to be remembered because of their ritual activities. The funerary epigram for the priest Phileratus in Cnidus (fourth century BC) specifically describes among his priestly duties the performance of rituals: when offering a sacrifice, he wore a wreath on his head. The most important of these sacrifices was the sacrifice of bulls offered to the immortal gods for the people of Cnidus; the thighs of the bulls were burnt on the altar (*SEG* 44.904).[29] Similarly, the funerary stele of Nike, a priestess of an anonymous deity in Beroea, is decorated with a libation scene (*IBeroia* 312).[30] The priest Philotas in Syria reports in a dedicatory inscription that he had erected the statues of gods "and represented himself making an incense offering" (*SEG* 40.1429);[31] the relief shows the representation of a priest in oriental dress offering incense in front of a statue of Heracles (unknown provenance, ca. 250-150 BC). Another priest, again in Syria (Babulin, near Alepo, ca. AD 250), had his tomb decorated with mythological scenes, divine figures, and cult scenes, which also include the representation of the priest himself performing a sacrifice.[32]

In a few cases we are fortunate enough to be able to see more clearly the importance played by the personal attitude towards a cult for the preservation, revival, augmentation, or more glamorous performance of rituals. In the mid-first century AD Tiberius Claudius Damas, president of the council in Miletus, proposed a decree concerning two banquets (*euōkhia*), to one of which the *prophētēs* (the priest of Apollo Didymeus) at Didyma invited the *kosmoi*

---

[26] Avram et al. 1999.
[27] French and Merkelbach 1997.
[28] Mantis 1990; see von den Hoff in this volume.
[29] Blümel 1994:158–159.
[30] Second century AD.
[31] Bordreuil and Gatier 1990.
[32] Chéhadeh and Griesheimer 1998.

(probably a board of sacred officials responsible for some kind of decoration in the sanctuary), while to the other the *stephanēphoros*, the eponymous magistrate, invited the *molpoi*, the old, respected priestly board of singers (*LSAM* 33 = *IMilet* 6.1.134). We happen to know Damas quite well.[33] Damas held the office of the *prophētēs* for at least two terms; in the year in which he served as *arkhiprutanis*, chief of the council of the *prutaneis*, the city—probably at his initiative—issued coins which bear his name and representations of the gods of Didyma: Apollo Didymeus by the river Canachus and Artemis Pythie. Damas was an individual with a particular interest in the old, revered sanctuary at Didyma and in its rituals, which were often neglected. His proposal obliges the acting *prophētēs* and the *stephanēphoros* "to organize the banquet of the *kosmoi* and the *molpoi* according to ancestral custom and in accordance with the laws and the decrees which have been previously issued." Those who violated this decree faced severe punishment, and the responsible magistrates were not allowed to substitute a monetary contribution for this celebration. We know that such substitutions occasionally occurred in cities of Asia Minor. An inscription at Tempsianoi records that a priest had funded the construction of an aqueduct (ca. AD 180-192); following the request of the city he provided the money he was supposed to spend for banquets for the construction of the aqueduct (*SEG* 49.1556). This is an interesting case of a city asking a priest not to follow the ritual traditions in order to secure funds for the aqueduct. The text from Tempsianoi shows exactly what Damas wanted to prevent. Damas was obviously afraid that his decree would be as persistently ignored by future magistrates as had been the many earlier laws which he quotes on the same matter. His concern must have been justified. Damas himself served as a *prophētēs*, voluntarily (*IDidyma* 237.2); in the text which records his first term in this office Damas underscores the fact that "he performed everything which his predecessors used to perform." Such statements in honorific inscriptions indicate that some priests were less diligent in the fulfillment of their duties; in fact, numerous inscriptions document a general unwillingness among the citizens to serve as *prophētai*, and an even greater unwillingness to perform *all* the traditional rituals. Damas served a second term later, after the office had been vacant for a year; not a single Milesian had been willing to serve as a *prophētēs* at Didyma. *IDidyma* 268 reports that Damas voluntarily served a second term as a *prophētēs*, at the age of eighty-one, and that he revived the ancestral customs and celebrated the banquet in the sanctuary at Didyma twelve days long. Similar references to the rites performed by the *prophētēs* appear occasionally

---

[33] See Chaniotis 2003.

in the inscriptions of the *prophētai*. I suspect that the explicit certification that the particular priest had fulfilled his duties indicate that this was not always the case. And some officials seem to have done more than their predecessors. An anonymous *prophētēs*, for example, provided the funds for a banquet for all the citizens for thirteen days; he distributed money to women and virgins at a festival; he provided a dinner for the boys who officiated in a celebration; and he distributed money to the members of the council on Apollo's birthday (*IDidyma* 297). And two other *prophētai* claim that they had revived ancient customs—their inscriptions are, unfortunately, too fragmentary to allow us to see what exactly the object of the revival had been (*IDidyma* 289, 303). These sporadic references to revivals seem to me to reflect failure rather than success. In any case, the inscriptions of Damas and other conscientious priests leave no doubt that some priests went beyond what most of their predecessors were willing to do.

The case of Damas reminds us that some of the temporary occupants of priestly offices attempted the revival of neglected rituals, motivated by a deep religiosity and a vivid interest in ancestral customs. Even after the end of their term of office they functioned, in this particular sense, as ritual experts. The fact that inscriptions which refer to these initiatives survive does not permit the conclusion that these initiatives were lasting. Damas' success, at least, was ephemeral. From his own inscriptions we know that at least *he* followed the custom; but otherwise we only find sporadic references to this celebration among the numerous *prophētai* inscriptions of the imperial period.[34]

The interest of priests in rituals is to be expected among the holders of hereditary priesthoods. Dryantianus, one of the Eumolpidae, represents such a case. Around AD 220 he proposed an Athenian decree concerning the Eleusinian procession, a cult that was an integral part of Athenian identity and self-representation from the fifth century BC onward (*LSCG* 8). Dryantianus' declared aim was to revive the customary rituals:

> because we celebrate the mysteries now, as we did in the past, and because the ancestral custom obliges us to see to it, together with the Eumolpidae, that the sacred things are carried from Eleusis to Athens and from the city back to Eleusis. (lines 4–9)

Further references to the ritual tradition follow: the supervisor of the ephebes should be ordered according to the ancient custom (*kata ta arkhaia nomima*; lines 9–11) to lead the young men in the customary manner (*meta*

---

[34] *IDidyma* 268, 291, 314, perhaps 322.

tou eithismenou skhēmatos; line 12); another official, the cleanser (*phaiduntes*), should announce to the priestess of Athena the arrival of the sacred things according to the custom of the forefathers (*kata ta patria*; line 16). The preoccupation with the maintenance of these customs implies that they were sometimes neglected. Indeed,

> the *kosmētēs* (the supervisor of the ephebes) who is in office, year after year, should take care that this custom will never be omitted and that the piety toward the goddesses will not be neglected. (lines 22–25)

Dryantianus is, however, not only appealing to piety and tradition. He is clearly interested in a spectacular performance of rituals in order to impress an audience. The ephebes should march in armor, wearing myrtle, "so that the sacred objects will be carried with a stronger escort and a longer procession" (lines 30–31). Other priests took steps in order to secure the funds customarily allocated to rituals,[35] proposed measures for the dedication of cult statues and *paraphernalia* of rituals,[36] or wrote down the customary cult regulations (for example, the Athenian *exēgētai*, the 'expounders of sacred law').

3. Ritual Experts for Local Rituals

Both Damas and Dryantianus repeatedly occupied religious magistracies; both men proposed decrees in the assembly as *experts*, in the sense that they had occupied themselves with the ritual traditions they aimed at preserving. Damas' motivation was his piety, while in the case of Dryantianus we are dealing with a ritual expert in an additional sense: a member of a family that had the hereditary privilege of transmitting and performing customary rituals. Both Damas and Dryantianus were concerned with local rituals, which were only performed in Didyma and in Athens and Eleusis respectively. It is reasonable to assume that local ritual particularities more likely required (or attracted the interest of) experts rather than common rituals such as sacrifice or libation. A Hellenistic decree of Tlos concerning the election of a priest (*TAM* 2.548; *LSAM* 78) required, for example, that the priest be experienced (*andra ton empeirotaton*), be present at all sacrifices (*dunēsomenon pareinai pasais tais thusiais*), and be careful that the traditional local sacrifices (*tas paradedom-*

---

[35] See e.g. Malay 1999 no.131 = *SEG* 49.1676. Cf. *IMilet* 1.9.360; *IEphesos* 213. See also Dignas 2002.
[36] E.g. *IMylasa* 895–897. Geagan 1991.

enas thusias hupo tōn progonōn) were performed in a worthy manner (*endoxōs*) and according to ancestral custom (*kata ta patria*).

Local rituals remained very popular throughout the Hellenistic and Roman imperial periods; in fact their popularity seems to have increased from the Hellenistic period onwards, because of the role played by rituals for the construction of a local identity. Dozens of designations of religious personnel active in local cults—such as the *kistiokosmos* (the adorner of the basket) of Athena Kypharissia in Messene (*SEG* 39.381), the *purphoros hieras nuktos* (the torch bearer of the sacred night) in the sanctuary of Apollo Maleatas in Epidaurus (*SEG* 39.358), the *diabetria* in the service of Artemis at Mopsuestia (see below), the *kunēgoi* 'hunters' in the service of Heracles Kunagidas in Beroea,[37] the *periaktria* (a person responsible for a procession?) in the service of Artemis in Cyrene (*SEG* 9.13), or the *essenes* of Artemis in Ephesus[38]—are only a faint reflection of a large variety of ritual practices.

Even a designation as common as that of the *loutrophoros*, the water-bearer (in the service of Artemis Boulaia in Miletus and Artemis Kindyas in Bargylia) may in fact be connected with very specific ritual practices. The cult of Aphrodite in Sicyon was served by a virgin called a *loutrophoros* and by a *neokoros* (temple warden) who was not allowed to have sexual intercourse (Pausanias 2.10.4). It has been suggested that the *loutrophoria* was a nuptial bath intended to promote fecundity.[39] Another ritual for which the expertise of a priestess was required is the enigmatic ritual of the *nuktophulaxia* (night watch) at Delos. Little is known about this ritual,[40] but what is known suggests that we are dealing with a unique ritual, probably at the Thesmophoria, during which a doorway in the sanctuary of Demeter was broken through and put back up again, under the direction of the priestesses of Demeter and Kore (*IG* XI 154, 287); this may refer to the opening and closing of the *megaron*, when a sow was thrown into it and when her remains were removed. A rather puzzling Hellenistic inscription from Cizicale (*SEG* 36.1235)[41] probably commemorates the performance of an uncommon ritual (a ritual dance?) by a priest ("Crateros, son of Hermocrates, priest, leaped").

Expertise was certainly required for the priesthood of the *hudroskopos* in Macedonia (*IBeroia* 509),[42] for the complex rituals of propitiation described

---

[37] Hatzopoulos 1994:101–110.
[38] On these see Bremmer in this volume.
[39] See Pirenne-Delforge 1994.
[40] See Robertson 1996; Schachter 1999; Salviat 2001.
[41] See French 1996:95–96.
[42] Casadio 1994:250.

in the confession inscriptions (see below), and probably also for the hereditary position of the *thoinarmostria* (the mistress of the banquet) in the cult of
Demeter in Sparta.[43] When a key bearer (*kleidophoros*) and priestess of Hecate
is praised in Stratonicea for the organization of the procession of the keys
(*kleidōn pompē*; *IStratonikeia* 1048M; *SEG* 38.1083), it is certainly not because she
had fulfilled a routine duty, but possibly for the performance of the ritual in
an aesthetically appealing manner.

A combination of generosity and respect for customary rituals that
required some expertise can be seen in the honorary inscriptions for two
women in first-century Mantinea (*IG* V ii 265–266).[44] Nicippa and Phaena were
honored for their active participation in the religious life of their city and for
their financial support of traditional cults. Nicippa assisted the priestesses of
Kore in dressing and decorating the cult statue, accepted und fulfilled with
generosity the liturgy of financing the sacrifices at the festival of the Coragia,
led the procession, dedicated a peplos to Kore, took care of the housing and the
proper performance of the mysteries, and financed the necessary construction work in the temple. Phaena was honored by the board of the priestesses
of Demeter for her generous contributions to this cult, which are described in
more general terms than in the decree for Nicippa; but it is interesting to note
that her generosity was continued for at least two more generations by her
daughter Theodora and her grand-daughter Phaena.

A special interest in ritual traditions can also be observed among priests
in late antiquity, when pagan rituals were in danger both because of lack of
faith and because of imperial legislation. A fourth-century honorary epigram
from Patmos is an instructive example of a priestess who was dedicated to the
revival of neglected rituals (Merkelbach and Stauber 1998:01/21/01). Vera was
selected by Artemis to be her priestess; as a *hudrophoros* (observer or finder
of water) she came from Lebedus to Patmus, where according to the local
tradition a statue of Artemis existed, brought by Orestes from Scythia. In this
holy place Vera celebrated a festival which included a very special sacrifice:
the sacrifice of a pregnant she-goat. Even later, probably in the fifth century,
a pagan priest in Megara, Helladius, set up an inscription in the monument to
the dead of the Persian Wars, restored an epigram attributed to Simonides,
and added the remark that "the city offered sacrifices up to this day" (*IG*
VII 53); it would be a mistake to take this statement as proof that this ritual
had been continually performed in Megara for ten centuries. Long after the

---

[43] Walker 1989.
[44] Jost 1996.

prohibition of pagan sacrifices, Helladius provocatively defied the laws of the Christian emperors; his performance of a heroic sacrifice was a revival rather than a survival.

Although the aforementioned examples allude to complex services, they still concern rituals that can be found almost everywhere: the decoration of the statue of a goddess, processions, sacrifices, banquets. A higher degree of expertise can be assumed in the case of unique rituals, such as fire-walking, attested for the priestesses of Artemis Perasia in Mopsuestia. A funerary inscription for a priestess (second/third century) is of special interest, since it combines two of the parameters that we have already seen: the performance of a unique local ritual and the use of onomastics in the self-representation of religious officials. The epitaph, published with a detailed commentary by H. Taeuber,[45] is dedicated to Eutychia, who was a *diabetria Perasias*, that is, priestess of the Anatolian Mother Goddess Perasia, who was worshipped in Hierapolis-Castabala and was associated with Artemis, Hecate, Selene, Demeter, and Aphrodite; the unique name of this priesthood is related to the ritual of walking on burning coals (Strabo 12.2.7);[46] Eutychia's agnomen, Metereine, derives from Meter (the Mother Goddess) and is also related to her office.

4. Ritual Experts for Exclusive Rituals

Most rituals are performed in order to establish communication between an individual or a group of persons and superhuman beings; the communication usually fulfills a very particular purpose. The results of initiatory rituals are, however, of a more permanent nature: life-cycle rituals change the status of a person, while initiation into certain mystery cults establishes a permanent and privileged relation with a divinity both during one's lifetime and after death. Given the secrecy of initiatory cults, it is not easy to determine the role of the priests, not as performers of rituals, but as ritual experts. One of the rare pieces of evidence that reveal an expertise in this respect is the epitaph of Alcmeonis, a priestess of Dionysus in Miletus (*IMilet* 6.2.733).[47] The statement that "she knew the destiny reserved for the virtuous" (*kalōn moira*) clearly shows that Alcmeonis combined the public office of the priestess with a religious experience relating to private eschatological expectations (probably beliefs related to the *Dionysiac-Orphic* mysteries). The case of Alcmeonis

---

[45] Taeuber 1992.
[46] Furley 1988:212–222.
[47] Cf. Villanueva-Puig 1998.

reveals the close interaction between public and private rituals.[48] One expected the priestess of Dionysus not only to preside over the *dēmosios thiasos* (public Dionysiac association) and to perform the rites on behalf of the polis, but also to exercise some control over the private *thiasoi*. The latter had to pay a fee for the initiation of women.[49] This stipulation is probably more than an effort to increase the revenues of *the* public cult of Dionysus: it seems to have aimed at putting the private *thiasoi* under some kind of public control, the more so given the orgiastic and potentially uncontrolled nature of the cult. But the expertise (*epistamenē*) of Alcmeonis does not exclude the possibility that we are dealing with a normative interference of the polis which wanted to guarantee the proper conduct of the ritual.

The case of the cult of the Corybantes in Erythrae is similar, both in the regulations and in the uncertainties of their interpretation. The regulations are included in a fragmentary cult regulation (ca. 350–300), of which a new fragment was published only a few years ago (*IErythrai* 2.206; *LSAM* 23, 25; *SEG* 46.1463; 47.1628).[50] The first lines seem to determine the sequence of sacrificial animals. Then the text stipulates that the purchaser of the priesthood (man or woman) would receive perquisites from all public sacrifices. The fact that the public priesthood could be purchased rules out the possibility that a ritual expert was needed; the priesthood required money, not expertise. The following regulations are also concerned with the perquisites the priest received from private sacrifices on public altars. The most revealing lines stipulate that when another priest performed the initiation or another priestess performed the rituals of washing (*louō*) and *krētēriazein* (mixing a bowl of wine?), he or she should give to the purchaser of the priesthood half of the revenues (lines 11–16). The law also stipulates that the purchaser of the priesthood had the right to swear in (*aporkisai*) the other priests and priestesses as well as the men and women who had been initiated (*telestheisas*) and washed (*loutheisas*). and who had performed the ritual of *krētēriazein* under the priests' supervision (lines 17–24). Himmelmann has observed that the text reveals the effort of the city to control the hitherto private worship of the Corybantes and to make all other priests and priestesses of the Corybantes pay dues to the purchaser of the priesthood.[51] Ritual expertise was needed, as the specific terminology implies (*teleō, louō, krētēriazō*), but the ritual expert was not the

[48] On this interaction see also Dignas in this volume.

[49] Cf. *LSAM* 48; *LSCG* 166.

[50] Cf. Voutiras 1996; Himmelmann 1997; Ustinova 1992–1998; Dignas 2002a; Herrmann 2002.

[51] With a different interpretation see Dignas 2002a.

purchaser of the priesthood; Y. Ustinova is *probably* right in her assumption that the priest was in charge of the sacrifices and the general supervision, while the ecstatic part was the responsibility of a religious expert. After the sacrifice a healer—the religious expert—drove the patient into an altered state of consciousness through music, incantation, and dance. R. M. Simms[52] has observed that a Phrearrhian cult regulation is exhaustively detailed in comparison to other *leges sacrae* (*SEG* 35.113).[53] According to his plausible explanation, this is so because the regulation describes rites connected with the Eleusinian mysteries; these rites obviously surpassed the sphere of common local priestly knowledge and required ritual experts.

The personal contribution of a priest and his family to a mystery cult can best be seen in an inscription honoring the priest Trocondas in Cremna.[54] Trocondas was hereditary priest (*kata diadokhēn dia genous*) of Artemis Ephesia. He was succeeded by his daughter Artemis; once again we observe the use of a personal name that underlines the personal relationship between priest(ess) and deity. The inscription informs us that Trocondas' family had provided the temple and the statue of Artemis, which suggests that the family had probably introduced the cult. Trocondas watched over the mysteries of Artemis with purity and in the manner appropriate to the goddess (*teterekota hagnōs kai theoprepōs*) and developed them further. The mysteries were introduced after the discovery of an item, for example, a written document—a cult regulation as in the case of the mysteries of Andania?—and were transmitted further within the family (*ta heurēthenta kai paradothenta hierotelē musteria*). The priest himself is represented in relief, wreathed, offering a libation in front of the temple and the statue of the seated goddess. The activity of Trocondas' ancestor who introduced the cult may be compared with that of Alexander of Abunoteichos in introducing a mystery cult modeled on the Eleusinian mysteries[55] or with that of Dionysius, the founder of an association of mystae in Philadelphia, who received the rituals and the rules of purity from Zeus while asleep.[56]

5. Ritual Experts for Body and Soul

Besides the expertise needed for the specific rituals of mystery cults, one may assume that rituals which went beyond the routine of public celebration

---

[52] Simms 1998.
[53] Ca. 300 BC.
[54] Horsley 1992 (first century AD).
[55] See Chaniotis 2002.
[56] Barton and Horsley 1981.

(procession, sacrifice, libation, prayer, and so on) and which corresponded to very individual needs were also tasks for ritual experts.

A dedication to Artemis Anaitis from Lydia reports that a woman made the dedication in fulfillment of a vow, because she had been cured from a disease by the priestess through incantation (*TAM* 5.1.331). Incantations are not necessarily performed by priests,[57] but in this particular case the diseased person entrusted her life to the hands of a priestess, obviously in expectation of better results through the performance of the incantation by a priestess as a ritual expert. It is from the same region (Lydia and Phrygia) that we get more information of specific rituals which required experts.

The confession inscriptions explicitly mention, allude to, or simply presuppose rituals involving priests.[58] The priests were responsible for cursing culprits; receiving written *prayers for justice*;[59] administering promissory and exculpatory oaths; and for explaining to visitors to the sanctuaries, who believed that they were being persecuted by the gods, the reason for their divine punishment (usually by means of oracles), and assisting them in atoning for their misdemeanors. Two rituals, in particular, reveal expertise: the public imprecation (to set up a scepter) and the transmission of sin to a triad of animals. The expression *to set up a scepter* appears in several variants in the inscriptions of Lydia and designates the erection of a symbol of divine power—probably in a sanctuary—during a ceremony of imprecation.[60] The erection of the scepter aimed both at preventing future crimes and at punishing offences already committed, usually by unknown offenders. We may assume that the ceremony was performed by the priests, who are in fact occasionally depicted on stelae with a scepter (the god's scepter?) in one hand. One of the rituals for which the sinners certainly needed assistance from priests is called a *triphonon* (triad of voices) in one text, and an *enneaphonon* (ennead of voices) in another, still-unpublished text. The confession of a certain Theodorus presents a description of the ritual.[61] After the mention of each sin we find the formula *he takes away* followed by a triad of animals—in the first case a sheep, a partridge, and a mole; in the second case, three kinds of fish; in the third case, a chicken, a sparrow, and a pigeon. The triads of animals probably represent various elements: the earth, the sky, and the area under the surface of

---

[57] Cf. Furley 1993.

[58] Cf. Chaniotis 2004b and 2008.

[59] Versnel 1991; Chaniotis 2004b:8–9.

[60] Robert 1983:518–520; Strubbe 1991:44–145; Petzl 1994:4, 89–90; Strubbe 1997:48; Gordon 2004:185–187.

[61] Petzl 1994:8–11; Chaniotis 2004b.

the earth. The object of the verb *to take away* is only once explicitly stated: it is the sin (not the illness). E. Varinlioğlu points out that the ritual transmission of the sin to animals recalls scapegoat rituals,[62] but finds its closest parallels in Hittite rituals which include the release of birds, fish, and mice supposed to carry an evil away.[63] Incantations accompany the ritual. The *triphonon* and the *enneaphonon* are hitherto unknown outside of Lydia, but there can be little doubt that in this case we have a ritual with a long local tradition expressed in Greek terms. The fact that the sinners had to receive instructions from the priests regarding the removal of sins shows that in this case the priests functioned as upholders of tradition and as ritual experts. This also applies to other rituals of atonement that could be performed only by priests and that are mentioned in the confession inscriptions. A text from Cula (?) dated AD 168/9 reports, for example, that the priests propitiated Men Axiotenus after supplication, following the god's command (Malay 1999 no. 111 = *SEG* 49.1720).

6. All Priests Are Zealous, but Some Are More Zealous than Others

This brief survey of the epigraphic evidence concerning the activities of priests confirms the *communis opinio* that, in general, persons in antiquity who acquired priesthoods by election, purchase, or lot were not ritual experts, while ritual expertise was to be expected among hereditary priests. And yet, some priests became ritual experts because of their personal commitment and their religiosity, sometimes because of their long service in a cult. Their expertise can be seen in their efforts to write down cultic regulations—as several *leges sacrae* suggest—in the proposal of measures for the restoration or more impressive performance of rituals, and in the performance of unusual rituals. This personal commitment is sometimes reflected by onomastic practices or by the self-representation of priests in their epitaphs. Such priests could even acquire the status of holy figures, either during their lifetime (compare Alexander of Abunoteichos) or after their death.

An inscription in Lydia records the dedication of an altar for a dead priestess by the association of *mustai* (*TAM* 5.2.1055). The deceased priestess was believed to have divinatory powers, and people seeking the truth were to pray in front of her altar in order to receive an answer by means of visions that would come either during the day or at night. It should not be surprising

---

[62] Varinlioğlu 1989:48–49.
[63] Cf. Wright 1987.

that this text—like much of the evidence mentioned in this survey—concerns a mystery cult.

Part Two

VARIATIONS OF PRIESTHOOD

2

Priestly Personnel of the Ephesian Artemision
Anatolian, Persian, Greek, and Roman Aspects

Jan Bremmer

THE INDO-EUROPEANS had neither a separate priestly class nor a specific term for priests or priestesses. This tradition may be one of the reasons why the Greeks had no clearly defined priestly class either. Every city could develop its own organization and vocabulary,[1] and the larger the city, the more specialized and developed priesthoods could become. In spite of this absence of an established order we tend to impose our own Judaeo-Christian ideas of priesthood on the Greeks. In other words, while we may be inclined to think of one particular kind of person, the Greeks included several kinds of religious officials within the term *priest(ess)*,[2] who had neither the same duties nor the same training as *our* priests.

The lack of a sharply defined function must have favored the incorporation of native institutions in areas like Ionia, where the Greeks were relatively late arrivals. One such example is undoubtedly the complex cult of Artemis at Ephesus. Hers was a particularly hospitable cult that in the course of time incorporated Anatolian, Persian, Cretan and Roman influences. The last full survey of all *priestly* functions within the cult of Artemis was presented in 1922, when Charles Picard published his still valuable study of Ephesus and Claros.[3] Since then we have seen only two more, if much less detailed, attempts at surveying the major priesthoods.[4] Recent decades have

I thank Beate Dignas, Jitse Dijkstra, and Stelios Panayotakis for information and comments.

[1] See the still useful survey in Kretschmer 1930:81–89.

[2] *Term*, of course, does not correspond to *vocabulary* here. The *one* person we might expect may be called *hiereus/hiereia* or by any other title. My discussion below gives many examples.

[3] Picard 1922:162–197 (*Megabyxos, essēnes,* priestesses), 277–287 (*Kouretes*).

[4] Talamo 1984:197–216 (no discussion of the priestesses); Burkert 1999:59–70 (no discussion of the *Kouretes*); on the *Megabyxos,* see also Burkert 2004:105–107.

witnessed an increasing interest in the Anatolian background of Greek religion,[5] a growing knowledge of ancient Persian onomastics,[6] a steady stream of newly published Ephesian inscriptions and new insights on the relation between myth and ritual.[7] A new analysis, then, is not out of place—the more so, since not even the literary evidence has been fully exploited. I shall therefore discuss the characteristics of religious functions at the Artemision in light of their complex background; the paper focuses on those officials who are referred to as priests in our sources[8], carried out tasks of priests, such as sacrificing,[9] or are called priests in modern discussions. In *Ephesian terms* this means that the study examines the *Megabyxos*, the male priests of the Roman period, the priestess, the *essēnes* and the *Kouretes*. Finally, I shall consider how my observations bear on the character of Greek priesthood in general.

1. The *Megabyxos*

As the Old Persian (DB IV 85), Elamite (DB elam. III 91), and Babylonian (DB babylon. 111) versions of Darius' famous inscription on the rock of Behistun attest, there was a Persian named Bagabuxša among the seven conspirators against the false Smerdis (§68). At least from Herodotus (3.70.3) onwards, the Greeks transcribed the name as *Megabyxos*, and the same name is attested as the title of the temple warden of Ephesian Artemis.[10] Although it literally means *He who serves (satisfies) God*,[11] there is no reason to assume that the warden demonstratively accepted the Persian title to stress his relation to the goddess.[12] After all, our oldest known *Megabyxoi* were no temple officers at all. We simply do not know how and when the Ephesian *Megabyxos* acquired his name. Yet his name strongly suggests that at some point a Persian had replaced a Greek after the Persian conquest of Ephesus around 500 BC, just like the Galatians had taken over the wealthy priesthood of Pessinous after their

---

[5] Burkert 1992, 2003 and 2004; West 1997.

[6] See especially the many studies of Rüdiger Schmitt; cf. the bibliography in Breidbach and Huyse 2000.

[7] See Bremmer 1992:265–276 and 2005:21-43; Burkert 2002:1–22.

[8] Again, this is not limited to *hiereis* but also refers to a Greek *equivalent* of this.

[9] For this and other priestly prerogatives in the context of daily ritual activities, see Chaniotis in this volume.

[10] See now Bremmer 2004a:9–10. For a discussion of the name and function of the *Megabyxos*, see Smith 1996: 323–335, which, however, is not very helpful.

[11] Benveniste 1966:108–117; accepted by Miller 1968:846; Mayrhofer 1979:16; Schmitt 2002:63.

[12] *Contra* Burkert 1999:63 and 2004:106.

invasion of Asia Minor in the third century BC.[13] Yet the fact that *Megabyxos* became a generic proper name may have been an Anatolian feature of the cult: the main priests of Pessinous called themselves *Attis* and those of Cilician Olba usually *Teukros* or *Aias*.[14]

Our oldest source for the *Megabyxos* probably is the comedy *Tolmai* of Crates (c. 450–430 BC), where a character says: "He cajoles the victual-seeker, but though shivering in the house of *Megabyxos* ..." (Crates F 37 KA),[15] clearly meaning "starving in the house of plenty" (thus Gomme on Thucydides 1.109.3). The Ephesian Artemision surpassed all other Greek sanctuaries— apart from Delphi—in wealth because of its extensive landed property.[16] Accordingly, its warden (see below) must have surpassed similar officials of other Greek temples; and indeed, his wealth long remained proverbial.[17]

The first, absolutely certain reference to the function of the Ephesian *Megabyxos* comes from Xenophon, who relates in the *Anabasis* that he left a tithe for Artemis with the *Megabyxos*, who later, perhaps in 384 BC, returned the money to him when he visited Olympia (5.3.6–7). Like many Greek sanctuaries,[18] the Artemision functioned as a bank,[19] as must have been the case in Menander's *Dis exapatōn*,[20] although, unfortunately, the context of the mention of the *Megabyxos* in the play (F 5 Sandbach) cannot be established.[21] Apparently, the *Megabyxos* was so important that he represented his hometown at the Olympic Games. In some way he may also have been involved in Xenophon's founding of the cult of Artemis Ephesia at Scillous, where his presence must have contributed not only to Xenophon's status but also to his own prestige.

An inscription from Priene dating to 334/3 BC speaks of "*Megabyxos*, son of *Megabyxos*" (*IPriene* 3). As he had helped to pay for the completion of the temple of Athena (one more indication of his wealth), the city had granted him

---

[13] See my detailed re-evaluation of the earlier stages of this cult in Bremmer 2004.

[14] Pessinous: see Bremmer 2004; Olba: Strabo 14.5.10; see also Gotter in this volume.

[15] Translation taken from Gulick (Loeb), adapted: the rest of the fragment is corrupt.

[16] Cf. Callimachus *Hymns* 3.250; Knibbe et al. 1979:139–147; Strelan 1996:76–79 ("The wealth of Artemis"); several studies in Muss 2001; Dignas 2002:141–156, 172–177.

[17] Cf. Apollonius of Tyana *Epistle* 2 Penella; Luc. *Tim.* 22.

[18] Bremmer 2003:32.

[19] Cf. Timaeus *FGrH* 566 F 150b; Caesar *Civil War* 3.33, 105; Dio Chrysostom 31.48, 54; *FiEphesos* I.261–262.

[20] As we can infer from Plautus *Bacchides* 306ff., where the *Megabyxos* is called Megalobulus. Plautus' dependence on Menander's *Dis Exapatōn* is now firmly established by E. W. Handley on *P.Oxy.* 64.4407. See also Zwierlein 1992.

[21] Menander, DE F 5 Sandbach, which calls him *zakoros* instead of *neōkoros* (see below). For the term, see J. Nollé on *ISide* 228.1.

the usual honors, such as a bronze statue (for which he had to pay himself).[22] At first sight, it is surprising that the civic decree did not extend the privileges, as is often the case, to the descendents of the *Megabyxos*. However, one need not look far for the reason of this omission, as in this case continuity in naming could have led only to the fiction but not the reality of filial succession. The explanation is supplied by Strabo, who relates that the Ephesians "had eunuchs as priests, whom they called *Megabyxoi* (they always tried to get from elsewhere some who were worthy of such a wardenship), and they held them in great honor" (Strabo 14.1.23). The castration is confirmed by the pseudo-Heraclitean letters of the second century AD that mention a trial against Heraclitus held at Ephesus ([Heraclitus] *Epistle* 9).[23]

Eunuch priests were common in Anatolia.[24] Those in the cult of Cybele and Attis in Pessinous were famous, and they are also attested for the cult of Hecate at Carian Lagina, and in the temple of the Galli in Phrygian Hierapolis.[25] Evidently, after their arrival at Ephesus the Greeks had incorporated (parts of) an existing indigenous cult; we may still have the name of the original indigenous goddess: Ûpis.[26] Yet it is also clear from Strabo's words that the Ephesians themselves were less keen to suffer "the unkindest cut of all"; they imported males from elsewhere to occupy this high position. The French king Henri IV may have thought that Paris was well worth a mass, but well-bred Ephesian males clearly did not think that the priesthood of Artemis was worth the loss of their testicles!

In the middle of the first century BC the *Megabyxos* was still so important that the Ephesians pleaded for him before Cleopatra when Marc Antony intended to bring him to court (Appian *Civil War* 5.1.9).[27] Soon after, the function must have been abolished. Strabo, who perhaps visited Ephesus in the very last decades of the pre-Christian era, speaks of him in the past. Around the year 30 BC Vedius Pollio, a freedman's son and *amicus* of Augustus, reorganized the cult of the Artemision (*IEphesos* 17.47–8; 18b.6; 18c.10–1; 18d.4),[28] and

---

[22] As is noted by F. Hiller von Gaertringen, *IPriene* on no. 231.

[23] Quintillian 5.12.21 mentions the *Megabyxos* as an example of effeminacy.

[24] For other Anatolian aspects of Artemis, see most recently Morris 2001:135–151 and 2001a:423–434, esp. 428–434.

[25] Pessinous: Bremmer 2004; Lagina: *IStratonikeia* 513, 544, 1101. Hierapolis: Strabo 13.4.14.

[26] See Timotheus F 778 Page/Hordern = Alex. Aet. F4 Magnelli (with Hordern and Magnelli *ad loc.*); Antimachus F 99 Matthews; Callimachus *Hymns* 3.204, 240, 4.292 (with the scholia *ad loc.*); Burkert 1979:130.

[27] This has been overlooked by LiDonnici 1999:201–214 and refutes her theses. Note also the reservations of Dignas 2002:190.

[28] Syme 1979:526 (date); Eck *DNP* 12.1 1154 s.v. *Vedius [II 4] P. V. Pollio.*

wealthy members of the Ephesian elite may well have bribed him to abolish the function of the *Megabyxos* for their own profit[29]—perhaps after the death of the last incumbent.

It is clear from this outline that we have only the sketchiest idea of the role played by the *Megabyxos* in the context of the Artemision and Ephesian society at large. The combination of castration and the name *Megabyxos* could mean that the first Persian was a court eunuch who had taken up the function after the Persian conquest of Ephesus.[30] Yet this remains speculation because we do not know if the Persians made any changes to the organisation of the Artemision at all. Regarding his function, Xenophon tells us that he was a *neōkoros*, a warden, the official responsible for the financial affairs of a sanctuary,[31] and the function is confirmed by the inscription from Priene (*IPriene* 231). In other words, the *Megabyxos* was not a priest proper and therefore perhaps not the one who sacrificed at Artemis' impressive altar.[32] That may well have been the priestess[33] because we know that in several sanctuaries the most important officials were the *neōkoros* and the priest(ess), functions that were sometimes combined into one hand.[34] However, in his summary of Xenophon's life, Diogenes Laertius (2.51) calls the *Megabyxos* a "priest", and male priests are attested after the end of the office of the *Megabyxos*.[35]

In spite of all these uncertainties our sources reveal that the *Megabyxos* was much concerned with his self-representation. Already around 400 BC we hear of Parrhasius painting his portrait (Tzetzes *chiliades* 8.400) and of Zeuxis commenting on his clothing and his slaves (Aelian *Varia Historia* 2.2). Unfortunately, the latter anecdote is also told of Apelles (Plutarch *Moralia* 58d; 471–472),[36] who certainly painted a procession of the *Megabyxos* (Pliny *Natural History* 35.93), just as, around the same time, Antidotus painted his grave (Pliny *Natural History* 35.132). The evidence is, of course, anecdotic,[37]

---

[29] See below.

[30] For the Persian eunuchs, see Briant 1996:I.279–288; Llewellyn-Jones 2002:19–49.

[31] For an interesting case, see Dignas 2002:139–140.

[32] For the altar, see now Muss and Bammer 2001, to be read with the devastating review by Kuhn 2003:197–226.

[33] See below.

[34] See e.g. also *SEG* 40.303 (Corinth); *IG* XII v 186 (Paros); *IAssos* 14; *IPrusias Hyp.* 53 (high priestess and *neōkoros*); *IPergamon* 3.152; *IMagnesia* 100a; *ILabraunda* 2, no. 45, etc.

[35] See below.

[36] For the anecdotes, see also Gschwantler 1975:123. For Zeuxis, see Ameling 1987:76 (probably from Heraclea Pontica).

[37] For stimulating reflections on the value of such anecdotes, see Saller 1980:69–83; Kortum 1997:1–29.

but the employment of the most famous painters of Greece indicates a feeling of self-esteem and importance that is rather unique among Greek temple officials.

2. Priestesses

Strabo supports the idea that the *Megabyxos* performed priestly functions by stating, "... maidens had to be joint priests with them [the *Megabyxoi*]" (Strabo 14.1.23). Burkert as well as Picard assume that these words prove the existence of a group of priestesses in the sanctuary.[38] Picard supports his case with the mention of the maidens,[39] whereas Burkert's view seems to rest on a misunderstanding of Strabo's reference to both *Megabyxoi* and priestesses. As Strabo clearly uses the plural in the case of the *Megabyxos* in order to refer to all former priests, this must apply also to the priestesses. Consequently, we should infer that there was a single maiden priestess serving the Ephesian Artemis in the Artemision.

In fact, both the literary and the epigraphical sources confirm the existence of a single priestess. According to Strabo, when the Phocaeans left their city in the context of the Persian conquest of Ionia, they first landed at Ephesus because of the oracular advice to accept a guide from Artemis Ephesia for their journey. At Ephesus, an upper-class woman named Aristarche told them that Artemis had appeared to her in a dream instructing her to join the Phocaeans and to take along a copy of the goddess' image. Aristarche became the first priestess in Massilia (Strabo 4.1.4),[40] and later the Massiliote cult image of Artemis was copied by the Romans and dedicated on the Aventine (Strabo 4.1.5).[41] Unfortunately, we do not know how old the Massiliote tradition is, but the lack of details suggests that it served an aetiological function, namely to explain the resemblance of the Phocaean cult image and its female priesthood to the Ephesian cult. It is noteworthy that there is no reference to Aristarche's husband, which suggests that the first Massiliote priestess was also a maiden. Evidently, the Phocaeans imitated the Ephesian profile of the priesthood. If they did this already when they founded Massilia, the institution of a maiden priestess must go back to the Archaic period.

---

[38] Picard 1922:182–190; Burkert 1999:73.

[39] See below.

[40] Cf. Malkin 1987:69–72; Scheer 2000:244–247.

[41] Cf. Turcan 2000:657–669.

A virgin priestess of Artemis also appears three times in the ancient novel.[42] The closing of Achilles Tatius' novel takes place in Ephesus and describes an ordeal in a cave of Artemis that no woman who was no longer a virgin could enter. The detail can be paralleled with the similar prohibition for women to enter the Ephesian temple of Artemis, which we are informed of by Artemidorus, an inhabitant of Ephesus (Artemidorus 4.4).[43] More importantly, however, the place was supervised by a virgin priestess (6.8.14)![44] The same function is also mentioned in Heliodorus' *Aethiopica* (1.22), which takes us to the first decades of the third century.[45] In this novel, Chariclea explains that she and her brother Theagenes, who belong to the Ephesian nobility, both became priests. Whereas her brother was a priest of Apollo, she became priestess of Artemis for the duration of one year. The evidence, then, suggests that at least during this period the priestess of the Ephesian Artemis was a maiden who was appointed for one year only.

Additional information is found in the *Historia Apollonii regis Tyrii*, a novel originally written around AD 215[46] but surviving only in two later, Christian recensions (RA, RB). In our present text, the young wife of Apollonius was sent to the *sacerdotes Dyane feminas* where *omnes virgines inviolabiliter servabant castitatem* (RA 27). Here the wife, a king's daughter, soon held *inter sacerdotes principatum* (RAB 48). After Apollonius had recognized her in the temple, she abdicated her priesthood and *ipsa vero constituit sacerdotem, que sequens ei erat et casta caraque* (RB 49).[47] It is striking that this notice confirms a hitherto isolated passage of Plutarch (*Moralia* 795e), who mentions that there were three degrees, the *melliera*, *hiera*, and *parhiera*, the *future*, *present*, and *past priestess*. We may safely conclude that at least from the second century onwards there was a group of priestesses of whom one was a *high priestess*. We also have a reference to a *parthenōn* at Ephesus, an institution that was not uncommon in (South-)Western Asia Minor[48] and that may have been the place where the maidens and, later, the priestesses were housed during their term of office.[49]

---

[42] For the passages, see also Thomas 1995:82–117, who neglects their mention of the virgin priesthood.

[43] Cf. Schwabl 1999:283–287. Similarly, Achilles Tatius 7.13; on the Ephesian background of Artemidorus, see Bowersock 2004:53–63, with prosopographical analysis on 54–56.

[44] For the ordeal, see Bremmer 1999:21–29, who overlooked Versnel 1994:152–153.

[45] For Heliodorus' date, see Bremmer 1999:26–27. See also Baumbach in this volume.

[46] For the date, see Bremmer 1998a:169–170

[47] For the passage, see Panayotakis 2002:112–114.

[48] Cyzicus: Michel, *Recueil d'inscriptions greques* 538. Didyma: *SEG* 35.1097. Magnesia: *IMagnesia* 100. Apollonia Salbace: L. and J. Robert 1954:281. Bargylia: *SEG* 44.868. Olymus: Robert 1935:159.

[49] Cf. *IEphesos* 900–900a.

The idea of a maiden priestess may seem surprising to us, but in several cults in the more conservative areas of Greece, such as the Central and Northern Peloponnese, youths could indeed function as priests. Given her importance as initiatory goddess, it is not surprising that Artemis' cult supplies the majority of adolescent priests. This is the case in the initiatory cult of Artemis Triclaria of Patrae,[50] the Artemis cult of Aegeira, where the priesthood ended with marriage (Pausanias 7.26.3), and the cult of Artemis Cnagia in Sparta.[51] An epigram in the *Anthologia Palatina* mentions a dedication of a statue of Artemis made by a priestess to an unknown sanctuary reserved for girls, and the fact that the priestess is named after her father, not her husband, also suggests a virgin priest (*Anthologia Palatina* 6.269).[52] Finally, we have a lacunose epigram from Patmus, which relates that Artemis herself made "Cydonia, the daughter of Glaucies, priestess and *hudrophoros* ... to bring minor sacrifices."[53] *Hudrophoroi* are well attested in Didyma and Miletus and it seems clear "both from consistent lack of reference to husbands, and from the fact that frequently the *hudrophoros'* father held the prophecy (at Didyma) at the same time, that normally the *hudrophoros* was a young, unmarried girl."[54] It will not have been different on Patmus or, for that matter, in Ephesus.

Our evidence regarding adolescent priests is almost exclusively late, but luckily we know that during the destruction of Siris in 530 BC the attackers killed fifty youths together with the priest, a male adolescent dressed as a girl, in the sanctuary of Athena Ilias (Lycurgus *Alexander* 984–92, with scholion on 984; Iustinus 20.2.3).[55] Apparently, the phenomenon of the adolescent priest developed from the directorship of choruses, as fifty is a well known number of Greek choruses. After the disappearance of the choruses with their initiatory function in the course of the Classical and Hellenistic era, the priesthood must have continued to exist.[56]

Apparently, the same development took place at Ephesus, where maiden choruses are well attested. However, the oldest testimonies do not concentrate on human maidens but on the Amazons. According to Pindar (F 174 Maehler),[57]

---

[50] Calame 1977:137 (with full bibliography); Baudy 1998:143–167.

[51] See Bremmer 1999c:189–190, from which I have taken over this paragraph, abbreviated and updated.

[52] Cf. Graf 1985:237–238.

[53] Merkelbach and Stauber 1998:169–170.

[54] SEG 39.855. Cf. van Bremen 1996:90n31.

[55] Cf. Graf 2000:267–269.

[56] Dowden 1989:157–158; Calame 1977:22–23 (choruses of fifty members); Bremmer 1999c:188–189 (development from initiation).

[57] Maehler wrongly ascribes the notice to Apollo's sanctuary in Didyma.

these had founded Artemis' sanctuary during their fight against Theseus. In his *Hymn to Artemis* (237-258), Callimachus supplies more details. He relates that Hippo, the queen of the Amazons, set up a statue dedicated to Artemis on the shore and performed a ritual for the goddess while the Amazons danced a war dance in full armor, followed by a circular choral dance. The description of the dance fits the way the *prulis* was danced on Crete, where the *Kouretes* shielded young Zeus with their dances (Hyginus *Fabulae* 193.3; Apollodorus 1.1.7). That the dance was rather ecstatic we can infer from the fact that it was accompanied by the *surinx* and that the feet loudly beat the ground.[58] Differing versions of the story about the Amazons exist[59] and competing stories claim that Coressus and Ephesus were founders of the sanctuary[60] but undoubtedly Amazons were at the heart of Artemis' cult and sanctuary.

Pausanias adds an interesting detail in his version of the sanctuary's foundation (7.2.8).[61] He relates that even before Theseus some Amazons came as refugees to Artemis' temple, fleeing from Dionysus. The combination of Dionysus and Artemis is not uncommon in Greek mythology and cult. More detailed parallels reveal that Artemis ends the marginal period caused by Dionysus through either healing a person or, further removed from the ritual, through killing him or her. Thus, Ariadne is killed by Artemis on Dionysus' indictment, and the Proitids are healed from their Dionysiac madness by Artemis, just like Eurypylus by Artemis Triclaria; the *katabasis* of Dionysus ends in the temple of Artemis Soteira in Troizen.[62] With regard to the Amazons, the return to normality is achieved by their being granted asylum, an important function of the Artemision.[63]

The dancing Amazons must have been the model for the real girls involved in the service of Artemis. Our sources start in the later fifth century with Aristophanes' reference to the "maidens of the Lydians" revering Ephesian Artemis (*Clouds* 598-600),[64] and they become more specific with

---

[58] For the dance and its relationship to the *purrhichē* of the *Kouretes*, see Ceccarelli 1998:135–136.

[59] See Pliny *Natural History* 34.53; Dionysius Periegetes 827–829, and schol. *ad loc.*; Hyginus *Fabulae* 223, 225; Pausanias 4.31.8.

[60] See Pausanias 7.2.7. Note also Coressus as Ephesian place name (Kreophylos *FGrH* 417 F 1; *Anthologia Graeca* 5.59.5); the Koressian gate (*IEphesos* 212, 425, 566); and the neighbourhood of the Koresseitai (*IEphesos* 9); Karwiese 1985:214-225; Knibbe 2002:207-219.

[61] See also Tacitus *Annals* 3.61; Pausanias 4.31.8.

[62] See Homer *Odyssey* xi 325 (Ariadne); Hesiod F 131 MW (Proitids); Pausanias 7.16.6–9 (Eurypylos); Pausanias 2.31.2 (Troizen). Graf 1985:242–243, who also compares Artemis' killing of Actaeon (Hesiod F 217a MW; Stes. F 236 Davies), but in that case Dionysos does not play a role.

[63] For this function, see now Rigsby 1996:385–393.

[64] Calame 1977:96 also compares Ion *TrGF* 19 F 22 and Diogenes Athenaeus *TrGF* 45 F1, but in both cases the reference is clearly to maidens from Sardis.

Autocrates in his comedy *Tympanistai* (F 1 KA), where he mentions the ecstatic, slightly lascivious dancing of the "maidens of the Lydians."[65] The maidens also appear in Menander's *Kitharistes* (93-97 Sandbach), where they participate in a "*deipnophoria* of maidens". This is perhaps the precursor of the *deipnophoria* attested for the reign of Antoninus Pius (*IEphesos* 221), which in turn may be the same as that referred to in another inscription dated to the third century AD (*IEphesos* 1577).

It seems plausible that the combination of maidens and a meal was inspired by the annual ritual in honor of Artemis described by the *Etymologicum Magnum* in an explanation of Artemis' epithet Daitis. The *aition* relates that once upon a time the maidens and boys of Ephesus under the leadership of the daughter of the king, Clymena, carried the statue of Artemis from the city to a field near the sea, where they danced and sung. When they failed to make the customary offering of salt the goddess became angry, and she was expiated only after the Ephesians repeated the ritual, which is still attested for the end of the first century BC (*Etymologicum Magnum* 402; *Anecdota Oxon.* II.435).[66] As Calame persuasively argues, the ritual's "substance is characteristic of several rites of adolescence, such as that begun by the *Proitides* at Lousoi or the one honoring Artemis at Brauron."[67]

A procession of boys and girls is also attested for the middle of the second century AD, namely in the famous opening scene of Xenophon of Ephesus (1.2.2-3).[68] We are told that all Ephesian boys and girls went in a procession from the city to the sanctuary. Each group was led by the most beautiful boy and girl respectively, Habrocomes and Anthea. As we are explicitly told that the festival was an occasion for match making between boys and girls, the event obviously marked the completion of adolescence. Although it was no longer "properly ritualized", the coming of age of the Ephesian adolescents was still firmly linked with the city goddess.

The various sources supplement one another and, as Calame has shown, all point to a scenario in which maidens collectively take part in a procession and choral dances celebrating the completion of their adolescence. Naturally, the leader of the girls in Xenophon's novel, Anthea, excels in beauty, because the Greeks customarily entrusted the position of the director

---

[65] For the dancing, see Calame 1977:93, who well compares Aristophanes F 29 (wrongly quoted as 30) and 147 (wrongly quoted as 148) KA.

[66] Heberdey 1904:210–215, *Beiblatt* 44 (*IEphesos* 14); Calame 1977:94–96.

[67] Calame 1977:95.

[68] For Xenophon's date, see Bremmer 1998a:170.

of the chorus to the most beautiful person.[69] Yet one element does not match the common descriptions. As we have seen, the *aition* of the ritual of Artemis Daitis mentions that both boys and girls were led by the daughter of the king, Clymena. Although we do hear of boys leading choruses of girls, there is no parallel of girls leading choruses of boys.[70] This pattern leads us to believe that the *aition* is of a relatively late date and perhaps reflects the situation where the priestess was the most important cult official.

Ephesian inscriptions from the Roman period confirm the institution of the priestess of Artemis. Evidently, the function was one of great honor and by far the most common office taken on by upper-class women, apart from the priesthoods of the imperial cult (*IEphesos* 104, 411, 492, 615 [improved text: *ITralleis* 87], 661, 892, 980–990, 982, 989, 994, 1026, 3059, 3072, 3232, etc.).[71] In all cases that furnish us with this type of information the priestess appears to be an unmarried woman, as she is regularly associated with her father but not with a husband.[72] Unfortunately, we are not well informed about her activities. The priestess adorned the temple and performed public sacrifice (*IEphesos* 987), reorganized the cult (*IEphesos* 3059), and shared out money to the *humnōdoi* on the birthday of Artemis (*IEphesos* 27). In the course of time priestesses started to hold multiple functions and became *prutanis* and/or *gumnasiarch* as well.[73] One possible explanation for this development could be a diminished status of the priesthood itself. Be this as it may, priestesses are still attested for the third century whereas male priests are not.[74]

3. Male Priests in the Roman Period

The disappearance of the *Megabyxos* did not entail that Artemis' sanctuary abandoned male priests altogether. For some reason these are neglected in recent studies of the priesthoods of Ephesian Artemis, but they are certainly attested in both epigraphical and literary sources. The edict of the Roman proconsul of Asia, Paullus Fabius Persicus, which was issued to the Ephesians in AD 44, talks about corrupt practices in connection with the personnel of the Artemision. Apparently, the civic authorities had started to create priesthoods

---

[69] See Athenaeus 13.565ff. Cf. Calame 1977:43, 72. Note also Bremmer 1999b:316–318.
[70] Calame 1977:48–73.
[71] Cf. van Bremen 1996:86.
[72] For a list, see Rogers 1991:75n73.
[73] See the list in van Bremen 1996:316–332.
[74] *IEphesos* 617, 892, 3233.

that enabled the elite to gain profit from the perquisites assigned to these priesthoods (*IEphesos* 18b).[75] The close co-operation between the two groups shows that they came from the same background, the Ephesian elite. Around AD 100 priests were still so prestigious that they belonged to the class of the "gold bearing" citizens (*IEphesos* 27.456), but inscriptions do not mention them afterwards.

The literary sources draw a somewhat different picture. The anonymous author of the apocryphal *Acts of John*, who wrote around AD 160, mentions a resurrection of the priest of Artemis (46). His contemporary Achilles Tatius describes a priest of Artemis who is clearly in charge of the sanctuary and who is much respected by the population (Achilles Tatius 7.12.15–16; 8.3). As both authors probably came from South-Western Asia Minor,[76] they must have been well informed about Ephesian institutions. In both cases, the reduction to only one priest could be a dramatization by the authors but it could equally signal a change in the organisation of the priesthood. As we have a lot more epigraphical testimonies regarding Artemis' priestesses than her priests, it seems likely that in the course of time most male aristocrats shifted their interests to the imperial priesthoods, even though Artemis' priesthood must have long remained prestigious due to its venerable age and wealth.

4. The *Essēnes*

Regarding the next group of religious functionaries, the *essēnes*, our sources are scarce and not always easy to interpret.[77] At one time, they must have been important figures in the temple, since they are mentioned in a series of Ephesian inscriptions, ranging from the late fourth until the later third century BC. They are commonly referred to as priests,[78] but as far as I can see they are never called that way in our tradition, even though they could perform sacrifices to Artemis on behalf of the city and were connected with the Artemision.[79] Although, unfortunately, the size of this group is never specified, their activities are reasonably transparent. Their main function was to assign new citizens via a lottery to their *phulē* and *chiliastus*, subdivisions of

---

[75] Cf. Dignas 2002:150–153, 188–193.

[76] For the date and place of origin of the *Acts of John*, see Bremmer 1998a:162 (= Bremmer 2001:153–154, 167–168). For Achilles Tatius, see Bremmer 1998a:167–168; Bowie 2002:60–61.

[77] Picard 1922:190–197; Talamo 1984:207–213; Burkert 1999:68; Dignas 2002:191.

[78] Picard 1922:190: "*un corps sacerdotal*"; Talamo 1984:208: "*esseni-sacerdoti*"; Burkert 1999:68: "*Priesterkollegium.*"

[79] See *IEphesos* 1448, 1473.

the Ephesian citizenry (*IEphesos* 1408f, 1413, 1440, 1443, 1447f, 1451, 1453, 1455 etc.); in addition, they sometimes handled money in connection with the sale of citizenship (*IEphesos* 2001). This is where our knowledge about their activities in the Hellenistic period stops. Burkert assumes that they also elected the *Megabyxos*, but I see no evidence for this.[80]

Callimachus uses the term twice. In his *Hymn to Zeus* he sings, "not a lottery made you *essēn* of the gods,[81] but the works of your hands" (66). It seems reasonable that in this case Callimachus means king because the same meaning occurs in one of his fragments (F 178.23 Pfeiffer) where he calls Peleus *essēn* of the Myrmidonians'.[82] Given that the lexicographical tradition interprets *essēn* as *king* or *king bee*,[83] it is not surprising that the *Etymologicum Magnum* (383.30) combines all this information and states, "king according to the Ephesians." Comparing the Athenian *basileus* and the Roman *rex sacrorum*, one scholar has suggested that Ephesus knew a group of sacrifical kings[84] but in Athens and Rome there was only one sacrificial king and the sacrificial duties of the *essēnes* are nearly negligible in our sources. In short, we should not be led astray by the imaginations of lexicographers, who evidently had no more reliable information than we have. Even though the bee is prominent on Ephesian coins,[85] we are totally in the dark about the associations of the Ephesians when they started to call this group of men *essēnes*. Our only certainty is that they derived the word from a neighbouring Anatolian language that has not yet been identified.[86]

After Alexander the Great we no longer hear of a connection between the *essēnes* and citizenship. Their function must have lost importance. Although particulars are lacking, they seem to have become the victim of the restructuring of the temple organisation that took place during the period of the *Diadochoi* (*IEphesos* 26). Our information starts to flow again with Pausanias, who notes the lifelong chastity of the priest and priestess of Artemis Hymnia in Orchomenus and observes, "I know of similar things that last a year and no more in the case of the *histiatores* of Artemis Ephesia, those called *essēnes* by the citizens" (8.1.13). Interestingly, the term *histiatōr* is found with this spelling

---

[80] Burkert 1999:68.

[81] The refererence is to *Iliad* XV 184–199. Cf. Burkert 1992:88–93 for its dependence on the Accadian epic *Atrahasis* (but note the reservations of West 1997:110).

[82] Pfeiffer wrongly writes *essēn* with a rough breathing in his edition. Cf. Masson 1962:49.

[83] King: Hsch. e 6335 Latte. King bee: *Et. Gud.*, *Suda* s.v. *essēn*

[84] van Berchem 1980:29–30.

[85] Karwiese 1995:152–164, 168–184, 197–207.

[86] Furnée 1972:172n118 with a collection of other words ending in -*ēn*.

only in a fragment of the Archaic lawgiver Charondas (*apud* Stobaeus 4.2.24). Yet the term was quite normal in the Greek world and even used by Apollonius of Tyana (*Epistle* 65 Penella) with regard to Ephesus. Apparently, the *essēnes* not only had to be chaste for a year but also had to host banquets. As in Greek religion the latter usually went concomitant with sacrifice, the notice may well be an indication of a sacrificing activity of the *essēnes*.

In the course of the late second and third centuries, the office seems to have lost even more of its importance. It became part of the functions of the *neopoioi*, and members often recorded that they had fulfilled two terms of *essēneia*. Moreover, we now regularly hear of only two *essēnes* so that it may be concluded that the corporation was limited in size in the later Roman period, just like the *Kouretes*[87], before it disappeared altogether (*IEphesos* 956–958, 963, 1582, 1588, 3263, 4330).

The origin of the office is lost in the dark of time. Yet the oldest known duties do not suggest that we are dealing with a major priesthood or a very important office. The obligation of remaining chaste for a year hardly fits the profile of an older male, as such a temporary celibacy during male adulthood seems to be totally out of place in the Greek world, even in an area that was influenced by Anatolian traditions. It would thus appear that the *essēnes* developed from a group of upper-class adolescents, who had to stay in the sanctuary for a year. This interpretation corresponds with a neglected notice by Aristophanes of Byzantium, who explains the term as *hēlikia tis* (F 100 Slater).[88] We hear indeed of young men officiating in the service of Artemis. Strabo relates that during an annual festival in Ortygia in honor of the goddess, *young men* (*neoi*) "vie for honour, particularly in the splendour of their banquets there" (14.1.20).[89] He does not use a technical term but it is possible that these *histiatores* were the *essēnes*.

5. The *Kouretes*

While the *neoi* were carrying out their office in the sacred grove of Ortygia another corporation was also active, the *Kouretes*. Strabo mentions that they held *sumposia* and performed some "mystic [probably: secret] sacrifices"

---

[87] See below.

[88] Slater (*ad loc.*) observes that no example of this usage exists, but that can hardly be an argument against the reliability of this gloss, as the same can be said about other glosses (F 11A, 14, 25, 30, 31, 103 etc.). He also approves the suggestion made by Nauck (1848:106) that the gloss is a corruption of the preceding one (F 99), but such a corruption is hard to imagine.

[89] Translation taken from Jones (Loeb).

(14.1.20).[90] The corresponding myth related that they had helped to keep Hera away from Leto when she gave birth to Artemis and Apollo in Ortygia. The *Kouretes* were thus connected with Artemis and it is therefore no surprise that they were also connected with the Artemision, which we learn from two inscriptions dated around 300 BC, one about a business in frankincense (*IEphesos* 4102) and the other about a request for citizenship (*IEphesos* 1449). In both cases, the *Kouretes* are mentioned after the *neopoioi*, who seem to have been their superiors.[91] From the names in the former inscription we can also infer that the corporation counted at least four members at that time, which suggests that the regular number of six in the imperial era went back to old times.[92] However, after the Augustan period we no longer hear about a connection with the Artemision. The building of the new *prutaneion* will have gone concomitant with a restructuring of the ancient corporation and with an assignment to cultic functions in the *prutaneion*.[93]

Originally, the *Kouretes* were groups of young men on the brink of adulthood, but their once widespread corporations had survived only in marginal areas of the Greek world, such as Acarnania, Messene and Aetolia. Yet the connection of the term with the process of coming of age was still felt in the Hellenistic period, witness the Greek-Egyptian term *mallokourētes*.[94] The *Kouretes* were especially worshipped on Eastern Crete, as is illustrated by the famous hymn of Palaecastro on Zeus and the *Kouretes*.[95] It is thus conceivable that the term was exported from Crete to Ephesus in the early Archaic period: architects from Cnossus built the Archaic temple of Artemis, and Cretan artistic influence on early Ephesus is well attested;[96] Zeus Cretagenes and the *Kouretes* appear in neighbouring Mylasa (*IMylasa* 102, 107, 806) and Amyzon (*IAmyzon* 14f).

Yet at Ephesus the *Kouretes* were not connected with Zeus but with Artemis. This tie may well be old, and in Aetolia the goddess was also closely associated with the *Kouretes*.[97] In contrast, in Cnossus the *Kouretes* were associ-

---

[90] For other connections of *Kouretes* with sacrifice, see Istros *FGrH* 334 F 48; Pausanias 4.31.9.

[91] For the Ephesian *neopoioi*, see Dignas 2002:192–193.

[92] For the number, see Knibbe 1981:97.

[93] Thus Graf 1999:258; Dignas 2002:200. For the social status of the new *Kouretes*, see also Rozenbeek 1993:103–105.

[94] See P.Oxy. 24.2407. Cf. Legras 1993:113–127.

[95] For text, translation and commentary, see now Furley and Bremer 2001:I.67–76; II.1–20. For a full enumeration of the Cretan worship of the *Kouretes*, see Sporn 2002:389.

[96] Muss 2000:149–155.

[97] See the excellent observations in Grossardt 2001:15, 238–239.

ated with Rhea,[98] and such connections of groups of men with a goddess, often with an initiatory background (as in the cases of the *Kabeiroi*,[99] *Kouretes* and *Korubantes*), regularly point to pre-Greek traditions.[100] Although in eastern Greece Artemis is occasionally associated with the mother of the *Korubantes* and the Meter,[101] the presence of the *essēnes* perhaps makes a Greek origin of the *Kouretes* more probable. Otherwise we would have to postulate the original existence of a goddess with two groups. However, the *Kouretes* were certainly no priests, even if they may have, on occasion, officiated as sacrificers in Artemis' cult.

6. Conclusion

The priesthood of Artemis had a complicated history. On the one hand Artemis' traditional supervision of the coming of age of girls is reflected in the choruses of maidens and the role of the priestess. On the other hand, her cult also incorporated elements of the cult of a pre-existing Anatolian goddess, namely a eunuch priest and a group of young men. It is even feasible that the Ephesians combined native (priestess) and Anatolian (eunuch) elements in the Artemis priesthood from a relatively early stage onwards.

What can we now conclude from our discussion with regard to general characteristics of Greek priesthood? I would like to single out four aspects of Artemis' cult that are typical for Greek priesthood but at the same time rather different from a concept of priesthood that stems from a monotheistic experience. First, it was evidently acceptable that a eunuch held one of the most important, if not the most important, functions in Artemis' cult. Whereas the organisation of the Christian Church has guaranteed that, before and after the Reformation, the Catholic priesthood and the Protestant ministry have remained identifiable and fairly strictly defined offices, Greek priesthood was clearly characterised by a flexibility that could continuously adapt to new circumstances.

Secondly, this flexibility made the Greek priesthood much more liable to political manipulation than the Christian one. We do not know how and when the *Megabyxos* received his name but it must have to do with the Persian conquest of Ephesus. Whereas the Orthodox Church in Greece preserved Greek

---

[98] Sporn 2002:124.

[99] For the initiatory background of the *Kabeiroi*, see Wachter 2001:326–327.

[100] See especially Graf 1985:115–120.

[101] See *IChios* 33. Cf. Graf 1985:55, 117.

identity in the times of the Ottoman Empire and the Polish priests sustained a sense of nationalism in the face of communism, the most important religious functionaries of Ephesus apparently had no trouble in co-operating with the occupying powers, be they Persian, Macedonian or Roman. In this respect, the Greek priesthood was perhaps more different from the clergy familiar to us than we might always have thought.

Thirdly, in many religions priests have managed to monopolize the performance of sacrifice. It was different in ancient Greece, where in principle everybody had this right.[102] The range and duties of the religious officials in the Artemision confirm that the performance of sacrifice alone is not sufficient to call somebody a priest or priestess.

Fourthly and finally, the existence of adolescent priests and the temporary character of many Greek priesthoods are confirmed by the profiles of the Ephesian priestess and, probably, the *essēnes*. This is a commonplace in the study of Greek religion but certainly forms a stark contrast with the Christian, Jewish, and Muslim traditions. Neither did the function require years of training, such as is obligatory for modern priests, ministers, imams, and rabbis. These factors contributed to the fact that pagan priesthoods were no competition for the Christian bishops when the confrontation between Christianity and paganism became of vital importance for the survival of paganism.[103] However, the Ephesian case is fascinating because it asserts very Greek characteristics of priesthood in the context of a very un-Greek genesis and context.

---

[102] Bremmer 1994:28. This is confirmed by Chaniotis; see Chaniotis in this volume.
[103] For the importance of the early bishops, see e.g. Brown 1992; Drake 2000.

3

Professionals, Volunteers, and Amateurs
Serving the Gods *kata ta patria*

Susan Guettel Cole

Alexandra Consults the Oracle

I N THE SECOND CENTURY AD, a priestess of Demeter Thesmophoros at Miletus consulted the oracle of Apollo at Didyma. A third-person account of her query survives:

> With good fortune.
>
> Alexandra, priestess of Demeter Thesmophoros, puts a question to the oracle, because, since the time when she took on the priesthood, never have the gods become so manifest through visitations, sometimes through maidens and women, and sometimes through males and children; (she asks) why this is so and if it is for some auspicious reason. The god spoke in oracle speech: "The Deathless Ones, coming among mortals [—], pronounce their judgment and the honor that [—]." (*IDidyma* 496a).

Alexandra does not identify the gods appearing to her constituents, but we can tell from her question that she is alarmed. The gods are not behaving predictably.[1] Concerned about change, she consults the oracle, aware that any change in divine behavior could be an ominous sign. The priestess assumes responsibility for examining anomalies in divine response because even the gods were expected to behave in traditional ways.

---

[1] Robert 1960:543–546 takes the expressions with "through" to indicate that the gods appeared in the form of women, young girls, males, and children. He adds that the text names the female worshippers of Demeter first, followed by males, not usually a concern to the *Thesmophoroi*, underscoring the unusual nature of the events that led Alexandra to ask her question.

As priestess of Demeter Thesmophoros, Alexandra represents a divinity whose rites were among the oldest the Greeks knew. Because Demeter was considered responsible for regulating food supply and diet, any irregularity in her attention, even in second-century Miletus, could be serious. The other side of the stone block on which Alexandra's question is paraphrased contains an oracular response describing the functions of Demeter, perhaps part of a reply to a second query of Alexandra:

> The god (Apollo) pronounced: It is necessary for the whole human clan to pay honor with sacrifices well moved by prayer to Deo, mother of a beautiful daughter and mother who gives flourishing fruit of food dear to mortals; for she is the first who sent wheat-bearing fruit on earth and put an end to the untamed and bestial spirit of mortals, when those dwelling among the naturally roofed mountain (caves) held a meal for gluttons in their raw meat-devouring jaws; and it is especially necessary for the residents around spear-holding Neleus (to give honor, too); for these people still possess the signs of hallowed birth that qualify them to perform here the rites of Deo and her daughter Deoïs. On account of this, with the [honor] of a divine service that cannot be divulged, you [showed yourself] to be a person sharing in the goal of a well-ordered way of life and [—] the rites of Eumolpus [—]. (*IDidyma* 496b)[2]

Demeter's regimen and Demeter's rites separate her worshippers from savages. The oracle claims for the residents of Miletus a special responsibility to the goddess, maintaining that their founder, Neleus, had brought from Attica the *sumbola* of the Eleusinian mysteries. These tokens confer on Milesians the privilege of performing Demeter's Eleusinian *orgia*, rites so sacred that they could not be described (*arrhēta*). Apollo's response enjoins the Milesians to do nothing that could jeopardize this relationship and permanent obligation.

Alexandra's title identifies her as the priestess of Demeter Thesmophoros, the priestess who officiated for women at the *Thesmophoria*. The second text calls Demeter's ceremonies the "rites of Eumolpus," naming the legendary ruler associated with the founding of the Eleusinian mysteries. In both texts, the main concern is tradition. The first text is concerned with traditional behavior. The second text stakes a claim to a long-established relationship with the divinity by evoking an ancient time and exhorting the Milesians

---

[2] The text (with translation) is included by Fontenrose 1988:207–208 no. 22, in his collection of *Historical Responses* at Didyma.

to remember their ties to the Eleusinian rites. A reference to an Eleusinian connection as late as the second century raises several questions. How did communities actually maintain the appearance of ritual continuity? Who judged that rituals were properly performed? Who inspected the process and outcome of female-only rituals and who was responsible for checking up on secret ceremonies? What role did priests and priestesses play in the process?[3] In what follows I am addressing these questions with a focus on female cult officials, and my frequent point of reference will be the rites of Demeter.

kata ta patria

Greek ritual was by nature conservative. Relentless repetition, the rigid calendar of festival schedules, and the formulaic patterns of ritual gesture and ritual speech gave to every performance the impression of great antiquity and long history. The experience of each reenactment of ritual implied that what was being done had always been done the same way. Claims of divine mandate for religious practice were simple to make. Such claims could be endorsed by cooperative oracles and were rarely challenged in public. The details of ritual practice were not a concern to historians or even to poets; we know only the barest outline of the rituals actually performed. We can tell from the epigraphical record, however, that practice was shaped by discussion, details were decided by legislative procedures, and disputes were subjected to the scrutiny of experts appointed to oversee public ritual.

Ancient administrators had a phrase they used when they wished to emphasize a solemn occasion or the long life and hallowed origin of a ritual. The expression *kata ta patria* (according to ancestral custom) was a phrase that made any violation not only an offense against the gods, but also an offense against the collective authority of the population past and present. There were many other ways to express this idea, but *kata ta patria* is a formula that seems to have carried special weight. The expression surfaces first at Athens and throughout the centuries appears more often in Athenian inscriptions than in all other city corpora combined. The phrase *kata ta patria* appears in public documents where it is important to imply that everything is as it should be, but it can also appear in contexts where legislation has resolved a dispute, changed a process, or established a new procedure. In the law courts this phrase and other similar expressions were used to register anxiety about

---

[3] For numerous observations and many answers to these questions, see Chaniotis in this volume.

proper performance of traditional ritual.[4] Such expressions were meant to soothe the reader or listener. As soon as a claim is made that something is being done *kata ta patria*, however, we can almost be sure that some kind of a change or challenge is already underway.

Inscriptions give us some idea of how procedures were supposed to be managed. Here we notice that administrators often relied on written texts preserved in local archives. Political changes were accompanied by an audit of ritual procedures. At Cos, for instance, the fourth-century synoecism required all sanctuaries of Demeter on the island to be managed from the central town. Purification ritual was standardized and the demes mirrored the *poleis*.[5] All the priestesses of Demeter had to follow the same regulations. Two *epistatai* were chosen to collect from the *nomophulakes* and the priests the regulations written down in the sacred laws about purification, and to display these rules in the sanctuaries of Demeter and Asclepius. The goal of the officials was to regularize public rituals according to the sacred and hereditary laws (*kata tous hierous kai patrious nomous*). Appeals to antiquity made the regulations stronger. At Ephesus, where Demeter Karpophoros was installed in the *prutaneion* in the imperial period, an inscription of the third century AD gives the regulations for care of the sacred fire and instructions for numbers of sacrificial victims. This late text reproduces two selections from an earlier sacred law. The first selection is called a summary of a hereditary law (*kephalaion nomou patriou*); the second is called another part (*allo meros*; IEphesos 10).[6] The first selection directs procedure for rituals entrusted to the *prutanis*. The hierophant is to lead him around "on the customary day" and teach him exactly what is "customary" for each god. In addition, the hierophant is to explain the singing of the paean at the sacrifice, the procession, and the *pannukhia*, which "must be performed *according to ancestral custom*" (*kata ta patria*). We rarely have such explicit detail about professional training for officials with part-time ritual responsibilities.[7]

As Angelos Chaniotis has shown, for the most part, the day-to-day administration of both public and private cult was left to officials and attendants who were not required to have special training. Those in charge were held accountable to public boards and local political administrators, but procedures for evaluation placed more emphasis on inventory of public property and auditing of accounts than on supervising the content of rituals. There was

---

[4] For instance, [Demosthenes] 59.75.

[5] *LSCG* 154 AI, for the procedure; AIIa for *Damatar Olumpia en poli*; AIIb for *Damatar en Isthmōi*.

[6] Suys 1998:174–175.

[7] See now Chaniotis in this volume on *LSS* 25 and *IdCos* ED 236, two texts with detailed instructions for ritual, available to priest and priestess.

a great deal of variety in demands of service. Some offices may have required as little as a single day of service in the entire year. Above all, although service could be lifelong or annual, there is no guarantee that longer service implied deeper ties, higher commitment, or even more responsibility.

Demeter at Erythrae

The evidence for priesthoods associated with Demeter provides an interesting test case for exploring issues of continuity in the context of sanctuary administration and traditional rituals.[8] Sanctuaries and festivals of Demeter were usually organized at the level of the smallest administrative unit, the deme or its equivalent. Demeter's sanctuaries were usually small and simple. Inscriptions associated with these sanctuaries tend to be short, even terse, and they are rarely informative about procedures of administration. Moreover, Demeter's ritual was so heavily cloaked in the requirements imposed by seclusion and segregation that we have little direct evidence for what was actually done and who was in charge. Some types of Demeter's worship required rituals that could not be described. But how much was restricted, how many people had to know the content, and where did the boundary between specialist and consumer lie? The *Thesmophoria* could not be viewed by males, but the rituals were often administered by legislative bodies made up of men. How were administrators informed about a particular festival? Who was responsible for seeing to it that all was performed *kata ta patria*?

In any city, Demeter could have more than one priestess. Taking Erythrae as an example, if we look at the epigraphical evidence, on first glance we have what appears to be a full dossier on cult practice: a catalogue of sale prices of the city's priesthoods, the most detailed and longest calendar of sacrifices outside of Attica, texts conferring honors on priests and priestesses, and records of dedications. When we look a little closer, however, there are, as usual, more questions than answers. The catalogue of sale of priesthoods gives us four separate offices for Demeter, two in her own right (Demeter Chloë and Demeter at Colonae) and two in tandem with her daughter Kore (Demeter and Kore; Demeter and Kore Pythocrestus (*LSAM* 25).[9] Prices can be compared as follows:

---

[8] Clinton 1974 collects the evidence for the Eleusinian organization of priestly duties. I will concentrate here for the most part on other examples.

[9] For a new fragment of a sale list, see *SEG* 37.921. I am indebted to Jonathon Strang's seminar report on the inscriptions of Erythrae for calling to my attention the significance of this dossier for rituals of Demeter. For a discussion of the list, see Dignas 2002:251–255.

Demeter Chloë	101 dr.
Demeter at Colonae	600 dr.
"	1300 dr.
Demeter and Kore	190 dr.
Demeter and Kore Pythochrestus	210 dr.

Even the most expensive of these offices (Demeter at Colonae; 1300 dr.), although the price reaches four digits, does not come close to that of Aphrodite in Embates (2040 dr.) or Hermes Agoraios (4600 and 4610 dr.). Does variation in price correlate with variation in prestige and authority? Were female priesthoods less likely than male offices to be considered important? Was Aphrodite more popular than Demeter? Such questions do not really get to the meaningful issues behind accounts such as these. We can notice that the cheapest priesthood at Erythrae (probably assigned to a female) was that of Ge (10 dr.), but the office of the priestess of the *Korubantes* who served females was priced higher than its partner office for the priest who served male constituents.[10] There was a priestess of Demeter Thesmophoros at Erythrae. A short inscription honors Zosime, priestess of Demeter Thesmophoros, for forty years of service:

> The *boulē* and the *dēmos* honored Zosime, daughter of _____, priestess of Demeter Thesmophoros and of Herse, who served as priestess for 40 years, for her reverence toward the gods and ...
> (*IErythrai* 69)

Forty years implies a lifelong office, *dia biou*. Zosime apparently lived long enough to preside over the institutional memory of the procedures for the *Thesmophoria* during a period of at least two generations. The records for the sale price of this priesthood, almost certainly once included in the catalogue, however, do not survive in the extant text.

The calendar of sacrifices at Erythrae lists prices for sacrificial victims designated for public rites, but the list turns out to be, for our purposes, just another dead end (*LSAM* 26).[11] The beginning and end of the original text are missing, and the list does not even contain the name of a single month. It is therefore impossible to correlate Demeter's festival program at Erythrae with the timetable of the agricultural year. Finally, although Demeter's name appears only once (Demeter Eleusinia, an adult sheep; 10 dr.), she and her

---

[10] Dignas 2002 suggests that the priestess was paid more because there were more female than male worshippers/initiates.

[11] Second century BC.

daughter were probably the ones who received a piglet "for the *pannukhis*"[12] and she herself was likely the divinity "in Leuce" (a place name) who received two piglets. Sheep and piglets are identified as sacrificial victims for Demeter and Kore elsewhere, and even the mandate to sacrifice to Kore an uncastrated male animal (ram, 10 dr.) is consistent with practice in other cities, where Persephone, Kore, and even Demeter herself could receive adult male victims.[13] Nevertheless, although there is nothing confusing about the evidence we do have, it is clear that we do not have enough to assume consistency of practice across regions and through time.

Eligibility for service seems to have been more a matter of status than a matter of experience, but if most priests and priestesses were in fact amateurs rather than professionals, who set the standards, who decided how ritual should be performed, and who was responsible for seeing that the rules were carried out? What happened on the ground on a day-to-day basis?

Professionals and Amateurs

The administration of Greek sacrifices, festivals, and sanctuaries was complex, and backstage maneuvers are rarely available for our consideration. The literary record tells us almost nothing about the administration of sanctuaries, and inscriptions tell us only about issues that needed to be spelled out locally. We know little about how worshippers interacted with temple staff and almost nothing about the responsibilities of individual offices. Contracts are more likely to spell out the rewards for priestly service than to give details about the actual duties. We are therefore poorly informed about qualifications for service. Sometimes one office seems to lead directly to another,[14] but family rank, wealth, and status were probably more decisive than experience. Reputation and attitude were not an issue. If hereditary office actually targeted those expected from birth to perform particular ritual service, this could have created opportunities for real training and long-term practice, but there is no indication that potential candidates for hereditary office ever received special training. In fact, Andocides' description of the private life of Callias indicates

---

[12] *Tais opisthē theais*, line 20, probably a reference to the location of their sanctuary, *behind the polis*, as opposed to *pro poleōs* at Smyrna, *ISmyrna* 655; and Paros, Herodotus 6.134.

[13] A ram for Persephone, Attica *LGS* I 26; a male piglet at Sparta, *IG* V i 364 line 11; a boar at Mykonos, *LSCG* 96, line 1, fourth century BC; and for Kore, a bull, Attic *deme* Phrearrhioi, Hesperia 1970:48, line 13.

[14] At Patmos a young female who had served as hydrophoros for Artemis graduated to rank of priestess: Kernos 2001 no. 175; *Steinepigramme* 01/21/01.

that questionable or even scandalous personal behavior did not compromise entitlement to hereditary priestly office (Andocides 1.124–128).

Did it matter that some were professionals, others only amateurs, and that, except for those who held long-term hereditary priesthoods, all others (whether appointed, elected, or competing to purchase) were in some sense volunteers? Like political office in Cleisthenes' Athens, priestly responsibilities often circulated among a wide group of qualified individuals. Who, then, actually did the work of sanctuary management; who decided what rituals should be performed; and who organized the cleanup of ash, blood, and fat of animal slaughter and roasting of meat after a major festival was concluded? Finally, who was responsible for maintaining the official record and who gave instructions for transmitting the details of cult practice to the next generation?

Administrative Structures

Organization of Demeter's ritual at the local level is illustrated by deme decrees from Attica.[15] Elsewhere requirements for service were not always uniform. Tradition was cited as the tie that bound one generation to another and created consistency for the decentralized rites of Demeter throughout the Mediterranean, but we are not always able to follow the exact history. Literary sources, especially the comments of Pausanias, indicate more variety than inscriptions do. At Olympia the priestess of Demeter Khamune had special duties and privileges (Pausanias 6.20.9).[16] She partook of the same purification rites as the *Hellanodikai*, and as the only married woman permitted to observe the athletic contests in the stadium, she watched from a special seat. Pausanias tells us that at the time of the foundation of Thasos from Paros Demeter's priestess, a young *parthenos* named Cleiobeia, was responsible for transporting the special ritual objects of the goddess to the new city (10.28.3). At Hermione Demeter's elderly female attendants regularly slaughtered with sickles four cows let loose in her temple (2.35.6–8).[17]

Inscriptions are concerned with procedure. On fourth-century Cos, as we have seen, deme priestesses of Demeter had to meet the same purity standards as the city priestesses of Demeter Olympia in town (*LSCG* 154).[18] The effects

---

[15] IG II² 1175 (Halai Axionides); 1177 (Piraeus); 1184 (Cholargus); Hesperia 1942:265–274. See Whitehead 1986: 79–81 for more examples.

[16] Compare 5.6.7.

[17] Only the four old women could identify the object of their worship. Pausanias says that he never saw it, and that neither foreigner nor local Hermion male ever did either.

[18] Comparing IIa with IIb, fourth century BC.

of synoecism are apparent in other ways. At Antimachia, where annual selection was offered by both purchase and sortition in the late fourth century, the system for selecting priestesses seems to have been spliced together from two different procedures at the time of the synoecism. Several priestesses were chosen at the same meeting, so individual demes of Antimachia must have been represented. The women who served swore an oath on assuming office (*SIG*³ 1006; *LSCG* 175).[19] Most towns had several priestesses of Demeter because Demeter was worshipped in every neighborhood. At Mantinea there was even a *koinon* (organization) of priestesses of Demeter and Persephone. The organization held meetings and passed motions to regulate banquets and to vote honors for their colleagues. The procedures guaranteed collective decisions and provided a means of publishing awards of public praise for the accomplishments of individual priestesses (*IG* V ii 266; *IPArk* 12, with commentary). Priestesses were required to meet the expectations of the community, and even the smallest divisions of the *polis* were considered "symbolic representations" of the whole.[20] In the Athenian deme of Melite, Satyra, another priestess of Demeter Thesmophoros, received public honors from the demesmen for her service and for her generosity in contributing more than one hundred drachmas for the annual sacrifices (Broneer 1942:265f no. 51).[21] In addition to commendation by the deme, Satyra is granted a crown of myrtle and the right to set up a painted portrait of herself in the temple of Demeter and Kore, the same privilege granted to other priestesses of Demeter.

Priestly status for females, however, was no guarantee of authority. Although priestesses of Demeter assumed responsibilities that conferred special status, that status was temporary and even a priestess could not act independently of her *kurios* (guardian). At the scheduled sortition for the priesthoods of Demeter at Antimachia, women unable to attend could be represented by a *kurios*. Husbands could therefore stand in for wives.[22] In the Attic demes wealthy husbands assumed in turn the obligations associated with the liturgies that subsidized deme banquets for the *Thesmophoria* (Isaios 3.80; 8.19f). Women's rituals were embedded in the deme calendar, but women were not deme members themselves.[23]

---

[19] Late fourth century BC.

[20] Sourvinou-Inwood 2000:40; for priestly responsibilities, see 38–44.

[21] Early second century BC.

[22] A woman did not necessarily purchase an office herself; at Halicarnassus the husband of the priestess of Artemis Pergaia, for instance, acted on her behalf: see *LSAM* 73.

[23] Whitehead 1986:81.

Local rules were set and ratified by local male assemblies. On Cos it was the husband of the priestess of Dionysus, not the priestess herself, who reported infractions to the local council (*LSCG* 166.28–30). A deme decree from Piraeus, recognizing the authority of the priestess of Demeter with respect to ritual, denied women the use of the sanctuary of Demeter if the priestess was not present (*IG* II² 1177). The deme assembly was prepared to recognize women's rites that could be called traditional, citing the *Thesmophoria*, the *Plerosia*, the *Kalamaia*, and the *Skira*; and they acknowledged the propriety of further events—"if the women come together on any other day *kata ta patria*." Alexandra was not the only priestess of Demeter to worry about precedent and appropriate behavior. The priestess of Demeter at Arcesine, concerned about women making free use of Demeter's sanctuary at forbidden times, requested that the local council and assembly fix a penalty for *asebeia* (*LSCG* 102).[24] She herself had no special jurisdiction. However, priestesses did have prerogatives protected by tradition. Archias, the fourth-century Eleusinian hierophant charged with impiety (*asebeia*) because he performed sacrifice *in defiance of ancestral tradition* (*para ta patria*), was executed for usurping the place of the priestess of Demeter at a sacrifice at the *eskhara* at Eleusis ([Demosthenes] 59.116; Athenaeus 13.594b).[25] Theano, priestess of Demeter at Eleusis who refused to perform the public curse of Alcibiades, apparently was not punished for her disobedience (Plutarch *Alcibiades* 22; 33).[26] The rights of priestesses were protected. Nevertheless, the fact that priestesses of Demeter were recognized as women of authority did not grant them special power. The authority of any priest or priestess did not reach outside the boundaries of the sanctuary.[27]

---

[24] Fourth century BC. Two other decrees issued in women's names, *LSAM* 61 and *LSS* 127, must refer to an assembly of women constituted for a festival. Neither preserves the name of the divinity concerned.

[25] He also sacrificed on a day when sacrifice was not permitted. The issues are discussed by Kron 1996:141n13. Clinton 1974:17n41 points out that the sacrifice in question (at the Haloa) was for Dionysus, not Demeter. If the speech known as *Diadikasia* of the Priestess of Demeter against the Hierophant (included in the fragments of Dinarchus) refers to the same case, the priestess of Demeter herself brought the charge. See Clinton 1974:23 with n85.

[26] By decree all the priests and priestesses of Athens were commanded to publicly curse Alcibiades, convicted of *asebeia* for impersonating the Eleusinian hierophant. The real hierophant, Theodorus, participated in the original public curse. When a second decree rescinded that curse seven years later, he claimed that because he had uttered the city's curse, not his own, he had meant no harm. As Clinton 1974:16 points out, *asebeia* was a state crime. For public curses as the responsibility of priests and priestesses on Delos, compare *SEG* 48.1037 and Chaniotis in this volume.

[27] Garland 1984:75: "The competence of the Greek priest extended no further than the enclosure wall of his sanctuary."

Even though rituals of Demeter were modest, protected by requirements of secrecy, and performed away from the eyes of the male community, ruling bodies and authorities had a stake in seeing to it that the rituals of the goddess were properly carried out. A deme decree from Attica about responsibility for supplying commodities for the *Thesmophoria* in Cholargus illustrates commitment to precedent:

> ... the *hieromnemones*;
>
> and with regard to those serving in common as leaders (*arkhousai*), both are to give to the priestess for the festival and for the care of the *Thesmophoria* the following:
>
> a twelfth *medimnos* of barley;
> a twelfth *medimnos* of wheat; a twelfth *medimnos* of barley meal;
> a twelfth *medimnos* of wheat meal (?)
> a twelfth *medimnos* of dried figs;
> 1 *khous* of wine;
> 1/2 *khous* of olive oil;
> 2 *kolutai* of honey;
> 1 *khoinix* of white sesame seeds
> 1 *khoinix* of black sesame seeds;
> 1 *khoinix* of poppy seeds;
> 2 fresh cheeses, not less than 1 stater each;
> a pine torch not less than 2 obols;
> and 4 drachmas of silver;
> and this is what the two leaders are to give.
>
> Further, those in office when Ctesicles is archon,[28] are to set up a stele of stone in the Pythium and to inscribe this decree on the stele, so that for the sake of the deme of the Cholargeis it might be available, letter by letter, for all time; whatever they spend is to be charged to the Cholargeis. (*IG* II² 1184)

The assembly paid for the inscription; the women who held annual office as *arkhousai* paid for the ingredients for the ritual cakes. The *arkhousai* were the women appointed in each deme to take charge of the annual banquet. The menu for Demeter was always prescribed. This particular inscription records the recipe "letter by letter" so that Demeter's cakes could be reproduced in precisely the same way every time the *Thesmophoria* took place in the deme.

---

[28] In 334/333 BC.

The *arkhousai* themselves probably served on an annual basis. The responsibility for ritual continuity did not rest on their shoulders because the deme assembly claimed authority to make decisions about the women's ceremonies and publicly claimed that their decisions were in effect forever. It should be no surprise to find that the men of Cholargos knew the recipe for Demeter's cakes so well that that their regulation reproduced the shopping list for the *arkhousai*.[29] The demesmen may have been excluded from the ceremonies of the *Thesmophoria*, but they were certainly familiar with the festival's menu.

For a festival of Demeter, Kore, and Zeus Bouleus on Mykonos, preparations were just as complicated (*SIG*[3] 1024). Here the *hieropoioi* paid for the wood and the sacrificial victims. For another festival for a female clientele, priests and archons had jurisdiction. The text issues an invitation to any of the women of Mykonos who wished to attend, as well as any of those women living in Mykonos who had completed the required cycles of special ceremonies for Demeter. No priestess is mentioned for these sacrifices (*LSCG* 96.15–20), but we may expect that a priestess officiated at the ceremony.

Good Girls, Bad Girls

Literature represents priestesses as female first and as sacred officials only second. Stories about priestesses seem to divide them into two groups: good girls and bad girls. Good girls are loyal to their families and city, bad girls are traitors. Alexandra belongs to the first class; Archidamia, a priestess of Demeter at Aegila in Laconia, belongs to the second. Archidamia let her affections for the Messenian leader Aristomenes overcome her loyalty to her own people.[30] Herodotus' account about Timo of Paros seems on first reading to be constructed on the same model. Timo was the sanctuary attendant blamed for encouraging Miltiades to violate the sanctuary of Demeter at Paros. Herodotus appears to imply that she betrayed her office (and therefore the goddess), and her city. There is, however, another possible interpretation of this episode.

It is instructive to examine the case of Timo closely. Subordinate temple-warden of the chthonic goddesses at the sanctuary of Demeter *pro poleōs* at Paros, Timo was taken captive when Miltiades laid siege to the city. In an interview with Miltiades she told him that the defense of the city could be broken

---

[29] Demeter has more cakes, more flavors of cake, and more shapes of cake than any other divinity. For discussion of ritual cakes, see Brumfield 1997 (thirty-nine varieties mentioned in epigraphical and literary sources); Kearns 1994.

[30] Taken captive as a result of the retaliation by women for male intrusion at their festival, as Pausanias reports, 4.17.1.

if he took a shortcut through the sanctuary of Demeter to reach the city gate. Miltiades followed her advice and attempted to examine the sanctuary even though it was off bounds for males. He jumped the precinct wall, but when he tried to open the *herkos* of Demeter Thesmophoros, he found the doors locked. Herodotus suspects that Miltiades intended to do something in the *megaron*, either to "move something that could not be moved or do something or other," but before Miltiades could even begin, a wave of fright and horror came over him, and he turned back the way he had come. In his fear, he hurt his thigh jumping back over the fence and thus incurred the injury that would lead to his downfall and death.

The Parians were distressed because Timo seemed willing to betray her *patris* and reveal to Miltiades sacred things that could not be spoken to the male *gonos*. When they consulted Delphi about dealing with her, however, they found that there were two sides to the story. The Pythia let Timo off without a reprimand. She would not allow the Parians to punish a priestess who was not the cause of these events, but only the facilitator.[31] According to the oracle, Miltiades was responsible for his own bad end.

Miltiades' panic and his experience of horror indicate confrontation with divinity. His experience of the goddess was not the experience described in epic, where the hero is overcome by the beauty, fragrance, and glow of a goddess,[32] but one more like Orestes' waking-nightmare vision of the Erinyes. It is almost as if the Pythia assumed that Timo had tricked Miltiades into walking into a divine ambush in Demeter's sanctuary. Did the Pythia protect Timo because she had deliberately created a situation where Miltiades could be defeated by Demeter herself? The issue of concern to Delphi is Miltiades' violation of Demeter's sanctuary, a violation inspired by arrogance, not Timo's tactical suggestion. The Parians were bound to accept the word of Apollo because the oracle was the board of final appeal and Apollo had the last word.

At Didyma, Alexandra was worried about an epidemic of epiphanies, but epiphany by day or night was a major mode of communication for Demeter. At Priene a man from Cyprus put up a plaque to memorialize an experience in which the two *Thesmophoroi* robed in white appeared to him three times in dreams, commanding him to honor the local hero Naulochus as founder of the city (*IPriene* 196).[33] In the *Homeric Hymn to Demeter,* the goddess appears

---

[31] Herodotus tells the whole story in 6.134–136. The actual events may not be as he reports, but the description of the sanctuary as "in front of the town" and of a *megaron* in a precinct surrounded by a wall, is consistent with many known sanctuaries of Demeter.

[32] As listed by Richardson 1974:252.

[33] With thanks to Gil Renberg for reminding me about this text.

twice in epiphany (188–211, 256–80).[34] The core experience of the Eleusinian initiate seems to have been based on an experience of divine epiphany, an experience that implies a special relationship between a god and a human individual. When Miltiades saw what a man should not see, he destroyed that relationship. Vision is an important element of the experience of Demeter, whatever the ritual, but ritual vision is regulated. Herodotus and Aristophanes both emphasize that the privilege of the ritual gaze could be contingent on gender. Aristophanes, commenting on the *Thesmophoria*, says, "It is not right for men to see" the rites of the women in the grove at the *Thesmophoria* (*Thesmophoroiazusai* 1150).

Demeter could appear in visions to order a temple, demand worship, or request a dedication. Other divinities could stand in for Demeter. At Cnidus a priestess of Demeter named Chrysina dedicated an *oikos* and a statue of her daughter Chrysogone because Hermes appeared to her in a dream and told her to minister to the two goddesses at Tathne (a place, probably a deme, at Cnidus; *IKnidos* 131).[35] Epiphanies of Demeter could happen with or without her attendants. In 345 Demeter appeared at Corinth in a dream to her own priestesses to promise that she herself would accompany Timoleon on campaign to Sicily (Diodoros 16.66.4; Plutarch *Timoleon* 8). Timoleon therefore named his trireme "The Two Goddesses" and when he sailed by night from Corcyra, it was noticed that a light from the sky touched his ship. For the interpreters (*manteis*) accompanying the general, this *phasma*, the appearance of light, confirmed the promise that the goddess had made to the priestesses at Corinth.[36]

Demeter appeared to Timoleon as she did to others in wartime to confirm support for those she favored. She was also present in the apparition perceived by Dicaeus and Demaratus on the Thriasian plain in 480 just before the battle of Salamis. These two men saw a cloud of dust moving from Eleusis and heard the ritual cries of the Iacchus song, normally sung by worshippers in procession from Athens to Eleusis. The perceptions of Dicaeus and Demaratus were stimulated by both sight and sound even though this was the year the mysteries could not have been celebrated. With the Persian fleet almost at the harbor of Athens, the Athenians had already abandoned Attica to the gods. The vision seen by Dicaeus and Demaratus, however, was a sign that the gods would protect Attica even when the Athenians themselves were

---

[34] Discussed by Richardson 1974:207–211, 252–256.

[35] Mid or late fourth century BC.

[36] Pritchett 1981:3.17 summarizes the account.

absent. Demeter indicated her concern for the Greeks again the next year at Plataea. Although fighting took place all around her sanctuary, she made her protection manifest by allowing no Persian to fall dead on her sacred ground (Herodotus 9.65).

Finally, at Argos in 272 Pyrrhus is said to have met his death at the hands of a woman who hit him with a roof tile. The slayer was no ordinary mortal, but the goddess herself, disguised as an Argive woman (Pausanias 1.13.8; Plutarch *Pyrrhus* 34; Strabo 8.6.18).[37] Demeter's retribution would have been appropriate for Pyrrhus because he was known to have violated a sanctuary of Persephone (Dionysius of Halicarnassus 20.9).

Three aspects of Demeter's interest in her worshippers stand out. In all three accounts, visions and divine epiphanies are contagious, but the three situations are not identical. Alexandra's request to the oracle describes clusters of visitations. Demeter's priestesses at Corinth all report the same dream. In the narrative about the procession to Eleusis, Herodotus gives us an example of the same waking vision experienced simultaneously by two people. From these examples it does not seem that the appearance of a god to a priest or priestess carried more weight than the same appearance to an ordinary person, but accounts of contagious dreams, serial epiphanies, and simultaneous visions make it clear that there was some advantage to a story that claimed a group experience. Finally, a laconic text from the grave of the priestess Ammas at Thyateira, promising visions (*horamata*) by night or day to those who made a sacrifice on the spot, seems premised on an assumption that divine epiphany could be summoned on demand (*TAM* 5.1055).[38]

Hereditary Priesthoods and Ritual Stability: Reviving the Old Woman

After the battle of Leuctra, the Messenians reclaimed sovereignty over their territory. Pausanias connects the reestablishment of Messenian political power in the fourth century with the continuity of Demeter's ritual.[39] As he tells the story more than half a millennium later, the Messenians could not legitimate their autonomy until they recovered the physical ritual object that confirmed their identity and validated their history. Dreams play an important part in

---

[37] For discussion of sources, see Pritchett 1981:3.34.
[38] Where the grave of a priestess is marked with an altar dedicated by her children and local *mystai* so that those in need of a vision can pray for one here.
[39] My account here is inspired by Alcock 2001.

Pausanias' narrative. Demeter's ancient hierophant (or a figure that resembles him) provides the necessary instructions. Direct from Eleusis at the time of the return of the Messenians, he appears in two instructive dreams that underscore the solemnity of the moment. His appearance to Epaminondas establishes the template for a *polis* (4.26.5–6.). His appearance to Epiteles reveals the hidden location of a text that preserved the ancient rituals of the Messenian people (4.26.7–8).

The Athenian hierophant is a powerful symbol in the narrative as Pausanias reports it. Because Epiteles followed the instructions of the hierophant "to revive the old woman" he was able to discover the vital message the Messenians needed. By excavating where the hierophant instructed in the dream, he found an inscribed sheet of tin rolled up like a bookroll inside a buried bronze *hudria*. Left by the ancient Messenian king, Aristomenes, the text preserved (and therefore restored to the Messenians) their own sacred rite (*teletē*) of the Great Goddesses. Because the story constructs an Eleusinian genealogy for this *teletē*, we can equate these Great Goddesses with Demeter and her daughter, the two goddesses Pausanias associates with the sanctuary in the Carnasian grove near Messene.[40] The Messenians needed the remnant of their cultural memory because exile and Spartan domination had kept them from maintaining the dedications and sanctuaries that would have testified to a historical tradition and validation of their claims to territory. Without this testimony, they had nothing they could claim as *kata ta patria*.

The integration of the sacred text into Messenian tradition required the cooperation of the hereditary priesthood of the goddesses. Pausanias tells us that the priesthood of Messenian Zeus at Ithome was an annual appointment (4.33.2), but he makes it clear that the priesthood of the Great Goddesses at Andania was controlled by a single *genos* whose line the Messenians traced back to Aristomenes' day. The chief Andanian ritual specialist, like the chief priest at Eleusis, had the title *hierophant*. Survival of the *genos* depended on a connection to Eleusis. Eleusis was both ancestral home and haven because the Messenians believed that their own mysteries had been brought from Eleusis to Andania by the Eleusinian hierophant Caucon at the time of the original foundation of the sanctuary (4.14.1). As the traditional account makes clear, the *genos* of priests took refuge at Eleusis during the first Messenian War and did not return home until the Messenian revolt. According to Pausanias, this *genos* was still marked as special almost three centuries later. The task of recording on papyrus bookrolls the ritual of the *teletē* preserved on the page

---

[40] Piolot 1999:207–223 discusses the problems of identifying the divinities.

of tin belonged to the priests of this *genos* because only the priests could have anything to do with the content of the ritual outside the performance of the mysteries themselves (4.27.5).[41] The actual rites could not be recalled without the discovery of the instructions on the tin tablet, but the family responsible for conducting those rites could still be identified. The survival of the *genos* of priests secured Messenian sovereignty over the land.

Even Pausanias admits that 287 years is a long time, but he is confident that the Messenians would have forgotten neither their customs nor their Doric habits of speech (4.27.9–11). Further, he recognizes the Andanian mysteries of the Messenians as belonging to the most sacred rites of all Hellas, surpassed in sanctity only by the Eleusinian mysteries (4.33.5). Like the oracle about Demeter at Didyma, the story Pausanias tells considers the connection to Eleusis a connection to a distant, but formative past. Both Miletus and Messene strove to represent themselves as specially designated ritual heirs in a direct line extending back to Eleusis. Caucon figures in both accounts. The Messenians recognized him in the hierophant who appeared in dreams to Epaminondas and Epiteles (4.26.8), the priest who had instructed them about the mysteries in the first place. He was a descendent of Phlyus, Athenian of the earth-born generation (4.1.5–9).[42] The Neleids at Miletus, who were called *Kaukōnes*, were said to have arrived at Miletus from Pylos by way of Athens. Both cities have grafted their rituals on an Athenian stem.[43] Pausanias does not believe everything he hears. He introduces the claim for the identification of the "aged hierophant" as Caucon with the qualifying verb form *legousin* (they say) because, like Herodotus discussing the rites at Samothrace or commenting on the *Thesmophoria*,[44] he is restrained by his own experience of ritual from disclosing everything he knows (4.33.5). Nevertheless, his Messenian narrative demonstrates that the institution with the strongest claim for preservation was not the mysteries themselves (because they required continuity of place and performance, and both had been lost), but the Andanian hereditary priesthood said to have been preserved with support from Eleusis. Genealogies could be fabricated and traditions conveniently altered. The oral histories recited

---

[41] For (re)discovery of a lost talisman of an interrupted mystery ceremony, compare the story about the priest Trocondas, who "discovered" something and handed over the "sacred mystery rites" of Artemis Ephesia to the Pisidians; Horsley 1992:119–150 (BE 1993.95; Kernos 1996:100). On Trocondas, see also Chaniotis in this volume.

[42] The tradition is confused, but one consistent feature is the tendency to associate the early history of the Messenian mysteries with Eleusis and Athens.

[43] The evidence is collected by Robertson 1988:230–261.

[44] For the reticence of Herodotus on mysteries and other restricted rites, see 2.51 (on the mysteries at Samothrace) and 2.171 (on the Thesmophoria).

locally in ceremonies or proudly summarized for tourists did not always have to be corroborated by documents. The prestige conferred on local cults by hereditary priesthoods may have offered enough evidence.

The Consolations of Narrative

The responsibility for creating and maintaining the appearance of ritual continuity was shared by hereditary priesthoods, public administrative bodies, written records, and, hardest to trace, ritual habit. Connection to a famous and long-lived regional or far-distant sanctuary could also confer prestige. Individual priests and priestesses could only imitate what they knew, and individual experience could not have reached very far. For both Messenians and Milesians, Eleusinian precedents were especially meaningful. Rules and regulations recorded on stone and texts like the one on the page of tin indicate deep confidence in the longevity of the written word.[45] I doubt, however, that the deme *arkhousai* in Cholargus made an excursion to the stone for autopsy before assembling the ingredients for Demeter's cakes at every annual deme celebration of the *Thesmophoria*. Reliance on the written word is a theme magnified again and again in the *leges sacrae*, but as the disputes surrounding the publication of the Athenian ritual calendar in the late fifth century should remind us, records were neither comprehensive nor always retrievable, and publication on stone was not always a matter of policy.

Narratives of divine epiphany offered models for ritual behavior. Priests took notes on epiphanies and wrote official accounts (*epistolai*) collected in local archives.[46] Oral tradition lies behind many narratives recounted in our sources. Narratives about divine epiphany are formulaic, many manufactured long after the experience they claim to illustrate, but the attitudes they represent were shaped by tradition. Constructed in response to crisis or to emphasize a special relationship with a god, such narratives give some indication of the attitudes and aspirations that shaped tradition. We can see why people relied on such accounts. Not every priestess was as sympathetic as Alexandra, as reliable as Zosime, or as clever as Timo, but their stories provided an opportunity for public display of collective human response to the divine. Repetition offered consolation and assurance that such responses were acceptable, and above all, *kata ta patria*.

---

[45] Henrichs 2002 and 2003 for distinctions between the various kinds of texts.
[46] Higbie 2003:199–201.

4

Greek Priests of Sarapis?

Beate Dignas

S TUDYING HELLENISTIC PRIESTS IS PIECEWORK. Given that the main body of
evidence comes from inscriptions, the questions, where is the best place
to start? and how can this study be structured successfully? seem almost
unanswerable. The task is extremely ambitious, but general statements on the
character and significance of priesthoods are such a desideratum that even
idiosyncratic examples must be evaluated, and comparison on various levels
must be allowed. But again, it seems almost impossible to establish the criteria
for evaluation. As several articles in this volume illustrate,[1] local idiosyncrasies
form part of even the most general conclusions. Starting in one place where
the evidence allows us to make statements, and then moving on to another,
and so forth, is thus a good idea—if successful, we can answer the question,
what was it like to be priest in X (be it Rhodes, Cos, Stratonicea, Delos, or
somewhere else)? The criteria *place, local political history,* and *religious tradition*
receive most attention when this approach is taken. Another approach, which
has to complement the one just described, is to examine certain aspects of
priesthood *across the board*; to give a few examples: the *revenues of priests,* the
duties of priests, the *mode of appointment,* the *social background,* and so on.[2] In
the most general terms, we can thereby answer questions such as these: was
it attractive to be a priest serving a Greek cult in the Hellenistic period? and
what was the character of the office with regard to element X?"

It might not suggest itself so readily, but it is also possible to look at
priests of the same deity in various places, in order to be able to say whether
a priesthood of Athena, for example, showed characteristics shared by her
priests everywhere. We tend not to undertake studies of this kind because

[1] See Bremmer and Gotter in this volume.
[2] This is the approach taken by Chaniotis, who explores the priests as "ritual experts."

our knowledge of a Greek pantheon within an individual *polis* suggests that Athena was a different Athena of different status in each community. A particular mythological tradition reflected in aspects of ritual may have a bearing on the topic, but supposedly not enough to justify an extended study devoted to *priesthoods of Athena.*

This attitude may change somewhat when it comes to nontraditional cults.[3] The Hellenistic period is generally said to be a time when new, foreign cults swept over the Greek world, which extended into areas that brought forward aspects of religion unknown in the traditional cults. Peculiar and exotic forms of worship; a new, personal attachment of worshippers to a particular deity; omnipotent gods with an array of characteristics that covered the realms of a number of traditional gods—these are but a few of the catchphrases used to describe the changes. *Priests*, or rather our assumptions regarding the character of priesthoods, form part of the description. The contrast between *priests in the oriental cults* and *Greek priests* is often the gist of the argument, although in many cases the supposedly new cults were firmly integrated among the official cults of a *polis* and in most respects resembled the traditional cults strikingly.[4] In more detailed studies, this resemblance is taken into account insofar as scholars seek the moment when such a cult was accepted as a public cult and when its features—and personnel—were thereby *Hellenized.*[5] To say it bluntly, *Greek priests* were created from one moment to the next. This essay examines one example of this type, namely the cult of Sarapis,[6] in order to show how unhelpful the dichotomy *private* versus *public* is and to illustrate how many factors contributed to the profiles of priests of Sarapis in the Hellenistic period.

[3] And this includes deities whose worship and *realm of authority* involved women in an exceptional way. See the essay by Cole in this volume, which focuses on the priestesses of Demeter.

[4] See Bremmer in this volume: his study of the priestly personnel at Ephesus reveals the complexity of labels such as *Greek* or *Anatolian*.

[5] Cf. e.g. Fraser 1960:22; Fraser's aim, however, is to show that the success of the Egyptian cults was not due to Ptolemaic influence, which would be reflected in the establishment of public rather than private cults. Roussel 1987 structures his description of the cults on Delos by contrasting the *private* and the *public* cults. See Brady 1978:18 (Delos) and 21–22 (Halicarnassus and Thera) and passim. Baslez 1977 emphasizes (in chapter 3) that the fact that the official acknowledgement of the cults was not decisive for the situation of the oriental religions on Delos, is an exception.

[6] The material relating to the Egyptian gods is now even more accessible through the corpus of inscriptions edited by L. Bricault (*Recueil des inscriptions concernant les cultes isiaques*, 2005 [= *RICIS*]), which updates L. Vidman's *Sylloge Inscriptionum Religionis Isiacae et Sarapiacae* [*SIRIS*]; equally helpful is the inventory of the archaeological material in the *Atlas de la diffusion des cultes isiaques* (2001), by the same scholar. In what follows, references are given to the numbers

In search of evidence that gives a full and lively account of Hellenistic priesthoods, I have come across a small number of epigraphical documents repeatedly. One of these is the so-called *Delian aretalogy of Sarapis* (*IG* XI 4, 1299),[7] a prose account of a priest of Sarapis, Apollonius (lines 1–28), and a hymn to Sarapis by the poet Maiistas (lines 29–94), both of which set out the history of the cult on Delos, starting with the foundation of the cult by Apollonius' grandfather of the same name, who had brought with him a small statue of the god from Memphis, and ending with the building of the first temple for the god (ca. 280–200 BC). As vivid and revealing as the inscription is with regard to the lives and doings of priests, I nevertheless set it aside several times on the grounds that it describes something that does not pertain to *Greek priests*.[8] Rightly so, it would seem, because here are a cult and priestly family that clash in all respects with what we expect from Greek priests. We are explicitly told that Apollonius' grandfather was an Egyptian, whose priesthood of Sarapis ran in the family.

> The priest Apollonius wrote this according to the command of the god. My grandfather Apollonius, who was an Egyptian and the offspring of a family of priests, came from Egypt and brought the god with him; and he continued to worship him as his forefathers had done, and he seems to have lived to the age of 97. (lines 1–6)[9]

This man carefully taught his son Demetrius how to carry out his priestly duties (lines 12ff.), and his grandson finally wrote down the history of the cult "according to the command of the god." When the god appeared to the author in a dream and ordered him to buy a piece of land on which to build a proper sanctuary, the priest encountered hostility and was involved in a public law suit, which—with the help of the god's miraculous powers—he won.[10] Hence

---

in *SIRIS* and *RICIS*; with regard to the Delian inscriptions references are also given to the respective numbers in P. Roussel's *Les cultes égyptiens à Délos du IIIe au Ier s. av. J.-C. [CE]*.

[7] Engelmann 1964 and 1975; *CE* 1 (French trans.); Totti 1985 no. 1 (German trans.); now also *RICIS* 202/0101 (with a French trans.).

[8] Above all, the *aretalogy* as such would be considered as a non-Greek feature by some scholars. I do not want to enter the discussion regarding the Greek or Egyptian origin of aretalogies. For a summary and bibliography see the introduction to Versnel 1990. Texts such as the Lindian *anagraphē* illustrate that the concept was certainly familiar in traditional Greek cults by the Hellenistic period.

[9] ὁ ἱερεὺς Ἀπολλώνιος ἀνέγραψεν κατὰ πρόσταγμα τοῦ θεοῦ· ὁ γὰρ πάππος ἡμῶν Ἀπολλώνιος, ὢν Αἰγύπτιος ἐκ τῶν ἱερέων, τὸν θεὸν ἔπαρεγένετο ἐξ Αἰγύπτου, θεραπεύων τε διετέλει καθὼς πάτριον ἦν, ζῶσαί τε δοκεῖ ἔτη ἐνενήκοντα καὶ ἑπτά.

[10] Cf. lines 23–28; we do not know on which grounds Apollonius was accused. Cf. Engelmann 1975:2: "A. II had omitted to obtain official permission for the building of the temple." With the

the inscribed column, a grateful testimony to his victory, accompanied by a votive tablet dedicated to Nike by the priest and a group of worshippers that call themselves *hoi sumbalomenoi tōn therapeutōn* (*CE* 3 = *IG* XI 4, 1290 = *RICIS* 202/0121).

Apparently, Apollonius' cult remained a small, private cult up to this point, but we do not know how the cult's popularity developed from then onwards.[11] Inscriptions from Sarapeum A, where the aretalogy was found, show that dedications were made not only by the *therapeuontes* (*CE* 2 = *RICIS* 202/0114–0120), who may have been a group of foreign worshippers, but also by a Delian citizen who was treasurer in 180 BC (*CE* 4 = *RICIS* 202/0122) and that the temple possessed a *thesaurus* (*CE* 6 = *RICIS* 202/0124). The epigraphic record furthermore reveals that shortly after the Athenians regained control over Delos in 166 BC the priest of Sarapis clashed with the authorities again. In a letter from the Athenian *stratēgoi*, the governor of the island was instructed to comply with a *senatus consultum* from Rome that allowed the priest of Sarapis, Demetrius from Rheneia, to reopen the sanctuary and be its servant just like before (*CE* 14 = *RICIS* 202/0195). The priest was now a Delian, who, as we learn from a dedication made shortly after this, was assisted by a man called Horus, son of Horus from Kasion, who "took care of the sanctuary and dealt with devotees' cures" (*CE* 15bis = *RICIS* 202/0198).[12] Over more than a hundred years, important features of the priesthood remained the same. Presumably, the priest continued to serve for life and the priesthood stayed in the same family. Twice, its holder was powerful and ambitious enough to defend his office against the authorities, even involving the Roman powers. Although no longer a foreigner himself, the priest was still assisted by an Egyptian so that specific tasks would be carried out in the traditional way. The priest must have

---

same explanation, Brady 1978:18 and Vidman 1970:36. Baslez 1977:215 argues that the Egyptian elements of the cult were responsible. Roussel, *CE,* pp. 246ff. points to the competition between private and public cults. Most recently, Siard 1998 argued that the conflict arose because the priest claimed access to a public water supply.

[11] Cf. Fraser 1960:22: "at this time the cult ... became public." Mikalson 1991:212 about Sarapeum C: "the only one to become a state cult," but 214; "Sarapis had by now at least one state cult on Delos." Siard 1998:482–483 clearly assumes that the sanctuary remained private when she points out the unique situation of an "*édifice privé racordé au réseau public de distribution d'eau*" (483). Baslez 1977:224–225 emphasizes the private setting. Brady 1978:18 assumes that the cult became public when a Delian became priest. Roussel, *CE,* 258 calls Sarapeum C the only public cult center. Jost 1998:303 emphasizes the contrast between the *public* interest/threat and the *private* cult setting.

[12] Dedication by a Delian couple on behalf of their son made during the priesthood of Demetrius, a Delian.

relied on a loyal group of worshippers who supported his claims when they were questioned and supported the cult and its priest financially.

Sarapeum A was not the only or even the main sanctuary of Sarapis on Delos. Two more cult centers have been discovered.[13] Sarapeum B appears to have been mainly a meeting place for associations of worshippers—the dedications that have been found were made by *eranistai*, (*CE* 20 = *RICIS* 202/0134), a *thiasos* (*CE* 21 = *RICIS* 202/0135), a *koinon tōn dekadistriōn* (*CE* 25 = *RICIS* 202/0139), and a *koinon enatistōn* (*CE* 26f = *RICIS* 202/0140–0141)[14]—but was also served by a priest. There is no evidence as to the character of the priesthood and the social or ethnic origin of its holders.[15] Sarapeum C, a monumental complex above the reservoir of the Inopus, was by far the largest of the three temples and prospered in particular during the second half of the second century BC.[16] The Delian inventories of the Athenian period include the objects from this temple just like those of any other public cult. Sarapis' treasure is the most extensive treasure aside from Apollo's.[17] The cult's origins, however, are not known to us. It seems plausible that it was also founded on private initiative, like Apollonius' cult and many other cults of Sarapis in the Greek world.[18] Inscriptions dating from before 166 BC do not characterize the clientele of this sanctuary any differently from that of Sarapeum A: dedications were made by *therapeutai* (*CE* 41f = *RICIS* 202/0161–0162) as well as the so-called *sumbalomenoi* (*CE* 45f = *RICIS* 202/0165–0167),[19] and references to ritual and personnel remind the reader strongly of Egyptian cults. One of the worshippers describes himself as "wearing linen" (*CE* 49 = *RICIS* 202/0170),[20] and a cult regulation prescribes abstinence from wine when entering the sanctuary (*CE* 50 = *RICIS* 202/0173–0174). Moreover, there are dedications by an *aretalogos* (*CE* 60 = *RICIS* 202/0186) and a *melanēphoros* (*CE* 58/58bis = *RICIS* 202/0183–0184). Unfortunately, there

---

[13] While all scholars distinguish between the three different temples of Sarapis on Delos, some go as far as to talk about three different cults, whereas others do not. Hamilton 2000:196 refers to the "unusually well-documented shift from private to public cult," and sees temples A and B as temples "built ... when the cult was still private," and temple C as "the large official temple of Sarapis."

[14] The reference to a κοινὸν τῶν θιαστῶν, an ἀρχιθιασίτης, and to a *leader* suggests that the associations had their own hierarchy.

[15] Cf. CE 21 (= *RICIS* 202/0135), various associations honoring the priest Kineas; and CE 22 (= *RICIS* 202/0136), a dedication dated by his priesthood.

[16] Cf. Bruneau and Ducat 1983:227–229.

[17] Cf. Hamilton 2000:196–197, 223–239.

[18] See Fraser 1960; Rigsby 2001; Voutiras 2005; and below.

[19] These dedicate, just as in Sarapeum A κατά πρόσταγμα.

[20] Or "carrying ritual objects wrapped in linen"?

is hardly any evidence regarding the priests who served this cult before the Athenian control of the island but an entry in an inventory from 182 BC lists a dedication made by the *Sarapiastai*, "whose leader was the priest Menneas" (*IG* XI 4, 1307, lines 7ff. = *RICIS* 202/0191).

It is generally assumed that Sarapeum C became the cult center of a state cult during the late phase of the Delian Independence (between 190 and 180 BC).[21] Unfortunately, the evidence regarding the actual shift from a private to a public setting is slight. A decree of the Delian people dated to 181 BC, which only by conjecture refers to the Egyptian deities, concerns the appointment of a *neokoros* (*CE* 215b, line2 = *RICIS* 202/0113). As to the reason for the *annexation*,[22] we can only speculate, but it may be safe to assume that the popularity of the cult made this move attractive to everybody involved.

Most of what we know about the structure and character of the cult dates from after 166 BC. This is problematic because the Athenian control changed Delian religion significantly and had a profound effect on Delian priesthoods.[23] With regard to my initial proposal, it is crucial that these changes do not quite capture the moment that saw the shift from *private* to *public* but took place about two decades later. However, our expectations regarding the character of a *public* cult and its priesthood are even more rigid when it comes to the Athenian period, and the changes at the beginning of this period certainly express the impact of state supervision: a list of Athenians serving on Delos as priests of Delian cults from 158/7 BC illustrates the immediate Athenian attempts to schematize and structure Delian religion and to integrate foreign cults such as that of Sarapis (*ID* 2605 = *RICIS* 202/0219).[24] In this somewhat hierarchical list of ten priesthoods, Sarapis features as number nine, followed only by the Delian hero Anius. Another priestly list, this time a diachronic one of successive priests of Sarapis, preserves the names and tribes of the Athenians who served between 137/6 and 110/9 BC (*CE* 73 = *RICIS* 202/0203).[25] The list reveals that the priesthood of Sarapis was an annual one; that many, if not all priests were chosen according to their tribes; and that prominent men, known also from other contexts in Athens and Delos, served as priests of Sarapis.

---

[21] An inventory of 183 BC (*IG* XI 4, 1307 = *RICIS* 202/0191) found in Sarapeum C lists many objects that reappear later in the Athenian inventories.

[22] Roussel 1916:256.

[23] For a detailed analysis of these changes, see Mikalson 1998 chapter 7.

[24] Cf. also *ID* 1499 (= *RICIS* 202/0228), 153/2 BC, in which nine out of the ten priests are honoured as a group.

[25] Many of the dedications found in the sanctuary can be dated on the basis of this list because the majority is dated by the priesthood.

These men were not attached to one cult exclusively, but sometimes held the priesthoods of two cults, even in successive years.[26]

My examination could end here, and I would have to draw the conclusion that as part of public religion the priesthood of Sarapis was shaped entirely by the Greek model that valued rotating annual offices and treated religious service just like any other civic duty, albeit an important one, to be carried out by prominent members of society. But are the priests of Sarapis fully characterized by the description given above? It is worthwhile to further investigate the matter. J. Mikalson, who looks at Delian religion from an Athenian perspective, expects from an Athenian priest of Sarapis after 166 BC exceptional "ingenuity and open-mindedness"[27] because he would be confronted with alien rituals and non-Athenian devotees. I would go further and claim that the priest's role would be largely shaped by traditions and expectations that had been in place for a long time and would not tend to change as dramatically as the administrative structures imposed in 166 BC or even before.[28]

The epigraphic record shows that the priests of Sarapis were by no means passive supervisors of a religious life that they were not personally involved in.[29] Dedications made by these priests or, to be more precise, by *hiereis*, are numerous and contributed largely to the prosperity of the cult.[30] The priests were frequently honored by cult associations and other religious personnel for being their benefactors,[31] sometimes even many years after they held

---

[26] For references see Dunand 1973, 3:185. However, unlike the situation on Rhodes, there was no *cursus honorum* of priests; and the apparent hierarchy of *ID* 2605 (= *RICIS* 202/0219) is not reflected in any other evidence.

[27] Cf. Mikalson 1998:229.

[28] The studies by Baslez 1977 and Dunand 1973 (vol. 3) focus on a question different from that of this essay, i.e. on how the Egyptian cults retained or changed their character when they spread to the Greek world (or Delos in particular), but their observations support my argument: see e.g. Dunand 1973, 3:186: "*partout où des prêtres d'origine égyptienne étaient en fonctions dans des sanctuaires grecs, ils devaient également y introduire leur mode de vie et il n'est pas impossible qu'ils aient été imités par les prêtres grecs eux-mêmes, dans la mesure où ceux-ci exerçaient leur fonction en permanence et étaient entièrement attachés à un sanctuaire.*"

[29] Cf. Mikalson 1998:229 who observes that the cult of Sarapis was "the Delian cult into which the Athenian priests threw themselves most wholeheartedly and which enjoyed, under the Athenians, the most prosperity."

[30] Cf. *CE* 90 (dedication of a *megaron*—a crypt?); *CE* 91; 97; 102–104 (the dedicants emphasize ἱερεὺς γενόμενος); 107; 108 (dedication of an *exedra*); 112/112bis; 113 (a fountain); 117; 121; 124; 133 (the priest heads a list of donors who each contribute considerable sums between 50 and 300 drachmas); 138–140; 142; 144; 160; 171; 179–180. For the corresponding numbers in *RICIS* see the concordance at the end of the second volume.

[31] Cf. *CE* 95 (by the σύνοδος τῶν μελανηφόρων); 105 (by the μελανηφόροι and θεραπευταί) 114 (by his father for having become priest); 115 (by the μελανηφόροι).

office.[32] They themselves pointed out their priesthood on many occasions, and their own daughters acted as *kanēphoroi*, often during their term of office.[33] Close, clearly paternal relations between *hiereis* and both individuals serving beside them and groups of worshippers attached to the cult emerge and point to religious structures that do not fit the conventional picture. The fact that these individuals and groups appear and thus participated in both the official cult and a private setting blurs the clear-cut distinction between cults A, B, and C.[34] In all three settings, a considerable number of people held cult titles associated with particular duties or, as a group, assumed a beneficial financial and organizational role, featuring in banquets and festivals, dedications and subscriptions.[35]

The existence of *kleidoukhoi, zakoroi, kanēphoroi, oneirokritai, aretalogoi,* and further cult titles in the public cult of Sarapis bears on the character of its priesthood and singles out the clergy as a whole. A hierarchy must have existed to some extent: the priests, as we have seen, were all prominent Athenian citizens, likewise the *kleidoukhoi*. In contrast, the *zakoroi* were often foreigners of a social status inferior to that of the priests. Their term of office was annual in most cases, and dedications and cult regulations were dated not only by the priesthood but also the zakorate.[36] The short term of office in these two cases may speak against a lifelong attachment to Sarapis, but this would have been made up for by intense involvement during the year of service.[37] It is probably not by chance that very prominent Athenian figures and governors

---

[32] Cf. CE 98 (the μελανηφόροι honor the priest of 130/29 BC in 123/2 BC); 144 (the priest of an earlier year makes a dedication during the term of office of another priest); 159 (a daughter honors her father who was priest seven years before).

[33] Cf. *CE* 112; 135; 141; 156; 171; 173a and b.

[34] This certainly applies to the associations of worshippers. We do not know whether Sarapeum A or B knew a *zakoros* or a *kleidoukhos* but we would expect a hierarchical structure in a private setting rather than in the official cult.

[35] Cf. esp. the inventories of the Athenian period where the *koina, Sarapiastai, sumbalomenoi thera-peutai* feature predominantly. See also *CE* 133, a list of donors.

[36] There are exceptions: *CE* 182 has a *zakoros* who held office for eighteen years; at Athens, however, in the first century BC the *zakoros* had to be appointed for life or two times (cf. *SIRIS* 33a).

[37] Annual priesthood was not necessarily the rule, not even in official cults, but during the Hellenistic period the Athenian and Delian evidence overshadows other cases. The sale of a priesthood of Sarapis in Magnesia on the Maeander (*SIRIS* 294) suggests service for life. See below; Dunand 1973, 3:148, emphasizes that in this respect the divide was not between private and public, but her examples of *priests for life* come from the imperial period. In 86/5 BC Sulla confirmed *asulia* to the sanctuary of Isis and Sarapis in Mopsuestia. From a letter of Lucullus to the magistrates, council and people we learn that the priest Diodotus had met Lucullus in person and in his role as priest had acted so prominently to evoke this decision that the city

of the island gave substantial financial support for cults but are hardly ever attested to have held priesthoods. Residence on the island if not in the sanctuary would have been important.[38] The role of the *zakoros* as *temple guard*, just like a *neokoros*, would certainly have required residence in the sanctuary, and a *pastophorion*, which provided lodgings for the servants of the cult, existed on Delos by 112/1 BC (*CE* 130 = *RICIS* 202/0296). The epigraphic record does not reveal much about the activities of the personnel, but their regular appearance and the emphasis on titles speak for themselves. The roles of *oneirokritēs* and *aretalogos* were part of the everyday life of the cult of Sarapis[39]—as is reflected not only in Maiistas' aretalogy following Apollonius' account: several dedications found in Sarapeum C were made "according to the command of the *oneirokritēs*."[40]

On the whole, it looks as if the multiple functions within the cult did not take away from the strong role of the actual *hiereus* but involved more worshippers in the administration of the cult and thereby created solidarity among those attached to the cult in various ways.[41] Whether one attributes the differentiated personnel attached to Sarapeum C directly to the Egyptian origin of the cult or not, it was accompanied by special cult regulations and customs that strike the observer as *foreign*. We do not know if the Delian priests of Sarapis shaved their heads as their Egyptian colleagues did,[42] but we do know that it was prohibited to wear wool in Sarapeum A (*CE* 16 / 16bis = *RICIS* 202/0199–0200) and that linen played a special role in Sarapeum C (*CE* 49 = *RICIS* 202/0170 and above). Here, it was also prohibited (for the priests or everybody?) to enter the sanctuary after having drunk wine (*CE* 50b = *RICIS* 202/0175).[43] Apollonius, the author of the *Delian aretalogy* and priest in Sarapeum A, justified many of his actions by claiming that he was acting

---

had granted tax exemption to him and his family. The editors of the text suggest that Diodotus may have been appointed for life (cf. *BE* 1995 no. 601; Sayar and Siewert and Taeuber 1994:113–130).

[38] Cf. Mikalson 1998:240.

[39] At one point, these two titles were held by the same person (cf. CE 119 = *RICIS* 202/0283, 115/14 BC).

[40] Cf. CE 169; 123 (= *RICIS* 202/0340 and 202/0289).

[41] Cf. Baslez 1977:309–310; it is remarkable that the structure of the cult personnel had an appeal also in the worship of Greek deities. Zeus Cynthios and Athena Cynthia were served by a priest, *zakoros*, and *kleidoukhos*: see Mikalson 1998:223, for further examples of this *orientalization*. For a table and prosopography of the personnel see Roussel 1916 appendix; Dunand 1973, 3:287–319.

[42] As Dunand suspects (1973, 3:187, and n1 with references).

[43] This may have applied to priests only. Cf. Plutarch *De Iside* 6. But cf. *SIRIS* 291 (= *RICIS* 304/0802, Priene), where the priest has the right of the ἐπίσπονδον οἴνου.

according to the god's command (*kata to prostagma*) and that Sarapis had appeared to him in a dream telling him what to do. Expressions referring to the god's command or epiphany are frequent in the Delian dedications to Sarapis in all three sanctuaries.[44] At first sight, they appear to be a feature atypical of Greek cults, known only in the worship of Asclepius (that is, incubation), but a closer examination reveals that they were common also in many other sanctuaries during the Hellenistic period. On Delos they can be found with regard to Zeus, Ares, Helios, Apollo, and Artemis. In every location, they were used predominantly by priests or other cult personnel, and often they were associated with the foundation of cults, private or public.[45] In all cases they were an important means of strengthening the authority of those claiming to act in accordance with divine wishes.

To sum up: even in the official cult of Sarapis, which was administered by annual priests and representatives of the Athenian state, many elements interfere with an easy description of the priesthood. By integrating a previously private cult of Sarapis into the public sphere, the Delians did not and could not do away with traditional structures and customs—these continued to exist throughout the Athenian period. The obvious popularity of the cult after 166 BC did not correspond to the low ranking given to it by the Athenians when they took control of Delos, which shows that the character and authority of priesthoods did not depend on state supervision.[46] One may attribute these phenomena to a conservative Egyptian spirit that prevailed on Delos and label them Delian idiosyncrasies.[47] In what follows, I want to compare the Delian priests of Sarapis to priests of Sarapis in other places and again ask whether the dichotomy of *private* and *public* should be emphasized or not. Within the scope of this essay I can only point to examples that would need a much fuller examination in their own individual contexts. They may serve, however, to question accepted views and to counterbalance the Deliocentric character of studies that focus on the religious life of only *one* place.

---

[44] Cf. e.g. *CE* 45; 66; 121; 169 (= *RICIS* 202/0165; 0223; 0287;0340). There are many more instances.

[45] For an almost complete table see van Straten 1976:21–27. A nice example is an epigram from Cnidus dated to the end of the fourth century BC in which a priestess of Demeter and Kore claims that Hermes appeared to her in a dream and commanded her to become the goddess' servant (*IKnidos* 131); famous are the origins of the games for Artemis Leucophryene at Magnesia (*IMagnesia* 16).

[46] Cf. Mikalson 1998:232, "Initially they [the Athenians] probably mistook the importance of the cult of Isis and Sarapis, of negligible importance back in Athens, and gave it only the ninth rank, but they quickly moved to promote this cult when they saw the support it had in the local community."

[47] Cf. Baslez 1977:309–310.

A public decree from Priene (ca. 200 BC), which deals with the sacrifices and priestly activities in the cult of Sarapis, is the kind of text that we miss for Delos (*SIRIS* 291 = *RICIS* 304/0802 = *LSAM* 36). Although form and content of the decree do not single out Sarapis as *atypical* in any way, the Egyptian origin of deities worshipped here is visible: the priest has to find and recruit "an Egyptian, who performs the sacrifice in a skillful way."

> The priest also provides the Egyptian who performs the sacrifice in a skillful way; nobody other than the priest is allowed to offer sacrifice to the goddess in an unskillful way. (lines 20–23)[48]

A large fine is imposed if someone offers sacrifice without the appropriate knowledge (lines 23–25). Apart from this very explicit regulation there are references to sacrifices on 20 *Apatourion* (lines 7ff.), which corresponds to the great festival of Osiris at the beginning of November; to the *lampadeia* in honour of Isis (lines 12–15), for which the priest has to provide oil and lamps; and to the *katekhomenoi tou theou* (line 29), a term that is almost entirely confined to Egypt. Just as we saw on Delos, there was a desire to preserve the traditional character of the liturgy, in particular the Egyptian way of carrying out sacrifice.[49] However, all of these elements are firmly integrated into the official description of the cult: even the *katekhomenoi*, devoted servants of the cult, if not temple personnel for life,[50] are guaranteed one fourth of the offering tables furnished by the *dēmos* (lines 29ff.). Two factors are thus responsible for shaping the priesthood of Sarapis in Priene: the local, official way of assigning priests their place and the traditional duties of priests of Isis and Sarapis.[51] That the former appears dominant may be expected from a public decree. Its purpose is to provide rules that guarantee the functioning of the cult and the remuneration of its personnel. We would have to know more about the origins and the life of the cult in order to assess the priest's attitudes or his personal involvement.

In many cases it is difficult to say whether a cult existed as a private cult before it was made public or why it was made public, let alone to establish why

---

[48] παρε[χ]έ[τω δὲ ὁ ἱερεὺς καὶ] τὸν Αἰγύπτιον τὸν συντελέσοντα τὴ[ν θυσίαν ἐμπείρως·] μὴ ἐξέστω δὲ μηθενὶ ἄλλωι ἀπείρως τὴ[ν θυσίαν ποιεῖν τῆι] θεᾶι ἢ ὑπὸ τοῦ ἱερέως·.

[49] Cf. Dunand 1973, 3:141.

[50] On the *katokhē* in Egyptian sanctuaries, see Dunand 1973, 1:282–283.

[51] It is remarkable that the archaeological evidence has been interpreted very controversially. Whereas some scholars describe the archaeological remains of the sanctuary as being very little adapted to the necessities of the traditional Egyptian cult but rather as being *Greek*, others underline the foreign character of the temple. For references, see Dunand 1973, 3:54–56.

it was founded in the first place—this is one of the reasons why the *Delian aretalogy* is such a crucial document. Even documents that appear to have orchestrated the shift from *private* to *public* leave many questions open, as is the case with an inscription from Magnesia on the Maeander (second century BC), which sets out the terms of the priesthood of Sarapis. An appended section reveals that the priesthood is sold and adds details that relate to the rights and duties of the buyer (*SIRIS* 294 = *RICIS* 304/0701 = *LSAM* 34). The opening lines of the text are lost, but there is a reference to a certain Pharsalius. He (?) is instructed to install a priest (?) "in the *temenos* dedicated to the god" (lines 10ff.). We learn that Sarapis is not to be worshipped/offered sacrifice in any other place (lines 12ff.). If this does happen, the place will become the property of the *polis* (lines 13ff.). It is generally assumed that a certain Pharsalius dedicated a privately owned piece of land so that the worship of Sarapis could be transformed from a private into an officially recognized cult.[52] If this is correct, the decree represents the result of the negotiations between the private founder (patron? priest?) and the civic authorities.[53] Unfortunately, the fragmentary state of the text leaves us to speculate as to the subjects of some of the sentences, so that Pharsalius' role and the identity of the priest of Sarapis are somewhat blurred. What we do see is that the civic *oikonomoi* guarantee the remuneration of the priest as well as his limits, whereas Pharsalius may even be the senior priest or at least responsible for the appointment of the priest;[54] the *dēmos*, however, has the right to change the details of the contract (lines 19ff.).[55] The terms of the priesthood of Sarapis in Magnesia resemble those of any other priesthood in many respects—the fact that its holder purchases his office is certainly representative for the area—but in particular the strong emphasis on the city's rights and the expressed fear of

---

[52] Cf. *LSAM*, p. 99; Vidman 1969:152: *Sunt duo decreta populi Magnetum, quibus cultus Aegyptius, primum privatus, Magnesiae permittitur rogante Pharsalio quodam, qui fundum suum huius rei causa dedicavit.*

[53] Sokolowski (*LSAM*, p. 99) compares the case to that of the priest Apollonius on Delos. If they are parallel, the establishment of a proper *temenos* with a temple would need civic approval—on Delos the priestly family defended their rights much more successfully than in Magnesia, where the future appointment of a priest is handled in the official way.

[54] Crucial is the restoration in line 9 ἱερέα; or, as Dittenberger, *Syll.*³ 578, followed by Robert, suggests, νεοκόρον.

[55] ἐξουσία δ' ἔστω τῶ[ι] δή[μωι ἀφελεῖ]ν ἢ [ὑπο]γράψαι ἕτερον ἕως τῆς ἀναφορᾶς. The sentence is very enigmatic and has been interpreted in various ways. Cf. Robert 1927. *REG* 40:222f, who suggests the submission to an oracle for *anaphora*. Sokolowksi, *LSAM*, p. 100, suggests *payment*. I understand the clause as meaning the following: "The *dēmos* has the right to amend this rider until it has been approved and become an official document."

the cult's *branching out* suggest official anxiety over the control of the priest of Sarapis.

Like so many other cult regulations, the inscription illustrates the details and significance of the sacred finances, and this touches on the most crucial difference between a *private* and a *public* priest of Sarapis: instead of being dependent on personal fortune or the generosity of worshippers, the *public priest* received his remuneration from the city.[56] The largest part of his income, however, would still be dependent on the popularity of the cult or rather on the number of offerings and sacrifices carried out in his sanctuary. State control over sacred revenues was always an important issue, cutting across *private* and *public* settings. A striking example regarding the cult of Sarapis comes from Thessalonice. Here the cult was supported by Philip V (187 BC) when the funds of the Sarapeum were used for purposes other than those connected with the cult (*SIRIS* 108 = *RICIS* 113/0503 = Hatzopoulos 1996 II: no. 15). In a *diagramma* that was forwarded by a royal official, the king imposed harsh fines on those who touched Sarapis' funds, and gave orders to immediately restore them to the sanctuary.

Nobody may divert any funds of Sarapis in any way, nor pledge them or any other dedications, and nobody may draft a decree regarding these matters. (lines 11–16)[57]

The inscription, above all its addressee, has been much discussed, and the discussion itself illustrates how difficult it is to label the cult as *public* or *private* and to identify those in charge of its administration.[58] Whether public priests or priests of a private association, what was their role in the dispute? Had the priests complained that sacred funds were diverted by civic magis-

---

[56] A decree from Samos (second century BC) grants permission to the priest of Isis to collect money for the goddess (*SIRIS* 250 = *RICIS* 204/1006).

[57] Τῶν δὲ τοῦ Σαράπιδος χρημάτων μηθεὶς ἀπαλλοτριούτω μηθὲν κατὰ μηθένα τρόπον μηδὲ ὑποτιθέτω μηδὲ τῶν ἄλλων ἀναθημάτων μηδὲ γραφέτω περὶ τούτων ψήφισμα μηθείς.

[58] Fraser 1960:38–39, n4, and n1 is convinced that the cult was a state cult and argues that the addressee has to be the *dēmos*. Hatzopoulos 1996:406–410 goes through various scenarios but apparently assumes that the sanctuary was administered by a religious association and that the text was addressed to the priests of the sanctuary. The text (lines 7-9) gives the reason for the public display of the king's decision as "in order that those in charge know how he [the king] ordains matters should be handled"; see now also Voutiras 2005:281–282; Voutiras explains the king's intervention as taking place at the moment when the city tried to impose itself on a private institution. He also takes note of a *public* character of the sanctuary, i.e. the fact that it was open to the public, integrated into the civic religious calendar, and of the (above all, financial) interest to the city; the author contrasts this with the closed community of its specialized clergy.

trates? Did the king have the priests in mind when he prohibited the opening of the *thesauroi* without the presence of an *epistatēs* and the *dikastai* (lines 21–24)? However we answer these questions, once more the *private* versus *public* scheme does not work.

Nothing in the text indicates that the inscription from Thessalonice was addressed to a private group of worshippers. But even if there was an explicit reference to such a group, its existence would not automatically refer us to a private or public setting.[59] Moreover, private associations, such as the *Sarapiastai* on Delos, functioned on the model of civic communities, which is nicely illustrated in a document from Thasus (second century BC) that records the sale of the *epōnumia* of a group of *Sarapiastai*.

> With good fortune. The *Sarapiastai* decided to honor the eponymous office of the *Sarapiastai*: the buyer of the eponymity receives the following privileges from the group. (lines 1–7)[60]

In structure and content, the decree is strikingly reminiscent of documents concerning the sale of official priesthoods in Asia Minor (or even the priesthood of Sarapis in Magnesia), and it looks as if these groups used civic documents as templates for describing their own offices and titles (*SIRIS* 265 = *RICIS* 201/0101).[61] The buyer receives *gera* from the association, he wears a headband at banquets, and he is crowned at every official gathering. During his lifetime, the buildings of the *Sarapiastai* will be named after him, and he gets to vote together with the priest and the secretary on certain occasions, as prescribed by the law. The installments paid by the buyer are used to pay for inscribing the decree, which is to be set up in the most conspicuous place. We can view the parallel as evidence either discrediting the position of office holders in private groups of worshippers or emphasizing the need for caution when it comes to the role of priests as defined in official decrees. Or, it may be the case that private associations took the imitation of the structure of the democratic city so far as to limit their priests' authority along the lines of what they

---

[59] Cf. Fraser 1960:22. See e.g. decrees of *Sarapiastai* in Athens (*SIRIS* 2 = *RICIS* 101/0201) and Methymna (*SIRIS* 262 = *RICIS* 205/0401); on the public and private character of Dionysiac *thiasoi* see Villanueva-Puig 1998:365–374.

[60] ἀγαθῆι τύχηι. ἔδοξεν τοῖς Σαραπιασταῖς τιμῆσαι τὴν ἐπωνυμίαν τῶν Σαραπιαστῶν· ὁ δὲ ἀγοράσας τὴν ἐπωνυμίαν ἕξει γέρα παρὰ τοῦ κοινοῦ τάδε·.

[61] Cf. Seyrig 1927. *BCH* 51:219–229. Seyrig, 228–229 insists, "*Aucun document, sans doute, ne permet de conjecturer un culte official des dieux égyptiens dans l'île.*" Whereas Seyrig stresses the modest character of the association Dunand 1973, 3:62 argues that the cult was firmly implanted in Thasian society and that important people were members of the group.

observed in the public sphere. In all these scenarios a dichotomy of *private* versus *public* would be unhelpful.

My final example comes from Syrian Laodicea by the Sea (174 BC). It throws light on the interaction between the civic authorities and three brothers who were the priests of Sarapis and Isis (*SIRIS* 356 = *RICIS* 402/0301).[62] In an appeal to the city the priests pointed out that the land on which the *temenos* was situated was their private property and that their rights as owners were violated. The scenario is the following:

> As a decree had been passed for those who asked the city to be assigned a place for the dedication of a statue to give a determined sum, and as some were asking also for places within the sanctuary, they (the three priests) suspected that in this way their property would be diminished and thus made an appeal to consider that it be looked after, in order that their property, to which it applied, should not be diminished. (lines 10–21)

The civic authorities responded to the priests' appeal by asking for payment for the statues themselves rather than for obtaining the space. Scholars have proposed various interpretations of the text, all of which focus on the status of the cult as *private* or *public*. Given the city's say in matters regarding the sanctuary, Dunand labels the cult *semiofficial* but *with good relations to the city*.[63] Fraser suggests there was "a stage in the transformation of a private into a state-cult, or it may be that a state-cult already existed."[64] Sosin's reconstruction of the scenario envisages an entirely *private* sanctuary, which was protected and managed by the *polis*.[65] The range of possibilities illustrates that the character of the priesthood—here clearly being a lifelong if not hereditary position, and including rights of ownership to the *temenos* and a very distinct role vis à vis the community—is not dependent on a private or public status (or vice versa).

Priests of Sarapis emerge in many places and contexts in the Greek world. Where they do not fit our conventional picture of priests, this is often explained by either the *foreign character* or the *private status* of the cult they

---

[62] The text was first published by Roussel in *Syria* 23 (1942/3), 21–32. See also Klaffenbach 1948:376–379; most recently Sosin 2005:133, who argues that the verb *anaskeuazētai* (line 16, cf. also *anaskeuazōntai* lines 20ff.) indicates a threat to the property itself, not to the property rights.

[63] Cf. Dunand 1973, 3:134n2.

[64] Fraser 1960:40.

[65] Sosin 2005:135.

served. Both aspects apply to the *Delian aretalogy*. Priestly status, knowledge, and family tradition matter enormously in the Egyptian priest's history of his private cult. However, the cult continued to exist and the priestly family continued to perpetuate their traditions, although at some point they became citizens of Delos. What would have happened if Sarapeum A had become the cult center of the state cult of Sarapis on Delos? Would the respective Apollonius or Demetrius immediately have become an entirely Greek priest? The epigraphic record from Delos and elsewhere shows that a priestly profile was very much shaped by local habit, by ways of administering and structuring the religious life of a particular city.[66] Obviously, public documents describe the activities of priests of Sarapis in the same way as activities of priests in traditional shrines, and there is no doubt that a community exercised considerable control over aspects of the priesthoods. However, I hope to have shown that the distinction between private and public priests of Sarapis is unhelpful with regard to a characterization of priesthoods. In particular, the widespread existence of organized groups of devotees of Sarapis, who were active in both private and public settings, renders the polarization impossible. Instead, one should pay attention to the origins and history of a cult, and should examine its personnel and internal structures carefully.[67] On Delos, and elsewhere, even *Hellenized* and public priests of Sarapis can then emerge as much more than annual magistrates who did not feel any personal attachment to the deity they served.

[66] A good and well-documented example is Rhodes, where the priests are firmly integrated in the religious *cursus honorum* (cf. Dignas 2003). But see Dunand 1973, 3:142, who assumes that the rather low place in the priestly lists suggests inferiority to the Greek cults. The approach to studying priesthoods becomes, once more, crucial. Dunand seeks the *oriental aspect* of the Egyptian cults whereas a student of Rhodian religion would emphasize the full integration of the cults in the idiosyncratic and quite remarkable religious *cursus honorum*.

[67] See the observations made by Bremmer in this volume on the religious officials in the Ephesian Artemisium.

5

Priests—Dynasts—Kings
Temples and Secular Rule in Asia Minor

Ulrich Gotter

THE AIM OF THIS ESSAY is to explore the complex relationship between sacred authority and secular power in Asia Minor, focusing exclusively on cases of personal rule. My dramatis personae will include rulers as priests and priests as rulers. More specifically, I will consider the role of sacred office for the exercise and mediation of "mono rule" in Asia Minor beyond the Greek *polis*; that is to say, in a territory which has been considered to display in principle a traditional tendency towards the integration of secular and religious power. To map the field, I have constructed three different case studies: first, the union of king and priest, figuring king Archelaus of Cappadocia at the Corycian Cave; second, the major examples of the so-called *Anatolian temple states*; and finally the dynastic priesthoods of Pessinous in Galatia and Olba in Rough Cilicia. At the core of the essay lie the expansion of priestly rule and the relationship between priestly rule and both cities in the immediate neighborhood and the superstructures (Hellenistic monarchies and Roman Empire) in which they were embedded.

1. Archelaus at the Corycian Cave

The most striking manifestation of the relationship between priestly and secular power in Asia Minor is the extreme case of regime change. An example of such a regime change and its significance for the local sacred office can be

For support of various kinds, I wish to thank Matthias Haake, Holger Hook, and Kai Trampedach.

found in an extraordinary monument in Rough Cilicia: the list of priests at the temple of Zeus above the Corycian Cave.[1]

The evidence is not unproblematic, as the temple was transformed into a Christian church in late antiquity.[2] Originally, the list of priests was attached to one of the antes of the pagan temple, before the blocks were incorporated into the north wall of the large Christian basilica. However, in the process of rebuilding, care was taken not to separate contiguous pieces at random,[3] so that, with two exceptions,[4] the parts remained in the correct order.

The monumental list of names consists of three clearly separated sections.[5] The first (A) covers the priests from the third to the first century BC; the second (B) and third (C) cover the office holders of imperial times (from the Hadrianic period onward, as the name *poplios Ailios* indicates[6]). In contrast to the later sections, the Hellenistic part, which will mostly concern us here, is complete. The first 130 lines are of one piece, while thereafter the hand changes from line to line.[7] The high point of this monument is that the Hellenistic list can be dated fairly precisely, assuming, as is more than likely, that the list records annual offices.[8] This not only allows us to date the erection of the shrine almost to the year, but also provides us with the uninterrupted annals of the priests of Zeus for (at least) 214 years.[9] The fixed point of reference for the list is the last name on the first section (A). On the lowest of the blocks, one can clearly read: *Arkhelaos Arkhelaou.*[10]

This combination of names is so rare that the identity of this priest is beyond doubt. He is Archelaus (son of Archelaus, son of Archelaus, son of Archelaus), king of Cappadocia. In 36 BC, the triumvir M. Antonius had

---

[1] First publication by Bent and Hicks 1891:243–258; advanced transliteration by Heberdey and Wilhelm 1896:71–79; text again published by Hagel and Tomaschitz 1998 Korykion antron 1. For the cult, see MacKay 1990:2103–2110.

[2] Feld and Weber 1967.

[3] Which is easily seen as the individual layers of the wall differ from each other in height. See also Feld and Weber 1967:256–257.

[4] Blocks IV and V from top: Heberdey and Wilhelm 1896:71–72.

[5] For a sketch of the situation, see Heberdey and Wilhelm 1896:71, 73–75.

[6] Hagel and Tomaschitz 1998 Korykion antron 1 B2 l. 8. For Asia, see Holtheide 1983:93–104. For Syria, see Sartre 1996:244–245.

[7] Heberdey and Wilhelm 1896:72.

[8] This assumption is strongly supported by the β after several names (cf. n16), indicating a second year of office.

[9] Nonetheless, it must be admitted that there is some uncertainty concerning the total time covered by the inscription, as the ending of eight lines has been lost (Hagel and Tomaschitz 1998 Korykion antron 1 A1 l.1; A1 l.9; A1 l.21; A2 l.22; A3 l.1; A5 l.1; A6 l.1; A7 l.19). Of course, some of these lines might have shown a β after the name.

[10] Hagel and Tomaschitz 1998 Korykion antron 1 A9 l.9.

invested him with this honor,[11] and Augustus had confirmed him after Actium, although Archelaus had fought on the side of Antonius (Plutarch *Antony* 61.1; Cassius Dio 51.2.1–2).[12]

After the death of Amyntas of Galatia (25 BC) Archelaus' territory was extended by imperial fiat: between 25 and 20 he was allocated the seaboard of Rough Cilicia, west of the river Lamos, as Strabo testifies (Strabo 12.2.1).[13] Only the *polis* Seleucia, with its generous fertile plain in the alluvial area of the river Calycadnus was exempt from this (Strabo 12.1.4; 14.5.6).[14] We need to assume that Archelaus took over the priestly office at the Corycian Cave pretty much at the same time as he assumed his rule over the territory: the imported dynast linked himself programmatically with the most dignified sacred place of the region, in the immediate hinterland of his residence at Elaioussa Sebaste. Such an act only seems to make sense at the start of his rule in Rough Cilicia. If we accept this premise, we can date the list with only a five-year margin of error. The first priest mentioned was in office between 239 and 235 BC, and the temple, which later was to be surmounted by the church, was erected between 82 and 77 BC.[15]

The list of priests is not only a convenient catalogue of letter forms in the first century BC and an immense collection of Luwian names. It also casts some light on a sparsely illuminated phenomenon: the significance of cults for secular rule. The key is the striking empty space below the name *Arkhelaos Arkhelaou*. With, or rather after, King Archelaus the list of priests was not continued on that ante. Since there is no evidence of a sudden change in the epigraphic habit, we are left with only two possible interpretations of that lacuna: (1) Archelaus held the office of priest once (that is for one year) and abolished it thereafter, at least in its traditional form; (2) with his rule, Archelaus also assumed the office of priest and remained, as long as he reigned, priest of Zeus in perpetuity.

I would tend towards the former solution: the annalistic list of priests was meant to demonstrate the tradition and continuity of the office. Within this framework it was possible to render in graphic terms—by adding a beta after the name—if and when a priest held the office for more than one year.[16]

---

[11] Sullivan 1980:1148–1149; Buchheim 1960:55–56; Hoben 1969:180–182. For Archelaus' family, see Sullivan 1980:1150–1154.

[12] Sullivan 1980:1154; Hoben 1969:182–183.

[13] For the dating, see Hoben 1969:184–185.

[14] See Cassius Dio 54.9.2.

[15] For the remaining hazards of any precise dating, see n9.

[16] Hagel and Tomaschitz 1998 Korykion antron 1 A1 l. 3.7.11.19; A2 l. 16.17; A3 l. 5; A4 l. 1.3.14.;

Archelaus did not use that possibility; there is no β after his name. Thus the permanent occupation of the office would have had to be planned from the start, and that again would have required a specification, for instance the formula *dia biou*. If Archelaus had tied the office of priest of Zeus firmly and permanently to his rule over the Cilician seaboard, one would moreover assume that his successor (Archelaus II[17]) should have done the same. But the inscription does not testify to that, and the empty space after *Arkhelaos Arkhelaou* would seem to speak against it.

In any case—and thus the decision between the two possible solutions hardly affects my argument—the rule of Archelaus in Rough Cilicia meant a decisive break for the priesthood at the Corycian Cave and its self-representation. Either an annual office was dynastically occupied and thus taken out of circulation, or it was ended symbolically. An abolition of the office in this sense, however, did not mean that with it the cult or its practices were ended as well. Yet, the change by Archelaus did affect the representation of the cult in the person of the priest, as it had been manifest in the keeping of the list at the ante of the temple of Zeus. The closure of the list did not affect the practice of the cult, but it affected the position of the priest in a regional context.

What can we conclude from this for the relationship between the priest and secular power on the Cilician coast? What rationale underlay the intervention of Archelaus in the morphology of the regional priesthood?

I can only read this as a calculated neutralization of a position which Archelaus must have seen as a latent risk for his rule. The nature of this handicap becomes clearer if one looks at who was priest of Zeus during the 213 years documented by the list. Although, apart from Archelaus, none of the others is known to us in any other context, much can be learned from the names themselves. Most importantly, the office holders appear to have been strongly rooted both in the region and within the regional elite. The list is full of (mostly theophoric) Luwian names. This holds true for the entire period covered by the list, although the proportion between indigenous and Greek names changes gradually in favor of the latter, especially towards the end of the list. The frequent combination of Luwian with Greek names in the same family indicates that even the bearers of Greek names should be considered as members of the regional and probably autochthonous elite. That the office holders belonged to a small, exclusive circle follows from the filiations

---

A5 l. 4.6.7.10.11.12.; A6 l. 4.7.8.9.10.11.13.14.16.18; A7 l. 1.2.5.6.7.9.10.13.15.18; A8 l. 1.2.3.7; A9 l. 3.4.6.8.

[17] For the rule of Archelaus II, see Sullivan 1980:1167–1168.

from which family links over generations can easily and safely be reconstructed.[18] And the exclusivity did not diminish over time. On the contrary, as the increasing incidence of tenure for a period of two years indicates,[19] the circle of acceptable candidates shrank from the beginning of the first century BC. Possibly, with *Zēnophanēs Teukrou*[20] the priests included a member of the Teucrid family, which, based on evidence at the temple of Zeus in Olba (see below), ruled over the mountainous territory to the north. His presence may be seen as another indicator of the prestige which the priests at the Corycian Cave enjoyed in the region.

Even if one cannot say anything specific about the practical functions of the priests, and about the role which they played beyond the cult, the constellation appears to be sufficiently clear from Archelaus' perspective. As a dynastic newcomer, not at all linked to the region, he was confronted with the most important sacred center of his new territory, whose personnel was deeply rooted in the region's traditional ruling elite. He sought to neutralize this structure of local authority, which threatened to become a problem for his as-yet-underdeveloped legitimacy, by taking on the priestly office himself and subsequently either changing its character or abolishing it.

This interpretation is rendered even more plausible by the fact that Archelaus acted similarly in Cappadocia, albeit by different means. The master of the temple and priest of Ma (Enyo) in Comana was not only the highest sacral authority in the kingdom of Cappadocia; in certain circumstances he could become a serious threat for a weak ruler (see below). This menace must have been quite real for Archelaus, since he became king solely by order of Antonius, without being visibly rooted in, or unanimously acclaimed by, the powerful local aristocracy (Strabo 12.2.11).[21] Against this background it can hardly be a coincidence that he founded a city in Comana,[22] which was not subject to the priest of Ma. In contrast to the renaming of Elaioussa in Sebaste and of Mazaca in Caesarea, the name *Hierapolis* indicates that the foundation was not addressing the Roman benefactor but rather staking a claim for the city's participation, within the Cappadocian context, in the cultic capital of the local temple of Ma.

---

[18] These family ties ought to be studied more carefully and comprehensively in another context. For some obvious examples of close relationships within the first blocks of the priest list, see Hagel and Tomaschitz 1998 Korykion antron 1 A2 l. 9.11.14.16; Hagel and Tomaschitz 1998 Korykion antron 1 A1 l. 4.5. 11. 17. 19. A2 l. 1.

[19] Cf. n16.

[20] Hagel and Tomaschitz 1998 Korykion antron 1 A 7 l. 4

[21] Hoben 1969:181–182.

[22] Harper 1968:99–100; Teja, 1980:1108.

In sum: Archelaus I did not become priest of the cult of Zeus at the Corycian Cave because he—as the son and grandson of priests of the Ma in the Pontic Comana—had a particular affinity to the priesthood. It makes equally little sense to assume that he possessed a particular sacral qualification for his promotion to king of Cappadocia and ruler of the coast of Cilicia.[23] The contiguity of territorial rule and sacral authority in the list at the Corycian Cave does not suggest any far-reaching concept, but was simply due to the specific situation—and was probably only very ephemeral.

2. *Temple States* and Kings

The textbook example of a close tie between sacral authority and secular power is supposed to be the so-called *Anatolian temple states*. It is generally thought that they manifested a traditional, structural, and permanent connection between local rule and priestly office. In what follows I will show that such a connection did not correspond with the regional concept of priesthood and that the combination of priestly authority and territorial power in one person was not the rule but the exception.

The literature considers the following to have been Anatolian temple states: Zela, Comana, and Cabira (Ameria) in Pontus; Comana and Venasa in Cappadocia; the temple of Men near Antiochia ad Pisidiam; Pessinous in Galatia; as well as Olba in Rough Cilicia.[24] Most of these formations were part of larger political units: Zela, Comana, and Cabira belonged to the kingdom of Pontus; Comana and Venasa to the Cappadocian king; Antiochia, until the treaty of Apamea, belonged to the realm of the Seleucids, as did Olba until the last of the Seleucids. How close the connection of Pessinous was to the Seleucid Empire before 188 is difficult to tell;[25] after the peace of Apamea it belonged, like the rest of Galatia, to Pergamum, until the Romans granted independence to the Galatians in 166.

In order to understand the relationship between priesthood and local territorial rule, it is important to note that there was not a single certi-

---

[23] So in fact Sullivan 1978:919–921.

[24] See the compilation by Boffo 1985:15–52. For the Men temple in Antiochia, see Brandt 1992:71–72. Boffo 1985:50, and Mitchell and Waelkens 1998:7, do not count the Men cult in Antiochia as an Anatolian temple state, the latter—not very convincingly—because "the actual remains of the sanctuary are Greek in character and provide no architectural evidence for an 'eastern' or 'Anatolian' cult." The degree of aesthetic Hellenization, though, is no indication of the political organization of the temple. There are *temple states* whose cultic centers show entirely Greek architecture—for instance, Olba—as well as *polis* cults with heavily Anatolian traits.

[25] Virgilio 1981:57–59, 70–74.

fied personal union of king and priest. This is all the more remarkable if one considers how important these priests and their territories were for at least some of those monarchies. Strabo reports, for instance, that in Cappadocian Comana the priest of Ma was appointed for life and—after the ruler himself—occupied the second rank in the kingdom (Strabo 12.2.3). The third highest rank was also occupied by a priest appointed for life, namely the priest of Zeus Dakiēos in Venasa (Strabo 12.2.5–6). Thus the Cappadocian king was flanked, so to speak, by priestly authorities.

The masters of the temple in the kingdom of Pontus were hardly less significant. The priest of Ma of (Pontic) Comana, which is supposed to have been modeled after the Cappadocian sanctuary, was, according to his rank (*kata timēn*), the second man after the king. During the *exodus* of the goddess, which was performed twice a year, he even wore a diadem (Strabo 12.3.32). It is possible that the king took off his own diadem for that period of time, thereby underlining the eminent role of cult and priest for the kingdom.[26]

The temples of Cabira and Zela, and their priests, who also served for life, likewise enjoyed great significance for the Pontic rulers. When swearing officially, the Mithradatids addressed the Men in Cabira, and the royal oath was: "by the Fortune (*tukhē*) of the king and by Men of Pharnaces" (Strabo 12.3.31). Finally, the temple of Anaitis in Zela, probably an old Persian cult, was marked by rites of particular sacrality, which, as Strabo writes, led the inhabitants of Pontus to Zela, where they made their oaths in relation to important matters (Strabo 12.3.37).

In extreme cases, the importance of these cults and the distinction of their priests in Pontus and Cappadocia could pose considerable problems for a ruler. We know of at least two situations in which priests became a direct threat to the king. The first case occurred in Pontus, when Dorylaos, the priest of Comana, took sides with the Roman Republic in one of the wars fought by Mithradates VI against Rome and tried to use his prestige to bring Pontus to abandon Eupator. Dorylaos' failure led to his execution and to the dishonoring of his family (Strabo 12.3.33). The second case occurred in 51 BC in the Cappadocia of King Ariobarzanes III, Eusebes Philorhomaios, whose rule was as insecure as had been those of his two predecessors.[27] Just one year earlier, in 52 BC, his father Ariobarzanes II had been assassinated by domestic opponents,[28] and the rule of Ariobarzanes III could only be stabilized through

---

[26] Trampedach 2001:281.
[27] Sullivan 1980:1127–1139.
[28] Hoben 1969:157–159.

the rapid intervention of the Roman proconsul Cicero (Cicero *Ad familiares* 15.2.4–8, 15.4.6). The most important antagonist of the Cappadocian kings in this tense situation was the priest of Comana, who played the Parthian card and, by gathering the disaffected, could threaten Ariobarzanes with force. The situation relaxed only when Cicero, supported by Roman troops, insisted that the priest had to leave the country (Cicero *Ad familiares* 15.4.6).

These two cases show how much power a priest of one of the important sanctuaries could accrue when the local king was weak, and what centrifugal consequences this could have for the monarchy. No wonder, therefore, that the kings tried everything in their power to neutralize the politico-religious capital of the temples, or to link it with their own persons. In Cappadocian Comana, the priests of Ma, as Strabo remarks, were usually recruited from the royal family (Strabo 12.2.3)—apparently not as a legally codified secondo-geniture, but in order to guarantee maximum loyalty of the priests towards the king. In Pontus at least, Mithradates VI appointed reliable followers as priests of Ma (Strabo 12.3.33),[29] hoping that these would also remain loyal to him. Under these circumstances a truly autonomous dynasty of priests could not develop either in Cappadocia or in Pontus. Yet the king never assumed the most important priestly office himself, either in those two countries, or in Antiochia ad Pisidiam. The demands which running the cult posed for the priest's way of life may have been a very practical obstacle. Thus rule and priesthood remained perpetually separate in the Hellenistic monarchies.

But what did the internal structures of the *temple states* look like? In what ways were sacred authority and secular rule connected with each other? Or to put it more precisely: what kind of rule did the priests exercise towards which subjects?

That the notion of *autocratic rule*, which is raised in the literature, is not unproblematic, is again suggested by Strabo. And Strabo, especially with reference to the Cappadocian and Pontic *temple states*, cannot be accused of not knowing what he was writing about. He characterizes the conditions in Cappadocian Comana thus:

> Its inhabitants are Cataonians, who, though in a general way classed as subject to the king (*hupo tō basilei tetagmenoi*), are in most respects subject to the priest (*hiereōs hupakouontes to pleon*). The priest is master (*kurios*) of the temple, and also of the temple-servants (*hiero-douloi*), who on my sojourn there were more than six thousand in

[29] Olshausen 1987:196.

number, men and women together. Also, considerable territory belongs to the temple, and the revenue is enjoyed by the priest. (Strabo 12.2.3)[30]

Strabo's description offers anything but a straightforward classification of the power relations. The only certainty is that the priest of Comana was the absolute master over the temple servants (*hierodouloi*) and that he commanded a considerable territory and its revenues. Much less clear is the situation of those living in Comana who were not temple servants. Here, Strabo avoids assigning a clear hierarchy between king and priest. The inhabitants of the town were *in principle* subjects to the kings and obeyed the priests merely in *most affairs*. This juxtaposition itself suggests that the priest possessed merely a de facto, but not a formal and regular commanding power.

This conclusion does not amount to an overinterpretation of the quotation. For it would have been more economical for Strabo at this point to have formulated a clear ruler-subject relationship between the temple master and those who were not temple servants; it would also have fitted better with his general line of argument. The fact that he did not do so therefore means that such a relationship did not exist.

This interpretation is supported by Strabo's description of the conditions in Zela, which points in a similar direction:

In early times [that is, pre-Roman] the kings governed Zela, not as a city, but as a sacred precinct of the Persian gods, and the priest was the master of the whole thing (*kurios tōn pantōn*). It was inhabited by the multitude of temple servants (*hierodouloi*), and by the priest, who had an abundance of resources (*periousia megalē*); and the sacred territory as well as that of the priest was subject to him and his numerous attendants. (Strabo 12.3.37)[31]

In this case, too, the priest—in effect acting as the plenipotentiary of the king—was master only over the temple servants (who were markers of the Pontic and Cappadocian *temple states* as well as of Pisidian Antioch), while he commanded the temple territory as well as his personal territory (as a fief?).

---

[30] Κατάονες δέ εἰσιν οἱ ἐνοικοῦντες, ἄλλως μὲν ὑπὸ τῷ βασιλεῖ τεταγμένοι, τοῦ δὲ ἱερέως ὑπακούοντες τὸ πλέον· ὁ δὲ τοῦ θ᾽ ἱεροῦ κύριός ἐστι καὶ τῶν ἱεροδούλων, οἳ κατὰ τὴν ἡμετέραν ἐπιδημίαν πλείους ἦσαν τῶν ἑξακισχιλίων, ἄνδρες ὁμοῦ γυναίξι. πρόσκειται δὲ τῷ ἱερῷ καὶ χώρα πολλή, καρποῦται δὲ ὁ ἱερεὺς τὴν πρόσοδον ...

[31] τὸ παλαιὸν μὲν γὰρ οἱ βασιλεῖς οὐχ ὡς πόλιν, ἀλλ᾽ ὡς ἱερὸν διῴκουν τῶν Περσικῶν θεῶν τὰ Ζῆλα, ᾠκεῖτο δ᾽ ὑπὸ τοῦ πλήθους τῶν ἱεροδούλων καὶ τοῦ ἱερέως ὄντος ἐν περιουσίᾳ μεγάλῃ, καὶ τοῖς περὶ αὐτὸν οὐκ ὀλίγοις χώρα τε ὑπέκειτο ἱερὰ καὶ ἦν τοῦ ἱερέως.

Where the problem of the *temple states* with respect to rule lay exactly, becomes unequivocally clear if we consider Pompey, after his victory over Mithradates, re-organizing the affairs of Pontus. He dissolved two of the three sanctuaries—not as cults, but as political units: he transformed Zela into a town, just like Cabira, which he renamed *Diospolis* (Strabo 12.3.37).[32] By incorporating surrounding territory (royal land?) the new *poleis* integrated temple territory and their own *khōra* into a single larger political unit (Strabo 11.8.4). In Comana, Pompey was somewhat more sensitive. He did not make the cult, which was rich in tradition, subject to the town of Comana, but appointed his comrade in arms, Archelaus, in the place of the priest who was loyal to Mithradates. At the same time, however, he created a political unit which, compared to the traditional organization of the temple territory, represented a radical innovation.

> When Pompey took over authority, he appointed Archelaus priest and included within his boundaries, in addition to the sacred land, a territory of two schoeni (that is, sixty stadia) in circuit and ordered the inhabitants to obey his rule. Now he [Archelaus] was governor (*hēgemōn*) of these, and also master (*kurios*) of the temple servants who lived in the city, except that he was not empowered to sell them. (Strabo 12.3.34)[33]

By describing Pompey's break with tradition precisely, Strabo sheds a brighter light on the traditional order of Comana than any other source. Central for our question concerning the rule of the priests in the *temple states* is the fact that Archelaus required a double competence—after the Pontic king had gone—in order to rule over a territory which exceeded the temple land and included a population which did not consist exclusively of temple servants. On the one hand, he became priest of Ma and master of the temple servants; on the other, he became leader (*hēgemōn*)—a strongly artificial title—of the remaining inhabitants of the territory. Effective rule over both groups could obviously not be achieved with the traditional priestly office in a temple state alone. This, however, allows only one conclusion for the pre-Pompeian period: even under the Mithradatids, the priests never possessed sovereignty over those who were not temple slaves; moreover, it was not within the horizon of

---

[32] Dreizehnter 1975:236–238; Olshausen 1991:449–454.

[33] παραλαβὼν δὲ Πομπήιος τὴν ἐξουσίαν Ἀρχέλαον ἐπέστησεν ἱερέα καὶ προσώρισεν αὐτῷ χώραν δίσχοινον κύκλῳ (τοῦτο δ' ἔστιν ἑξήκοντα στάδιοι) πρὸς τῇ ἱερᾷ, προστάξας τοῖς ἐνοικοῦσι πειθαρχεῖν αὐτῷ· τούτων μὲν οὖν ἡγεμὼν ἦν καὶ τῶν τὴν πόλιν οἰκούντων ἱεροδούλων κύριος πλὴν τοῦ πιπράσκειν·

expectations of the participants, for otherwise the artificial title of Archelaus would simply have been unnecessary. In these circumstances we cannot speak of a traditional connection between sacred authority and territorial rule in the temple state of Comana. Archelaus, who, unlike the priests in the kingdom of Pontus, was expected to exercise real rule under Roman auspices, had to be more than a priest.

This conclusion is confirmed by sources other than Strabo. For under Mithradates VI, Comana struck its own so-called semiautonomous coins. This is a mere town coinage with the inscription *KOMANŌN*, and resembles the coinage of other Pontic towns, which were probably also initiated by the king.[34] By contrast, the coins bear no reference to the priest. This strongly suggests that the inhabitants of the town Comana were not subjects of the master of the *temple state*. Thus during the time of the Mithradates, there were two separate units exercising political power in and around Comana: a settlement behaving like a *polis*, and the temple with its land and slaves.

This reconstruction also solves a problem connected with the history of the Men-temple at Antiochia ad Pisidiam. For in the third century BC, Antiochos I or II founded a colony with settlers from Ionia, at a distance of just three and a half kilometers from the sanctuary.[35] The hierarchical relationship in which this Antiochia may have stood to the old temple state has hitherto caused some headaches. As S. Mitchell and M. Waelkens state:

> There is no reason to believe that a priestly state existed alongside and in competition with the Greek Polis at Antioch.[36]

Yet this notion collides head-on with Strabo's report, which makes it unequivocally clear that the end of the traditional priesthood came only with the reduction of Antiochia to a Roman colony in the time of Augustus (Strabo 12.8.14).[37] If one accepts the interpretation of a temple state put forward

---

[34] Olshausen 1987:187–212.

[35] Mitchell and Waelkens 1998:5–7.

[36] Mitchell and Waelkens 1998:7.

[37] "Now Phrygia Paroreia has a kind of mountainous ridge extending from the east towards the west; and below it on either side lies a large plain. And there are cities near it: towards the north, Philomelium, and, on the other side, the Antiochia near Pisidia, as it is called, the former lying in a plain, whereas the latter is on a hill and has a colony of Romans. [Antiochia] was settled by the Magnetans who lived near the Maeander River. The Romans set them free from their kings at the time when they gave over to Eumenes the rest of Asia this side of the Taurus. Here there was also a priesthood of *Mēn Arkaios*, which had a number of temple-slaves and sacred places, but the priesthood was destroyed after the death of Amyntas 'by those who were sent thither as his inheritors' (*hupo tōn pemphtentōn epi tēn ekeinou klēronomian*)."

above, the problem solves itself: for the question, in what power-relationship the new *polis* stood to the old temple state, does not pose itself *strictu sensu*. Because the priest of Men could not exercise an overarching territorial rule just as his colleagues in Pontus and Cappadocia could not, and because the temple with its land and slaves was not dissolved in pre-Roman times, both units coexisted in the same place, like other combinations which were or would become common elsewhere in Asia Minor. Given the configuration we know about, anything else can simply not be expected.

In summary, we can note the following for the temple states in Cappadocia, Pontus, and Pisidia: their priests did not, by the standards of the Hellenistic world, exercise political power. On the one hand, they were closely integrated with the surrounding kingdoms; on the other hand, they could not integrate different types of subjects under their aegis. They might have been *autocratic*, but only towards the temple slaves and only with respect to the temple's own land. Under these circumstances the term *temple states* for these formations is in principle misleading, and actually obsolete. The most important priests in the kingdoms of Pontus and Cappadocia and at Antiochia ad Pisidiam were—to put it pointedly—nothing other than particularly privileged administrators of temple possessions—masters of a domain, as it were—invested with the kind of authority which allowed them to be extraordinarily functional in the context of the sacred household of their respective monarchies. The fact that the combination of sacred authority and aristocratic provenance occasionally turned these office holders into a considerable danger for the ruler was inevitable, but it has nothing to do with the temple masters having had a traditional competence to rule.

3. Priest-Dynasts: Pessinous and Olba

This negative result regarding the combination of sacred authority and secular power in Asia Minor notwithstanding, the file on *Anatolian temple states* cannot yet be closed. For there are two exceptions, regarding significantly different constellations: the Cybele-temple of Pessinous in Galatia, and the cult of Zeus of Olba in Rough Cilicia.

The characterization by Strabo of both situations is in itself remarkable. While he regularly mentions the existence of *hierodouloi* with regard to the remaining temple states, he denies us any such information with respect to both Pessinous (Strabo 12.5.3) and Olba (14.5.10). Instead, the term *dunasteia is used in connection with* both priesthoods, *which suggests hereditary rule.*

Moreover, in the case of Pessinous one can deduce from his correspondence with the Pergamene king Attalus II that he possessed the freedom to take autonomous decisions and room for political maneuvering.[38] The correspondence documents the joint plans of priest and king for political and military intervention in Galatia.

Yet while the information for the temple rule of Pessinous in general, and particularly for the first century BC, is very sparse, we are on much more solid ground with respect to Olba. In order to put alternative relationships between cultic authority and secular power into sharper profile, the dynasty of priests in Olba will take center stage in the following considerations. It makes sense to start again with Strabo, who offers the only available synthetic treatment of the Cilician temple state.

> And above this [Cyinda] and Soloi is a mountainous country in
> which is a city *Olbē*, with a temple of Zeus, founded by Aias the son of
> Teukros. The priest (*hiereus*) of this temple became dynast (*dunastēs*)
> of Cilicia Trachaea; and the country was beset by numerous tyrants,
> and the gangs of pirates were organized. And after the overthrow
> of these they called this country the domain (*dunasteia*) of Teucrus,
> and called the same also the priesthood (*hierosunē*) of Teucrus; and
> most of the priests were named Teucrus or Aias. (Strabo 14.5.10)

Despite a whole series of mistakes and imprecisions,[39] Strabo here provides a framework within which other evidence can be accommodated. Several relevant points can thus be made:

1. The temple rule of the Teucrids was organized as *dunasteia*, as a hereditary rule, based at the sanctuary of Zeus Olbius. The master of the temple was at the same time priest and dynast.[40]

2. Rule over a cult meant the rule over a territory, which Strabo here seems to conceive as the whole of Rough Cilicia.

3. Near the sanctuary was a city, Olba, which the cult could be understood to belong to.

Even though Strabo is wrong in his statement that the Teucrid dynasty ruled over all of Rough Cilicia,[41] a considerable amount of territory was linked

---

[38] Welles 1934 nos. 55–61.
[39] Trampedach 2001:270–272.
[40] For the foundation myth of the Teucrid dynasty, see Trampedach 1999.
[41] Gotter 2001:299.

to the political domination over the temple. This is indicated by inscriptions and signs on dozens of towers between the rivers Lamus and Calycadnus, which refer to the temple of Zeus Olbius and thereby circumscribe the expanse of the Olbian *dunasteia*.[42] This Olbian territory was a patchwork of different elements. As shown by honorary inscriptions for the priestly dynast of the early first century BC, as well as by later coins,[43] the temple state consisted—on the level of organized groups—of the tribes of the *Kennatai* and *Lalasseis* as well as the *polis* Olba. In this way, the rule of the Teucrids in Rough Cilicia in many respects, albeit on a smaller scale, resembled the monarchical regimes in Hellenistic states. The coherence of the territory and its subjects was essentially provided by the person of the ruler. Those subject to his rule were and remained disparate: a city, tribes which were organized as *koinon*, and a rural population that lived in villages and small settlements surmounted by towers and fortresses of the dynast. In contrast with the Hellenistic monarchs, however, it was not merely, or primarily, the much-lauded victoriousness of the ruler that had an integrating function,[44] but the common cult, which apparently represented the central communicative platform of the curious union between Lamus and Calycadnus. The temple of Zeus Olbius was and remained the point of reference for both ruler and subjects. In this sense the priestly rule among the Teucrids was indeed a temple state.

Against the background of the conditions outlined for the remainder of Asia Minor, the question poses itself—how was it that the exceptional combination of religious authority and secular power occurred in mountainous Cilicia of all places? One essential facet, surely, is the specific embedding of the Olbian temple state in the Seleucid kingdom. Unlike the temples of Pontus and Cappadocia, the temple of Zeus Olbius possessed no cult function for the Seleucid monarchy overall.[45] The Syrian kings were obviously less interested in the religious capital of the Teucrids than in their politicomilitary potential in an inaccessible mountainous area, which always remained peripheral for the Seleucid realm. Thus all the evidence suggests that the career of the Teucrid dynasty began with the foundation of Seleucia at the Calycadnus by Seleucus Nicator in the early third century BC. The location of the town and of its fertile plain immediately below the slopes of the Taurus made well-ordered and amicable conditions in the adjacent mountainous area an absolute necessity. And in the first century BC the priests themselves referred to a connection

[42] Durugönül 1998; Trampedach 2001:270–271.
[43] Hagel and Tomaschitz 1998: OlD 86, 100; Staffieri 1978 nos. 2–34.
[44] Cf. Gehrke 1982.
[45] Trampedach 2001:282.

between their shrine and Seleucus Nicator, who was said to have dedicated a building (or a part of it) in the Zeus-Olbius-complex.[46] Yet, a permanent and direct intervention of the Seleucids in the Olbian territory cannot be found, and this too may be attributed to functional causes. In the perspective of the Seleucids and their foundation of Seleucia at the Calycadnus one rather needed a power that was independent and capable of acting in the mountainous region of the Taurus.[47] Thus, the chief priest in Olba—unlike, for instance, those in the temple states of Pontus and Cappadocia—was not appointed by the monarch. Instead, his rule was the product of dynastic hereditary succession.

With the bankruptcy of the Seleucid Empire, the relationship between the priestly dynasts and the monarchs changed again. When strife arose over the succession during the first century BC, the mountainous area of Olba temporarily became the last refuge of Seleucids in distress.[48] In return for their loyalty, the priestly dynasts were made titular *Brothers of the Kings* (that is, of the Seleucid rulers Philip I and Philip II).[49] Perhaps the change in the title of the Olbian dynasts was also related to their altered role in the Seleucid kingdom. Originally simply called *hiereus*,[50] from the early first century BC at the latest, they began to call themselves *arkhiereus megas*.[51]

The close connection between rule and priesthood within the Teucrid state also dictated the choreography of regime change. When the dynasty of the Teucrids ended (probably in the early Tiberian period[52]) it was not enough for the new man in the Olbian territory—like Archelaus at the Corycian Cave— merely to neutralize the religious authority of the sanctuary of Zeus Olbius in ephemeral ways. Indeed, the Roman favorite Markos Antonios Polemon, who had no power base in the region,[53] clad himself in the traditional robes of the Olban priestly dynasts and called himself on his coins as they did: *ARKHIEREUS MEGAS*.[54] In Olba, unlike in the remaining temple states, religious authority and secular power were indeed inextricably linked. It ought to be stressed, though, that this mélange was—even by Anatolian standards—the exception, not the rule.

---

[46] Hagel and Tomaschitz 1998:OlD 36.

[47] Sayar 1999:129: "*Die frühen seleukidischen Könige waren anscheinend an einer echten und effizienten Urbanisierung in der Kilikia Tracheia nicht interessiert.*"

[48] Keil and Wilhelm 1931:66.

[49] Verilhac and Dagron 1974:238–239; Hagel and Tomaschitz 1998 OlD 100, OlD 91, OlD 92.

[50] Hagel and Tomaschitz 1998 OlD 1; Hagel and Tomaschitz 1998 Kan 8.

[51] Hagel and Tomaschitz 1998 OlD 91, OlD 92, OlD 100, OlD 36.

[52] Gotter 2001:301.

[53] Gotter 2001:301–302, 310. For the identity of this Polemon, see Gotter 2001:315–319.

[54] Staffieri 1978 nos. 29–34. For the end of the dynastic priesthood in Olba, see Pani 1970:327–334; Gotter 2001:302–303.

Part Three

VISUAL REPRESENTATION

6

Images and Prestige of Cult Personnel in Athens between the Sixth and First Centuries BC

Ralf von den Hoff

IN THE *POLEIS* OF ANCIENT GREECE, priests and priestesses rarely had permanent political, social, or economic power as a group and outside their sanctuaries.[1] On the other hand, everyone would agree that priests were an essential component of every Greek *polis*.[2] One aspect of their position was their high prestige; that is, their reputation and informal authority.[3] In ancient Greece, prestige was defined by and recognizable through various cultural practices. Images set up in the public sphere—statues, reliefs, or paintings initiated by the depicted persons or by others—were focal means of demonstrating prestige. Indeed, a large number of such portraits of cult officials are preserved from the Greek *poleis*. These *testimonia* have been catalogued and analyzed. But considering the debate about the roles of priests and priestesses in Greek *poleis*, it seems decidedly unusual that they have not been studied under the specific perspective of prestige presentation.[4] In this essay, I will try

I would like to thank Beate Dignas and Kai Trampedach for inviting me to participate in the conference and for the atmosphere of inspiring communication they created together with all the other participants of the colloquium. I also owe thanks to Anja Klöckner for her—as always—precise information about votive reliefs, to Shelby Wells (San Antonio), Andreas Scholl (Berlin), Susanne Pfisterer-Haas, Inge Kader, and Heide Glöckler (Munich) for providing photographs, and to Kris Giannotta and Stephen Lake for correcting my English. The remaining faults are, of course, my own responsibility.

[1] Feaver 1957:123; Garland 1984:75; Bremmer 1994:6–7; Bremmer 1996:10; cf. A. Chaniotis and U. Gotter in this volume.

[2] Price 1999:67; cf. Sourvinou-Inwood 1988:259–260.

[3] Burkert 1977:161. Witness, for instance, the advice of the priestess of Athena in favor of Themistocles' plans in 480 BC: Herodotus 8.41. The distinction between power and prestige is crucial and needs further investigation.

[4] Mantis 1990; cf. also Clinton 1974; Aleshire 1989; Aleshire 1991 and now *ThesCRA* 5:1–65. Priest-

to do so in a chronological overview. My purpose is to trace the changing role and importance of images of cult personnel in relation to their prestige. Those elements of priestly functions and qualities will be discussed which were crucial for the setting up of these images, in order to understand the basis on which the reputation and authority of priests was founded and to describe the public discourse that used this reputation as social capital. The category *cult personnel* includes all persons responsible for *cult activities* who held a certain *office* which was not solely administrative in function.[5] I am going to examine portrait images of cult personnel, although other—and possibly more important—means of defining prestige did exist and would also be worth studying. However, I will not restrict my interest to preserved images. Rather, all epigraphic, literary, *and* archaeological records will be studied, insofar as they refer to images. Such a synoptic approach has for long been neglected and thus appears particularly necessary and fruitful.[6] Athens between the sixth and first centuries BC has been chosen as a case study due to the large corpus of surviving records, which allows us to trace historical changes over this period. I will focus primarily, but not exclusively, on the Acropolis as Athens' most important sanctuary, in which public roles and the prestige of cult personnel can be expected to be expressed best, although other contexts such as grave monuments and other sanctuaries would need further investigation.[7] Two questions will guide me through the relevant *testimonia*:

1. What were the changing functions and aims of images of cult personnel?

2. Which qualities of the depicted cult personnel were emphasized in these images, that is, how was prestige defined and how was it articulated visually?

---

esses have received particular attention recently: Kron 1996; van Bremen 1996; Dillon 2002; Lindner 2003. On grave reliefs with images of cult personnel: Scholl 1996:135–148; Kosmopoulou 2001:292–300.

[5] Cf. Plato *Statesman* 290c–d; Aristotle *Politics* 6.1322b12–28; cf. Price 1999:67–73; A. Chaniotis in this volume.

[6] Cf. von den Hoff 2004, where some of the ideas touched on here have also been worked out from a different perspective; Clinton 1974.

[7] Such as the Asclepieum (with reference to Aleshire 1989; Aleshire 1991) or the sanctuary at Eleusis (with reference to Clinton 1974). A study of the grave reliefs (cf. above n4) from the point of view of the demonstration of their prestige by cult personnel, is still a desideratum; see the remarks below. I will not discuss the depiction of priests and other cult personnel on vases here, because they follow different rules, in that, for instance, they are not individualized; cf. van Straten 1996; Gebauer 2002, and the remarks in Bremmer 1994:28; Bremmer 1996:33; below n27.

Starting with the Archaic period, we do not know of any statues of cult officials, explicitly defined as such, from Athens in the sixth century BC. It has been claimed that the more than seventy *korai* from the Acropolis were images of servants of Athena, such as *ergastinai*, *kanēphoroi*, *arrhēphoroi*, or priestesses of the goddess.[8] Yet these figures could also be dedicated to Poseidon (*IG* I³ 828), who had no female cult officials, and they do not display any attributes identifying them as divine or mythological figures or as cult personnel.[9] Equally significant is the fact that they bear no individual names. Rather, in the inscriptions, they are simply called *korē*, *aparkhē*, or *perikallēs agalma*. This is in contrast to named statues on the Acropolis, and to named *korai* in other sanctuaries, which, however, are also never identified as cult personnel by their inscriptions. Thus, it remains the most plausible explanation that the Athenian *korai* were primarily dedications to Athena (or to other gods), rather than being intended to represent living persons.[10] Neither any identification as specific individuals nor any clue to cult functions is readily recognizable. As precious and expensive *agalmata*, the *korai* served to demonstrate the wealth and *piety* (*eusebeia*) of their male dedicators. Wealthy male citizens also used these votives as visual confirmation of the social role of women as objects of exchange and as visual demonstration of normative female behavior.[11]

---

[8] See now Hurwit 1998:125–129; Karakasi 2001:115–144; Keesling 2003:3–161; Holtzmann 2003:55–62 (all with further bibliography); Stieber 2004. For suggested identifications, cf. for example, Ridgway 1977:108–112 (*arrhēphoroi* or *kanēphoroi*; but note that she altered her opinion, cf. below, following note); Shapiro 2001:3–5 (*kanēphoroi*); Shapiro 2001:92-94 (young Athenians); Karakasi 2001:134–139 (*arrhēphoroi*); Brinkmann 2003:71 ("*Frauen aus reichen attischen Häusern*", which is also suggested by Stieber 2004); further bibliography: Kron 1996:145n36; Keesling 2003:100–102. That some *korai* have been found near the alleged house of the *arrhēphoroi* (Pausanias 1.27.3) is no argument for an identification. For other find-spots, cf. Karakasi 2001:130 fig. 19. Insofar as Archaic images do not attempt to depict age accurately, the argument that the *korai* look too old for girls like *arrhēphoroi* (Langlotz 1939:7–8; Martini 1990:80) is not valid.

[9] Dedication to Poseidon: Keesling 2003:112. The so-called Peplos Kore from Athens, Acropolis 679 (Ridgway 1990:602–611; Keesling 2003:135–139; Brinkmann 2003 cat. no. 100) wears a garment different from those of the other statues, and seems to be a goddess. Ridgway 1982:126–127; Ridgway 1990:601–602; and Harrison 1988:53–54, identify the *korai* as nymphs or similar semidivine figures. Keesling 2003:97–161 now identifies the *korai* as statues of Athena, but this remains debatable because almost all (!) of them lack Athena's principal attributes of the Archaic period: weapons and aegis (for exceptions: Keesling 2003:129–140). These omissions must have been intended to distinguish the *korai* from statues of Athena.

[10] Lechat 1903:270; Graindor 1938:202–211; Payne and Young 1936:9–10n3 (reference to goddess rather than to dedicator); Langlotz 1939:7–8; Richter 1968:4; Schneider 1975:2–3; Floren and Fuchs 1987:262; Pandora 1996:129–131 no. 1; Martini 1990:80–82; Ross Holloway 1992:268; Kron 1996:145; Dillon 2001:12; Holtzmann 2003:56; cf. Keesling 2003:107–121. Keesling 2003 and Stieber 2004 have recently challenged this point of view.

[11] Schneider 1975:2–3; Osborne 1994:90–91.

The lack of explicit depictions of cult personnel on the Archaic Acropolis is the more noteworthy because statues of specific individuals were placed in this sanctuary during the sixth century. Even statues of civic officials were set up there, such as the sitting "scribes," possibly *tamiai*.[12] Furthermore, elsewhere in Greece, identifiable portraits of cult officials are known from the Archaic period. From Didyma, the marble figure of a man is preserved, who wears an unusual mantle and is holding a scepter (fig. 1). This possibly identified him as a seer in Apollo's sanctuary.[13] His sitting posture was a common pattern of representation for members of the political elite, especially in the East. *Key-bearers* (*kleidoukhoi*) were depicted in small, *korē*-like terracotta figurines from the Artemis sanctuary in Cercyra,[14] while in Miletus, the marble statue of a *korē* could be equipped with a *lituus*-like staff to demonstrate the cult function of the woman being portrayed.[15] These images document the fact that conventional statue types (a *korē*, a sitting man) did serve to depict cult personnel in Archaic Greece, while distinct attributes, related to sacred authority (scepter, key), were used as symbols of their specific cult functions. Since such portraits are completely lacking from Athens, it appears that, in this *polis*, cult officials did not choose to represent themselves or to publicly define their status in this way during the Archaic period, even if concern with cult status was not entirely excluded from the competitive practices of Athenian aristocrats. Nevertheless, the prestige associated with cult and ritual itself was high, considering the scenes of processions and sacrifices on Attic vases of this period.[16]

In the fifth century, according to Pliny's *Natural History* 34.54 and Cicero's *Against Verres* 2.5.5, statues of both *kanēphoroi* (by Polyclitus) and

---

[12] For named statues of dedicators, see only the image of Rhombus (Fuchs and Floren 1987:276 pl. 22.1; Holtzmann 2003:63 fig. 41); further evidence in: Krumeich 1997:23–24; Holtzmann 2003:50–55, 63–66; Keesling 2003:117, 180–185. For the *scribes*: Krumeich 1997:22–23 figs. 1–4; Trianti 1998:1–33; Shapiro 2001a:94-96 (*"heilige Männer"*); Keesling 2003:182–185; Brinkmann 2003 cat. no. 22, 66; Holtzmann 2003:65–66 fig. 43.

[13] Istanbul, Archaeological Museum 1945: Höckmann 1996:93–102 pl. 18–19.1; Kopanias 2001. On the sitting posture: Nagy 1998. For the role of seers in the Archaic period, see K. Trampedach in this volume.

[14] Cercyra, Archaeological Museum: Lechat 1891:32 fig. 4, 79 fig. 13; Mantis 1990:30–31 pl. 5.

[15] Now lost, *ex* art market: Mantis 1990:31–32 pl. 6a; Karakasi 2001:35n9 cat. no. M10, 38–39 pl. 45. For the unusual attribute, cf. Özgan 1978:133–135. See also Archaic statues of priests from Cyprus: Senff 1993:54, 70–71 pl. 37, 61d–e; Karageorgis 2000:109–110 no. 172.

[16] Vases: Gebauer 2002. Among extant Attic grave monuments of the Archaic period, only the painted stele of Lyseas can be related iconographically to a cult context, on the basis of the attributes depicted; however, these could also be signs of his *eusebeia* rather than pointing to a position as priest of Dionysus: Mantis 1990:92–93 pl. 42b. For the dominance of the elite in Athenian state religion: Ober 1989:57, cf. also 290n73.

Figure 1. Statue of a seer (?). From Didyma, sixth century BC. Istanbul, Archaeological Museum 1945. Photo by H. P. Laubscher, courtesy of the Institut für Klassische Archäologie, Ludwig-Maximilians-Universität, Munich.

kleidoukhoi (by Phidias) existed in Greece.[17] If the relief from Mantinea with a woman inspecting the liver of an animal was set up in honor of a female seer,

[17] Palagia 1980:41; Mantis 1990:52–56; 74–75; Phidias' statue could also have been a mythical figure. Cf. the *kleidoukhos* of Euphranor (Pliny *Natural History* 34.78; Palagia 1980:40–41) and late Classical or early Hellenistic *kleidoukhoi* from Cyprus (Connelly 1988:21–22, 27 fig. 32–33). We do not know the date of the statues of priestesses in front of the temple of Hera in Argos: Pausanias 2.17.3.

this would be further evidence for images of cult personnel in the Classical period.[18] But still no such records from Athens have been preserved—either from the Acropolis or from other areas of the city. This is astonishing, because, also in this period, we know of votive statues of other Athenian individuals, such as athletes, civic servants, and *stratēgoi* being set up on the Acropolis.[19] The statue group of the *stratēgos* Tolmides with his seer beside him (Pausanias 1.27.4–5) is a revealing example.[20] Placed on the Acropolis around the middle of the fifth century, the purpose of this group was to demonstrate Tolmides' military success. The seer was not meant to be a cult official in his own right, but represented the *eusebeia* of Tolmides himself.[21] In Athens, mention of individuals as holding cult offices was avoided even in inscriptions, as is evidenced by the case of Callias, son of Hipponicus. He fought successfully at Marathon in the position of Eleusinian *dadoukhos*, while he was, indeed, wearing his priestly garment (Plutarch *Aristides* 5). Despite this highly renowned act, he did not mention his priestly office in a dedicatory inscription on the Acropolis some years later (*IG* I^3 835).[22] Instead, he calls himself *hipponikos* in reference to his Olympic victories, which obviously were more prestigious than his position as *dadoukhos*.

It is on the Acropolis, in the frieze of the Parthenon (447–438 BC), that the first explicit representations of Athenian cult officials appear in the public sphere. In the Panathenaic procession, depicted in the northern, southern, and western parts of this frieze, distinct cult officials cannot be identified, although some participants carry cult objects and all are engaged in the rites of the cult.[23] In the most prominent eastern frieze, the women leading the procession are also carrying cult utensils (East 2–15, 55, 57–63).[24] Although here younger *parthenoi* and older women are distinguished by dress and hairdo,[25] we are

---

[18] Athens, National Museum 226: Mantis 1990:51–52 pl. 18; Kron 1996:142–143 fig. 1; Kaltsas 2002:132 no. 254. The statue of a priestess made by Phradmon from Argos is attested by an inscription from Ostia: Zevi 1969–1970:110–114.

[19] Krumeich 1997:63–150; Keesling 2003:170–180, 191–198. For the difference between private votive statues and official honorific statues, which, in Athens, were not set up between 477/6 and 394/3: Demosthenes 20.70; Himmelmann 2001:51–53n79.

[20] Krumeich 1997:110–111, 244 cat. no. A58; Keesling 2003:258n81.

[21] For seers in Athens: Garland 1984:81–82; 1996:93–94; cf. Trampedach and Flower in this volume. Cf. a statue of a *splankhnoptēs*: Pliny *Natural History* 34.81: Robertson 1999.

[22] Krumeich 1997:92; 231–232 cat. no. A20.

[23] For the frieze as a whole: Berger and Gisler-Huwiler 1996; Neils 2001.

[24] Berger and Gisler-Huwiler 1996:147–169 pls. 128–130, 138–140; Hurwit 1998:184–186; Neils 2001:154–158 fig. 118; Dillon 2001:42–50; Holtzmann 2003:131–133; Lindner 2003:58–59.

[25] Berger and Gisler-Huwiler 1996:151, 152, 167, 168, 169; Neils 2001:158; cf. Beschi 1984:180–183; Harrison 1989:51–53.

Figure 2. *Archon basileus* (?) and priestess of Athena with servants. Central part of the east frieze of the Parthenon, 447–432 BC. London, British Museum. Photo, Erich Lessing / Art Resource, NY.

still unable to identify holders of distinct cult offices, except for two possible *kanēphoroi* (East 50–51).[26] It is only in the central scene—above the entrance and framed by the gods themselves—that priests are depicted (fig. 2). One male figure (East 34) wears the long, ungirded *khitōn* which was the typical dress of priests.[27] This dress and the very prominent position point rather to an official representative of the *polis* than to a member of the *genos* of the Praxiergidae without an official priestly position, as has been recently suggested.[28] Thus, he is probably best identified as the *arkhōn basileus*.[29] He holds Athena's *peplos*. Behind him, two girls (East 31–32) are welcomed by a larger woman (East 33). In such a position, related to the Panathenaea and above the entrance to Athena's temple, the priestess of the goddess must be depicted. She is slightly smaller than her male counterpart and is not clothed distinctively. Thus, iconographically, the priest is highlighted and distinguished from usual civic images, while

[26] Roccos 1995:641–668, esp. 657–658; Neils 2001:157; *contra*: Mansfield 1985:354–355n130. Other identifications of cult personnel: Beschi 1984:193; Harrison 1989:53; Berger and Gisler-Huwiler 1996:167.

[27] Berger and Gisler-Huwiler 1996:157–161 pl. 134; Neils 2001:166–171 figs.127, 197–200; Neils and Oakley 2003:159 fig. 24; for the dress, cf. Miller 1989:319–323; on vases, the long priestly *khitōn* is rarely depicted: Mantis 1990 pls. 35b, 43; van Straten 1995 figs. 135, 145–146.; cf. Gebauer 2002:471–478.

[28] Steinhart 1997.

[29] Berger and Gilser-Huwiler 1996:159, 172–174 (table with suggested identifications).

the priestess is not. This will become a common pattern in Athenian images of cult personnel. The two girls in front of the priestess are carrying stools, but it is uncertain whether they are the official *diphrophoroi*.[30] Because of her size, the girl on the left (East 31) is certainly the youngest female participant in the entire frieze. She is highlighted by her frontal posture, which would make an identification as *arrhēphoros* probable, except that the stool may militate against this conclusion.[31] Taken all together, in keeping with the Archaic Attic tradition, the Parthenon frieze was not intended primarily to depict individual cult officials by means of well-defined iconographical patterns. Instead, it staged the whole *dēmos* of Athens as active participants in the cult: an icon of *tōn Athēnaiōn eusebeia*. Indeed, the Athenians later claimed that their *eusebeia* towards the gods made them superior to all other *poleis* (Lycurgus *Against Leocrates* 15). Only in the eastern frieze are two high cult officials present, framed by and close to the gods, and thus distinguished: the most important woman in Athena's cult, who was a member of the *genos* of the Eteoboutadae, with two girls as her attendants, and the most important man in the *polis*-cult as a whole, who was chosen by lot each year, with a male attendant. This choice programmatically included both hereditary and democratic priesthoods.[32] Further, the fact that the priest is taller than the priestess, and that his bearing of Athena's robe makes his role more prestigious, points to the precedence of men in the *polis*-cult. At the same time, both the presence of two female attendants in this scene, as opposed to only one male attendant for the priest, and the prominent position of women in the Panathenaic procession as a whole, were certainly due to the female gender of the deity to whom the temple was dedicated, and suggest that women were by no means unimportant in the Athenian cultic context. Thus, gender and sociopolitical roles were distinguished precisely: they resulted in hierarchies and different ways of participation in the cult, as well as in different priestly dress. Yet these first public Athenian images of cult officials were still not meant to be depictions of historical individuals. Rather, they were *signa* of civic *eusebeia* embedded within the *Athēnaiōn dēmos* as a whole. They represented positions rather than individuals, and signified the importance of cult activities in the *polis* and the idea that cult officials acted primarily in the service and on behalf of the city and her piety, and not according to their own desire for prestige.

---

[30] Schäfer 1987; they really carry stools, *pace* Wesenberg 1995.

[31] Cf. Sourvinou-Inwood 1988a:58–59; von Heintze 1993; Berger and Gisler-Huwiler 1996:158–159; Neils 2001:168; Holtzmann 2003:134. For the age of *arrhēphoroi*, see below. For the shoulder cord worn by East 31: Harrison 1977; Roccos 2000:245–247 (but with crossbands).

[32] Schäfer 1987:211.

Figure 3. Grave relief of a priest. From Athens, late fifth century BC. Berlin, Staatliche Museen, Pergamonmuseum K 28. Berlin, Staatliche Museen, Pergamonmuseum.

It was immediately after the erection of the Parthenon, in the late fifth century, that this situation began to change. From this time on and through the fourth century, priests and priestesses were depicted on Attic grave reliefs (figs. 3–4).[33] Here, for the first time, cult personnel were individually named

---

[33] See above n4; cf. Bergemann 1997:45; *ThesCRA* 5:30 nos. 136–138 pls. 4–5; and now Ajootian 2007.

Figure 4. Grave relief of the priestess Polystrate. From Athens, early fourth century BC. Athens, Kerameikos Museum I 430. Deutsches Archäologisches Institut, Athens; neg. no. Ker 6164.

on public images, although in this genre of monument, references to professional activities were normally very rare. Priests (fig. 3) wear the long *khitōn*, which is already known from the Parthenon frieze, and they usually hold a knife in their hand as a sign of their ability to perform sacrifices. Priestesses, on the other hand (fig. 4), are represented in common civic dress, as in the frieze, but now they frequently hold a temple key.[34] Again, gender distinctions are obvious: priestesses are not distinguished by their dress, but defined by their administrative authority (key), while priests are clearly distinguished by their garment as well as being defined as performers of bloody rituals (knife). It is noteworthy that, in Athens, such individualized images of cult personnel were introduced in funerary art, albeit in small reliefs rather than in the elaborate *naiskoi* of the wealthy families. Thus, the members of the elite—in charge of the hereditary priesthoods and monopolising ritual expertise—did not use their prominent grave monuments to advertise their role in the cult. Rather, they did so only in smaller reliefs, and it was the middle class who visually represented their *eusebeia* and services for the *polis* in prestigious priestly positions, which they certainly gained by way of lot or election.[35] Not everyone who was in a position to do so, however, actually took the opportunity: witness the grave *stēlai* of a family of seers from Brauron, and the grave *lēkuthos* of Myrrhine, first priestess of Athena Nike. She is depicted without any attributes referring to the position she held. Instead, the image focuses on her relationship to the gods—that is, her *eusebeia*—which in itself seems to have been more prestigious than the cult office.[36]

Despite the increasing number of grave reliefs with cult personnel, priests or priestesses do not appear on Attic votive reliefs of the fourth century, although the preparation of sacrifices is depicted.[37] This is certainly due to the

---

[34] Lindner 2003:55, 61–63. Temple keys and sacrificial knife: Mantis 1990; Scholl 1996:136–137, 143; Kosmopoulou 2001:294. For the dress: Kosmopoulou 2001:296–297 (women); above n27 (men). However, knives are also known as attributes of female cult personnel in graves: Kron 1992:650.

[35] Scholl 1996:138–139, 147–148; cf. the grave monuments of the Lycurgus family, below n52.

[36] Brauron: *SEG* 23, 161; Bergemann 1997:202 Q3 pl. 11. Although members of this family are explicitly named as *mantis* on the large inscription stelae of this precinct, the reliefs do not refer to this position. Myrrhine, Athens, National Museum 4485: Turner 1983:82–96; Rahn 1986; Clairmont 1993:163–165 no. 5.150; Kaltsas 2002:148–150 no. 289; Holtzmann 2003:224 fig. 196; cf. *IG* I^3 35 and *IG* I^3 1330, Hansen 1983:54 no. 93; Parker 1996:125–127; Price 1999:175–176 nos. 4–5; *ThesCRA* 5:10 no. 31. On *eusebeia* (cf. above) and honoring the gods as important qualities mentioned in grave epigrams: *IG* II^2 5501 = Hansen 1989:88–89 no. 600; *IG* II^2 6551 = Hansen 1989:90–91 no. 603; *IG* II^2 7227 = Hansen 1989:49 no. 543; *IG* II^2 8593 = Peek 1960 no. 106; Blümel 1994:158–159; further evidence: Peek 1960:371 s.v. *Frömmigkeit*.

[37] Van Straten 1995; Edelmann 1999. The exception which proves the rule is the priest wearing a

Figure 5. Document relief in honor of a woman. From the Athenian Acropolis, early fourth century BC. Athens, Acropolis Museum 2758 + 2427. Photo, Gösta Hellner, Deutsches Archäologisches Institut, Athens; neg. no. Ath. 1985/3.

fact that these reliefs were dedicated by citizens who were not priests. Thus, by showing the dedicator's autonomous sacrificial act, they aimed at demonstrating his *eusebeia*, which did not necessitate the presence of a priest. It is also in the early fourth century that the first honors for Athenians as religious officials are recorded (*IG* II² 1140). This happened at the same time as the first honorific statues for Athenian citizens after the Tyrannicides were also set up.[38] This change is also discernible on the Acropolis, for example, on the fragments of a marble relief from this sanctuary which was carved during the early fourth century (fig. 5).[39] Accompanied by other divine figures, Athena is

---

long *khitōn* on a votive relief in Eretria, Museum 631: Edelmann 1999:190no. B32 (I owe this reference to A. Klöckner); cf. Mantis 1990:36 Taf. 9b (votive relief in Malibu, Getty Museum 73.AA.124); Geominy 1989:255 (votive relief in St. Petersburg, Hermitage PAN 160).

[38] Awards of wreaths: Blech 1982:153–161. For honorific statues after 394/3, see above n19. The inscription for the priest Aristokrates (*IG* II² 3454; Meritt 1933:155–156 no. 4; Davies 1971:60 no. 1926) does not belong to this period, nor is it a statue base: Ma and Tracy 2004:121–126.

[39] Athens, Acropolis Museum 2758 + 2427: Meyer 1989:287 cat. A76 pl. 27,1; Mantis 1990:41–42, 88; Lawton 1995:125 no. 91 pl. 48. Priestesses on document reliefs: Lawton 1995:61.

Figure 6. Document relief in honor of a priestess of Athena, second half of the fourth century BC. Berlin, Antikensammlung Sk 882. Drawing after *Archäologische Zeitung* 15 (1857), pl. 105.

adorning a smaller woman (with a wreath?), who is piously raising her hand towards the goddess in a gesture of prayer. Considering the provenance of the relief, and that it was the upper part of an honorary decree in which the woman must have been the *honorée*, it is reasonable to conclude that a female member of the Acropolis cult personnel is depicted here. She may have been

119

the priestess of Athena herself, although no key is depicted as a definite sign of this position. In the mid-fourth century and the era of Lycurgus, the number of honors awarded to Athenian cult personnel increased (*IG* II^2 354; 410; 1199). The relief of an honorific decree for a priest of the tribe Antiochis is additional visual evidence of this trend.[40] Also from the Acropolis comes another relief recording honors for a woman (fig. 6).[41] Dated on stylistic grounds to around 340–320, Nike, flying from Athena's hand, crowns a smaller woman, who is holding a temple key and who again raises her hand towards the deity. She must be a priestess of Athena and thus a member of the *genos* of the Eteoboutadae.[42] These fourth-century *testimonia* reveal the growing prestige attached to cult offices in terms of awards granted by the *polis*.[43] Now, individual honors, especially for the old *genē* holding the hereditary priesthoods, were documented visually on the Acropolis. However, honorific statues for cult personnel set up by *dēmos* and *boulē* were yet to be placed in this sanctuary.[44]

Private votive statues depicting cult officials seem to have compensated for this absence. The base of the life-size bronze statue of Lysimache is the earliest surviving example from the Acropolis (*IG* II^2 3453; fig. 7).[45] As a priestess of Athena, Lysimache came from the *genos* of the Eteoboutadae. Her bronze statue was set up posthumously around 360, most probably by a member of her family. The inscription especially highlights the fact that she had seen generations of children; she died after sixty-four years in office, at eighty years of age. So far, efforts to identify copies of this portrait statue

---

[40] Athens, National Museum 3482: Meyer 1989:289–299 cat. A86; Lawton 1995:143–144 no. 145 pl. 77. Cf. also the honors for a priest in an Attic *dēmos*: SEG 42, 112; ThesCRA 5:28 no. 121.

[41] Berlin, *Antikensammlung* Sk 882: Meyer 1989:289 cat. A85; Mantis 1990:41–43 pl. 12; Lawton 1995:151–152 no. 164 pl. 86; Scholl 2002:193 no. 90; ThesCRA 5:29 no. 124 pl. 3.

[42] It is uncertain whether it perhaps depicts Phanostrate, priestess of Athena, known to have been in office in 341/0: Mantis 1990:41–43; Aleshire 1994:336 no. 2 note b.

[43] It is doubtful whether the document relief in Athens, National Museum 1396 (Lawton 1995:147–148 no. 153 pl. 81; Kaltsas 2002:236 no. 496) portrays a priest of Amphiaraus, as the honored Articlides is not wearing priestly dress.

[44] Other official honorific statues were also rare on the Classical Acropolis: *IG* II^2 3822, 4321 (cf. Hansen 1989:179 no. 761); the provenance of *IG* II^2 4330 is uncertain; *IG* II2 3827 is Roman: Ma and Tracy 2004:121–126. On the other hand, official honorific statues did exist in sanctuaries outside Attica: Eule 2002:213–214.

[45] Jahn and Michaelis 1931:pl. 28 no. 9; Reisch 1919:303–306 fig. 192; Lewis 1955:1–12 fig. 2; Hansen 1989:175–176 no. 757; Mantis 1990:70–71 pl. 29; Georgoudi 1993:157–196; Kron 1996:143–144 fig. 2 (with bibliography); Löhr 2000:198; Bielman 2002:22–25; Holtzmann 2003:221; ThesCRA 5:10–11 no. 32. It remains uncertain whether this was the same Lysimache, mother of Telemachus, founder of the Asclepieum, who dedicated a silver *phialē* on the Acropolis in 398/7: Harris 1995:171 cat. V 317, 246 no. 31; Hurwit 1998:251; Bielman 2002:22; Holtzmann 2003:221; cf. Davies 1971:170–171.

Figure 7. Statue base of the priestess Lysimache. From the Athenian Acropolis, ca. 360 BC. Athens, Acropolis. Photo by Feiler, Deutsches Archäologisches Institut, Athens; neg. no. Akr. 2300.

Figures 8a–b. Plaster cast: portrait of a priestess (?). Roman marble copy after a Greek original of the early fourth century BC, London, British Museum 2001. Cast, Munich, Museum für Abgüsse Klassischer Bildwerke 127. Photos, H. Glöckler, Museum für Abgüsse Klassischer Bildwerke, Munich.

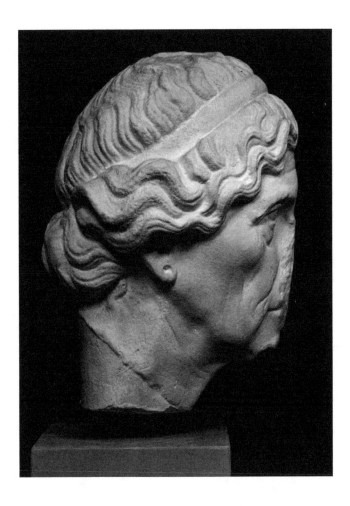

made by Demetrius of Alopece (Pliny *Natural History* 34.76) have not been convincing,[46] but a female head of possibly slightly earlier date, preserved in Roman copies in London (figs. 8a–8b) and Rome, gives an idea of such a portrait of an old priestess.[47] Her old age, like that reflected in this portrait, her

---

[46] Cf. Pfisterer-Haas 1989:101–105; Kron 1996:144; Schulze 1998:98–99. Nonetheless, the fact that Pliny mentions the statue speaks in favor of the existence of Roman copies.

[47] London, British Museum 2001: Reisch 1919:312–316 fig. 195; Pfisterer-Haas 1989: 102–103 Abb. 164–165; Mantis 1990:70–74 pl. 30γ–31; Todisco 1993:61–62 pl. 89; Hurwit 1998:251 Abb. 205; Holtzmann 2003:221 fig. 195. The *strophion* relates the head to the portrait of the priestess Aristonoë (below n68); originally, earrings were attached on both sides, which also distinguishes the woman from conventional mythological figures; but cf. the identification as mythological heroine: Pfisterer-Haas 1989:104–105.

lifelong service for Athena and for the *polis*, proved Lysimache's *eusebeia* and thus made such an extraordinary (and, as far as we know, hitherto unknown) statue of a priestess on the Acropolis possible. Nonetheless, as is seen from the epigraphic formula, it was not an official honor granted by *dēmos* and *boulē*. Instead, the Eteoboutadae themselves took the opportunity to demonstrate their particular religious engagement for the *polis* with such a prominent votive monument.[48] They emphasized their own prestige in religious affairs, while at the same time approximating this statue to the honors awarded by the *polis* to other priestesses of the same *genos*, which were documented on the Acropolis in the reliefs mentioned above.

Lysimache's statue, the grave-reliefs, and the public honors indicate that, in the late fifth and fourth century, for the first time, the prestige associated with a cult office became the subject of individual representation in the Athenian visual culture. By the same token, an element of competition in demonstrating this prestige emerged, a trend which the *eupatridai* seem to have reinforced. Yet, if we consider the grave reliefs and other individual records, it becomes clear that this phenomenon had broader dimensions.[49] In contrast to ordinary Athenian citizens, who used these reliefs merely to document their cult positions, the elite sought to demonstrate their *eusebeia* in Athena's sanctuary itself, which thus became the locus of the display of prestige associated with cult offices. In view of the fact that the elite could parade themselves in the central sanctuary of the city, religious representation on their prominent grave monuments may have been redundant.

The sociopolitical changes of the late fourth century were not without consequences for the representation of cult personnel on the Athenian Acropolis: the elite sought to preserve its religious hegemony, while the middle classes tried to display elite-like qualities. From 317/07 on, grave reliefs were forbidden by law: thereby, the opportunity to document cult engagement in the *nekropoleis* vanished altogether.[50] At the same time, the Acropolis became a focal point of Athenian identity construction, especially in the religious sphere, and also the preferred setting for official statues of the most highly honored Athenians.[51] Such a context led the members of the wealthy *genē* to maintain

[48] Compare the dedication of a small temple by the priestess Menecrateia in the sanctuary of Aphrodite Pandemos around 350–320: *IG* II^2 4753; Hansen 1989:183–184 no. 770; Kron 1996:154–155 Abb. 8.

[49] For the definition of *eupatridai*: Ober 1989:55–59. Cf. the votive statue of the priestess Chaerippe made by Praxiteles and set up by her brothers, possibly in the city Eleusinion: Ajootian 2007.

[50] Later, in the Hellenistic period, this is done again by depicting keys on *columellae*: Mantis 1990 pl. 14–15.

[51] See von den Hoff 2003.

the position they had established in this sanctuary by means of votive images of cult officials. The Eteoboutadae imposed this competitive demonstration of prestige on the Acropolis to an unprecedented degree.[52] Habron, Lycurgus' son and successor as hereditary priest of Poseidon, shortly before his death around 305, dedicated a *painting (pinax)* on the Acropolis (Pausanias 1.26.1).[53] In this painting, Ismenias of Chalcis depicted *the family's genealogy (katagōgē)* in life-size figures,[54] including the last three priests of Poseidon: Lycomedes, his son Lycurgus, and Lycurgus' son Habron ([Plutarch] *Moralia* 843e–f). Habron, the dedicator, is seen handing over the trident to his brother Lycophron. Habron did not have any children, and so had to make other arrangements for his succession: Lycophron had a son.[55] Thus, the monumental painting was an assertion of the Lycurgus family's legitimacy and of the continuity in holding their hereditary priestly office.[56] The *pinax* was located inside the Erechtheum, which was also the principal office of the Eteoboutad priests of Poseidon and, at the same time, the cult place of their ancestor Butes with the throne of his priest (*IG* II² 5166). Later, the painting hung beside a gallery of *images (graphai)* of the Eteoboutad priests of Poseidon in the same room (Pausanias 1.26.5), but it is unclear if the first of these images was dedicated in the Classical period or later.[57] Nonetheless, in the late fourth century, Ismenias' painting was not enough for the Eteoboutadae: also inside the Erechtheum, a statue group of Lycurgus with his three sons Habron, Lycurgus, and Lycophron was dedicated ([Plutarch] *Moralia* 843e–f). The lifetime of these subjects suggests a date after around 330/20; since the sons of Praxiteles, Timarchus and Cephisodotus, carved the statues, a date before around 290 is probable, although we do not know which of those depicted was the dedicator.[58] The group is a further

---

[52] For the *genos*: Davies 1971:351–352; Merker 1986:41–50; Matthaiou 1987:31–41; Aleshire 1994:28; Parker 1996:290–293; Mikalson 1998:22. For the priesthood of Poseidon: Garland 1984:106; Aleshire 1994:330–332; Lycurgus very probably held the priesthood until his death in 325/4. The grave *lekuthos* of Lycophron has been found: Matthaiou 1987:35–37 pl. 10; *SEG* 37.160. It must have been set up after the law of Demetrius prohibiting large grave monuments.

[53] Marcade 1948:697–698; Hölscher 1977:378–379; Merker 1986:47, 50; Hintzen-Bohlen 1990:152–153; Löhr 2000:147 no. 167; cf. von den Hoff 2003:179–180 for the following argument.

[54] Lippold 1916:2141.

[55] Marcade 1948:697–698; Hintzen-Bohlen 1990:153; cf. Merker 1986; Matthaiou 1987.

[56] Hintzen-Bohlen 1990:153. Ideas about the appearance of the painting remain speculative: Robert 1895:86; Löhr 2000:147, 156, 163–164, 177.

[57] It remains unclear if these images were wall paintings (Dörpfeld 1911:48, 95; Lippold 1916:2141). Pausanias' plural proves that the painting by Ismenias, at the most, was *one* of them, if not a single dedication, which seems more probable: Robert 1895:87; Hölscher 1977:378; Hintzen-Bohlen 1990:152–153n178; Löhr 2000:163; *contra*: Jeppensen 1979:385. For portrait paintings in temples in the fifth century: Pausanias 1.1.2; Woodhead 1997:390–391 no. 277.

[58] Timarchus and Cephisodotus: Matthaiou 1994:175–183; Ajootian 1996:94–97; Andreae 2001;

demonstration of the family's genealogy. During the second half of the fourth century, it was not unusual to set up such family monuments on the Acropolis.[59] What was unusual was the material of the Eteoboutadae's statues: wood. This linked them to the old and venerable wooden *xoana* on the Acropolis, such as the cult image of Athena not far from the statues themselves (Pausanias 1.26.6; Apollodorus *Library* 3.14.6).[60] A wooden statue of Hermes also stood in the Erechtheum, supposedly dedicated by Cecrops, the mythical king of Attica (Pausanias 1.27.1). In this local and material context, the wooden statue group of Lycurgus and his sons must have connoted the sacred tradition and antiquity of the Eteoboutadae's cult engagement. In the years before 290, a statue of a priestess of Athena added to the visual presence of this *genos* (IG II^2 3455).[61] She was a member of the other line of the family, in charge of the priesthood of Athena Polias,[62] and was most probably called Lysimache like her well-known predecessor. The portrait statue was dedicated by her son and set up during her lifetime. Besides the Eteoboutadae, other families also sought to advertise their cult position by setting up votive statues on the Acropolis. The statue of Pheidostrate, priestess of Aglauros from the *genos* of the Salaminioi and sister of the politically active Chremonides, was placed there sometime around 300 BC (IG II^2 3459).[63] Not far away, Pheidostrate herself dedicated a statue of her father Eteocles (IG II^2 3458); he had previously been honored for his engagement in the Eleusinian cult (IG II^2 1933.11), and was one of the first *agōnothetai* of Dionysus after 317/07. He himself dedicated a statue in the theater of Dionysus (IG II^2 3845).

In short, between around 330/20 and the early third century, the families of the Athenian elite tried to enhance their visual presence on the Acropolis by dedicating multiple portraits of family members—statues and paintings, of

Schultz 2003. For the lifetime of Lycurgus and his sons: above n52. Lippold 1921:236; Bieber 1923-1924:270; Morricone 1991:196-197, prefer a date for the group late in Habron's lifetime (310/04), while Marcade 1948:698 suggests a date in the early third century, but only because of the artists' floruit, which Löhr 2000:160, thinks is possible. Against a dedication made by Habron: Hölscher 1977:378n23. Indeed, the possibility cannot be excluded that the statues were dedicated by Lycurgus himself: Hintzen-Bohlen 1990:153.

[59] Löhr 2000.

[60] Wooden statues: Oelmann 1957:15n11; Romano 1980:357-364; Donohue 1988:147; Arafat 1996:54-57; Pritchett 1999:168-182. Archaic wooden votives: Kyrieleis 1980. Cf. the wooden statue of Sarapis from the Roman Imperial period: *LIMC* 7 (1994) 669 s. v. Sarapis no. 8b.

[61] Lewis 1955:8; Davies 1971:171-172 no. 4549 (stemma and dedicator); Mantis 1990:74; Aleshire 1994:336-337 note d; von den Hoff 2003:180n62-63.

[62] Garland 1984:91-94.

[63] Ferguson 1938:20-21; Mikalson 1998:165n87; von den Hoff 2003:180. Chremonides himself appears as dedicator on the Acropolis: Immerwahr 1942:344-347 no. 3.

individuals and groups, in and outside prestigious cult offices. This trend was new in terms of quality and quantity. In the case of the Eteoboutadae, material and context reveal that this demonstration was ideologically based on the family's long genealogy, which ostensibly provided a link to Athens' mythical past. It also touched on the legitimacy of the hereditary character of their priesthoods, that is, on traditional claims of expertise and power. At the same time, such dedications were now often set up while the depicted cult official was still alive,[64] so that they lent luster to the living families. This went far beyond the two prevailing interests of the earlier period: to demonstrate *eusebeia* and to document service on behalf of the *polis*. In the case of *genē* like the Eteoboutadae or the Salaminioi, this development cannot be separated from political pretensions. The Acropolis thus became a point of crystallization, where families competed to visually consolidate their prestige within society through the recording of their cult activities.[65]

Unfortunately, we lack precise information about how such Athenian statues of cult officials—mostly made of reusable bronze—looked. To infer from the evidence of the Parthenon frieze and the grave reliefs, we might suppose that priests were portrayed wearing the long *khitōn*, although this dress is not previously recorded for freestanding statues. Klaus Fittschen has suggested that the head of a beardless man from Athens with a myrtle wreath belongs to the late third century BC (figs. 9a–9b).[66] Such wreaths were typically worn by the Eleusinian hierophants, but often in addition to a *strophion*. The fact that nonpriestly officials could also receive such a crown casts into question the statement that the depicted person was indeed a priest.[67] However, if this were the case, it would demonstrate that such images followed the modern fashion of shaving in contrast to the traditional appearance of, for instance, bearded philosophers in this period. In light of the visual *testimonia* discussed above, statues of priestesses should have worn the conventional *khitōn* with a *himation* above it during the fourth and third

---

[64] This was not previously completely unknown (Keesling 2003:192), but as far as is known, it is new for cult personnel.

[65] Cf. Geagan 1996:155: "transformation of the cult away from personal piety to status display."

[66] Athens, National Museum 351: Arndt und Bruckmann 1891–1942 no. 343–344 (era of the Diadochi); Buschor 1979:87 no. 218 Abb. 60 (first century BC); Harrison 1953:14 (first century BC); Stewart 1979:82–84 no. 1 Abb. 26 a (first century BC); Fittschen 1988:26n155 pl. 133 (late third century BC, myrtle wreath); Stewart 1990:fig. 781 (200 BC); Andreae 2001:115–116 fig. 75; pl. 86 (190 BC, archon); Kaltsas 2002:297 no. 621 (first century BC).

[67] *Hierophants*: Clinton 1974:23n96, 32–33, 46; cf. Clinton 1974:104–106 figs. 11–14; Goette 1989. Honorific statues for *hierophants* set up by the Eleusinian priesthood: Clinton 1974:23–24 (*IG* II^2 2944); for other honors awarded to *hierophants*: Clinton 1974:22–27. Myrtle wreaths for other nonpriestly personnel: Woodhead 1997:329 no. 228.

Figure 9a-b. Plaster cast: portrait of a priest (?). From Athens, late third century BC, Athens, National Museum 351. Cast, Munich, Museum für Abgüsse Klassischer Bildwerke 354.Photos, H. Glöckler, courtesy of the Museum für Abgüsse Klassischer Bildwerke, Munich.

century. This is also illustrated by the early Hellenistic statue of Aristonoe, priestess of Nemesis from Rhamnus (fig. 10).[68] She has a rounded *strophion* in her hair, like the head compared above to Lysimache's portrait. This was apparently a priestly attribute. With a *phialē* in her right hand, Aristonoe is

[68] Athens National Museum 232: *IG* II² 3462; Mantis 1990:109–110 pl. 47β; Eule 2001:141–143, 185 cat. 57 fig. 63; Petrakos 1999:108 no. 133; Himmelmann 2001:8 fig. 2 (with further bibliography; for a later dating of the inscription: Tracy 1990:165); Kaltsas 2002:274 no. 574; *ThesCRA* 5:29 no. 126 pl. 3. Cf. the early Hellenistic statuette of a herd initiate (?), Eleusis, Museum 111: Mylonas 1961:203 fig. 80; Clinton 1974:104–105 C. It is unclear if the early Hellenistic statue in Athens, National Museum 255 (Kaltsas 2002:256 no. 535), depicted an Eleusianian *dadoukhos* (Geominy 1989:253–264) or the divine Iacchus (Clinton 1992:70, 137 no. 3 fig. 64).

Figure 10. Statue of the priestess Aristonoe (on base, *IG* II² 3462). From Rhamnous, third century BC. Athens, National Museum 232. Institut für Klassische Archäologie, Ludwig-Maximilians-Universität, Munich.

pouring out a libation; obviously, the temple key was not the only attribute of statues of priestesses in this period. Rather, other utensils and gestures could also underline the cult activities and, by the same token, the *eusebeia* of the depicted person.[69] Finally, Aristonoe's portrait—and possibly also the male head mentioned above—demonstrates that marble as well as bronze was used for statues of cult personnel in Attic sanctuaries.

During the third century BC, possibly as a reaction to the conspicuous visual demonstration of cult activities by the elite, the practice of setting up images of cult officials on the Acropolis changed its character. For the first time, we now find even statues of less important cult personnel, like the small-scale statue (or relief) of Syeris, the *aged servant* (*diakonos*) of Athena's priestess Lysimache. In view of the epigram inscribed on the base, a Hellenistic date is more convincing for the statue than the identification of Syeris' mistress with the fourth-century priestess Lysimache.[70] The image was set up by Syeris herself. Her age certainly justified her doing so: old age was a topos for the qualification of cult officials (Plato *Laws* 759d). The scale of the image reflected Syeris' minor role in holding a secondary office; furthermore, she was possibly of Egyptian origin. By its comparatively smaller size, the votive also enhanced the high status of the real priestesses, who were visually present in the same sanctuary; indeed, a statue of Syeris' superior was set up not far away (*IG* II² 3455).

It was also in the third century that, for the first time, statues of *arrhēphoroi* were set up on the Acropolis. These four young girls, between seven and eleven years old, were elected every year and lived on the Acropolis for the time of their office. They were in charge of the traditional ritual of the Arrhephoria (Pausanias 1.27.3); two of them, chosen by the *arkhōn basileus*, attended to the weaving of Athena's *peplos*.[71] Only the inscribed bases of their bronze statues are preserved. The first of this series belong to the

---

[69] Compare the statue of the priestess of Demeter, Niceso, from Priene (Berlin, *Antikensammlung* Sk 1928), who once, as a sign of her function, held a hydria(?) on her head: Mantis 1990:98–99 pl. 44β; Kron 1996:146–148 fig. 4; Eule 2001:43–44, 179–180 cat. 43 fig. 71; *ThesCRA* 5:30 no. 131 pl. 3.

[70] Reisch 1919; Lewis 1955:8 (also for the date); Stewart 1979:115, 118 (epigram); Aleshire 1994:337 note d; Hurwit 1998:356n23; Bielman 2002:22–23; *contra* Mantis 1990:75–76; Holtzmann 2003:221. For an impression of the appearance of the image, cf. the bronze statuette in Reisch 1919 pl. 6. Todisco 1997:121–123 takes the object mentioned here for a relief, and, indeed, the preserved base is much longer than it is deep: Reisch 1919:302. For the earlier priestess Lysimache, see above.

[71] Jordan 1979:28–36; Turner 1983:121–122; Mansfield 1985:260–357; Brulé 1987:79–98; Lefkowitz 1996:78–91; Berger and Gisler-Huwiler 1996:193–194; Donnay 1997; Dillon 2001:57–60; Holtzmann 2003:222, Aleshire, and Lambert 2003:77; Neils, and Oakley 2003:149–151.

second quarter of the third century (*IG* II^2 3470, 3471, 3472). Later examples date from the late third through the first century BC (*IG* II^2 3461, 3466, 3473, 3488, 3496, 3497), and from the imperial period.[72] Hence, this is in fact the largest group of portrait statues from the Hellenistic Acropolis. A statue of an *arrhēphoros* was dedicated either to Athena or to Pandrosus, who was related to the Arrhephoria. It was usually set up shortly after the end of the girl's official duties, and her father was the dedicator, thus highlighting the families' rather than the girls' prestige.[73] In the fourth century, paying for the *Arrhēphoria* was a *leitourgia* (Lysias 21.5), a privilege of the wealthiest families, while the *arrhēphoroi* themselves had to be of *good birth* (*eugenēs*). This does not refer to a legally defined social group, and may imply nothing more than a long Attic ancestry. Further, the fact that the *arrhēphoroi* were elected is a sign of the originally nonaristocratic character of her office.[74] Consequently, they were not necessarily members of the *eupatridai*, although they certainly belonged to the middle or upper classes of Athens, who could afford to set up a bronze statue on the Acropolis.[75] At first glance, it is quite astonishing that, given the traditional prestige of the *arrhēphoroi*, statues of these girls were not set up earlier. However, this development confirms the view that now, in the early Hellenistic period, the practice of demonstrating religious prestige had widened its scope and was adopted by other prosperous groups of Athenians, who used for this purpose the highest office accessible to them.[76]

Statues of other minor cult officials are also known from the Hellenistic Acropolis, such as images of *kanēphoroi*. These girls were slightly older than the *arrhēphoroi* (ten–fifteen years old: Aristophanes *Lysistrata* 642–647) and had to carry the baskets with sacrificial utensils in the various cults in Athens, and at the Panathenaea.[77] *Kanēphoroi* seem to have been members of the *eupatridai*, witness the sister of Harmodius in the sixth century (Thucydides 6.56),

---

[72] List of *testimonia*: Donnay 1997:204–205. For the dates: Aleshire 1994:336 *ad* no. 6–7note f; cf. Donnay 1997:181, 204–205; Mikalson 1998:199, 206, 256 (who postulates a date after 229 for the first statues); Geagan 1994:167–170; Geagan 1996:153–155; von den Hoff 2003:178–179; for the dates of *IG* II^2 3470–3472: Tracy 2003:141. *Arrhēphoroi* are not attested with certainty in the cult of Asclepius: Aleshire 1989:90–91; Mikalson 1998:266 *ad IG* II^2 974 = *SEG* 18, 26.18–19.

[73] Some fragmentary inscriptions belong to the same series because of their characteristic dedication formula: *IG* II^2 3465, 3482, 3486; Donnay 1997:180n11.

[74] Turner 1983:52–119, 120–128. For the concept of *eugeneia*: Ober 1989:248–259.

[75] Geagan 1994:170 ("wealthiest"); Donnay 1997:197 ("aristocracy"); Wilson 2000:42–43, with critique in Ober 2000; cf. Feaver 1957:146; Burkert 1976:4; Turner 1983:121–122; Mansfield 1985:270–271. Cf. priests as *eugenetoi*: Demosthenes 57.46, 48.

[76] Cf. Geagan 1994:170.

[77] Roccos 1995:641–666; Brulé 1996:47–50; Lefkowitz 1996:78–91; Berger and Gisler-Huwiler 1996:194–195; Dillon 2001:37–42; Neils, and Oakley 2003:17–19, 158.

and the fact that fathers of *kanēphoroi* had *leitourgia* duties in the Athenian Asclepieum.[78] These fathers were also obliged to pay their daughters' costs, and nominated them without democratic procedure, which is additional evidence for the exclusive nature of this office.[79] The first Athenian record of a statue of a *kanēphoros* comes from the Acropolis and is dated to the fourth or third century BC (*IG* II² 3457);[80] the girl was also active as *kanēphoros* in Eleusis. The wreaths on the marble base testify to an official honorific statue;[81] if the early date is correct, then this is the first statue set up by *dēmos* and *boulē* for a cult official on the Acropolis. The second statue of a *kanēphoros* likewise comes from the Acropolis and was an official honor (*IG* II² 3477); it was set up during the second century BC. In contrast to statues of *arrhēphoroi*, then, statues of *kanēphoroi* were rare and not private dedications, but honors granted by the *polis*.[82] This was due perhaps to the higher social status of the girls and to the financial support which their fathers provided to the *polis* cult. Lycurgus had also been honored for adding to the equipment of the *kanēphoroi* ([Plutarch] *Moralia* 852a–b). To judge from these cases, the *polis* would seem to have occasionally acknowledged the financial engagement of the elite in the cult with honorific statues of elite families' daughters on the Acropolis.[83]

On the third-century Acropolis, the new statues of minor cult officials like the *arrhēphoroi* signify an increasing and socially more broad-based interest in demonstrating engagement in religious offices—which had been originally an elite privilege—by imitating (originally) elite practices.[84] They also testify to a new social differentiation. While a broader spectrum of Athenians set up statues—possibly as an imitation of elite practices well established since the fourth century—leading families were less interested in dedicating images of their members who had been only minor cult personnel. Rather, the elite had two other possibilities open to them for asserting their prestige: they dedi-

---

[78] Aleshire 1991:90–92.

[79] Cf. Zopyros: *IG* II² 896, and Wilson 2000:25–26; Ober 2000

[80] Outside Athens, statues of *kanēphoroi* had existed since the later sixth century, see above nn14, 17. Pliny *Natural History* 34.69 (Praxiteles) does not refer to a *kanēphoros* with certainty: Corso 1988:75; 201n365. For statues of *kanēphoroi* in Athens: Geagan 1994:167–170.

[81] Compare Burnett, and Edmonson 1961, and: *IG* II² 3207, 4330.

[82] Cf. *IG* II² 3489, 3498; Geagan 1983:155–158 nos. 1–2.

[83] Daughters serving as *kanēphoroi* must have enhanced their fathers' prestige: see *IG* II² 668.31–33, 896.9–10, i 14–15, 21–28, where this is mentioned explicitly; cf. Mikalson 1998:198–199.

[84] Cf. what Ober 1989:259–261, 289–292 has called "democratization" and "subversion" of elite ideals, attested by the desire of many "to portray themselves in the role of aristocrats and their use of terminology that specifically recalls the aristocratic code of behavior" (289). In Athens, this trend may have begun earlier, during the fourth century, in the political arena rather than in the religious context.

cated statues of their high-ranking priests, and they were awarded statues of minor cult officials by the *polis*. At the same time, from the third century onwards, honorific statues of cult personnel granted by the *polis* served to pay honor to their financial rather than merely to their religious engagement. Furthermore, compared to the small number of statues of mostly mature men and women produced in the fourth century, the considerable increase in the number of statues of young female cult officials after this period defined the sanctuary as an especially female space and as a sphere of activity for young Athenian girls. This aspect in turn added an educational dimension to the design of the sanctuary: the holding of cult offices was visually defined as the most prestigious activity of Athenian maidens, while the *ephēbeia* was defined as the most prestigious service of young boys by statues and honors set up in other places during the Hellenistic period. On the Acropolis, a similarly gendered pattern of normative behavior had been displayed in earlier periods, notably by the Archaic *korai* and by the Classical Parthenon frieze, with its clearly distinguished tasks for youths and maidens.

Again, it is quite difficult to decide about the appearance of the new images of *arrhēphoroi* and *kanēphoroi*. Since statues of *kanēphoroi* were still renowned in the imperial period (Pliny *Natural History* 36.25; Cicero *Against Verres* 2.5.5), and since some of the *arrhēphoroi* bases from the Acropolis have artists' signatures, it is probable that Roman copies of such statues are preserved, although they have not yet been identified. One possible candidate is the statue of a maiden in the Glyptothek in Munich (fig. 11), with a replica in San Antonio (fig. 12), recently identified by Christiane Vorster.[85] The girl appears to be ten–fifteen years old, which would fit either a *kanēphoros* or an *arrhēphoros*. The fact that such a statue of a girl was copied in Roman times suggests its importance either in terms of artistic value or of local fame, which might be explicable if it came from the renowned Athenian Acropolis; female statues in such prominent public places very often depict cult personnel. The slightly-larger-than-life size of the figure, compared with other statues of children, would further signify the importance of the girl.[86] Finally, the figure

---

[85] Munich, Glyptothek 478 (preserved height without plinth: 1.23 m): Hiller 1965:43–46 pl. 20–24; Vorster 1983:78–79, 127–133, 348 no. 51; von den Hoff 2003:179 fig. 4. San Antonio, Museum of Art 85.137.2 (preserved height: 0.66 m): unpublished; Fine Antiquities, Sotheby's New York, Auction 9.12.1985, lot 139; I owe this reference to C. Vorster. The existence of two replicas makes it probable that the Munich statue is a very good Roman copy and not a Hellenistic original, cf. Furtwängler 1907:7.

[86] Compare the size of statues of children from Brauron, which do not exceed 1.20 m: Vorster 1983 cat.; cf. Sourvinou-Inwood 1988a, for defining the age of girls in statues.

Figure 11. Statue of an *Arrhēphoros* (?). Roman copy after a Greek original of the third century BC. Munich, Staatliche Antikensammlungen und Glyptothek 478. Staatliche Antikensammlungen und Glyptothek, Munich.

Figure 12. Statue of an *Arrhēphoros* (?). Roman copy after a Greek original of the third century BC. San Antonio, TX, San Antonio Museum of Art 85.137.2. Courtesy of the San Antonio (TX) Museum of Art.

resembles the young girl carrying a stool in the Parthenon eastern frieze (East 31; fig. 2), who must be a member of the Acropolis cult personnel, although we do not know which. On stylistic grounds, the statue in Munich has been dated to the third century, which accords well with the date of the earliest *arrhēphoroi* bases. In view of the large number of statues of *arrhēphoroi*, it seems reasonable to identify her as an *arrhēphoros* rather than as a *kanēphoros*.[87] Hence, although distinct iconographic features are lacking, the statue type from *Munich-San Antonio* could well depict an early Hellenistic statue of one of these maidens, as Vorster has suggested in her dissertation. At least, the resemblance to the figure on the Parthenon frieze makes an identification as a cult official on the Acropolis highly probable. The statue demonstrates that undistinguished dress was still common for female cult personnel in the third century, and that the iconographic tradition created by the Parthenon was still alive in this period.

The images of cult personnel on the Athenian Acropolis during the second and first centuries BC can only be touched on here.[88] In this period, the total number of honors awarded to cult officials was growing.[89] As Riet van Bremen has observed for late Hellenistic Asia Minor, the *poleis* increasingly took over the role of private dedicators in the cultic sphere.[90] By the same token, it was the financial engagement of the persons honored which became increasingly important.[91] The *polis* was now anxious to secure adequate funding for the cult, and the prestige associated with cult offices consequently came to be contingent on such engagement. At the same time, Athenian families active in this context intensified the advertisement of their service on behalf of the *polis* by commissioning inscriptions and statues at various places in the city.[92]

---

[87] Identification as a *kanēphoros* can probably be excluded because of the dress: Roccos 1995. A suggested depiction of an *arrhēphoros* which occurs on a fourth-century votive relief (Acropolis Museum 2554: Palagia 1990:351–352 fig. 16; Jenkins 1994:28 fig. 15; I owe these references to Olga Palagia), is not wearing a *himation*, but a *peplos*, though its identification is unclear, cf. von den Hoff 2003:179n51.

[88] Cf. van Bremen 1996; Eule 2001:125–127 (Asia Minor).

[89] See only: *IG* II² 689–690, 776, 783 (for the date, see now Tracy 2003:155), 788, 863, *SEG* 33.115; Woodhead 1997:390–391 no. 277; Holtzmann 2003:221; Ma and Tracy 2004, 121–126 (from the *Agora*).

[90] Van Bremen 1996:174–180.

[91] Cf. *IG* II² 776.17; *IG* II2 788. The frequent honors granted to the priests of Asclepius in the second century BC were possibly due to the fact that this office was a *leitourgia*: Aleshire 1991:72–75; *SEG* 18.21–22, 26–29; Mikalson 1998:203–204, 261–262; cf. *IG* II² 968; Mikalson 1998:258. The growing importance of selling priesthoods could also be mentioned in this context: Turner 1983:141–173; Wörrle 1990:43–49. For the decline in the difference between religious and civic *leitourgiai*: van Bremen 1996:25–34.

[92] Chrysis, priestess of Athena: Acropolis: *IG* II² 3484; *IG* II² 3485; Delphi: *IG* II² 1136.7, 12, 27–32;

The first honorific statue of a priestess set up by *dēmos* and *boulē* on the Acropolis belongs to this period. It was the portrait of a priestess of Pandrosus, from the *genos* of the Salaminioi, dating from the second century BC (*IG* II² 3481).[93] This portrait added to the visual presence of this family in the most prestigious sanctuary of the *polis*. Furthermore, the relation of Pandrosus to the Arrhephoria underlined the importance of this old and exclusively Attic ritual, which is also revealed by the large number of statues of *arrhēphoroi* on the Acropolis. The new awards of wreaths to the *ergastinai* signify the same interest in traditional and local cult offices in this period (*IG* II² 1034, 1036, 1060; *SEG* 28.90).[94] The fact that even *arrhēphoroi* received official honorific statues on the Acropolis in the first century AD illustrates the continuity of this trend (*IG* II² 3554, 3556). Since the second century BC, references to local *polis* traditions were also expressed in private votive statues, witness the statue of Philtera, priestess of Athena (IG II² 3474).[95] Her image expanded the statue group of Eteoboutadae on the Acropolis, but the inscription also mentioned the name of this *genos* for the first time. The text not only reminded the viewer of Philtera's father, who had been *stratēgos*, but also of two of her most renowned (but long dead) ancestors: Lycurgus, the reformer of Classical Athens, and Diogenes, who liberated the *polis* in 229. Thus, family tradition and *polis* tradition became explicitly intertwined, transcending the immediate religious context in which they were publicized. In the high and late Hellenistic period, most of the cult officials honored or depicted on the Acropolis still came from the upper strata of Athenian society, though certainly not exclusively from the wealthiest *eupatridai*.[96] The increasing number of their images and of documents of honors awarded to them in this sanctuary made very blatant how broad the engagement of these Athenian families in cult affairs was: indeed, Acropolis cults appeared to be practiced and financed almost exclusively by

---

her father was priest of Asclepius (*IG* II² 950 = *SEG* 18.22), her grandfather priest in Eleusis (*IG* II² 3857); cf. Aleshire 1989:175–176 table 9 (stemma); Mikalson 1998:256. Panariste: *arrhēphoros* and *ergastinē*: *IG* II² 3488; *IG* II² 1034 col. II.9; for other members of her family: Clinton 1974:98–101 with no. 1, 13; Mikalson 1998:260. Further examples: Geagan 1983:155–161 nos. 1–2; Mansfield 1985:284–286, 288–289; Geominy 1989:257–258; Mikalson 1998:239; 266; 258; Aleshire 1991:89–92; compare also the multiple offices of *ergastinai*: Tracy 1990:219; Aleshire and Lambert 2003:85–86.

[93] Raubitschek 1945:434–435.

[94] Tracy 1990:217–219. For the *ergastinai*: Mansfield 1985:277–281; Brulé 1987:100–105; Berger, and Gisler-Huwiler 1996:194; Mikalson 1998:256–258; Holtzmann 2003:222; Aleshire, and Lambert 2003.

[95] Aleshire 1994:336 no. 11; Mikalson 1998:171–172, 206, 256. For the artists: Despinis 1995:333–338; Linnemann 2001.

[96] Cf. for the *ergastinai*: Aleshire, and Lambert 2003:86.

these affluent Athenians, though they were no longer the monopoly of the *eupatridai.*

Primary visual evidence for the appearance of statues of cult personnel on the Athenian Acropolis is also lacking for the late Hellenistic period. Only images from other contexts can be used in order to obtain an idea of what such portraits may have looked like. The bald head of a man from the Agora, dated to the first century BC, may represent a priest—possibly of Isis—because the *strophion* was very often a priestly attribute.[97] Beardlessness and verisimilitude adopt fashionable elements of late Hellenistic civic portraiture. We do not know what kind of statue belonged to this head, but grave reliefs from Asia Minor with similar portraits indicate that now priests could wear a common civic *himation.*[98] This change (earlier, the long *khitōn* was their significant dress) further reduced the visual distance between male cult officials and other citizens, and reveals the incorporation of priestly offices into the civic interests of the *polis.* Unfortunately, we do not know if this was also true in Athens. Nonetheless, the most impressive document of priestly self-representation in this period comes again from Athens, although not from the Acropolis. It is the monumental votive relief which Lacratides, priest in Eleusis, dedicated around 100 BC.[99] Compared to the portraits we have discussed so far, the dedicator, wearing the *strophion*, appears in a very unusual manner: he has a long beard and long hair, which is in contrast to the contemporary portrait fashion, but which relates his image to portraits from Athens' Classical past. The classicizing style of the relief similarly reminds the viewer of a relationship to the great Classical era of Athenian power. Lacratides is shown standing in the middle of a group of gods and goddesses and is the same size as these

---

[97] Athens, Agora Museum S 333: Harrison 1953:12–14 no. 3, 84–85 pl. 3; Stewart 1979:80–81 fig. 24; Smith 1991:257 fig. 326; Pakkanen 1996:55n186. Cf. another late Hellenistic portrait with a wreath, but in Corinth, Archaeological Museum 1445 a: Harrison 1953:13 pl. 43 c (possibly a priest). A survey of the *strophion* as priestly attribute is a *desideratum.* The presence of a *strophion*, however, does not necessarily define a priest: cf. Rumscheid 2000:2–4 and above n47 and n68 for *strophia* as attributes of priestesses. A bald head as a sign of a relation to the cult of Isis: Fittschen 1977:67–69 no. 22; Isis cult in Athens: Pakkanen 1996:47–63; Mikalson 1998:276–277.

[98] Leiden, *Rijksmuseum* Pb. 27: Pfuhl, and Möbius 1977:93 no. 170 pl. 37; Känel 1989:56–57; Schmidt 1991:83–84, 138 (priest?). Images of priests are otherwise unknown on Hellenistic grave reliefs, but images of priestesses are preserved from Smyrna: Pfuhl, and Möbius 1977:136–138; Känel 1989:57; Mantis 1990:99–101; see also the second-century grave *columellae* with temple keys from Athens: Mantis 1990:44–45.

[99] Eleusis Museum 5079: Heberdey 1899:111–116; Mylonas 1961:197–199 fig. 71; Stewart 1979:53–55, 78 pl. 23c (head of Lacratides); Palagia 1987:82–83 fig. 1; Clinton 1992:51–53, 135 no. 3 figs. 5–7; Papangeli 2002:243 figs. 246, 253 (head of Lacratides). For the dedicator: Clinton 1974:97 no. 1.

deities. This is neither the pious and humble documentation of *eusebeia* in the service of the *polis*, nor a representation of family traditions—the two principal concerns which stood at the beginning of the development of Attic images of cult personnel. Rather, Lacratides claims a powerful and exceptional individual role as being near to the gods and representing and revitalizing a glorious past.[100]

This brings us to the end of the period under investigation. Looking back, it appears that, in the Archaic period, the prestige of cult offices had not been used for visual self-representation and social competition in Athens. Being a priest seems to have been perceived merely as a *technical* duty. Thus, generic rather than individualized images of cult personnel could be neutral signs of civic *eusebeia* in this *polis* in the late fifth century. The radical democracy under Pericles and the following crisis of the Peloponnesian War were the starting points for an individualized competition in the holding of cult offices. At this time, the middle class, eligible only for nonhereditary priesthoods, started to document cult activities in the service of the *polis* through images of priestly figures on grave reliefs. From the fourth century, this competition for prestige was pursued especially by the *eupatridai* through their private dedication of portraits of members of their own family as cult personnel, which were set up on the Acropolis.[101] Obviously, the Athenian elite saw their social position challenged and were looking for new ways of maintaining their privileged role in the religious sphere. Social distinctions and gender roles were clearly expressed in these late Classical Athenian images of cult personnel by means of attributes and dress and by their different settings. What we know about the early Hellenistic votive statues of priests on the Acropolis reveals that, for instance, Lycurgus and his sons justified their expertise and prestige by alluding to cult traditions and family genealogy. In the third century, however, Athena's sanctuary saw the demonstration—through portrait statues—of a less exclusive engagement in the field of cult activities by other wealthy Athenian families. Statues of minor cult officials appeared with increasing frequency. This could be read as a sign of a *democratization* of this particular cult space, or at least of a broader conception of who was responsible for this space and of who constituted the religious elite.[102] As in the Archaic period, so also during the third century, the *female* character of the cult of Athena was demonstrated by a large number of statues of young girls in the service of the

---

[100] A painting of Alcibiades in Nemea's arms on the Acropolis was taken as a sign of *hubris* in the late fifth century: Plutarch *Alcibiades* 16.5.

[101] Cf. van Bremen 1996:178; Geagan 1996:155.

[102] Cf. Ober 1989:259–61, 289–292.

goddess. Establishing a relationship to Athens' great past became an important feature of dedications of statues in the high and late Hellenistic period. The *polis* secured the existence of its cults by awarding honors increasingly to those who were financially engaged and not only to those who traditionally inherited religious prestige: being a priest became very much a question of funding cult activities. Wealth had replaced birth as the definition of the elite. Consequently, in the late Hellenistic period, for Lacratides, expertise and family were no longer of primary importance. His prestige was based on wealth—evidenced by the large format of the marble relief—and on claims of individual power and status in reference to the past and the gods. The increasing importance of cult officials as civic donors in the Hellenistic period had made this change possible, as a result of which, new means for self-confident demonstrations of personal prestige became even more necessary.[103]

---

[103] Unfortunately, this phenomenon cannot be examined in its relation to other changes in late Hellenistic culture here; cf. various contributions in Wörrle and Zanker 1995.

Part Four

IDEAL CONCEPTS AND THEIR TRANSFORMATION

7

Philosopher and Priest
The Image of the Intellectual and the Social Practice of the Elites in the Eastern Roman Empire (First–Third Centuries AD)

Matthias Haake

1.

T HE EPICUREAN PHILOSOPHER LYSIAS OF TARSUS was something of a monster. At some point in the late Hellenistic or early Augustan period,[1] he was appointed *stephanēphoros*, that is, priest of Heracles, the founder-hero of the Cilician *metropolis* and one of its principal gods.[2] Six months later, when his magistracy expired, he held on to it and used his position as a stepping stone to seize absolute power, becoming tyrant of his *patris*.[3] Athenaeus, who

---

I wish to thank the participants of the conference for their comments as well as N. Luraghi (Cambridge, MA) and A.-C. Harders (Freiburg) for reading the article and improving my English text. The article of Bendlin 2006 appeared too late to be fully taken into account.

[1] For his dating in the late Hellenistic period, see Welles 1962:56–58 and the brief remarks by Smith 1996:121–122. On his dating in the early Augustan Period, cf. Ruge 1932:2423. On Lysias of Tarsus in general, see Goulet 2005b.

[2] See Dio Chrysostom *Oration* 33.45. On Dio's Tarsian orations, see Jones 1978:71–82. On Heracles as mythical founder of Tarsus, cf. Scheer 1993:294–305. On the cult of Heracles and his place in the local pantheon, see Chuvin 1981:319–324 and Ziegler 2002:364.

[3] Lysias, not mentioned by Strabo in his paragraphs on Tarsus (*Geography* 14.5.12–15), is characterized by Athenaeus as one of those military leaders who arose out of a milieu devoted to philosophy (*Deipnosophists* 5.215c). Strabo's omission of Lysias (as well as that by other relevant sources, such as Dio Chrysostom and Lucian) is surprising, because Strabo refers in his passage on Tarsus to domestic troubles in this city during the reign of Augustus. In these political conflicts was involved, besides the minor poet Boëthus (cf. Susemihl 1891:2n6, 408n194), the Stoic Athenodorus, son of Sandon, called Cananites (cf. Goulet 1989), who is possibly mentioned in an inscription from Rome (*IGUR* 4.1543; see Moretti 1976 and also Follet 1989a:659). The Academic philosopher Nestor (cf. Goulet 2005c) succeeded Athenodorus as *lord of the city* on behalf of Augustus. On the historical context, cf. Welles 1962:53–57; Berve

has handed down this story in his *Deipnosophists* (5.215b–c), wrote that Lysias manifested his new standing by his outer appearance: he wore a purple *khitōn* with white stripes, a sumptuous *khlamus* around his shoulders, white Laconian shoes on his feet, and his head was adorned with a golden crown of laurel leaves. According to this story, Lysias acted the way a Greek tyrant had been supposed to act since time immemorial: he distributed the property of the rich to the poor and put to death all those among the rich who were unwilling to surrender their possessions.[4]

In spite of its extreme brevity, the story reported by Athenaeus has two interesting aspects. First, Lysias became tyrant by using his priesthood to his advantage. It is not clear exactly how he was able to use his position as *stephanēphoros*—possibly the eponymous priesthood of Tarsus[5]—for his coup d'état; indeed, it is not certain whether or to what extent the prestige of the *hiereus* of the Tarsian *hērōs ktistēs* was an important asset for Lysias and his takeover. Secondly, and more importantly in the present context, Lysias is an example of a philosopher who was elected by his *patris* to be the priest of a cult—and one should add that Lysias was an Epicurean philosopher. This seems at first sight surprising, because common conceptions of the relation-ship between religion and philosophy in Greek culture would not initially lead us to expect a follower of Epicurus—or, in fact, a philosopher of any other school—to act as a priest. The following story should underline this point.

In Arrian's *Discourses of Epictetus*, Epictetus of Hierapolis reports a conver-sation between himself and a citizen of Nicopolis (1.9.26–29).[6] The dispute concerned the priesthood of the city's imperial cult. Epictetus advised his interlocutor not to agree to become *hiereus* of the emperor, because he would have to come up with a lot of money for nothing. However, the man of Nicopolis replied that his name would be recorded on every official document. When Epictetus asked whether the man would be present every time his name

---

1967:439–440; Kienast 1999:467–468; and especially Bowersock 1965:47–48, who is fundamental for the personal relations between the two Tarsian philosophers and the first Roman emperor.

[4] On this aspect, see e.g. the brief remarks of Berve 1967:483. Cf. Luraghi 1997, an instructive case study on one particular element of the constructed *image* of Greek tyrants—their death. The same is true *mutatis mutandis* for the dealings of other tyrants with the wealthy inhabit-ants of their cities.

[5] Cf. Stier 1929:2345. For a skeptical view of Lysias of Tarsus and of the historical value of Athenaeus' story, see Sherk 1992:223.

[6] Cf. Wehner 2000:56 on the form of address in this passage. On Epictetus' life and his historical, social, cultural, and intellectual context, see Fuentes González 2000; Long 2002:10–37. On the *Discourses of Epictetus,* see Long 2002:38–66. The relationship between Arrian (see note 64 below with main text) and Epictetus is examined especially by Brunt 1977. The short commentary on our passage by Dobbin 1998:181–182 is not convincing in every respect.

was read aloud from a document and would thereby be able to confirm that it was indeed his name, and whether he knew what would happen after his death, the citizen of Nicopolis answered that his name would outlast his own life. Epictetus tried to counteract this statement by urging his interlocutor to inscribe his name on a stone, for in this way his name would outlast him, too. And, in any case, who would remember the name of any imperial priest of Nicopolis outside of that *polis*? The man from Nicopolis does not give any real and concrete answer to this question; rather, he adds a new aspect: the golden crown that he would wear during his lifetime. The dialogue, a clear failure in communication, is closed by Epictetus with the suggestion that the man of Nicopolis would do better to acquire a crown of roses and put it on his head—it would look more beautiful.[7]

This passage is a *locus classicus* for analyzing the attitude of Greek philosophers towards the ritual worship of the Roman emperor as well as for the sociopolitical function of the priesthood of the imperial cult in Greek *poleis*— or at least, for the way in which both aspects are reflected in literary texts, for the social practice is something else, as I will discuss below.[8] The imperial priesthood was clearly held by local elites to be very important: the recording of one's name in public documents, the perpetual commemoration, and—as expressed by the golden wreath—the position of honor in the *patris*, were worthwhile aims. This perspective represents the common opinion, to which the position of the philosopher is diametrically opposed: from a coherent philosophical point of view, the external phenomena connected with the imperial priesthood were empty vanities.

The utterances of Epictetus demonstrate that philosophers had—at least according to literary statements—precise conceptions about how a philosopher should regard the priesthood of the imperial cult. The rejection of this office depends on considerations of two different kinds. On the surface, there are the social—but not the religious—aspects of the priesthood: the amount of money required for the priesthood and the honors connected with it were considered to be incompatible with the *habitus* of the philosopher as it was constructed in literature. However, this argumentation certainly implies a criticism of the imperial cult. Such criticism does not focus exclusively on the imperial cult itself, but is also leveled by different philosophical schools at

---

[7] Against the background of this narrative it is a good punchline that Puplius Memmius Leo, *philopatris* and *philosophos*, was honored because he had been *inter alia hiereus* of the *Sebastoi* and *agōnothetēs* of the *Aktia* at Nicopolis (AD 244–248); see Riemann 1877:294 no. 89; Sarikakis 1965:153, 155; cf. Puech 2005a.

[8] See e.g. Bowersock 1973:182–183. Cf. Millar 1965:147.

the traditional cults in general: ultimately, it always targets the absence of a developed theological system, the exaggerated importance attached to ritual correctness, the anthropomorphism of the pantheon, the question of the individual's relation to the divine, and the outward appearance, which was seen as inherent to the priesthoods.[9]

Literary texts therefore suggest an incompatibility of priestly functions with philosophical conduct: according to the philosophical *doxai* and *dogmata*, a person could pursue one career or the other, but not both. In the following discussion, this image will be analyzed in terms of its true relevance to the social activity of persons who were philosophers and its correspondence with reality. Such scrutiny is suggested by various extant examples of discrepancies between philosophical theory, the practice of philosophers, and their legal status. Two instances may suffice here. First, the case of Favorinus of Arelate. According to Philostratus' biography in his *Lives of the Sophists* (490), Favorinus tried to avoid being elected to the imperial priesthood by his native city by referring to the fact that this would not be in accordance with his position as a philosopher. In support of his position, he appealed to a law which exempted philosophers from public service.[10] When Favorinus realized that Hadrian did not consider him a philosopher—and that he therefore had no legal basis for refusing the office—he said to the emperor that his teacher Dio had appeared to him in a dream and told him that men come into the world not only for themselves but also for their *patris*. Therefore, Favorinus decided to obey Dio's alleged advice and to become priest of the imperial cult. Before the Roman emperor, the man of Arelate did not bring any original philosophical arguments into play—he tried to hide behind the legal status of philosophers but did not refer to philosophy *per se* as being incompatible with a priesthood.[11] In other words, for Favorinus it was possible, under special circumstances, to be both philosopher and priest.[12] The second case is that of the Stoic philosopher

---

[9] On Greek philosophers and their attitude to religion, cf. e.g. Attridge 1978; Frede 1999:41–44; Price 1999:126–142; Most 2003. It is important to emphasize the fact that my investigations do not deal with philosophical theologies, which are very different from common religious conceptions, but only with philosophical attitudes towards public cults.

[10] Cf. also Cassius Dio *Roman History* 69.3.4–6; see Bowersock 1969:35; Hahn 1989:106; Fein 1992:142–145; Gleason 1995:145–147; Bowie 1997:6–8. On the relationship between Hadrian and Favorinus, cf. Swain 1989; on Favorinus in general, see Follet 2000; Amato 2005:1–192.

[11] According to this passage, the Athenians decided to destroy a bronze statue of Favorinus in Athens as if he were an enemy of the emperor when they learned of the philosopher's refusal to accept the office of the imperial priesthood. The Athenians were unconvinced by Favorinus' argument: the fact that the man from Arelate called himself a philosopher was in their view not an obstacle to his becoming an imperial priest.

[12] Favorinus did not act like the philosopher Secundus, who remained silent even in front of

Gaius Iulius Theon from Alexandria, who was imperial *arkhiereus* at Alexandria and of the whole of Egypt (*POxy* 12.1434): Theon was a member of Augustus' milieu, and the first Roman emperor granted him Roman citizenship as well as vast tracts of land in Egypt.[13] Obviously, nothing prevented Theon from being a philosopher as well as holding the office of the *arkhiereus* at Alexandria with its attendant duties.

In sum, there were persons who were philosophers and who also served as priests. Neither from their own perspective nor in the public view of the *poleis*—the communities in which these *philosopher-priests* lived—were they placed in a paradoxical situation when they combined in their own persons two ostensibly irreconcilable activities. But are we dealing here only with isolated examples, or is this a more widespread phenomenon?

2.

The following enquiry into philosophers who also acted as priests will foreground one kind of source that is located in a completely different context of communication from that of literary texts, namely, inscriptions.

Two considerations suggest this approach. Since we are dealing with the public perception of philosophers and their public role—especially in the *poleis* of the eastern part of the Roman Empire—as well as with public expectations, evidence that comes from the public realm is particularly relevant and more revealing than literary products. Public decrees—passed by *boulē*, *gerousia*, or *dēmos*—reflect directly the commonly accepted norms of the *polis*-world. Inscriptions initiated by *private* individuals—such as grave inscriptions, dedicatory inscriptions, or the Didymaean prophet-inscriptions—are elements of self-representation, but they are set in the same space of communication of the *polis*-community as the public inscriptions. This framework guarantees that private inscriptions, too, will reflect accepted social norms.[14]

Hadrian; see Anonymous *Life of Secundus the Philosopher* pp. 70.16–72.13 Perry. On this passage, see Hahn 1989:182–185; Fein 1994:250–253.

[13] On Theon, in addition to the Oxyrhynchus papyrus, from which we have the information about his imperial priesthood and his possession of land, cf. Suida, s.v. (203), where he is mentioned as a Stoic philosopher. See generally Bowersock 1965:37–38 on Theon (Pros. Ptol. VI.iii.A.4.B, no. 16763) and his relationship to Augustus; on Theon and his family, cf. Musurillo 1954:103–104. On the *archiereus Alexandriae et totius Aegypti* and the character of this office, cf. Demougin 2006; even if her characterization of this "priesthood" as a secular office can be accepted (although I am not entirely convinced by her remarks), it remains remarkable that it was a Stoic philosopher who was chosen for this function.

[14] I examined these aspects in greater detail and with additional references in Haake 2007:1–12.

Before analyzing the relevant epigraphic material, it is necessary to investigate the use of the word *philosophos* in the Greek inscriptions of the Roman imperial period. A first glance at the dozens of examples in which the word *philosophos* occurs demonstrates that *philosophos* does not always have the same meaning, but that, depending on the context, there is a spectrum of semantic interpretations of this word. It therefore seems appropriate to divide the epigraphic evidence into different groups.[15]

There are a great number of inscriptions in which the word *philosophos* is found, but the meaning in all of these cases does not seem to be the same. In some cases, the word is used as an adjective; *philosophos* is then combined with other honorable attributes like *philopolis*, *philopatris*, or *philokaisar*. In a private honorary inscription from Ancyra, dating from the mid-second century, Gaius Aelius Flavianus Sulpicius is called the first of the *ethnos* and twofold *galatarkhos*, and then labeled as *philodoxos*, *ktistēs*, and *ploutistēs*, *polustephanos*, *philosophos*, *philopatris*, and *aleiptos* (D'Orbeliani 1924:42f Orb. 76 = Bosch 1967:211–214).[16] Iulius Nicetes is mentioned in an honorary inscription from Claudiopolis in the second century as *philosophos*, *philokaisar*, and *philopatris* (*IKlaudioupolis* 67).[17] The dedication of a statue from around 300 for Aurelia Leite of Paros, wife of Marcus Aurelius Faustus, the first of the *polis*, *arkhiereus* of the *Sebastoi* and *Kaisares* says that she is *philosophos*, *philandros*, *philopais*, and *philopatris* (*IG* XII v 292 = Pleket 1969:40 no. 31).[18] The use of *philosophos* as an adjective is demonstrated clearly by the usage of the superlative *philosophōtatos* and *philosophōtatē* respectively: in an inscription dating from the third century, the Spartan Aurelia Oppia is called *philosophōtatē*, her father Calli[crates(?)] *philosophōtatos* (*IG* V i 598), and in a further inscription, her daughter [Aur(elia)] Herakleia is also designated *philosophōtatē* (*IG* V i

---

[15] On the meaning of the word *philosophos* in inscriptions, see Hahn 1989:161–164; Lendon 1997:91; Barnes 2002:293–298, 303–304; Puech 2002:10–15. Cf. in general Veligianni 2001 on *philos*-composita in Greek inscriptions during the Roman imperial period.

[16] Cf. Hahn 1989:161, 163. On Gaius Aelius Flavianus Sulpicius, who is also mentioned—without the epithet *philosophos*—in three further inscriptions (*IGR* 3.196–197; Mordtmann 1874, 21 no. 8), see Puech 2000a.

[17] Cf. Hahn 1989:162 and Fernoux 2004:494 on this inscription; on Iulius Nicetes, see Puech 2005m. Publius Avianus Valerius is called *philosophos* and *philopolis* in a second-century honorary inscription from Hadrianoi (*IHadrianoi* 51 = *IPrusa* 18; cf. Şahin 1977:257–258 on the origin of the inscription). On philosophers at Hadrianoi—in addition to *IHadrianoi* 51, also evidenced in *IHadrianoi* 52 = *IPrusa* 17—see Fein 1994:254–255; Fernoux 2004:493–494.

[18] On Aurelia Leite, see van Bremen 1996:71; Levick 2002:134; Puech 2005; Stavrianopoulou 2006:222–223., 239–240. On her husband, see Berranger-Auserve 2000:76, 171. Aurelia Charilampiane Olympias is called *philandros*, *sophron*, and *philosophos* in an epitaph from Heraclea Pontica (*IHeraclea Pontica* 10; second/third century AD); cf. Puech 1994b.

599).[19] Clearly, in all of these cases, the people praised in the inscriptions were not philosophers in the strict sense of the word, but lovers of wisdom just as they were lovers of their *patris*. The word *philosophos* in these contexts is then to be understood as an adjective with an encomiastic meaning: it could form part of a set of values that expressed the ideal of the good *politēs*, and it testifies especially to the moral character of a person. At the same time, though, it should be emphasized that—even when the word *philosophos* is used as an adjective—for the ancient *reader*, an allusion to the noun *philosophos* must have been implied.

In a large number of inscriptions, persons are also called *philosophos* without any further epithets. Examples of this type of inscription include a private honorary inscription from Caesarea Maritima for Titus Flavius Maximus (*ICaesarea Maritima* 12);[20] a dedication from the territory of the Cilician *polis* Epiphania for Demetrius Tullianus (*IdC* 125; second/third century AD);[21] an epitaph for Mateinianus from Nicomedia (Grélois 1998:383 no. 58 [fig. D 14 on pp. 254-255]; second century AD?);[22] the base of a statue for Ctesiphon from Thasus (Empereur-Simossi 1994:408-410 no. 1; second/third century AD);[23] an honorary inscription by the *boulē* and *demos* of Pergamum

---

[19] All three of them received further honorific titles besides this noteworthy epithet. On Aurelia Herakleia and Aurelia Oppia, cf. Rizakis et al. 2004:71–73 nos. 61 and 64; on Callicrates, see Bradford 1977:223 s.v. Kallikrates (63). Quintus Aufidenus Sextus, uncle of Quintus Aufidenus who was accorded the epithet *philosophos*, is called *philosophotatos theios* in a Spartan inscription honoring his nephew and dating from the early Severian period: Woodward 1927–1928:33–34 no. 56; cf. Hahn 1989:163; Cartledge and Spawforth 2002:180 with 263n6; see also Rizakis et al. 2004:65–66 nos. 44 and 46. What is especially interesting about this aristocratic family from Sparta is their kinship background (cf. Cartledge and Spawforth 2002:183): Aurelia Oppia's husband Marcus Aurelius Teisamenus was a seer, and their daughter is designated in her grave inscription as a descendant of Heracles, Apollo, and the Iamidae (*IG* V i 598; for this text, see Peek 1978:254), the latter being one of the most famous families of seers in ancient Greece. On Marcus Aurelius Teisamenus, cf. Rizakis et al. 2004:128 no. 192; on the Iamidae, see Flower in this volume.

[20] This inscription—dating from between AD 71 and the third century AD—has been published by Burrell 1993:291-292 no. II 1, with some considerations on the identity of the honorand; see Puech 2005k. If it is possible to identify Titus Flavius Maximus with another known person, then it seems most reasonable to identify him with a homonymous philosopher from Cretan Gortyn, whose gravestone has been found at Carthage (*CIL* 8.12924; see Liesenfelt and Le Bohec 1974–1975:127–128 no. 5; Hahn 1989:143–144n33; Puech 2005i), rather than with the *procurator Augusti* of the same name from Urbs Salvia in Italy (*CIL* 9.5529); against this latter proposal, cf. Eck 1992–1993:107n100.

[21] On Demetrius Tullianus, cf. Puech 1994c.

[22] On the form of the name, cf. Feissel, BE 2000 no. 33 and especially Solin 2002:112; on Mateinianus, see Puech 2005g.

[23] On Ctesiphon, see Follet 2003:86–87.

for Tiberius Claudius Paulinus from Antiochia Pisidiae (*AvP* 8.3.32);[24] an honorary inscription from Troizen for Marcus Aurelius Olympiodorus (*IG* IV 796);[25] a Spartan inscription for Iulius Phil‹oc›ratidas (*IG* V i 116; between 165 and 170 AD);[26] and an honorary inscription *post mortem* from Chaeronea for Sextus Claudius Autobulus, a descendant of Plutarch (*IG* VII 3425).[27] In all of these cases, it is difficult to decide, due to lack of sufficient evidence, in which sense the word *philosophos* is used. Similarly, in cases in which more than one member of a family is called *philosophos* without further epithets in the same inscription, it is not absolutely clear whether *philosophos* is used as an adjective or as a noun. Examples include a private dedication from Thessalonice by Sosibius, son of Sosibius—both men are called *philosophos* (*IG* X ii.i 145; before the mid-third century AD)—and an honorary inscription from Apollonia ad Rhyndacum in Mysia for Magnilla *philosophos*, daughter of Magnus *philosophos*, and wife of Menius *philosophos* (*IGR* 4.125 = Pleket 1969:40 no. 30; second/third century AD).[28] Clearly, when the word *philosophos* is accompanied by the article, it is to be understood as a noun; but it is not always obvious whether the person is to be understood as a philosopher in the true sense of the word. For instance, Sosibius, son of Sosibius, calls himself *philosophos* without an article, whereas in the case of his father, *philosophos* has the article (*IG* X ii.i 145). Even if there is no article, it is still possible that *philosophos* is to be understood as a noun, as in an honorary inscription from Aphrodisias for the philosopher Titus Aurelius Alexander, the father of the famous Peripatetic philosopher Alexander of Aphrodisias, in which both are designated *philosophos* without an article.[29] It is also important to differentiate between public

---

[24] His Latin grave inscription is known from his native town, Antioch, where he is designated not only as philosopher, but also as *hērōs*: *CIL* 3.302 = *ILS* 7777; cf. Hahn 1989:146n48.

[25] Müller 1968:217–218 thinks it is unreasonable to include this *curator* from Troizen as a member of the leading family of the sophist Marcus Aurelius Olympiodorus from Thespiae; cf. Jones 1970:223–224; Gregory 1979:264 no. 9; Jones 1980:377–380; Puech 2002:308–312, on this family.

[26] On this person and his name, cf. Cartledge and Spawforth 2002:180 with 263n6; Rizakis et al. 2004:320–321 no. 497.

[27] On Sextus Claudius Autoboulos, who lived in the third century, cf. Puech 1989c. It is only because of the reference to the ancestor Plutarch and the content of the text that it seems plausible to understand *philosophos* in this inscription in its sense as philosopher.

[28] On Magnilla, see Puech 2005e; on her father, Puech 2005f; and on her husband, Puech 2005l. A similar case is represented by Pompeia Polla, who called herself daughter of Pompeius Pleistarchus *philosophos* in an Eleusinian honorary inscription for her husband, Titus Flavius Euthykomas, from c. AD 166/7 (*IG* II² 3984 = *IEleusis* 487); cf. Follet 1976:249–252.

[29] The statue of Titus Aurelius Alexander was erected in accordance with a decree of the council and the people by his homonymous son, who was "one of the heads (*diadokhos*) of the philosophical schools at Athens"; see Chaniotis 2004a:388–389 no. 4, and 2004:79. The *diadokhos* Alexander is the famous Peripatetic philosopher, on whom cf. Goulet and Aouad 1989.

decrees and private inscriptions. Only in the case of Delphi does it seem to be possible to hypothesize that the word *philosophos* is never used as an adjective.[30] This indicates that it is equally necessary to consider local specifics in the usage of the word *philosophos*.

However, in other cases, it is clear that the words *philosophos* and *philosophia* are meant as a distinct reference to the subject of *paideia*. Three cases among many may be mentioned: an honorary decree from Olbia for Callisthenes, son of Callisthenes (*CIRB* 42);[31] the epitaph of Gaius Calpurnius Collega Macedo from Antiochia Pisidiae, called *rhētōr*, *philosophos*, and *arkhiatros* (Ramsay 1919:2; cf. Jones 1982:264—fourth century AD);[32] and the base of a statue for Quintus Statius Themistocles, son of a permanent priest of Asclepius and descendant of *philosophoi*, consuls, and Asiarchs, which bears a dedicatory inscription—based on a *psēphisma* of the *boulē* of the Areopagus—dedicated by his relative Titus Flavius Glaucus, *poiētēs*, *rhētōr*, and *philosophos*, as well as *fisci advocatus*.[33] The statue was erected in the Athenian Asclepieum next to the

---

[30] The epigraphic evidence for philosophers at Delphi during the imperial period is as follows: an honorary inscription for Gaius, son of Xenos, who is mentioned as *philosophos* (*F.Delphes* III iv 103; about AD 130; on Gaius, see Whittaker 2000); Gaius may have been the adoptive father of Bacchius of Paphus, son of Trypho and adopted son of Gaius (*F.Delphes* III iv 94; on Bacchius; cf. Puech 1994). This Bacchius, one of the teachers of Marcus Aurelius (*Meditations* 1.6), and the Athenians Zosimus, Sotimus, Claudius Nicostratus (cf. Byrne 2003:185 s.v. Claudius no. 301; Goulet 2005d), and Marcus Sextius Cornelianus from Mallus, are called *philosophoi platōnikoi* in an honorary inscription (*F.Delphes* III iv 94; between AD 140 and 155; cf. Puech 1998:262). Lucius Calvinus Taurus, teacher of Aulus Gellius and Herodes Atticus and a friend of Plutarch, is called a *philosophos platōnikos* (*F.Delphes* III iv 91; on Taurus, cf. Lakmann 1995:207–228); similarly, the otherwise unknown Isidor of Thmouis (*F.Delphes* III ii 116; late second/early third century AD; cf. Puech 2000). Sextus Claudius Aurelianus from Smyrna is called *puthagorios* (*F.Delphes* III i 203; late second/early third century AD; cf. Puech 1989b). Whereas Marcus Atilius Maximus is designated as *philosophos platōnikos* (*F.Delphes* III i 199; for the text, see Daux 1959:493–495 no. 22 with J. and L. Robert, BE 1961 no. 346 and Daux 1978:610–612; cf. Puech 2005h), Publius Cornelius Lupus of Nicopolis (*F.Delphes* III iv 115, also mentioned in *F.Delphes* III iv 114; cf. Puech 2005c) and Tiberius Iulius Rufus (*F.Delphes* III iv 89; for the text, cf. Vatin 1970:684) are both called only *philosophos*. In those cases in which *philosophos* is written without any specification of a philosophical school, no further epithets are ever given. On the Platonic philosophers at Delphi, cf. Marek 1984:212-213; Hahn 1989:146; on philosophers at Delphi during the imperial period in general, see Weir 2004:113–116; Haake 2006:533–536.

[31] On Callisthenes, cf. Puech 1994a.

[32] On this inscription, see Trombley 1993:172–174, and also the brief remarks by Lorenz 1999:763; cf. now Samana 2003:432–434 no. 334; Nutton 1977:219 no. 25; on the title *arkhiatros*, see Nutton 1977:215. On Macedo, cf. Puech 2005d.

[33] This inscription is *IG* II² 3704, on which cf. Aleshire 1991:59–70; Puech 2002:270–272 no. 122; Geagan 1991:159–160. On Titus Flavius Glaucus (Byrne 2003:233–234 s.v. Flavius no. 20), see Puech 2002:270–283 nos. 122-127; Quintus Statius Themistocles (Byrne 2003:443–444 s.v. Statius no. 11) served with distinction as *kleidoukhos* of Asclepius.

monument of their common great-grandfather Quintus Statius Sarapion—
poiētēs, iatros, rhētōr, and philosophos stōikos—who was a friend of Plutarch.[34]

Of course, the word philosophos is also used in a specific sense, to refer to
people who were professionally active as philosophers. Suffice it to mention
an Athenian honorary inscription, which, incidentally, also belongs to the
dossier of persons who are mentioned as both philosopher and priest in the
same inscription: the honorand, Titus Coponius Maximus from the dēmos
Hagnon, was hiereus of the cult of Demos and Charites, agōnothetēs of the
Megala Kaisareia, and Stoic diadokhos (IG II^2 3571; before AD 117/118).[35]

Before turning our attention to persons who are mentioned as both
philosopher and priest in the same inscription, it is necessary to consider one
last group of inscriptions in which we can be certain that the word philosophos is used as a noun, because it is accompanied by a specification that indicates the philosophical school. A few examples for the different schools may
illustrate this point. In an honorary inscription from Egyptian Antinoöpolis,
Flavius Maecius Se[verus] Dionysodorus is mentioned as Platonic philosopher (SB 3.6012 = GIBM 4.1076 = IPortes 14);[36] Lucius Peticius Propas is called
a Stoic philosopher in a private dedication of a portrait statue by his mother
at Olympia, based on a psēphisma of the Elean boulē (IvO 453);[37] a certain
Apollonius, otherwise unknown, is attested as a Peripatetic philosopher in a
Greek inscription from Rome (IGR 361 = IG XIV 1088);[38] at Brundisium, a public
grave inscription calls Eucratidas of Rhodes an Epicurean philosopher (IG
XIV 674 = ILS 7780);[39] Marcus Po[r(cius)?] Sopatrus is called a Pythagorean in

---

[34] On the Sarapion Monument, see Kapetanopoulos 1994 with the older literature. Cf. Jones
1978a:228–231; Puech 1992:4874–4878; and Follet 2001 on the Stoic Sarapion (Byrne 2003:441–
442 s.v. Statius no. 4); see also Samana 2003:128–130 no. 022.

[35] Cf. Hahn 1989:123, 125, 129–130; also Byrne 2003:203–204 s.v. Coponius no. 3: He was archon
eponymus in AD 99/100 (IG II^2 1072). On his father, who was hierokērux of Hagnous and who held
many of the most important and prestigious offices in Athens, cf. Byrne 2003:200f s.v. Coponius
no. 2.

[36] On this inscription, cf. Cauderlier and Worp 1982, who propose that the name of the Platonic
philosopher should be restored with Se[verus]; cf. also more generally, Hahn 1989:139, 162.
Proposals for the date of this inscription range from the second to the fourth century AD. On
Dionysodorus, see Puech 1994e.

[37] Cf. also Schörner 2003:444–445 cat. 841. See Zoumbaki 1996: 202–203, and Rizakis and Zoumbaki
2001:510 nos. 290, 612, and no. 298 on Lucius Peticius Propas and his mother Occia Prisca. On
Lucius Peticius and the Peticii, cf. the brief remarks by Salomies 2001:165–166; further, Lo
Monaco 2004:295–296.

[38] This inscription is dated between the first and third century AD; cf. Hahn 1989:149; Riess
2001:185; Solin 2003:295. For Apollonius, see Puech 1989a.

[39] On Eucratidas, cf. Puech 2000, and see Haake 2007:235–236, on this probably late-Hellenistic
inscription.

an inscription from the Illyrian *polis* Apollonia (*IApollonia* 260);[40] Menecles is attested in a grave epigram from Cyme as Pyrrhonian philosopher (*IKyme* 48 = *IGR* 4.1740); Uranius called himself a Cynic in an epigram from the tombs in the Royal Valley at Egyptian Thebes (Bernand, *Inscr. métriques* 141);[41] and finally, there is a mention of an eclectic philosopher from Alexandria in an Ephesian inscription dating from the early first century AD (*IEphesos* 3.789).[42]

This survey of the use of the word *philosophos* in Greek inscriptions dating from the Roman imperial period shows that the word was not used exclusively in its substantive meaning of *philosopher*, but also in its adjectival sense of *lover of wisdom; the latter application is always honorary, but not literal.* Generally, when the context is taken into account, it is possible to establish in which sense the word *philosophos* is used.

3.

In the following section, selected epigraphic testimonies for individuals who are mentioned explicitly as priests as well as philosophers will be discussed. The analysis will embrace a variety of cults and members of different philosophical schools distributed geographically across the whole of the eastern part of the Roman Empire, in order to illustrate the diffusion and the nonspecific character of the union of philosopher and priest in one person.

We begin with three Samian inscriptions relating to Gaius Iulius Amynias from the Augustan period. One of these inscriptions, on the base of a statue dedicated by *boulē* and *dēmos*, says that Amynias was called Isocrates and that he was an Epicurean philosopher (*IG* XII vi, i 293). From a second inscription, we learn that he held the eponymous magistracy of *dēmiourgos* in AD 6/7 (*IG* XII vi, i 190), while a third epigraphic testimony gives information about Amynias as a member of a Samian embassy to Augustus in 6/5 BC to reassure the emperor of the loyalty of Samos (*IG* XII vi, i 7). This last inscription shows that Amynias was *hiereus* of the *Autokratōr Kaisar Sebastos*, son of the god, of his son Gaius Caesar, and of Marcus Agrippa. Apart from this evidence, nothing else is known about Gaius Iulius Amynias.

---

[40] Second century AD; cf. Cabanes 1996:93–94.

[41] On Uranius, cf. Goulet-Cazé 1996:400; Goulet-Cazé 2005. There is some evidence that Cynics called themselves in inscriptions *dogs* to express their affiliation; see e.g. Diocles, who denotes himself in the royal tombs of Thebes four times as *dog*: Baillet 1926:1542, 1611, 1721, 1735; cf. Goulet-Cazé 1996:394.

[42] On this eclectic philosopher, see Runia 1988:241–242, who plausibly suggests identifying him with Potamo of Alexandria, known from Diogenes Laertius' *Lives of Eminent Philosophers* 1.11; cf. also Hahn 1989:138–139.

These three inscriptions are certainly remarkable. It is striking, for example, that an Epicurean philosopher held the highest and most prestigious offices of his *patris* and rendered important services to the *polis* of Samos—in other words, his actions did not really reflect the Epicurean doctrine. The point is underlined by the statement implied in Amynias' nickname Isocrates, which certainly refers to his rhetorical skill. Even though no single inscription tells us that Amynias was a *hiereus* of Augustus, of Gaius Caesar, and of Agrippa while also being an Epicurean philosopher, it is beyond doubt that the Samian *boulē* and *dēmos* realized that Amynias combined in himself a cultic office and a commitment to Epicureanism. And neither he himself nor the Samian community seems to have seen in this an obstacle to Amynias' acceptance of public offices and duties—such as the priesthood of the imperial cult.[43]

Further epigraphic evidence confirms that there was no essential impediment to *polis*-communities in the eastern part of the Roman Empire designating an honorand in one and the same inscription as *hiereus* and Epicurean philosopher.[44] An honorary inscription from Cyprian Palaipaphos, dedicated to Aphrodite Paphia and expressing the city's gratitude to one of her citizens, dates from between 15 BC and AD 14. The text is badly damaged and only a preliminary publication is available: Plous, the honorand, was a philosopher—probably an Epicurean—who was appointed for life as *arkhiereus* of the *Theos Autokratōr Kaisar Sebastos* (Mitford 1980:1352n321; see now Mitford 1990:2196n105).

There are a number of cases of persons who were priests and also philosophers, but who are not designated as both in any extant inscription.[45] Only through Lucian's *Alexandros* or *Pseudomantis*, for example, is it known that Tiberius Claudius Lepidus—attested in an honorary inscription from Amastris as *arkhiereus* of Pontus and *epistatēs* of the *polis* (*IGR* 3.88 = Marek 1993:162 Amasra no. 12)—was an Epicurean philosopher and, as such, an adversary of Alexander of Abunoteichos. According to the literary tradition, the opposition between the Epicurean and the *seer* Alexander resulted from the Epicureans' general rejection of oracles, which were one of the central media of Alexander

---

[43] I have dealt with Amynias and the three Samian inscriptions in greater detail in Haake 2007:190–194.

[44] On Epicureans as imperial priests, see now Koch-Piettre 2005:269–270; on Epicureans as priests of *traditional* city cults, Koch Piettre 2005:266–269.

[45] In addition to the following examples, one might also mention the Epicurean Quinctilius Maximus, whose career is known from *IAlexandreia Troas* 39 and who is attested in Arrian's *Discourses of Epictetus* as being an Epicurean (3.7); cf. Puech 2005j.

(Lucian *Alexandros or Pseudomantis* 25).[46] A dedication from the Numidian city of Madaura mentions Apuleius as an adornment of the city and as *philosophus platonicus* (*ILAlg* 1.2115), but it is attested only in literary sources by himself and another author that he was also a priest.[47] Another case is Plutarch, who is called *philosophos* (*IEleusis* 650 = *IG* II^2 3814) on an Eleusinian statue base for a descendant, the Sophist and sacred herald Nicagoras, which dates from the mid-third century, while in a Delphic inscription, he is mentioned as *hiereus* (*Syll.*^{3} 829A = *CID* IV 150).[48]

Thanks to three inscriptions from Didyma, we know that at least three philosophers—an Epicurean, a Stoic, and a Platonist—acted during the imperial period as *prophētai*.[49] The first testimony comes from one of the so-called prophet-inscriptions for a *prophētēs* and *philosophos epikoureios* by the name of Philidas, son of Heracleon, from an otherwise unknown *genos* which traced its origin back to Ajax (*IDidyma* 285). The dating of this inscription is uncertain, but it is nonetheless possible to point out some important aspects. *Authors* of the prophet-inscriptions were the Didymaean prophets themselves, the highest priests of Didymaean Apollo and descended from the noblest families of Miletus,[50] who were appointed by lot after the five Milesian demes had nominated one candidate each. The functions of the *prophētēs* were, on the one hand, the ritual performance of the sacrifices to Apollo and, on the other hand, representative duties as well as announcing and interpreting the answers of the oracle. The *prophētēs* Philidas, who left behind only an inscription of four lines as testimony of his office, did not see any inconsistency in being both an Epicurean philosopher and a prophet, or in publicly commemorating this aspect after the end of his term as prophet. Those who selected him as their candidate evidently had no reservations about this situation, either, for there can be no doubt that they knew about his Epicurean background.

---

[46] On this passage, cf. Victor 1997:149–151; for a better understanding of Lucian's *Alexandros*, see now Elm von der Osten 2006, and especially Bendlin 2006:197–203. On Alexander of Abonouteichos, see Robert 1980:393–421; Jones 1986:133–148; Miron 1996. On Tiberius Claudius Lepidus, cf. Piettre 2002:140–141; Goulet 2005a.

[47] See Apuleius *Florida* 25.38 with the commentaries by La Rocca 2005:239–240 and Todd Lee 2005:156; cf. also Augustinus *Letters* 138.19; on Apuleius, see Flamand 1994; on his priesthood, cf. Rives 1994; Harrison 2000:8.

[48] On the Eleusinian inscription, cf. Puech 2002:357–360; on the Delphic inscription, see Jones 1971:28. On Plutarch as philosopher and priest, see Feldmeier 1998; Bendlin 2006:172–177. In a second Delphic inscription (*Syll.*^{3} 843 = *CID* IV 151), Plutarch is mentioned neither as philosopher nor as priest.

[49] On the Didymaean *prophētai*, see Günther 1971:118–119; Fontenrose 1988:45–55.

[50] Cf. Günther 2003:447, on the character and intention of the prophet-inscriptions. On the social elite of Miletus, see Andreou 2000.

Besides Philidas, one Aelius Aelianus (*IDidyma* 310) is attested in a Didymaean funerary inscription as *prophētēs* and *philosophos stōikos*.[51] Finally, Phanis, too, *diadokhos* of a local (Platonic?) philosophical school and dedicator of a herm of Plato (*IDidyma* 150), was *prophētēs* of Apollo's oracle at Didyma (*IDidyma* 127).[52]

To return to Epicurean *hiereis*, modern scholars have been particularly impressed by Aurelius Belius Philippus, *hiereus theou megistou hagiou Belou* and *diadokhos* of the Epicureans at Apamea ad Orontem (Rey-Coquais 1973:66–68 no. 3; cf. now Smith 1996:120). The relevant inscription is preserved only in a very fragmentary state and is dated to the second or third century AD. In spite of its poor condition, it is possible to gather from the text that Aurelius Belius Philippus had done something at the god Belus' behest. Therefore, the Epicurean publicly recognized the god as the inspirer of his own acts. Since Aurelius Belius Philippus was *diadokhos* of the Epicureans at Apamea, there must have been an institutionalized Epicurean school, which is not otherwise attested. The sanctuary of Zeus Belus at Apamea was an important oracle sanctuary,[53] which was consulted, for example, by Septimius Severus (Cassius Dio *Roman History* 70.8.5–6). Little is known about this sanctuary, and nothing about the Epicurean *diadokhos*, except what the inscription tells us; yet Aurelius Belius Philippus, whose name contains Latin, Semitic-theophoric, and Greek elements,[54] has captured scholars' interest for two reasons: first because, although being an Epicurean philosopher and therefore an exponent of Hellenic culture, he had strong relations to the cult of Belus,[55] and second, because of the supposed inconsistency between his Epicureanism and his priesthood.[56] However, rather than perceiving Aurelius Belius Philippus as a person enmeshed in inner paradoxes, we should perhaps question whether the supposed inconsistency might not prove to be an error of perspective on our part. For the issue whether an *orthodox* Epicurean should be a priest of Belus is relevant if, and only if, the postulate is valid that Epicurus' *doxai* were determinant for his followers in their public life.

---

[51] Cf. Puech 1989; Andreou 2000:9.

[52] See again Andreou 2000:9.

[53] Cf. Balty 1981 and 1997 on the sanctuary of Zeus Belus.

[54] It is not possible to say anything specific about the unique and striking name Belius because of insufficient evidence, although it is clear that this theophoric name is to be seen in the context of the relation between Aurelius Belius Philippus and the god Belus, whose priest the Epicurean was. However, we cannot tell when he received this name, so it remains an open question as to what specific meaning should be ascribed to it.

[55] Cf. Millar 1993a:262–263; see Rey-Coquais 1997 on culture in Roman Syria.

[56] See Smith 1996:127–130. An instructive ancient source in this context is a grave inscription from Miletus, in which Epicurus and his *doxai* are connected with pleasure and atheism (*IMilet* 734); on this inscription, cf. Haake 2007:227–229.

From Lycian Rhodiapolis comes an honorary inscription dating from the first century AD, granted by the local *boulē*, *dēmos*, and *gerousia* for Heraclitus, son of Heraclitus Oreius (*TAM* 2.3.910),[57] who was most likely an adherent of Epicurus' doctrine, even if this detail is not mentioned explicitly in the text. Heraclitus was not only *hiereus* of Asclepius and Hygieia, but also a physician, the author of medical and philosophical writings in verse, a Homer of medical poetry and a man bedecked with honors by the Alexandrians, the Athenians, the Rhodians, the Epicurean philosophers at Athens, and the sacred Thymelic synod, among others. This text was inscribed on the base of a statue plated with gold and formed part of the honors granted to Heraclitus, together with a statue of *paideia*, which probably means that this statue represented Heraclitus with insignia of *paideia*. A second inscription informs us that he was *hiereus* for life; had built a *naos* for Asclepius, Hygieia, the *Sebastoi*, and the *patris*; and had dedicated the corresponding *agalmata* (*TAM* 2.3.906).[58] Heraclitus clearly had a strong association with philosophy, but acted without any reference to philosophical ideas in the conduct of his life, which was formed rather by his social background as a member of the local elite of Rhodiapolis.

It was long assumed that the Sophist Lucius Flavius Hermocrates—known from Philostratus' *Lives of the Sophists* 109–112 and an inscription from Erythrae (*IErythrai* I 43)—who lived during the reign of Septimius Severus, was mentioned in an honorary inscription from Pergamum (*IPergamon* 8.34).[59] In this inscription, *boulē* and *dēmos* of Pergamum honored a Lucius Flavius Hermocrates, *philosophos* and *arkhiereus* of the *naoi* of Asia. Recent scholarship, however, has convincingly argued that the Hermocrates honored at Pergamum descended from the same family as the Sophist mentioned by Philostratus, but that he is not identical with him (being perhaps his grandfather?) and probably lived already during the reign of Marcus Aurelius.[60] Of special interest in this context is the fact that the honorand is called both philosopher and *arkhiereus*. Unlike the cases analyzed above, here, the word *philosophos* is not accompanied by any further specification. Despite the lack of further adjectival epithets, it seems likely that *philosophos* is here used as a noun. If this is the case, then this document is further proof of the fact that it was entirely possible to be both a philosopher and a priest. However, Hermocrates was not merely philosopher and priest: an oracle of the great god Asclepius announced

---

[57] On this inscription, cf. Robert 1990:582; see now Samana 2003:397–399 no. 290; Puech 2000b.
[58] On this inscription, see also the remarks by Oliver 1975.
[59] Cf. e.g. Campanile 1994:56 no. 34c.
[60] Cf. especially Jones 2003; also, Puech 2002:297–307 nos. 137–139.

that "He was not immortal, being mortal born, but long ago he alone was the best of hero-men." (*IPergamon* 8.34 = *Steinepigramme* I 06/02/03).[61]

For one final example, we turn to an honorary inscription from Stratonicea in Caria, dated to around AD 160, which was set up by *boulē*, *dēmos*, and *gerousia* for Hierocles of Hieracome. Apart from Hierocles, the *arkhiereus* of the *Sebastoi* and holder of many further priesthoods, his two sons were also honored: Thrason Leon, *arkhiereus* of the *Sebastoi*, *gumnasiarkhos* and *hiereus* of Zeus Panamaros, and Leon Thrason, likewise *arkhiereus* of the *Sebastoi*, *gumnasiarkhos* of the *neoi* and *hiereus* of Zeus Chrysaorios (*IStratonikeia* 2.1.1028). Both sons were explicitly called *philosophos*—and this, in spite of their youth.[62] For this reason, we should not assume that in this inscription, Thrason Leon and Leon Thrason were called philosophers in the strict sense of the word, but rather that they were represented as adults—as adults belonging to the social elite of their *polis*.

To conclude: it was clearly possible to be both a philosopher and a priest. This was true not only for those who combined both roles in their own lives, but also for the various societies which provided the social context within which to combine two—at first sight, diametrically opposed—callings.[63]

---

[61] For a translation and interpretation of the oracle, cf. Jones 2003:130; Bendlin 2006:180n64.

[62] Cf. Robert 1978:402n57; see also Montserrat 1997 on an inscription on a mummy (*SB* 18.13645), where *philosophos* is also used as a laudatory epithet for an educated young man of the local elite in a funeral context. On Leon Thrason, cf. Puech 2005b.

[63] Without pretending to completeness, further epigraphic evidence could be added as follows: the *diadokhos* Titus Flavius Pantainus (cf. Byrne 2003:237–238 s.v. Flavius no. 39) was priest of the philosophical Muses in Athens (Meritt 1946:233 no. 64; around AD 100; cf. Parsons 1949:268–272; Oliver 1979; McK. Camp 1989:50–51); Tiberius Claudius Sospis, priest of the altar (*ho epi bōmos*), is mentioned by Philostratus as an illustrious philosopher (*Lives of the Sophists* 591) and was honoured by the Athenians because of his *aretē* and *philosophia* (Meritt 1961:272–273 no. 110; cf. Follet 1976:290–292); Gnaeus Claudius Severus, son-in-law of the emperor Marcus Aurelius, consul, and *pontifex*, is called *philosophos* in a newly discovered fragment of a known Ephesian inscription (*IEphesos* 5.1539 with Engelmann 2000:78; for the text, see Jones 2002:113—last quarter of the second century AD). On Gnaeus Claudius Severus and his family from Paphlagonian Pompeiopolis—his father had also been consul and was one of the teachers of philosophy of the young Marcus Aurelius (cf. Jones 2002:112n21)—see the fundamental article of Groag 1902; also, Syme 1968:102–103; Halfmann 1982:643. Hadrian, who dedicated the statue of Gnaeus Claudius Severus and wrote an appendant epigram, is the famous sophist Hadrian of Tyre, on whom see Campanile 2003. A further example is the Alexandrian Lucius Septimius Trypho, *philosophos*, twice priest of Dionysus, *arkhiereus* for life of Dionysus Kathegemon and *arkhiereus* for life of the emperor Marcus Aurelius Antoninus *neos Dionusos* (*CIG* 4.6829 = *IGR* 4.468; between AD 198 and 209; on this inscription, cf. Merkelbach 1985). The restoration *[The]o[k]ritos Ariste-[ou phil]osophos Epi-[koureios]* in a list of *molpoi* from Aigiale is not without its difficulties (Duemmler 1886:102–104 no. 6 = *IG* XII vii 418 = *IGR* 4.998; cf. Robert 1937:53–54n5—dated by Robert to the Roman period).

4.

Following the description and analysis of these case studies, it is necessary to ask whether it is possible to give an explanation for our observations.

In view of the large number of examples, it is clear that persons who were philosophers and who also served as priests were not uncommon. The chronological and geographical distribution of our examples indicates further that this phenomenon was not limited to one region or to a particular period in time. Finally, given the variety of types of cult—imperial cult, oracular cult, and a wide range of *polis*-cults—as well as the affiliation to various philosophical schools, a satisfactory explanation cannot be based on the specific peculiarities of any given cult or philosophical doctrine.

An alternative approach to interpreting this phenomenon would appear to be more promising, namely, one that avoids perceiving those who were at the same time philosophers and priests as embodying a paradox, and which instead considers the social background of the philosophers. Epictetus, mentioned at the beginning, is not a typical example as far as the social status of philosophers in the Roman imperial period is concerned, because he was a slave, probably by birth; as such, he was an exception among the philosophers. In general, philosophers were descended from the (local) upper classes of society—as was, for example, the author of the *Discourses of Epictetus*, the consul and historian Lucius (or Aulus) Arrianus from Bithynian Nicomedia, who is called *philosophos* in inscriptions from Athens (Peppas-Delmousou 1970:378) and Corinth (*ICorinth* 8.3.124).[64]

The examples we have considered substantiate this general statement. Gaius Iulius Amynias was undoubtedly descended from the Samian elite and acted according to the common expectation of members of the upper classes of the Greek *poleis* during the Hellenistic and imperial periods that they should serve their *patris*. It was clearly compatible with this expectation that Amynias presented himself and was seen by his fellow citizens as an Epicurean, that is, a follower of a doctrine that focused on personal *ataraxia* and not on acting on behalf of the community of the *polis*. The same can be said with regard to the question of religion. Like Amynias, the imperial priest from Palaipaphos, Plous, and Tiberius Claudius Lepidus from Amastris were certainly members of the upper class. The office of the *prophētēs* in the temple of Apollo at Didyma was one of the most prestigious and expensive priesthoods of the *polis* of

---

[64] On Arrian, see the overview by Follet 1989; on his career, see Syme 1982; and with particular reference to the epigraphic evidence on Arrian, Oliver 1982; Chaniotis 1988:331–332 E 47.

Miletus. As for Aelius Aelianus, we know from an inscription, set up by his daughter Aelie Aeliane when she was *hudrophoros* of Artemis Pythie, that this family belonged to the Milesian upper class and that its members held numerous important offices in the *polis* (*IDidyma* 310). In the case of Aurelius Belius Philippus, it is only an assumption, although a very likely one, that he belonged to the local elite. It is absolutely certain that Heraclitus of Rhodapolis descended from a family of leading citizens of his *patris*. Finally, Hermocrates, honored at Pergamum and attested as *stephanēphoros* and called *philosophos* in an inscription from Phocaea (*CIG* 3414b), was a member of a family known from many inscriptions to have belonged to the provincial elite of Asia.

The public behavior of the various actors examined was always determined by their social background and corresponded with the expectations of the *polis*-communities towards a member of the upper classes and the system of norms in which they were socialized; duty to the *polis* and honorable deeds performed for the *patris* formed central aspects of an upper-class man's way of life.[65] An important role in this context was played by cultic offices, which generally required no special qualifications in the religious field, but which were rather an expression of a distinctive social prestige within the society of the *poleis*. The eminent importance of acting as a civic benefactor of one's own *polis* finds one of its most eloquent examples in a very long and famous inscription from a small town in the Lycian mountains: Oenoanda. Diogenes of Oenoanda—a member of the local elite of his *patris*—wrote and published the so-called Epicurean inscription at his own expense on the front of the stoa in the agora and explains his motivation at the beginning of the text.[66] Addressing his fellow citizens, he states that, even though he is (at the present time) not engaged in public affairs (that is, he follows the Epicurean doctrine of *ataraxia*), the teaching expressed in the inscription is the equivalent of such actions (Diogenes of Oenoanda *The Epicurean Inscription* fr. 3 I 4–8 Smith). Of course, Diogenes declares that "joy [of real value is generated not by theaters] and [... and] baths [and perfumes] and ointments, [which we] have left to [the] masses, [but natural science]" (fr. 2 III 8–14). With this statement, he denies

---

[65] On the Greek *polis* in the Roman period, see Millar 1993, and Meyer-Zwiffelhoffer 2003 on the *politai* in Greek cities during the Roman imperial period; see Pleket 1998 on political culture and practice in the Greek cities of Asia Minor in the Roman Empire. On the social elites, cf. Quass 1993:149–178, 210–229, 253–269, 303–347; Stephan 2002:59–113.

[66] On this inscription, cf. Gordon 1996; Warren 2000:144–148; Scholz 2003:208–227; Bendlin 2006:159–165. For text and translation, see Smith 1993 and 2003. The identity of Diogenes is not certain; for a discussion of the various proposals, cf. Smith 1993:35–48; Scholz 2003:210; Puech 1994d.

traditional elements of euergetic acts performed by members of the local upper classes. Yet the social framework for his public activity is the *polis*, just as it is for Demosthenes of Oenoanda, who instituted and funded the festival of the Demostheneia.[67] Demosthenes and Diogenes wanted the same thing, expressed through different means: to benefit their *patris*. Being an Epicurean, appearing as such and preaching *ataraxia*, did not prevent Diogenes from acting for his own *polis*, even if in a most unusual way.[68]

This point concerns a central aspect of Greek philosophy, and explains the reason why the opposition between *doxai* and *dogmata* on the one hand, and social action on the other, only appears to be a problem. It is possible to explain this situation by considering the conceptual separation of theory and practice in Greek thought. The philosophical discourse constructed with respect to *theōria* was not necessarily the authoritative guide for everyday social conduct. In the Greek world, the pursuit of philosophy was characterized by *theōria*, which was radically dissociated from the practical sphere. That does not mean that philosophical ideas had no influence on ordinary life and bore no relationship to reality, or that they could not develop a discursive influence. The strict separation of *theōria* and practice implies that the notion of realization in practice was not automatically inherent in philosophical concepts, and that philosophical opinions did not necessarily influence the social behavior of an individual who was a follower of a philosophical school.[69]

In the light of this distinction, it was therefore not a problem of principle if a philosopher also held a priesthood—neither from his own point of view nor from that of his social environment. The interesting question is rather: Why, in some cases of priests who were also philosophers, do the inscriptions mention both roles, while in others, such as that of Tiberius Claudius Lepidus from Amastris, they do not? Unfortunately, it is difficult to find a generally applicable answer to this question, because we are not sufficiently well informed.

We are confronted with a conceptual gap between the position of Epictetus outlined at the beginning of this paper, and the social practice of all those attested in inscriptions who were at the same time priests and philosophers. We may introduce a distinction among those called *philosophoi*, which can be illustrated by comparing, for example, Euphrates of Tyre and Plutarch

---

[67] The inscription relating the foundation of the Demostheneia has been published by Wörrle 1988:4–17.

[68] On Epicureanism as a philosophical trend which appealed particularly to the upper classes of the *poleis*, see Timpe 2000:61.

[69] On this aspect, see Gotter 2003:175.

of Chaeronea. Euphrates lived in the late first and early second century and was a very successful man, especially in Rome—but also a Stoic philosopher. While Pliny the Younger praised him because he put into practice what the philosopher only taught (Pliny the Younger *Letters* 1.10.10.), Euphrates had quarrels with people like Apollonius of Tyana, who accused him of enjoying a lifestyle which was not consistent with his status as a philosopher (Philostratus *Life of Apollonius* 5.39).[70] Yet it was precisely his conduct, at once commended and criticized, which made him such a respected person amongst the Roman elite.[71] Plutarch of Chaeronea was a Platonic philosopher: he is mentioned as *philosophos* in an inscription from Eleusis (*IEleusis* 650 = *IG* II² 3814),[72] but in his native city and at Delphi, performing public duties and serving as a priest, he always acted as a member of the local elite and even wrote *Precepts of Statecraft*, as well as *The Oracles at Delphi No Longer Given in Verse* (Plutarch *Moralia* 798a–825f; 394e–409d).[73]

Euphrates, Plutarch, and the other individuals discussed above who were called philosophers and who acted as priests—and who often also held other magistracies—were members of the social elite of their native cities. They belonged to the ruling classes and acted not only in their *patris*, but sometimes also on a provincial or imperial level. As men with an upper-class background, they had acquired *paideia* and were *pepaideumenoi*.[74] They saw themselves and were seen as philosophers, which implies that they were acknowledged to possess a particular set of values in theory and practice; yet being a philosopher was for most of them not the exclusive role of their social *persona*, as seems to have been the case with people such as Epictetus or Secundus.[75] These two—and others, such as Cynic philosophers—were primarily intellectuals, which means that they personified the opposition of *spirit and power*.[76] Such an exclusive role of the intellectual, however, could not be embraced by

---

[70] On this passage, see Flinterman 1995:72–73

[71] On Euphrates, cf. Frede 1997; Flaig 2002:129–131; Jones 2003a:160–162; for a general overview on Euphrates, see Robiano 2000.

[72] See note 48 and main text above.

[73] On Plutarch's career, see Jones 1971:13–38. On the importance of religious matters as an element in the lives of members of the upper classes in Greek *poleis*, see e.g. Galli 2001.

[74] On the relationship between *paideia* and power in the Second Sophistic, see e.g. the monograph by Schmitz 1997; also, Jones 2005 on the relevance of culture in the careers of eastern senators. Cf. Anderson 1989:104–136 on the term *pepaideumenoi*; see Borg 2004 on portraits of *pepaideumenoi*.

[75] No *persona* is characterized by one role exclusively, but each is composed rather by a set of roles; on this point, cf. Haake 2003:97; Bendlin 2006:178; see also the methodological remarks by Burke 1980:50–53.

[76] See Haake 2003:97–100 on the concept of the social figure of the intellectual.

people like Plutarch or Euphrates in everyday life: they were confronted with expectations that reflect above all the norms of the elite, and which they felt themselves obliged to fulfill. To be depicted as *philosophos* could serve to represent a virtuous leading citizen,[77] but these philosophers did not follow the models of the *true* philosopher established in literary sources.[78]

In the Roman imperial period, as in the Classical and Hellenistic eras, the application of one's self to philosophy was an occupation of members of the local elites of Greek *poleis*, which was considered to be advantageous for one's status and prestige.[79] While certainty on this point may remain impossible, it nevertheless seems probable that being designated a priest and at the same time a philosopher was understood to augment the social capital of such figures in the public's estimation. In any case, professing to be a philosopher was not an impediment to being a priest. For the present, however, it must remain an open question as to why it was only sometimes explicitly stated that the same individual was both a priest and a philosopher.

Members of the local upper classes in the eastern Roman Empire were characterized by *multiple identities*; for example, as *politai* of their particular *patris*, as possessors of Roman citizenship, and as Greeks under Roman rule.[80] In the same way, they were also assigned different social *personae*, such as *philosophos* and priest, which did not exclude one another, but which constituted the ideal of nobility in Greek *poleis* in the Greco-Roman world.

---

[77] On this theme, cf. Bowersock 2002; Dillon 2002.

[78] See Diefenbach 2000:101–112 on such models.

[79] For a more detailed discussion with additional references, see Haake 2007:279–281.

[80] On *multiple* identities in the age of the Second Sophistic, see Jones 2004; cf. more generally, Stephan 2002, especially 114–260.

165

8

An Egyptian Priest at Delphi
Calasiris as *theios anēr* in Heliodorus' *Aethiopica*

Manuel Baumbach

1. The Discovery of the Priest in the Greek Novel

WHEN WE CONSIDER THE FIGURE AND ROLE of the priest in the Greek romantic novel, there is a conspicuous discrepancy among the five extant novels. Whereas priests and priestesses do not appear at all within the three earliest novels (Longus) or are only incidentally mentioned as attendants at sacrifices or cultic processions (Chariton, Xenophon),[1] in those of Achilles Tatius and Heliodorus, the figure of the priest is integral to the plot. At the end of his *Leucippe and Clitophon,* Achilles Tatius introduces an anonymous priest of Artemis who proves to be the savior of the two lovers. Heliodorus goes even further: his novel is precisely about priestly figures. The hero and the heroine, Theagenes and Chariclea, are a priest and a priestess, and their fate (and the plot of the novel) is largely determined by the action of another priest, Calasiris. Admittedly, we have only a small sample of the genre to work with, while the extant texts cannot be very exactly dated, and to this extent, our interpretation must be regarded as tentative. Yet it does appear that there is a development in the use of the priest-motif in the Greek novel: from the third century AD onward, authors identified their protagonists less

---

I would like to thank the editors for their critical suggestions, and I am very grateful to Stephen Lake for helping me with the translation.

[1] For the dating of the Greek novels, cf. Bowie 1999:40–41: Chariton's *Kallirhoe* (ca. 50 BC–AD 50); Xenophon of Ephesus' *Ephesiaca* (early second century AD); Longus' *Daphnis and Chloe* (late second century AD); Achilles Tatius' *Leucippe and Clitophon* (late second century AD); Heliodorus' *Aethiopica* (third/fourth century AD). For the dating of Heliodorus, cf. also Bowersock 1997:149–160. Chariton: 3.9.1 and 3.9.4 (priestess), 8.2.9 (priest); Xenophon: 1.5.6 (priest), 1.10.6 (priestess).

with the political than with the religious elite,[2] and they expanded their material with a discussion of religion and cult.[3]

Whether this focus in the novel as a genre and especially in Heliodorus is connected with a stronger religious awareness in the third and fourth centuries,[4] or whether it is due to the personal circumstances or intentions of the individual authors,[5] cannot be decided with certainty. The present essay will concentrate on the depiction of priests in the *Aethiopica* and the function they assume within the narrative, in order to show what kind of effect the text (and the priests in it) is intended to have on the reader. Of course, the character of the priest in the novel is a literary construct which has to be understood primarily in its function within the fictional plot. Nevertheless, the effectiveness of the priest as a literary construct depends on many aspects of stylization and contextualization, and his portrayal cannot be so unrealistic or improbable that no dialogue between the text and its audience is possible. In the analysis of priest-figures, both literary and historical models must therefore be taken into account in order to ascertain which models the priests in the novel might correspond to or be in dialogue with. The priest in literature can only be understood in relation to the many voices of possible cultural and literary references.[6]

Let us begin with a short summary of the *Aethiopica*, which narrates the love story of Theagenes and Chariclea, the priestess of Artemis, in ten books. Abandoned by her Ethiopian parents, Chariclea is raised by Charicles, a priest

---

[2] Despite the fact that a priest always had an important function in both the political and the religious life of a *polis*, in literary fiction the emphasis can be placed upon one or the other of these spheres alone. Thus, for example, in his description of the events in Memphis, Heliodorus (books 7 and 8) creates a distinction between the religious and the political (i.e. nonreligious) influence of a priest.

[3] A similar focus on the priest can be found in Philostratus' *Life of Apollonius of Tyana* and the two satires of Lucian, *Peregrinus* and *Alexandros*. Although these works do not belong to the genre of the novel, a direct influence on the authors of Greek novels in the third century AD cannot be ruled out. For possible connections between the *Apollonius* and Heliodorus' *Calasiris* figure, see n37 below. For the historical dimension of the *Apollonius* with emphasis on the religious and cultural changes in Greek culture in the third century, cf. Swain 1999a; Elsner 1997.

[4] Cf. Bowie 1999:55.

[5] The *sphragis* at the end of the novel—"So concludes the *Aithiopika*, the story of Theagenes and Charikleia, the work of a Phoenician from the city of Emesa, one of the clan of the Descendants of the Sun, Theodosios's son, Heliodoros" (10.41; all translations from Heliodorus are taken from Morgan 1989)—and Photius' note that Heliodorus "later became a bishop" (*Bibl. Cod.* 73) have given rise to the scarcely verifiable assumption that a personal religious belief of Heliodorus is reflected in the novel; see e.g. Weinreich 1962:239, who writes that Heliodorus, "a religious man and a priest of Helios of Emesa, who had a serious moral attitude in a time of religious syncretism, found his way from Helios to Christ as the *Sol salutis* and converted to Christianity" (my translation).

[6] For Bakhtin's concept of polyglossia, cf. Whitmarsh 1998:95.

of Apollo at Delphi. When the protagonists first meet at the sacrifices held in honor of Neoptolemus during the Pythian celebration, they fall in love and decide to flee from Delphi, as Chariclea is promised to another man. They are assisted in their plan by Calasiris, the Egyptian priest of Isis, who recognized Chariclea's true descent by signs of identification and who wants her to return to Egypt, as it has been prophesied that she would. The trio arrive in Egypt, where Theagenes and Chariclea are separated several times and the strength of their love is put to the test. With the assistance of Calasiris and the Athenian Cnemon, whose biography is included in the novel as a kind of novella, they finally come to Memphis, where Calasiris, shortly before his death, decides the quarrel between his two sons as to which of them will succeed him as high priest. Having successfully evaded an intrigue of the Persian governor's wife, who had fallen in love with Theagenes, the two protagonists are taken prisoner by the Ethiopian king, Hydaspes, who does not recognize Chariclea as his daughter and decides that they are to be sacrificed to Helios and Selene. This rite, however, is prevented by the *anagnōrisis* of Chariclea and her parents together with the local priests, the gymnosophists, who demand the abolition of human sacrifices. At the end of the novel, Theagenes and Chariclea are made priest and priestess of Helios and Selene.

The fact that the story is told chronologically only from book seven onward, when the protagonists arrive at Memphis, makes the *Aethiopica* especially interesting from a narratological point of view.[7] The preceding events consist of flashbacks and inserted stories about Cnemon and especially about Calasiris, who emerges not only as protagonist but also as narrator: Calasiris accompanies the fictional characters from the second up to the seventh book and narrates the events in the first person. The importance of his tale is marked not only by its length but also by the fact that Calasiris' story—although told later—contains the basic information on which the remainder of the novel is constructed. Thus, having opened the story with an ecphrastic riddle (1.1–3), the omniscient author recedes behind the fictional character of Calasiris, and "reading" Calasiris becomes the crucial step in decoding the novel.

2. The Poetics of Reading in Heliodorus' *Aethiopica*

Having finally overcome the persistent prejudice that it was little more than the pulp fiction of Antiquity,[8] the ancient novel can now be regarded

---

[7] For an analysis of the narrative structure, cf. Morgan 1999; Winkler 1999.

[8] So e.g. Rohde 1914:IX, who excuses himself in the preface of his *Der Griechische Roman und*

as literature intended for cultivated readers.[9] Although primarily intended as entertainment, the novels' literary quality is high. We find extensive use of unmarked intertextuality, which assumes the readers' *paideia*; an artful mixture of genres; and—as in the case of Heliodorus—a highly sophisticated text "playing the game of literature."[10] His novel can thus be read as a history of reading, in both the concrete and the abstract senses of the word. The plot becomes transparent only by the deciphering of a headband given to Chariclea when she was abandoned; written in sacred letters (*hieratikois*, 4.8), it reveals her true descent from Ethiopia.

In a similar fashion, various characters try to read dreams and oracles, and whenever the meaning is uncertain, the reader is invited to participate in the narration by interpreting the text for himself.[11] As the story unfolds, the reader must emancipate himself from the position of being, as it were, part of the audience within the story itself. This situation is exemplified by the figure of Cnemon. After telling his own love story, which can almost be regarded as a classic of the genre, Cnemon himself joins the audience and, like the reader of the novel, listens to Calasiris' story. However, as Cnemon becomes more emotionally involved in events, yet fails to understand circumstances and oracles whose meaning seems to be clear to the reader, the latter distances himself from the position of Cnemon.[12] At the same time, the reader's anticipation of a traditional love story is replaced by an awareness of something new and unusual in the *Aethiopica*. This shift centers around the figure of Calasiris, who mercurially appears as trickster, philosopher, priest, and holy man. His story must also be read from multiple perspectives: as a listener within

---

seine Vorläufer for having dealt with an unliterary subject written by "many bad and mediocre authors" *("Die vielen schlechten und mittelmäßigen Autoren")*. Cf. also Hägg 1983:90, who defines the readership of Greek novels as "the population outside the big cities, women, people looking for romanticism and idealism."

[9] For the readership, cf. Stephens 1994, who rules out a widespread circulation of the novels in Greco-Roman Egypt on the grounds of comparatively small papyrological evidence, and Bowie 1994, who argues for an educated readership after analyzing the literary quotations in the novels and their dialogue with other works of literature.

[10] Cf. Winkler 1999:350: "There are many ways to play the game of literature, and a sophisticated player is now and then caught alluding to his private sense of being an author ... and to the ironies of communication ... Heliodorus is such an author, and the *Aithiopika* is an act of pure play, yet a play which rehearses vital processes by which we must live in reality—interpretation, reading, and making a provisional sense of things."

[11] Winkler 1999:313 stresses the way in which the reader's reception is controlled by means of oracles: "Poised somewhere between the perfect interpreter (Kalasiris) and the inadequate interpreter (Thyamis, the Delphians, *et alii*) stands the actual reader, who must be taught how to read the *Aithiopika*."

[12] For Cnemon as a reader, cf. Morgan 1991:95–100.

a fictional plot; as an object of our literary and cultural knowledge, which is independent of the story; and through his own self-perception.

a) Calasiris as priest: the perception from the outside

The first time we see Calasiris through Cnemon's eyes, we are offered an important clue to his character as a priest: his outward appearance. Cnemon meets Calasiris on his way to Chemmis, and describes him as follows:

> ... an old man walking aimlessly along the river bank, pacing to and fro, to and fro, beside the river, like an athlete in a long-distance race running length after length of the track, apparently confiding his cares to the river. His hair was long, like a priest's, and pure white; his beard grew long and thick, lending him an air of dignity, while his cloak and the rest of his clothes were of a Greekish appearance. (2.21)

Cnemon can immediately identify the stranger as a priest by his long hair. Obviously, his awareness is based on his Greek knowledge of priests. Yet even apart from Cnemon's *Greek* knowledge, the appearance of the hair and clothes are frequently mentioned as important characteristics of priests, who thus form a clearly defined and identifiable group, as far as their outward appearance is concerned. Hence, Heliodorus depicts the priest as a *type* which is easily recognizable in any context and which even surpasses national borders.[13] Indeed, it is striking that in his first description of Calasiris through Cnemon, Heliodorus does not follow Herodotus' well-known depiction of Egyptian priests, a near *topos* which nonetheless occurs frequently elsewhere in the novel, but prefers a strongly un-Herodotean image: while Herodotus writes that "everywhere else, priests of the gods wear their hair long; in Egypt they are shaven" (2.36) because of strict purification rules,[14] Heliodorus amends this representation, ascribing Greek traits to Calasiris, yet intending that he assume a certain universality. Thus, both the Greek Cnemon and Calasiris' own estranged Egyptian sons at Memphis recognize Calasiris as a priest because of his outward appearance:

> But finally the old man realized that it was his shabby appearance that was preventing his sons from recognizing him, whereupon he

---

[13] For a discussion of Herodotus' account of Egypt and his reliability, cf. Hartog 1988:297–300. The presentation of Egyptian religion in the Greek novel is analyzed by Várhelyi 1997.

[14] All translations from Herodotus are taken from Godley 1920.

> threw off his disguise of rags, untied his priest's hair, cast aside the
> pack from his back and the staff from his hands, and confronted
> them, revealed in all his sacerdotal dignity. (7.7)

By establishing a type of priest whose *phusis* is universally recognizable, the
novel not only establishes a constant which guides a Greek reader through
unfamiliar terrain during the fictional journey from Greece to Egypt,[15] but
it also alerts the reader to the religious dimension: by being reminded of
Calasiris' identity as a priest, the reader is directed towards the larger religious content of the plot, which is shaped by a priest as the representative of
the divine will and who therefore seems to be especially sacred.[16]

Closely related to the universal recognizability of priests is their absolute and unquestioned religious authority, which is respected equally by all
nations and individuals. This applies to Egyptian robbers, who live outside
of society (or the *polis*) and who honor Calasiris' son, Thyamis, by inviting
him to lead the group precisely because he is a priest (1.19), as well as to the
people of Delphi, who allow the Egyptian priest to live on the temple site,
grant him a free living at the expense of the community and honor him like
one of their own priests (2.27). Likewise, a ruler such as the Ethiopian king,
Hydaspes, submits to the advice of the priests; that is, his gymnosophists. In
this respect, neither the origin nor the kind of priesthood is relevant. On the
contrary: in the persons of the three *traveling* priests, Chariclea, the Ethiopian
priestess of Artemis, Calasiris, the Egyptian priest of Isis, and Chaireas, the
Greek priest of Apollo, the novel transgresses borders and nationalities and
argues for the universality of the position of priest. Calasiris holds a preeminent position among other priests only insofar as his relationship with
the gods seems to be extraordinarily close.[17] Thus, he is able to interpret a

---

[15] This also applies to Chariclea, who is perceived as a priestess by the Egyptian Thyamis because
of her clothes (1.20): "But, most important, she seems to me to be the priestess of some god.
Even in dire adversity she thinks it altogether wrong to remove her sacred crown and robe."

[16] Calasiris justifies his proposal to flee from Delphi together with Chariclea and Theagenes by
stressing that this was the wish of the gods, who were guiding and instructing him by way
of prophecies and signs (4.16). Cf. also 3.11: "Apollo and Artemis appeared to me, so I imagined—if indeed I did imagine it and not see them for real ... They called me by name and said:
'It is time now for you to return to the land of your birth, for thus the ordinance of destiny
demands. Go then and take these whom we deliver to you; make them the companions of your
journey; consider them as your own children. From Egypt conduct them onwards wherever
and however it please the gods'."

[17] Calasiris frequently emphasizes this special relationship; for example, at his arrival in Delphi,
when "the place's own oracular voice sang in my ears in tones that truly were heaven-sent"
(2.26), or at 2.25, where he mentions "the god-sent wisdom of which I may not speak."

prophecy correctly upon his arrival at Delphi, which decisively strengthens his religious authority:

> The large crowd of onlookers was loud in their praises of the god for granting me an oracle the very first time I approached him. They pronounced me blessed and thereafter lavished all kinds of attention on me: they said that only one person had ever been more warmly received by the god—a certain Lycurgus from Sparta. (2.27)[18]

The authority of a priest seems to derive entirely from his religious profession, whereas neither his social nor his political position is taken into account. No political functions are ascribed to either Calasiris or Chariclea, nor are they singled out because of any notable descent—in fact, their background is scarcely mentioned; only their priesthood in the *polis* is important.[19] For Heliodorus, it is the profession alone which brings honor to the individual. Thyamis can justify his forthcoming marriage to Chariclea, who is completely unknown to him, thus:

> I put it to you, my friends: what better match could there be than one between a high priest and a consecrated priestess? (1.21)[20]

The "objective" depiction of priests serves to remind the reader of the religious dimension of the love story of Chariclea and Theagenes, who, having submitted themselves to a divine will, are constantly accompanied by priests who help to bring the divine *telos*, that is, the consecration of Chariclea and Theagenes as priest and priestess of Helios and Selene, to its fulfillment. Calasiris seems to be the appropriate person for this task, since he is on good terms with the gods and is able to recognize their will and to realize it. For a listener such as Cnemon, who is primarily interested in the love story of Theagenes and Chariclea, it is conceivable that his understanding of the religious element of the story is confined to the view that Chariclea and

---

[18] Heliodorus is referring to the Spartan lawgiver, whose visit to Delphi is narrated by Herodotus (1.65) in a way which is similar to the portrayal of Calasiris' reception by the priestess: "Lycurgus, a notable Spartan, visited the oracle at Delphi, and when he entered the temple hall, straightway the priestess gave him this response ... Some say that the priestess moreover declared to him the whole governance of Sparta which is now established."

[19] The information that Calasiris' elder son would follow him as high priests of Isis in Memphis (7.2) hints at the traditional inheriting of priesthoods in Egypt, where it remained the privilege of certain upper class families for generations; cf. Thompson 1990:101.

[20] Of course, Thyamis (and the Greek reader) correctly assumes that a beautiful woman is freeborn (cf. Menander, *Heros* fr. 2 K-T), and that a priestess cannot have come from the lower classes.

Theagenes are loved by the gods because they are priests, and that they are aided by priests who are able to interpret the divine will correctly. Yet as the story progresses, and as the reader distances himself from Cnemon, another aspect of the figure of the priest gradually comes to prevail.

b) Calasiris as philosopher: his self-perception

Let us return briefly to Cnemon's first impression of Calasiris:

> ... an old man walking aimlessly along the river bank, pacing to and fro, to and fro, beside the river, like an athlete in a long-distance race running length after length of the track, apparently confiding his cares to the river. His hair was long, like a priest's, and pure white; his beard grew long and thick, lending him an air of dignity, while his cloak and the rest of his clothes were of a Greekish appearance. (2.21)

Cnemon may not observe anything here which is particularly odd, but this figure will strike the reader as being at least a little ambivalent. The long hair, dignified beard, and Greek attire are strongly suggestive of the type of a Greek philosopher, the more so as Calasiris walks up and down the river bank like a peripatetic,[21] pondering and lost in thought. The ambivalent significance of his outward appearance will lead the reader immediately to view Calasiris not merely as a priest but also as a philosopher. As the reader steps back from the perspective of Cnemon and more critically evaluates the latter's account of Calasiris—and if one accepts Calasiris' self-perception as philosopher, explorer, and wise man—this double identification will appear justified. Although at several points Calasiris mentions the close association of scholarship with the priesthood, it is scholarship in which he and the reader are especially interested. Thus he explains his journey to Delphi:

> But I learned that in Greece there was a city called Delphi, sacred to Apollo but a holy place for the other gods too, a retreat where philosophers could work far from the madding crowd. Here I made my way, for it seemed to me that a town devoted to holy rites and ceremonies was a place of refuge well suited to a member of the priestly caste. (2.26)

---

[21] Another possible association could be that of an orator, which, as a figure in the Second Sophistic, was also a familiar sight and whose outward appearance corresponded to that of a philosopher.

Here, Calasiris is partly motivated by religion, but contact with philosophers proves to be the more important interest. His position in Delphi is assured by an oracle from Apollo, but he devotes only part of his time to religious activities:

> In short, my happiness was complete, for I spent my time either performing holy rituals or taking part in sacrifices, which a host of people, both native and foreign, perform each and every day in great numbers and in many forms to win the god's favour; or else in discussions with philosophers, for that type of person congregates in great numbers around the temple of the Pythian Apollo; the whole city is literally a palace of the Muses, permeated by the Apolline spirit of the god who leads them. (2.27)

In what then follows, Calasiris' account of Delphi becomes a speech in praise of his own achievements in the fields of science, art, and philosophy. His report is revealing: after making a general statement about the Greek thirst for knowledge,[22] Calasiris claims that many people came in order to learn something about unfamiliar, Egyptian religious customs; he apparently declines, however, to elaborate further on this subject. Instead, he gives Cnemon and the reader but a hint of his learning. Thus, through the medium of Calasiris' audience within the novel, the reader's curiosity to learn more about Egyptian religion is aroused—only to be disappointed. Calasiris tells us something about the flooding of the Nile (whereby, for the Greek reader, the Herodotean question about the true reasons for the flooding is finally answered by an Egyptian priest),[23] and we learn that Homer was actually of Egyptian descent (3.14). However, even if the religious customs of Egypt are of interest to the Delphian audience which is ostensibly questioning Calasiris, for Heliodorus' reader, they cannot be. The focus on religion deliberately fades, since the only religious festival that Calasiris tells Cnemon and his (Greek) readers about is not an Egyptian but a Greek rite, namely, the popular and well-known Pythian ceremony. In this way, Calasiris directs attention away from himself as priest, and

---

[22] "In short, their questions covered everything there is in Egypt, for Greeks find all Egyptian lore and legend irresistibly attractive" (2.27).

[23] This evident intertextual dialogue with Herodotus *solves* a Herodotean *aporia*: whereas Herodotus cannot offer his readers an explanation which a priest cannot reveal to him (2.19: "Concerning its [the Nile's] nature, neither from the priests nor from any others could I learn anything yet I was zealous to hear from them why it is that the Nile comes down with a rising flood ... Concerning this matter none of the Egyptians could tell me anything"), it is Calasiris who willingly answers the reader's Herodotean question.

towards the scholar and philosopher that he desires to be regarded as. It could almost be said that Calasiris, the priest, is merely a facade for Calasiris, the scholar, who, moreover, seems to dissociate himself verbally from the circle of Egyptian priests by betraying their secret knowledge:

> And so the days passed, until one day one of the more sophisticated ones started to question me about the Nile: what are its sources, what unique power does it have that makes it so different from other rivers, and how is it that, unlike all others, it floods in the summer? I told him everything I knew, all that is recorded about this river in sacred texts, things of which none but members of the priestly caste may read and learn. (2.28)

Emphasizing the close—and for an Egyptian priest, typical—connection between priesthood and scholarship, Calasiris at the same time undermines this relation by revealing fragments of secret knowledge known only to priests, thereby violating their group identity. The longer we listen to Calasiris, the weaker becomes the religious aura that surrounded the priest of Isis at the beginning of the novel and in the portrayal of him by Cnemon. Moreover, in the course of his story (and his transformation into a scholar), Calasiris does not merely qualify his earlier claim to priestly divine inspiration by classifying science as an art of prognostication;[24] in fact, the strongest proof of his own divinity, the correct interpretation of the oracle for Theagenes and Chariclea (a riddle that nobody in Delphi, not even the local oracle priest, could solve), turns out to be nothing more than the crafty invention of a clever man with sufficient experience in life to unravel the prediction without the aid of the gods.[25]

In short, it proves misleading to look at the Egyptian priest through Cnemon's Greek spectacles, so to speak, and to regard Calasiris as if he were a Greek priest, who would perform cult rituals for a certain deity and thus might have a particularly close relationship to the god he represents. On the contrary, Calasiris is not to be associated with any single divinity. He is a universal priest who can be called in anywhere, and who can therefore also participate in sacrificial ceremonies for Apollo in Delphi:

> In short, my happiness was complete, for I spent my time either performing holy rituals or taking part in sacrifices. (2.27)

---

[24] Science "studies the movements of the stars and thus gains knowledge of the future" (3.16).
[25] Cf. Baumbach 1997.

In this respect, the comparison between Calasiris and Charicles is illuminating, since Charicles is expressly presented as a Greek priest. He is associated with only one deity (Apollo) and one sanctuary (Delphi), performing the rituals there as they are prescribed. He has not received any special education, which was neither characteristic of nor a precondition for a Greek priesthood.[26] Schooling, however, becomes the most important criterion of a priest, especially in a novel which abandons all other features which would distinguish a priest. Hence, apart from providing the opportunity to witness the activity of an Egyptian priest in Greece, the confrontation between Charicles, the typical priest, and Calasiris, who is independent of both place and cult, encourages the reader to question familiar notions of the Greek priest and to look at him through Egyptian spectacles, from the point of view of Calasiris, for whom education is the main criterion even for priests. In this respect, two points are particularly interesting.

First, on several occasions Charicles implores Calasiris—because he is an Egyptian priest and scholar—to help him convince Chariclea to marry the Greek he has chosen for her. He is convinced that Calasiris can use magic to bewitch Chariclea.[27] Calasiris agrees,[28] although he does not believe in magic, which he has previously dismissed as a sign of a lack of education. By demanding an enchantment from him, Charicles disqualifies himself as entirely uneducated, at least according to Calasiris' classification of the two different types of wisdom:

> There is one kind that is of low rank and, you might say, crawls upon the earth; it waits upon ghosts and skulks around dead bodies; it is addicted to magic herbs, and spells are its stock-in-trade ... But there is another kind, my son, true wisdom, of which the first sort is but a counterfeit that has stolen its title; true wisdom it is that we priests and members of the sacerdotal caste practice from childhood; its eyes are raised towards heaven. (3.16)

---

[26] For the Greek priest, cf. Beard 1990:45: "the Greek term *hiereus* (priest) at least evoked one well-defined category of religious official, within a standard cult framework. The hiereus was the functionary of one particular deity (the 'priest of Apollo') and was traditionally attached to one particular sanctuary of that deity."

[27] For example in 2.33: "Be with me, Calasiris, my dear friend. Use your magic and cast an Egyptian spell on her."

[28] Cf. Calasiris' performance in 4.5: "Having secured our privacy, I launched into a sort of stage performance, producing clouds of incense smoke, pursing my lips and muttering some sounds that passed for prayers, waving the laurel up and down, up and down, from Chariclea's head to her toes, and yawning blearily, for all the world like some old beldam."

Since, according to Calasiris, true priests reject the use of magic, Charicles cannot be one.

Second, it becomes obvious that even as priest of a Greek oracle, Charicles does not, and should not, have any authority. Not only does he fail to help Chariclea, although he claims that "priests are quite capable of putting even the greatest wrongs to right" (3.18); he is also unable to interpret oracles and dreams at his own shrine. When he calls on Calasiris to consult him about a dream, he is told:

> For a priest, and the priest of the god with the greatest powers
> of prophecy at that, you strike me as a pretty poor interpreter of
> dreams. (4.15)

Hence, Charicles is systematically dismantled before the eyes of the reader and shown to be uneducated, unqualified, and unsuited. He simply cannot compete with Calasiris, and is therefore left in Delphi while Calasiris takes over the responsibility for Chariclea and Theagenes. Calasiris' wisdom and knowledge of human nature (the two qualities which enable him to interpret the oracle) make him an appropriate guide for the protagonists. As such, he can be, and desires to be, acknowledged less as a priest than as a wise man, and the figures in the novel increasingly recognize him as such: Cnemon, Theagenes, and Chariclea repeatedly address him as *sophōtate* (wisest) or as *sophos anēr* (wise man),[29] and thus lead the reader towards the identity of the *divine man* that—as a concept—seems to be hidden behind the figure of Calasiris.

c) Calasiris as *theios anēr*: the reader's perception

If we consider both his self-portrayal as philosopher-priest and the perception of him by others who render him as a priest loved by god, the figure of Calasiris combines certain traits of the divine man (*theios anēr*), who as a *type* appears in the second and third centuries AD.[30] The original reader, familiar with these traits from the cultural environment and from *paideia*, is encouraged here to evaluate Calasiris according to the conventional characteristics of a wise man. In this context, the following aspects are to be taken into account.

In literary sources dating from the third century AD and later, the divine man appears as both a Christian (Origen)[31] and especially as a pagan figure (Apollonius, Plotinus, Iamblichus). Besides conspicuous beauty, a benevolent

---

[29] So, in 3.11 *ō sophōtate* (Theagenes), 3.93, and 4.10 *ō sophe Kalasiri* (Chariclea).
[30] For the appearance of the *theios anēr*, cf. Bieler 1935; Du Toit 1997; and Fowden 1982.
[31] See Tloka 2003.

nature, and divine election, the main characteristic feature is his extraordinary (pagan) education (*paideia*), which is acquired from early childhood by his contact with philosophy and which finally becomes the decisive factor for his qualification as *theios anēr*.[32] A significant criterion that pagan and Christian divine men share, as it were the *conditio sine qua non*, is the rejection of magic. For this reason, Philostratus, for example, in his description of Apollonius, must first clear him of the accusation of being a magician before he can establish him as a *theios anēr*.[33] From the early third century at the latest, the figure of the divine man became a permanent role model in pagan philosophical circles, especially among the Neoplatonists, and the term is often used to express admiration for teachers (for example, in Diogenes Laertius or Porphyry). In this respect, Plato and Pythagoras can be recognized as prototypes who combined exemplary philosophy (Plato) with an exemplary way of life (Pythagoras).[34]

When we compare this figure with Heliodorus' representation of Calasiris, there are several points of contact. In its content, Calasiris' story displays an impressive number of references to Plato,[35] by means of which he is made to resemble Plato.[36] Calasiris is also directly associated with the prototypes of the divine man. Charicles, for example, notices at a festival that Calasiris does not drink wine, which is explained as follows: "He does not drink wine nor eat any creature that is endowed with a soul" (3.11). When Theagenes asks for the reason, Charicles answers: "He comes from Memphis, in Egypt, where he is a high priest of Isis" (3.11). The refusal to eat meat because of its origin is a characteristic feature of a Pythagorean, whose way of life forms a model for the divine man of the third century AD.[37] In spite of the frequent use of Herodotus in the novel, Charicles, in his ignorance, supposes Calasiris' practice to be an Egyptian peculiarity.[38] Calasiris' strict rejection of magic is emphasized repeat-

---

[32] In the case of Christian *divine men,* orthodox religious belief combined with a sound knowledge of the Scriptures is a further characteristic, as their reliability as mediators between God and men must be ensured.

[33] See Hahn 2003:91.

[34] Cf. Fowden 1982:34, 36.

[35] Cf. Hilton 1996:192–193.

[36] The allegorical interpretation of the novel by the Neoplatonist Philip also indicates that Heliodorus was already associated with Plato in Antiquity.

[37] Cf. also the parallel with Apollonius, whose presentation in Philostratus is analyzed by Hahn 2003:92: "To the popular and at the same time strongly attacked tradition and admiration of Apollonius Philostratus opposed a totally different Apollonius, a Pythagorean philosopher ... whose divine nature and whose extraordinary ability to perform miracles and to forsee the future are based on an unprecedented wisdom which was gained not least by a strict Pythagorean lifestyle" (my translation).

[38] Herodotus 2.37: "they [the Egyptian priests] neither consume nor spend aught of their own;

edly, and is articulated in his distinction between true wisdom (*alēthos sophia*) and common wisdom (*dēmodēs sophia*),[39] a distinction which is typical of a *theios anēr*. As Charicles urges him to bewitch Chariclea, he puts him, as it were, to the test, while in book 7, Calasiris' attitude towards black magic becomes apparent when he witnesses a séance:

> But he [Calasiris] refused, saying that the mere sight of such things was unclean and that he could only tolerate it because he had no alternative; it was not proper for a priest either to take part in or to be present at such rites; the prophetic powers of priests proceeded from legitimate sacrifice and pure prayer, whereas those of the profane were obtained literally by crawling upon the ground and skulking among corpses, as the accidents of circumstances had permitted them to see this Egyptian woman doing. (6.14)[40]

Calasiris, however, is not a perfect *theios anēr*. In general terms, the description of him in the *Aethiopica* conforms to that of a divine man, but it diverges in various details. Besides the lack of a beautiful, indeed of any extraordinary, outward appearance,[41] he displays an at times somewhat dubious manner, which reminds us of a fraud or "trickster" (Winkler); for example, when he lies to Charicles or allows him to believe that he uses magic. Moreover, Calasiris himself seems to be seeking perfection as he travels to broaden his knowledge. Thus, as noted above, he desires to meet with wise men in Delphi precisely for the same reason he claims to have come to Ethiopia, namely, to learn the wisdom of the country and its people.[42] It was also characteristic of a *theios anēr* that he have a group of students about him.[43] Calasiris seeks out other scholars in Memphis and in Delphi, but he does not appear to want his own students. Theagenes and Chariclea, who seem to be "glad to

---

sacred food is cooked for them, to each man is brought every day flesh of beeves and geese in great abundance, and wine of grapes too is given to them."

[39] See Bieler 1935:75.

[40] Heliodorus seems to share Calasiris' attitude towards black magic, to judge by the course of the events (the old woman dies shortly after), as well as by an accompanying authorial statement: "So she died, bringing instant and fitting fulfillment to the prophecy that her son had given her" (6.15).

[41] This criterion is frequently mentioned and regarded as proof of a holy man: cf. Bieler 1935:51; and Philostratus, *VA* 1.7; Porphyry, *Vita Plotini* 10; Iamblichus, *VP* 5.20.

[42] Cf. 4.12: "my travels took me as far as the land of the Ethiopians, whose wisdom I was eager to learn."

[43] See Fowden 1982:38: "The pagan holy man's primary social function was that of a teacher of philosophy; and his primary social milieu was provided by his own disciples."

receive [Calasiris'] assistance" (3.19), are the first and only ones who follow him. Finally, he lacks any deeper understanding of cult rites, and perhaps even of their reform, which is often mentioned in the portrayal of divine men and which distinguishes Apollonius of Tyana as a *theios anēr*.[44]

The type of the *theios anēr*, then, does not find its perfection in the figure of Calasiris, who is himself still seeking perfection. Yet he serves as a forerunner and signpost in the novel: he brings Chariclea and Theagenes to Ethiopia, the symbol of true wisdom, where alone the two are recognized as divine people, and where they will realize in themselves what is merely pointed to in Calasiris.

Calasiris himself—and this is a decisive point for my interpretation—has never been in Ethiopia, but only invented the story of his journey to Meroë in order to convince Chariclea to leave Delphi.[45]

3. The *Aethiopica* as a Program of Education for a *theios anēr*

In Heliodorus' *Aethiopica*, the destination of the journey of Chariclea and Theagenes is Ethiopia, a country which must be the destination of everyone seeking to "bring about the apotheosis of the wisdom of Egypt by supplementing it with the wisdom of Ethiopia" (4.12), as Calasiris puts it. In the tenth and final book of the *Aethiopica*, we encounter truly divine men such as the Ethiopian gymnosophists and especially their leader, Sisimithres. They are depicted with all the attributes of the *theios anēr* and, as it were, as a final proof of their divinity, they reform the Ethiopian cult in an important way, by eliminating human sacrifice.[46] The novel therefore leads the reader as well as the protagonists to the inner circle of divine people. For Chariclea and Theagenes, the way to this *telos* was paved by Calasiris, who picks them up in Delphi and takes them to Egypt. This journey is marked out by three priests, each of whom is characterized by a greater degree of perfection. First, there is the ordinary Greek priest (Charicles), then Calasiris, and finally, a truly divine man

---

[44] Fowden 1982:52: "But it was the pagan holy man's direct involvement with pagan cults that most deeply compromised his social position. The centrality of this development to the holy man's self-image should not be underestimated ... Apollonius of Tyana never missed an opportunity to reform and purify the temple rites wherever he went."

[45] Cf. Baumbach 1997.

[46] Cf. 10.7–9. Sisimithres rejects the sacrifice as sacrilegious: "Now we [the Gymnosophists] shall withdraw into the temple, for neither can we ourselves approve of anything as barbaric as human sacrifice nor do we believe that it is pleasing to the divinity. I only wish it were possible to put an end to all animal sacrifices as well and be satisfied with offerings of prayers and incense such as we make" (10.9).

(Sisimithres). With all three men, Chariclea has a father-daughter relationship,[47] which becomes clear at the end of the story. As an abandoned child, she was raised by Sisimithres until she was seven, before he gave her to Charicles, from whom she went to Calasiris, who brought her back to Ethiopia. Like the reader, she got to know all three figures of priests and stages of knowledge. She was taught by them, and finally together with Theagenes she returns to her homeland to receive the highest consecration of a priestess, that of Selene, while Theagenes becomes the priest of Helios.

In mentioning these deities, Heliodorus not only alludes to their symbolism of light, which provides the protagonists as well as the reader with an all-embracing illumination, but he completes the religious syncretism which is presented in the figure of the priest. With Selene and Helios, he makes the Ethiopians worship the same deities who were worshipped in Delphi right at the beginning of the novel and whose cult can also be represented by an Egyptian priest (Calasiris). Thus, for his Greek readers, Heliodorus creates a syncretistic *kosmos* in which religious differences are marginalized or do not exist, and which extends from the *omphalos* in Delphi to the edge of the civilized (because Greek-speaking) world in Ethiopia.[48] From this point of view, it is only consistent that the priests as representatives of this syncretistic religion also have syncretistic characteristics: like Calasiris, they become universalists who can be employed everywhere and who serve the one religion in an exemplary fashion. They become role models with whom all Greeks can identify without any difficulty. At the same time, the leveling of differences in cult and religion in the persons of Heliodorus' priests releases a potential which in turn makes a more far-reaching equality ultimately possible: education. The more the priest loses his specific identity through his association with a cult and a nation, the more important his education—as an identity-creating element—becomes. Like Calasiris, who recognizes the omnipotence of Apollo (Helios) earlier than the other characters in the novel, the reader is intended to recognize education as being the only means of establishing a religious syncretism, and his own education leads him to this recognition.

---

[47] Chariclea emphasizes her close relation with the priests by calling both, Calasiris and Charicles, father; cf. for example, 4.5 and 7.14 (after the death of Calasiris): "No more may I call anyone Father, the best of names, for heaven has made it its sport at every turn to deny me the right to address anyone as my father. My natural father I have never seen; my adoptive father, Charicles, alas, I have betrayed; now I have lost the man who took me into his care, cherished me, and saved my life."

[48] Cf. also Merkelbach 1962:235, who states that Heliodorus wrote his novel—which he interprets as a novel about the Mysteries (*Mysterienroman*)—"not for Syria alone but for the Roman empire as a whole."

Heliodorus' story, which began as a typical romantic novel, written for Cnemon, a romantic listener, has become a discourse about the (new) role of the priest in a syncretistic religion and about his transformation into a divine man.[49] Thus, the love story becomes a superstructure for reflection about the perception, the self-image, and the cultural importance of divine men, who alone succeed in doing their job regardless of national and cultural differences, and in solving worldly and religious problems (concerning, for example, issues such as love and human sacrifice) as role models in Egyptian, Greek, and Ethiopian society. Accordingly, for Heliodorus, crossing religious boundaries does not mean that an Egyptian priest comes to Greece to comment on Greek conditions, or to criticize or abolish them. Instead, Heliodorus deliberately eliminates all religious differences, whether they exist in the cult, in the clothes, or in the mentality of the people involved, so that he can propagate a new type of priest, the *theios anēr*. For such a man, religious and cultural boundaries do not exist, and priests' identities are not tied to particular, local cults; instead, such a man can become a role model for readers of all religious persuasions and beliefs in the entire Roman Empire,[50] even for the Christians, who, as it happens, made Heliodorus a bishop.[51] The question as to what extent this concept of a divine man originates from a search for role models in a society which in the third and fourth centuries AD was inundated with cults and religions must remain unanswered. The story was told in fiction by a direct descendent of Helios: Heliodorus, who eventually numbered himself among the priests. Thus, he wants to provide his work with particular authority, and he tries to surpass other works of literature about divine men, like Philostratus' *Life of Apollonius*. As author, he has the authority of a *theios anēr*:

So concludes the *Aethiopica*, the story of Theagenes and Chariclea, the work of a Phoenician from the city of Emesa, one of the clan of the Descendants of the Sun,[52] Theodosius' son, Heliodorus. (10.41)

---

[49] There is also epigraphic evidence for a new *type* of priest from the second century AD onward, which suggests that education became a more important criterion for the election of priests, who were likewise described as philosophers; cf. Haake in this volume.

[50] For the tendency in the literature of imperial Rome to construct universal, polytheistic figures, see Elsner 1997:34–37.

[51] Cf. Socrates Scholasticus, V 22; and Photius, *Bibl. Cod.* 73: "later he [Heliodorus] became a bishop."

[52] For the dynasty of priests in Emesa and the link between the Emesian god and Helios, cf. Fick 2002; Altheim 1942.

Part Five

MANTEIS: PRIESTS AT ALL?

9

The Iamidae
A Mantic Family and Its Public Image

Michael A. Flower

E VERY STUDENT OF GREEK HISTORY knows that the Peloponnesian War was brought to an end when Lysander, the brilliant and ruthless Spartan admiral, captured the entire Athenian fleet at Aegospotami in 405 BC. What is less well known, perhaps familiar only to a handful of scholars with an interest in Greek divination, is that Lysander was not given the full credit for this victory. For Pausanias the travel writer tells us something that other sources leave out:

> They say that Agias while acting as seer to Lysander captured the Athenian fleet at Aegospotami except for ten ships." (3.11.5)

Pausanias' opinion that it was Lysander's seer who captured the Athenian fleet is partly confirmed by a monument which was erected at Delphi and which has been partially recovered (Pausanias 10.9.7): on the so-called Navarchs monument, Lysander dedicated a statue both of himself and of his seer Agias.[1] There was also a bronze statue of Agias in the marketplace in Sparta itself (Pausanias 3.11.5). This Agias was obviously a famous person at Sparta and perhaps throughout the whole of Greece. And yet he was the grandson of an even more famous seer, that Tisamenus of Elis who, as Herodotus says, "won" the battle of Plataea and was "commander with the Spartan kings" (Herodotus 9.33–35). In this essay I will not be as interested in what particular seers actually did or said as in recovering what it meant to be a seer and how a seer might represent himself. How did seers fashion an image for themselves? What kind of image was important? What was the relationship between image making and actual success in one's career? And given that the rituals of divination consti-

---

[1] The manuscripts at Pausanias 10.9.7 mistakenly read "Abas."

tuted a type of public performance, how did the seer go about scripting his own role? Our ancient sources do not address these types of questions directly, and thus the answers must be inferred through a close reading of texts. Recent work on the anthropology of divination can provide both a theoretical framework and clues for how to read our sources.[2] As a case study, we will consider the most famous mantic family of the fifth century BC and the one about which we have the most information, the Iamidae, the family to which both Agias and his grandfather Tisamenus belonged.[3] Although this is a study in microhistory, I will attempt to situate my conclusions within a larger macro framework.

At the outset it will prove useful to clarify exactly what it meant to be a seer. The Greek word is *mantis*. A *mantis* (variously translated as 'soothsayer', 'diviner', 'prophet', or, as here, 'seer') was an expert in the art of divination.[4] Because Greek religious terminology is inexact, the person called a *mantis* dealt with a broad range of religious activities, and the term embraces a variety of prophetic types, ranging from the interpreters of signs, to ecstatic mediums, to purifiers and healers.[5] Although the Pythia, who served as the mouthpiece of the god Apollo in his oracular seat at Delphi, like other priestesses may be called a *mantis*,[6] I am concerned here only with the mobile *mantis* who usually, although perhaps not always, was male.[7] He practiced what the Greeks called a craft or skill (*mantikē tekhnē*);[8] and the aim of this craft was to ascertain the will and intentions of the gods in relation to human actions. Seers tended to move from city to city, attaching themselves to prominent generals

---

[2] Especially useful are Peek 1991, LaGamma 2000, and Pemberton 2000, which explore both the social function of divination and the performative aspects of divinatory rituals.

[3] The main treatments of the Iamidae are Bouché-Leclercq: 1879–1882, 2:59–69; Weniger 1915:66–76; Hepding *RE* IX 685–689 s.v. *Iamos*; Löffler 1963:27–28; Kett 1966:84–93; Parke 1967:174–178; Roth 1982:222–231.

[4] On the role of the *mantis* in Greek society, see esp. Kett 1966; Lonis 1979:95–115; Pritchett 1979:47–90; Roth 1982; Jameson 1991; Bremmer 1993; Bremmer 1996a. I explore this topic more fully in *The Seer in Ancient Greece* (University of California Press, 2008).

[5] For brief discussions, see Roth 1982:7–9; Bowden 2003:257–264.

[6] The term *mantis* is applied to the Pythia (Aeschylus *Eumenides* 29), the Sibyl (Suda, s.v. *Sibyla Chaldaia*), and to Cassandra (Aeschylus *Agamemnon* 1275). Herodotus calls the priestesses of the oracle of Zeus at Dodona *promanties* (2.55).

[7] Both artistic remains (a remarkable fifth-century BC grave stele from Mantinea depicts a woman holding a liver in her left hand: see Möbius 1967) and epigraphic evidence (*SEG* 35.626: the epitaph of the third-century BC *mantis* Satyra from Larissa) suggest that there were at least some female seers who fulfilled a social function similar to that of the male seers discussed in this essay. Although Plato does not call her such, his Diotima, who delayed the onset of the plague at Athens by ten years (*Symposium* 201d), would seem to be a *mantis*.

[8] For the term, see Aeschylus *Prometheus Bound* 484; Sophocles *Oedipus Tyrannus* 709; Herodotus 2.49, 83.

and statesmen as their personal advisers; the most successful seers were what Walter Burkert has called "migrant charismatic specialists."[9] With this combination of skill and charisma, *manteis* were the most authoritative experts on religious matters: they were religious specialists, or "agents of control within their religion's symbolic universe."[10] Their competence was exceptionally broad, encompassing all of the various forms of divination that were practiced in Archaic and Classical Greece: these included the interpretation of bird signs, dreams, portents, and entrails. Nonetheless, sacrificial divination was the principal art of the seer who assisted generals on campaign and who won battles in partnership with them. The military seer was responsible for two types of sacrificial divination that necessarily preceded an engagement: the camp-ground sacrifice called *hiera* and the battle-line sacrifice called *sphagia*. The former (*hiera*) was usually performed by examining the victim's liver (the victim was usually a sheep), and the latter (*sphagia*) was performed by slitting the victim's throat (often a young she-goat) while observing the animal's movements and the flow of blood.[11]

It is essential to distinguish seers from priests since, although they performed different functions in Greek society, they are often confused. A priest (*hiereus*), whether male or female, was an appointed public official who obtained office by lot, election, birth, or purchase. Priests usually had no special religious training or knowledge, and their function was principally concerned with ritual. The priest's prime responsibility as *hiereus* was to manage the offerings, sacrifices, and the sanctuary itself and its property, all of which were *hiera* (sacred).[12] The difference between priest and seer has been well expressed as follows:

> In contrast to the priest, whose prestige derived from the renown of the cult he administered, the seer owed his prestige to the success and reliability of his prophecies."[13]

Of course, both seer and priest could derive prestige from their membership in an aristocratic clan or lineage (*genos*), such as the Athenian families of the Eumolpidae and Ceryces who were the hereditary priests of the Eleusinian Mysteries. But unlike a priest, a seer was not merely a performer of prescribed

---

[9] Burkert 1992:42.

[10] See the insightful analysis of religious specialists by Rüpke 1996.

[11] For these sacrifices, see esp. Szymanski 1908; Pritchett 1971:109–115; Pritchett 1979:73–90; Jameson 1991; Parker 2000.

[12] Mikalson 2004:11.

[13] Harris 1995:27.

rituals; he had to be successful in the practice of a skill or craft that depended on expertise and experience, and which might involve considerable personal danger. The priest, insofar as his authority depended on his office, had no need to possess personal charisma; for the seer, such charisma was the basis of his authority and an essential aspect of his persona.[14]

We know the names of about seventy historical seers of Archaic and Classical Greece, but for most of them we simply do not know if their fathers and grandfathers had been seers as well. The evidence that we do have, however, indicates that it was highly desirable to be able to advertise that one's ancestors had also been seers. For instance, a stele from an Attic peribolus tomb of the classical period bears the inscription:

> Here I cover a wise and just man, Calliteles, the *mantis*, son of the honored *mantis* Meidoteles." (*SEG* 23.161)[15]

Although by the end of the fifth century BC it was possible to acquire books on divination, we know of only one seer who apparently was completely self-taught and had a successful career.[16] Thrasyllus, a Siphnian, was bequeathed books on divination, as well as some property, by his guest-friend the seer Polemaenetus. With those books in hand, he became an itinerant seer and acquired a large fortune. All of this is reported thirdhand some fifty years later by the speaker of Isocrates' forensic speech *Aegineticus* (5–7, 45). It is important to note that the speaker's testimony cannot be taken at face value, since his version of their relationship provides a precedent for the very type of transfer of property that he is seeking to defend. He initially says (6) that Thrasyllus was self-taught ("taking those books as his starting point, he practiced the craft"), but he later states (45) that he "learned his art from Polemaenetus." Perhaps we can speculate that Polemaenetus actually had adopted Thrasyllus and trained him as his apprentice, in which case Thrasyllus could have represented himself to his clients as the latter's son. Yet even if a Greek seer was able to obtain various technical handbooks through which he could acquire some basic knowledge, it is impossible that these books could have contained the elaborate and comprehensive lists of omens such as were recorded on the many hundreds of cuneiform tablets that have been discov-

---

[14] The classic treatment of charismatic authority is Weber 1978, 1:241–254 (first published in 1922). The seer is endowed with personal charisma, which is due to his *personal* qualifications, as opposed to the charisma of office (a type of institutionalized charisma) that may be possessed by a priest. Note also Lindholm 1990.

[15] *SEG* 23.161. See Mastrokostas 1966:282; Garland 1982:168–169.

[16] See Pritchett 1979:73; and Dickie 2001:68, 70.

ered in Mesopotamia.[17] All seers in the Greek world by necessity had to rely on their own skill in interpretation, a skill that was validated by personal charisma rather than by book learning.[18]

The most respected and sought-after seers belonged to families that had practiced seercraft for many generations, reaching back to an eponymous ancestor who had acquired prophetic power either as the gift of a god (usually Apollo) or by some other supernatural means. The prophetic gift that endows the family did not necessarily have to belong to the mythical or legendary past. Herodotus (9.92–94) tells the story of how Zeus and Apollo, in the generation before the Persian invasions, gave to Euenius of Apollonia as a gift "the innate faculty of divination." In the eyes of his clients, a seer's authority and credibility depended on his belonging to an established family of seers. This, we may presume, had a double purpose. First, it was proof that the craft of divination had been acquired in apprenticeship to a master who was a member of one's own family. Second, the seer must have represented himself as possessing an innate capacity for divination, a prophetic gift that he had inherited.

The four most distinguished clans of Greek seers were the Melampodidae, Iamidae, Clytiadae, and Telliadae.[19] Each of these clans claimed descent from legendary seers of the heroic age: Melampus, Iamus, Clytius, and Tellias respectively. Nothing is recorded about Tellias and exceedingly little about Clytius (his genealogy is given by Pausanias at 6.17.6), but the story of how Melampus learned the language of birds, when his ears were licked by snakes, apparently was told in some detail by Hesiod in his lost poems *Melampodeia* and *Greater Ehoiai* (F 261 MW).[20] Members of all these families figure prominently in the pages of Herodotus. Megistias, an Acarnanian said to be a descendant of Melampus, served and died with the Spartans at Thermopylae (7.219, 221, 228). He took his only son with him, and then sent him away before the Greeks were surrounded; it is a fair inference that the boy was serving as apprentice to his father. The Elean seer Tellias (surely one of the Telliadae), by devising a clever

---

[17] On the complex subject of Mesopotamian divination, a good place to start is Oppenheim 1977:206–227.

[18] The difference between Mesopotamian and Greek divination is succinctly expressed by Trampedach 2003a:266–280. See further Trampedach in this volume.

[19] There was also a famous clan of hereditary seers at Telmessus in Caria, among whom was that Aristander who so successfully served both Philip II and Alexander the Great: see Herodotus 1.78, 84; Aristophanes fr. 554 Kassel–Austin; Cicero *On Divination* 1.91, 94; Arrian 2.3.3; with Harvey 1991. Another famous non-Greek mantic clan was the Galeotae of Sicily: see Cicero *On Divination* 1.39; Pausanias 5.23.6; with Parke 1967:178–179, 191–192.

[20] On Melampus, see especially Suarez de la Torre 1992.

stratagem, helped the Phocians to defeat a Thessalian army that had invaded Phocis a few years before the invasion of Xerxes (8.27). The most renowned of the Telliadae was Hegesistratus, who served Mardonius at Plataea (9.37.1).

It is often remarked on, but difficult to explain, that with the exception of the Melampodidae, all of these families came from Elis in the northwestern Peloponnese. There was, however, something unique about the self-representation of the Iamidae that set them apart from these other mantic families. They alone claimed an immediate divine descent, since Iamus was the son of Apollo and grandson of Poseidon. The importance of belonging to one of the established families of seers seems obvious enough, but does it actually tell us who these seers were? Given that there surely was no historical seer named Iamus, is it still possible that all of the Iamidae were related in the sense that they belonged to a single clan linked by connections of blood? Genealogies are malleable entities. Even when people sincerely believe them to be accurate, they may be false.[21] The function of such claims to kinship and descent is of far greater interest to us here than their truth or falsehood (which cannot be recovered in any case).

Herodotus says that the seer Deïphonus, who was serving with the Greek fleet in 479, passed himself off as the son of the famous seer Euenius of Apollonia:

> I have before now heard that trading on the name of Euenius he was contracting work throughout Greece, although he was not the son of Euenius." (9.95)

This single sentence tells us two important things: that a blood connection to a successful seer was helpful for gaining upscale employment, and that such claims were not accepted uncritically. Society was not a tacit accomplice in a sham, nor were seers merely the members of guilds, such as the Homeridae or Asclepiadae, among whom the adoption of an apprentice by his master was clothed in the language of kinship. It was fundamentally important that the seer was believed to be what he claimed to be, literally the blood descendant of another seer.

The foundation myth of the Iamidae is told by Pindar in his sixth *Olympian*.[22] This poem was written for Hagesias of Syracuse, an Iamid who served as seer to the tyrant Hieron and who was victorious in the mule-cart

---

[21] See Thomas 1989:155–195 on the nature of Greek genealogies.

[22] For the substantial bibliography on this poem, see Hutchinson 2001:371n16. Carne-Ross 1979, and Goldhill 1991:146–166, are particularly noteworthy as literary analyses.

race at Olympia in 472 or 468 BC. As Pindar tells the tale (*Olympian* 6.57–74), Apollo bestowed upon his son Iamus "a twofold treasury of divination," and "from that time the clan of the Iamidae has been much renowned among Hellenes." That twofold treasury was "to hear the voice that is unknowing of lies" (most probably the voice of Apollo[23]) and "to establish an oracle on the summit of Zeus' altar" at Olympia. Whether an Iamid actually established the oracle is beyond historical recovery, but during the imperial period, and probably as far back as the fifth century BC, the Iamidae shared the stewardship of Zeus' oracle with the Clytiadae, a post which they jointly held through the third century AD.[24] At least one Iamid in each generation had fixed employment at Olympia, where later sources tell us that they practiced divination atop Zeus' altar by examining the cracks in the burnt skins of sacrificial animals.[25] In the case of these particular seers, the general distinction between seer and priest becomes blurred; for in addition to practicing divination, they were responsible for the care of the great altar of Zeus and for certain monthly sacrifices, and those were duties of a kind that usually belonged to priests, not to seers.[26] Since only one seer was chosen from each of the two families to work the oracle, other members might seek employment as itinerant diviners throughout the Greek world.

And indeed we do have evidence that members of the Iamidae were active throughout the Greek world as migrant charismatic specialists. On occasion a seer might settle in the community that he had successfully served, and there may have been branches of the Iamidae not only in Syracuse and Sparta but also in Messenia; in Croton in South Italy; and in Arcadian Stymphalus.[27] Previous scholarship on the Iamidae has been highly positivist in nature, and has concentrated on recovering who was and who was not an Iamid, where members actually settled, and what they actually did. But what our sources tell us is perhaps more useful for recovering the self-representation both of the Iamidae as a clan and of its individual members than it is for establishing historical truth. Charismatics authorize their activities and establish confi-

---

[23] Scholion 113a says of this line: "to hear the voice of the gods or of birds." Löffler 1963:28 rightly interprets the phrase as the unerring voice of Apollo: so also Hutchinson 2001:404–405.

[24] Inscriptions from Olympia (for which see Weniger 1915) only list the officiating seers from 36 BC to AD 265, but Pindar calls Hagesias "steward of the mantic altar of Zeus in Pisa." Schachter 2000 argues that the Clytiadae came into prominence only at a relatively late date, but this seems unlikely given the epigram of Eperastus discussed below.

[25] See Parke 1967:184–185.

[26] See Pausanias 5.13.11; 5.15.10; with Weniger 1915:104ff; Roth 1982:181–183.

[27] The evidence for a Messenian branch of the Iamidae is highly suspect, since it is found in Pausanias' account of the Second Messenian war (4.16–23).

dence in themselves by projecting an image, and it is that image which our sources reflect.

Pindar, for instance, describes Hagesias thus:

> If someone were an Olympic victor, steward of the mantic altar of Zeus in Pisa, and joint-founder of famous Syracuse, what hymn of praise could such a man escape, if he should find his fellow townsmen ungrudging in the midst of delightful songs? (lines 4–6)

Now Hagesias, living in Syracuse, could not literally have been one of the seers in charge of the oracle at Olympia; what Pindar must mean is that as an Iamid he was theoretically eligible to hold that position. So much is obvious. But the last claim has been the cause of considerable modern controversy. What did Pindar mean by "joint-founder"? Should we believe the scholiasts to Pindar in their assertions that this word alludes to the fact that members of the Iamidae had followed Archias, the *oikist*, to Syracuse in ca. 733 BC?[28] Or did Hagesias somehow deserve the title in his own right because Syracuse had been refounded by the tyrant Gelon? Perhaps these are the wrong types of questions to ask. As a matter of fact, we cannot hope to know when Hagesias' ancestors had migrated to Syracuse, nor even if he really was an Iamid by ties of blood and kinship. This is because we are not dealing with facts that could be authenticated, but with family tradition, or even with a tradition that was invented by Hagesias himself. And indeed we can see that Pindar is stressing what was important to Hagesias' self-projection as a successful *mantis*: that he was an Olympic victor, that by hereditary right he was steward of Zeus' oracle, and that he came from one of the oldest Syracusan families. The only established fact is his Olympic victory; the rest is merely unverifiable assertion and the projection of an image.

The Syracusan branch of the Iamidae, whatever its antiquity, seems to have come to an end with this Hagesias, who apparently was murdered after the fall of Hieron.[29] The Iamidae fared better, at least in the long term, at Croton. The Iamid Callias, whom Herodotus calls an Elean, assisted Croton

---

[28] I am not persuaded by Malkin 1987:96–97 that the term *sunoikistēr* is applied to Hagesias himself on the grounds that the tyranny of Gelon was regarded as a refoundation of Syracuse; cf. Hutchinson 2001:378–379. Luraghi 1997a argues that Hagesias' father and mother both came from Stymphalus (his father had been granted citizenship there and his mother was a native Arcadian). Hornblower 2004:182–186 suggests that the scholiasts are right, and that "the compliment consists, not of granting Hagesias a fictitious title of oikist, but of transferring the ancestral role of the Iamids as co-founders of Syracuse to Hagesias the Iamid of Pindar's own time" (185).

[29] See scholion 165 with Kett 1966:18–20.

in her war with Sybaris in 510 and was richly rewarded with select estates (5.44–45). Herodotus claims that his descendants still possessed that land in his own day. But this Callias must have needed to explain something that was especially awkward and embarrassing: that is, how did he end up serving the Crotoniates when he had been hired by the tyrant of Sybaris? I cannot think of a single seer who changed sides in the middle of a conflict, and one imagines that there was some unofficial code of conduct which dictated against such high-handed acts. His justification, I would suggest, is embedded in Herodotus' narrative:

> The people of Croton say that Callias ran away from Telys the tyrant of the Sybarites and came to them, since the sacrifices (*hiera*) were not turning out favorable for him when he was sacrificing against Croton.

One might be tempted to rationalize this explanation by conjecturing that the Crotoniates had offered Callias more money or that he calculated that Sybaris would lose the war. But Herodotus himself takes this explanation at face value, and he apparently expects his readers to do the same. Within the Greek divinatory system of knowledge and belief, in which system Callias was a specialist, unfavorable omens from sacrificial divination were a necessary and sufficient explanation for human action. We see this time and again in the works of Xenophon, particularly in the *Anabasis*.[30] The imperfect tense in the phrase "were not turning out favorable" indicates that Callias tried repeatedly to obtain good omens, but that the gods were unwilling to grant them. He thus represented himself as having fully discharged his duties to his original employer; the will of the gods was clear, and there was no need to perish in a doomed cause.

In the Hellenistic period, we find an Elean Iamid named Thrasybulus serving with the Mantineans against the Lacedaemonians under King Agis IV (244–241 BC). He "both foretold victory to the Mantineans and himself took part in the fighting" (Pausanias 8.10.5). He must have been a person of great wealth and influence, since he dedicated a statue of King Pyrrhus of Eprius at Olympia (Pausanias 6.14.9). If Pyrrhus was another of his employers, as seems likely enough, then the dedication of this statue was a means of advertising the success of that employment. But Thrasybulus had an even more conspicuous means for showing off his talents. Pausanias (6.2.4–5) saw a remarkable and

---

[30] *Anabasis* 6.1.31; 6.6.35–36; 7.6.43–44. See further, Pritchett 1979:78–81, who, however, tends to take his examples out of context.

iconographically unique statue of Thrasybulus himself at Olympia: a gecko was crawling toward his right shoulder and a dog was lying beside him, cut in two with its liver exposed. The divinatory significance of both animals is uncertain. Pausanias thought that Thrasybulus established his own personal method of divination in which he uniquely examined the entrails of dogs; Pausanias does not discuss the lizard, but it is a reasonable inference that Thrasybulus claimed to understand the language of animals, or at least of lizards.[31] It has been suggested, however, that the description "cut in two" refers to the rite, as practiced in Macedonia and Boeotia, of purification of an army, whereby the troops passed between the parts of a severed dog.[32] Since some seers still performed rites of healing and purification in classical times,[33] it is not impossible that Pausanias has misinterpreted the iconography of the statue. Or it may be that Thrasybulus used the dog both for purposes of divination (and thus the depiction of the exposed liver) and for purification. What is clear is that even within an extended mantic family, individual members might represent themselves quite differently. Indeed we should expect that a seer would want to emphasize that although he belonged to a particular clan, all of whose members shared inherited and proven abilities, he nevertheless was exceptional in some way. The dog and the lizard mark Thrasybulus as different from other seers and even from other Iamidae; they are emblematic of his claim to be someone with a special access to the supernatural world.

Another statue at Olympia bears comparison with this one, even if it is of a Clytiad rather than of an Iamid. In the late fourth or early third century BC an Elean *mantis* by the name of Eperastus, who won at Olympia in the race in armor, emphasized his claim to belong to two mantic families. Pausanias records the inscription on his statue as follows:

> I boast to be a seer of the race of the prophetic-tongued Clytidae, blood from the god-like Melampodidae." (6.17.5–6)

This may not be elegant poetry (and Clytiadae seems to be spelled Clytidae in order to fit the meter), but Eperastus has managed in a single couplet to attribute to himself the qualities of being "prophetic-tongued" and "god-like," as well as belonging to two illustrious families of seers (since Clytius, the progenitor of the Clytiadae, was in turn a descendant of Melampus). If Eperastus was intending to attract clients (as I presume that he was), then this statue with its

---

[31] See Pritchett 1979:54, 196–202; Parke 1967:168.

[32] So Pritchett 1979:54; following Nilsson 1955–1967, 2:230n1. The main texts are Plutarch *Moralia* 290d, for Boeotia; and for Macedonia, Livy 40.6; Curtius 10.9.11.

[33] Xenophon *Anabasis* 5.7.35; Plato *Republic* 364b–e; Hippocrates *Diseases of Women* 1.

inscription would have served as a very effective and conspicuous advertisement of both his martial abilities and his prophetic credentials.

Before moving on, one other statue at Olympia is worth mentioning. Satyrus, the son of Lysianax, whose statue Pausanias (6.4.5) also saw at Olympia, won five victories in boxing at Nemea, two at Delphi, and two at Olympia, probably in the late fourth century BC.[34] Unfortunately, Pausanias only says that he was from the family of the Iamidae, but he does not specify if he was a *mantis*.[35] Even if he did not practice as a *mantis*, his nine panhellenic victories certainly would have added to the prestige of this family.

The Iamid *mantis* about whom we have the most detailed tradition concerning his life and career is Tisamenus of Elis. In fact, there is no historical Greek *mantis* who figures more prominently in our sources. The story of how Tisamenus became a Spartan citizen and was launched on what was arguably the most successful mantic career of all time is imbedded in Herodotus' account of the battle of Plataea in 479 BC.[36] In mid-July of that year the largest Greek hoplite army ever to take the field met the army of Mardonius, cousin and brother-in-law of King Xerxes, in Boeotia. Herodotus moves in his narrative from the dispositions of the troops to the activities of the seers on each side, and this includes an account of how Tisamenus came to be with the Spartan army:

> Tisamenus, the son of Antiochus, was the one sacrificing for the Greeks. For he was following this army as its seer. Although he was an Elean and a Clytiad of the family of the Iamidae, the Lacedaemonians had made him their fellow citizen. For when Tisamenus was consulting the oracle in Delphi about having offspring, the Pythia answered that he would win the five greatest contests. Failing to understand the oracle, he turned his attention to gymnastic exercises, thinking that he was going to win gymnastic contests. Practicing the pentathlon and entering into competition with Hieronymus the Andrian, he came within one fall [in the wrestling] of winning an Olympic victory. The Lacedaemonians, however, learned that the oracle given to Tisamenus was not referring to gymnastic contests but to contests of Ares, and by persuading

---

[34] Pliny *Natural History* 34.51, assigns Silanion, the artist who made the statue, to the 113th Olympiad (328–325 BC).

[35] But as Kett 1966:67 observes, it is likely enough that he was one.

[36] On Herodotus' treatment of him, see Flower and Marincola 2002:164–175; the present essay goes far beyond the notes in that commentary, and represents further thoughts. For a different type of analysis, see Munson 2001:59–72.

him with pay they were attempting to make Tisamenus the leader in their wars, together with those of the Heracleidae who were their kings. But when he saw how concerned the Spartans were to acquire him as their friend, he began to raise his price, indicating that if they should make him one of their own citizens, with a share in all privileges, he would do what they wanted, but not for any other payment. When the Spartans first heard this they thought it monstrous and they completely let go of their need for him; but in the end, with the great fear of this Persian army hanging over them, they agreed and went after him. When Tisamenus recognized that they had changed their minds, he said that he was still not satisfied with these things alone, but that it was necessary in addition for his brother Hagias to become a Spartan citizen on the same conditions as himself. In saying these things he was imitating Melampus, to make a guess, in demanding both kingship and citizenship. [Then comes a digression on Melampus.] Thus indeed the Spartans, since they were terribly in need of Tisamenus, yielded to him completely. And after the Spartans had yielded, Tisamenus the Elean, who had become a Spartan citizen, served as their seer and helped them to win the five greatest contests. And alone of all men these became citizens with the Spartans." (9.33–35)

As the text of Herodotus now stands, Tisamenus is called "a Clytiad of the family of the Iamidae." Most scholars have claimed this to be impossible and have accordingly labeled "Clytiad" as a scholiast's gloss, [37] but I see no reason to rule out the possibility of intermarriage between the leading mantic families: that is to say, one of his parents was an Iamid and the other a Clytiad. There was an unimpeachable mythic paradigm for prophetic power passing from mother to son, since Teiresias had a daughter named Manto, who was the mother of the seer Mopsus. And it is easy enough to imagine why someone would have wanted to represent himself as belonging to both of these families. The Clytiadae, as mentioned above, claimed to be descendants of Melampus, the most famous of all legendary seers, and a blood connection with Melampus was an obvious vehicle for mantic self-advertisement and self-promotion.

Herodotus does not explain here how an Iamid could be so stupid or Lacedaemonians so uncharacteristically intelligent. Moreover, the internal logic of the story presupposes that Tisamenus had not acted as a profes-

---

[37] On this problem, see Schachter 2000; Flower and Marincola 2002:166–167, 321–322. But I here offer a different solution.

sional *mantis* before his consultation of Delphi; otherwise, he surely would have understood what kinds of "contests" the Pythia had in mind. We are thus expected to imagine something that might seem unlikely on the face of it—that the Spartans hired someone who had no previous experience in his craft and was completely untested. Nonetheless, the story of this consultation of Apollo is in keeping with how the Greeks imagined that Apollo sometimes acted. In Greek tragedy it is certainly the case that Apollo, by giving certain oracles at certain times, is able to stage-manage events so as to achieve the desired consequences. The plots of certain plays, such as *Oedipus Tyrannus* and *Ion*, hinge on Apollo's capacity for so arranging and manipulating events. In the case of Tisamenus, if Apollo had not delivered the oracle that he did, Tisamenus might never have become a seer. Thus, when Apollo predicted that Tisamenus would win the five greatest victories, he in a sense also caused him to win those victories. Implicit in Herodotus' story is the subtext that not just any seer trained in the craft of divination could have won those victories, but only a divinely selected Iamid in whom the prophetic gift given to Iamus by Apollo himself was particularly potent.

It is certainly possible, of course, that what Herodotus has given us is in fact a case of the effect being substituted for the cause. In other words, what may have happened is that Tisamenus was granted Spartan citizenship after the battle of Plataea as a reward for his services. At a much later date (394/3), Sthorys of Thasos was awarded Athenian citizenship for his assistance during the battle of Cnidus.[38] It is, then, easy to imagine how the oral tradition about Tisamenus might have displaced the reward. On grounds of probability, the grant should have come after the services had been rendered, not before, especially when one considers that the Spartans were notoriously parsimonious with grants of full citizenship (that is, to Spartiate status). Nevertheless, the story, as Herodotus reports it, reveals what was credible to his contemporaries: to them it was a real possibility that Apollo, through the medium of his oracle, might intervene spontaneously and unpredictably in human affairs, even if he did not do so very often. And it was also credible to them that the Spartans, who were intensely religious as a society and who had a special relationship with Delphic Apollo,[39] would have paid any price to get the best possible seer.

Setting aside the issue of historicity, let us now consider how the clan of the Iamidae represented the career of their most illustrious member in their collective memory. Herodotus does not say this, but there may have been a

---

[38] See *IG* II² 17, lines 26–29; with Osborne 1970.
[39] For Spartan religious attitudes, see Parker 1988; Richer 1999.

Michael A. Flower

rather specific reason why the Spartans were so eager to hire Tisamenus on the eve of Plataea, quite apart from their generalized fear of the Persian war machine. The seer Megistias, an Acarnanian who was said to be a descendant of Melampus, as mentioned above, had perished with the Spartans at Thermopylae (Herodotus 7.219, 221, 228). His death may have created the vacancy filled by Tisamenus, in which case it was not the fear of Xerxes' imminent invasion which impelled the Spartans, but rather their lack of an expert seer for the specific confrontation with Mardonius. Could it be that the career of Tisamenus marked a turning point in the fortunes of the Iamidae?[40] Did they now eclipse the Melampodidae and other mantic families? The work of the seers attending the oracle at Olympia must have been fairly mundane, most of it dealing with questions put by hopeful athletes, and it would appear that Olympia was seldom consulted about important matters of state or ritual.[41] Thus it was military employment outside of Elis that brought fame to the family. The destruction of Sybaris, aided and abetted by Callias, was a dramatic event to be sure; but the defeat of Mardonius at Plataea by the regent Pausanias was "the fairest victory of all those we know," as Herodotus calls it (9.64.2). It was only now, I suggest, that the Iamidae became the most celebrated of all mantic families. Pindar's statement that since the time of Iamus "the race of the Iamidae has been much renowned among Hellenes" (line 71) should rather be referred to Tisamenus.

If this is correct, it helps to explain something rather peculiar. Pindar's account of Iamus in the sixth *Olympian* is not only the fullest source for this myth, it is the only independent source, and that is striking given that other seers (such as Melampus, Mopsus, Teiresias, and Amphiaraus) figured so prominently in early Greek poetry.[42] Nor are there any certain artistic representations of Iamus.[43] Moreover, there are at least two features of the story of Melampus that Pindar has borrowed and applied to Iamus, and the obvious

[40] Apart from Plataea in 479, his other victories were at Tegea in ca. 473–470, at Dipaea (or Dipaeis) in ca. 470–465, either at Mt. Ithome or the Isthmus of Corinth (the text of Herodotus is corrupt) in the 460s, and at Tanagra in 457. See Herodotus 9.35.2; with Flower and Marincola 2002 *ad loc.*

[41] See Pindar *Olympian* 8, lines 1–8; Parke 1967:186–190.

[42] Pausanias at 6.2.5, for instance, cites Pindar for the story of Iamus as if he were the only source.

[43] Art historians have speculated that the old man on the East Pediment of the temple of Zeus at Olympia, which depicts the preparation for the chariot race between Pelops and Oenomaus, is the seer Iamus: see *LIMC* 5.1:614–615. This figure well may be a seer, but the identification with Iamus is made solely by reference to Pindar's sixth *Olympian*. In any case, the temple was constructed ca. 470–457, and thus the carving of this pediment was most probably later than Pindar's ode.

explanation is that Pindar was attempting to suggest that Iamus was as great a seer as Melampus.[44] It is possible, therefore, that Pindar, in celebrating the ancestry of Hagesias, needed to make up most, perhaps virtually all, of the myth.[45] He is simultaneously establishing a mythological basis for the prominence of the Iamidae and reflecting their new status in the larger Greek world.

However that may be, there is one aspect of Pindar's treatment that provides the key to understanding the self-representation of Tisamenus and his descendants at Sparta. As Pindar tells the story (6.28–30), Iamus, the son of Apollo, was also the grandson of Poseidon by the nymph Pitana. This type of double descent from the gods is unparalleled in Greek myth, and must have been introduced by Pindar for a specific reason. Now, Pitana was the name of one of the five Spartan villages, and anyone who became a Spartan citizen would necessarily have become domiciled in one of those villages. The inference to be made is pretty obvious.[46] Pitana must have been the village to which the Iamidae, beginning with Tisamenus and his brother Hagias, belonged; and Pindar is here providing a mythological legitimization for their membership. One does not want to make Pindar a mere cipher for Iamid self-promotion, but his reworking of the myth fits the situation of the family so nicely that he must have had a very clear idea of what suited the interests of his patrons when he gave the Iamidae a Laconian ancestry.

There is an obvious danger of circularity in using Herodotus to explain Pindar in order to explain Herodotus, but I want to suggest that the ultimate source for the story which Herodotus reports about Tisamenus, even allowing for his own remodeling of it, was Iamid family tradition.[47] Herodotus claims to have visited the Spartan village of Pitana (3.55.2), and he might have encountered there one or more members of Tisamenus' family. If such were the case, then the right conditions would have been present for the reliability of the oral tradition about Tisamenus. The memories of a closed group, such as a

---

[44] Both Melampus and Iamus acquired the art of sacrificial divination as the result of an encounter with Apollo in the Alpheus River (compare Apollodorus 1.9.11 with Pindar, lines 57–63), and both had an encounter with snakes. Pindar records that two snakes tended the infant Iamus and fed him honey, whereas Hesiod has snakes lick Melampus' ears when he was asleep so that when he awoke he could understand the language of birds. None of this is noticed by Hutchinson 2001.

[45] The many peculiar features in Pindar's story are succinctly treated by Parke 1967:176–177 (largely following Wilamowitz 1886:162–185).

[46] As suggested by Wilamowitz 1886:162–185; followed by Parke 1967:176–177; see also Thomas 1989:107; Luraghi 1997a.

[47] A less plausible explanation is that Herodotus is drawing on a Delphic story that was intended to ridicule the rival oracle of Zeus at Olympia (argued by Crahay 1956:102–104).

particular family or a religious community, tend to be more fixed than those of larger entities. This does not mean, however, that the oral tradition would then be *true*, since accuracy of transmission is not related to the truth or falsity of a tradition.[48] A tradition is remembered because it serves a useful purpose for the receiving generation, and in the case of the Iamidae that purpose is obvious. The function of Apollo in Herodotus' tale is analogous to his role in Pindar's story of Iamus. In Pindar, Apollo endows the first Iamid as a seer, and here he does the same for Iamus' descendant Tisamenus. Herodotus' story not only explains why Tisamenus was so successful, but it also validates and confirms the status of his descendants, both as seers and as Spartan citizens. In the end, it is the self-representation of the Iamidae, rather than the truth or falsity of the story itself, that is most accessible to us.

There is one thing, however, that is strangely missing from Herodotus' account of Tisamenus' exploits, if indeed that account ultimately goes back to Iamid family tradition in a reliable chain of oral transmission. There is no mention of his martial prowess. Pindar, for instance, emphatically stresses that Hagesias was due the same praise that Adrastus had given to the seer Amphiaraus:

> I long for the eye of my army, one who was good both as a seer and
> to fight with the spear." (lines 16–17)

The association of mantic and warlike abilities was fairly common, and the phrase "good both as a seer and to fight with the spear" had a long history both before and after Pindar.[49] Perhaps the story of Tisamenus' near victory in the *pentathlon* was sufficient to suggest his martial valor, as well as his personal wealth and aristocratic status. Herodotus, moreover, does not as a matter of course tell us all that he knows, and it would not be surprising if a more elaborate version of Tisamenus' exploits at Plataea circulated orally.[50]

Whatever the circumstances under which it came about, Tisamenus did serve as the seer for the Spartans at Plataea, and it is possible that his name can be restored in an inscription which records the dedication of a statue to

---

[48] For this important point, see Murray 2001:316–317; in general, Vansina 1985.

[49] According to scholion 26, Pindar borrowed this sentence from the epic *Thebaid*. It reappears in a grave epigram of the early fourth century for the seer Cleobulus (note 51 below). Note also the roughly similar description of Amphiaraus in Aeschylus *Seven Against Thebes* 568–569 (performed in 467 BC).

[50] Pausanias 3.11.6–8 gives an account of Tisamenus' career which is a loose paraphrase of Herodotus, except for one detail: that the Spartans allowed the Messenians who had rebelled to depart under truce, "being persuaded by Tisamenus and the Delphic oracle." This perhaps reveals that various accounts of Tisamenus' exploits were in circulation.

Demeter and which was found near the likely location of the battle.[51] But just how important was his role? According to Herodotus, the Spartans wished "to make Tisamenus the leader (*hēgemōna*) in their wars, together with those of the Heracleidae who were kings." Since it was the prerogative of the kings at Sparta to command the army, the Spartan offer comes as something of a surprise. Indeed, the language here suggests a position tantamount to "joint commander with their kings," and this notion is reinforced by the verbs "would win" and "helped them to win" which Herodotus uses of Tisamenus' activities. Yet Herodotus does not depict Tisamenus as having any active role in the actual battle, either in marshalling the troops or in the fighting. Herodotus must therefore mean that Tisamenus was the leader in the same way as was Calchas, the seer of the Greeks at Troy. Homer speaks of him as the one who "led (*hēgēsato*) the ships of the Achaeans into the land of Ilium through that seercraft (*mantosunēn*) which Phoebus Apollo had given him" (*Iliad* I 71–72). Like Calchas, then, Tisamenus *leads* the army and practices the art of divination as Apollo's gift. So too in Euripides' *Phoenissae*, the seer Teiresias claims the credit for securing Athens' victory over Eleusis:

> I made the sons of Cecrops victorious, and, as you can see, I possess this golden crown, which I received as the first fruits of the enemy spoils." (*Phoenissae* 854–857)

Turning to the fourth century, Aeschines (*On the Embassy* 78) says that his uncle Cleobulus, who we know from his grave epigram was a *mantis*, "along with Demaenetus, won the naval victory over Cheilon the Lacedaemonian admiral."[52] One strongly suspects that seers depicted themselves not just as advisers to kings and generals, but as individuals who literally could *win* battles for their clients.[53]

In terms of Herodotus' narrative the great service that Tisamenus performed at Plataea was his declaration that "the omens were favorable for the Greeks if they remained on the defensive, but not favorable if they should cross the Asopus river and begin battle."[54] Herodotus claims that Mardonius

---

[51] This inscription, *IG* VII 1670, has been republished by Flower and Marincola 2002:320–322.

[52] On this passage, see Harris 1995:23–27. For the inscription, see *SEG* 16.193; Daux 1958; and Pritchett 1979:57.

[53] This notion of *leading* an army may go back to the Near East; for an analogous expression was used of the Babylonian seer, who was said to "go in front of the army." See West 1997:349.

[54] Although Herodotus does not mention him again, he surely also performed the *sphagia* (battle-line sacrifice) in the moments before the Persian and Spartan armies joined battle some eleven days later: see Plutarch *Aristides* 18. I have elsewhere discussed the possibility that Simonides of Ceos gave a fuller and much more elaborate version of Tisamenus' prophecy in F 14 (West,

was eager for a battle, but that he was prevented from crossing the Asopus by the unfavorable omens that were reported to him by his own Greek seer Hegesistratus of Elis. The medizing Greeks had their own seer, Hippomachus of Leucas, and he too was unable to obtain omens that were favorable for an offensive. These omens fit the tactical situation perfectly, and thus moderns have been quick to assume that the seers on each side must have engaged in a conscious manipulation of the omens when they gave their interpretations. But to explain the actions of seers in terms of "conscious manipulation," either of their own devising or at the behest of their commanders, is far too simplistic and grossly misconstrues the function of divination in Greek society.

We cannot recover the actual psychological processes by which a seer inspected and interpreted the omens, and it is certainly the case that almost all methods of divination are open to manipulation, whether conscious or unconscious, on the part of the diviner.[55] The degree of such manipulation will of course vary from one individual to another and will be conditioned by the nature of the divinatory procedures that are employed. But we can say that the Greek seer represented himself as divining by virtue of his art and by aid of his innate prophetic gifts. When the seer sacrificed the victim and then interpreted the entrails, he was engaged in a public performance before an audience of mortals and of gods; both his immediate success and his prospects for future employment depended on how well and how convincingly he played his role as expounder of the divine will. His value to society as the practitioner of a socially useful craft in turn depended on his human audience's faith in his ability properly to interpret the signs sent by the gods.[56] Thus the worst accusation that one could level against a seer was that he was influenced by greed to give knowingly false interpretations. Such accusations, which are fairly common in Greek literature, reveal both the high value that society placed on divination and an attendant anxiety about its proper performance.[57] That the Spartans indeed had faith in Tisamenus is demonstrated by their further employment of him and by their unique grant of citizenship.

IEG²) of his recently restored elegiac poem on the battle of Plataea, but the fragments are so lacunose that it is impossible to tell whether it is some god or a mortal who is speaking, or indeed exactly what is being said (Flower 2000:67n9; Flower and Marincola 2002:318). So Simonides is best left out of the discussion.

[55] See Collins 1978:237.

[56] For the social function of divination, see Park 1963; and the important collection of articles in Peek 1991. For the performative aspects, see also LaGamma 2000 and Pemberton 2000.

[57] So Oedipus says of Teiresias, "he has sight only when it comes to profit, but in his art is blind" (Sophocles *Oedipus Tyrannus* 388–389); cf. Homer *Odyssey* ii 184–186; Sophocles *Antigone* 1054–1055; Euripides *Bacchae* 255–257. See further Morrison 1981:106–107; Smith 1989.

Tisamenus went on to win four more great victories for Sparta, the last being at Tanagra in 457. As mentioned at the beginning of this essay, his grandson, Agias (II), was seer to Lysander in 405 at the battle of Aegospotami. But for reasons unknown to us, his great-grandson (or perhaps great-nephew), also named Tisamenus (II), was involved in the conspiracy of Cinadon at Sparta in 397.[58] He was executed along with Cinadon and the other conspirators after being paraded through the streets of Sparta in a dog collar, while being whipped and goaded (Xenophon *Hellenica* 3.3.11). It is an ironic testament to the family's fame that "Tisamenus the *mantis*" is the only one of Cinadon's fellow conspirators who is named by Xenophon. The Spartan branch of the Iamidae then disappears from the historical record.[59] Although it reemerges in inscriptions of the first century BC and second century AD, it is highly unlikely that the individuals who are named Iamus and Tisamenus in these inscriptions were actually related to the victor of Plataea. The problem is that late Hellenistic and Roman imperial times saw a renewed interest in Sparta's past. Individuals traced their ancestry to Heracles, Perseus, the Dioscuri, both royal houses, Lycurgus, Brasidas, and many other famous personages from Sparta's mythical and historical past. Such lineages were undoubtedly invented links with a past that was, strictly speaking, unrecoverable.[60] Given the social and political upheavals that afflicted late Classical and Hellenistic Sparta, by the time of this inscriptional evidence there can have been very few individuals who could trace their ancestry back to Spartans of the Classical period, much less to the elite of Spartan society. At Olympia, on the other hand, the family disappears after AD 265.

The mantic Iamidae nevertheless had a long and successful run: if we take our sources at face value, they were one of the most preeminent families of seers from the foundation of the Olympic games in the eighth century BC right through to the end of the third century AD. A thousand years of successful employment is a long time for a single clan, even by modern standards. This

[58] Figueira 1986:193n70, suggests that he may have been an inferior (*hupomeiōn*), one of those Spartiates who had lost their citizen status due to an inability to pay their monthly mess dues.

[59] A Lacedaemonian named Agias is named in a Delphic inscription as *prostatēs* of the *naopoioi* (president of the temple builders) under the Delphic archon Theucharis in the spring of 351 BC (Poralla 1913 no. 23; *CID* 2.31, line 65). This indicates that he must have been a man of considerable wealth and high social status. Whether he was related to Lysander's seer of the same name (his grandson perhaps), it is not possible to tell.

[60] I cannot agree with Spawforth (in Cartledge and Spawforth 1989:163–165), who argues that such families were actually descended from the *old* aristocracy of Classical Sparta and that there was an unbroken continuity of hereditary religious authority. He argues by analogy with the Athenian priestly families of the Eumolpidae and the Ceryces, but the social conditions in Attica were far different from those at Sparta.

success was due not merely to the victories garnered by its members on the field of battle; it was maintained and perpetuated by the calculated self-promotion that is reflected in our various ancient sources. As we have seen, the Iamidae managed that self-promotion in terms of traditional aristocratic claims to excellence, as athletic victors, the dedicants of statues, as warriors and *commanders* of armies, the founders of cities, and as the direct descendants of gods and heroes.

Family Tree of the Iamidae at Sparta
(showing probable descent from father to son)

Antiochus — Tisamenus I (victor of Plataea) — Agelochus — Agias II (Lysander's seer at Aegospotami) — Tisamenus II (implicated in conspiracy of Cinadon in 397).

10

Authority Disputed
The Seer in Homeric Epic

Kai Trampedach

ICHAEL FLOWER HAS ALREADY OBSERVED that we know a number of Greek seers of Archaic and Classical Greece by name.[1] When we compare this situation with priests, the transmission of seers' names, at least for the historical context of the pre-Hellenistic period, is much richer. The reason for this situation is obvious: the profession of seer depended much more on personal abilities. Do these personal abilities also lend themselves to a certain political authority? In my opinion, the answer is no: Greek seers in general exercised no more political authority than the priests, albeit for different reasons. Rather, they are professional interpreters of the divine will, whose social position appears to have been precarious and impermanent. In the following essay, I wish to substantiate this thesis by analyzing both the narrative and the practical applications of the conduct of the Homeric seer. It is not sufficient merely to assemble the statements of the poet concerning seers: each specific situation in the *Iliad* and the *Odyssey* in which the poet presents the seer in relation to other figures in the story must be more closely examined. The results will show that the later historical transmission of the concept of the seer (in so far as it has a public significance) is consistent with the lineaments of the Homeric paradigm.

For assistance with the translation and for helpful suggestions, I wish to thank my dear colleague Stephen Lake. I am also indebted to Michael Flower (Princeton) for a series of constructive comments. The argument of this paper is based on my *Habilitationsschrift*, *Politische Mantik: Studien zur Kommunikation über Götterzeichen und Orakel im klassischen Griechenland*, which was accepted in 2003 by the Department of History and Sociology of the University of Constance, and which is forthcoming.

[1] See above, in this volume. The evidence for the historical seers in Archaic and Classical times was collected by Kett 1966.

1. Calchas at Troy (*Iliad* I 53–117)

In the Achaean camp before Troy, plague has broken out. After ten days, Achilles summons the men to a meeting and proposes that a seer or a priest or an interpreter of dreams be consulted to find out whether Apollo is angry because of a broken vow or an imperfect hecatomb, and if he can be appeased with a pure sacrifice.

> When he had thus spoken he sat down, and among them rose up Calchas, son of Thestor, far the best of bird diviners, who had knowledge of all things that were, and that were to be, and that had been before, and who had guided the ships of the Achaeans to Ilios by the gift of prophecy that Phoebus Apollo granted him. (I 68–72)[2]

Before Calchas addresses the question of the cause of the plague, however, he requests a promise of protection from Achilles, because he fears that some day he may fall victim to the vengeance of someone powerful. After Achilles has promised him protection, Calchas says what the audience already knows: the wrath of Apollo, manifested in the plague, was provoked by the contempt shown towards Apollo's priest at Chryse, whose daughter was abducted by Agamemnon, who refused to surrender her even when he was offered a generous ransom. The conciliation of the god requires the unconditional return of the maiden to her father, and a hecatomb in the sanctuary of Chryse. The reaction of Agamemnon fulfills expectations, and is directed first against Calchas:

> Prophet of evil, never yet have you given me a favorable prophecy; always it is dear to your heart to prophesy evil, and no word of good have you ever yet spoken or brought to fulfillment. (I 106–108)

In spite of this insult, Agamemnon agrees and declares himself willing to return the maiden in the interests of the army, though not without justifying himself in a rather offensive manner, and then demanding a suitable compensation for the loss of his honor gift, which provokes the wrath of Achilles. The doom of the *Iliad* takes its course.

Achilles seeks out a specialist, because he suspects that a ritual mistake—an unfulfilled vow or an impure sacrificial victim—is the cause of the plague, and he wishes to find appropriate means of expiation. This initiative assumes

---

[2] Unless otherwise indicated, quotations from Homer are taken from the Loeb translations by A. T. Murray, revised by W. F. Wyatt (*Iliad*, 1999) and G. E. Dimock (*Odyssey*, 1995) respectively.

that a knowledge of ritual falls within the competence of the seer. The leading seer among the Achaeans feels himself thus addressed. His answer then indicates, as might be expected, a "holy hecatomb" as a ritual means of appeasing the god, though this certainly does not exhaust the options. Calchas has in fact revealed that the cause of Apollo's anger lay not in the sphere of ritual, but rather in Agamemnon's breach of a social norm, in that he had insulted a priest, who is under the protection of a powerful god. Any other noble could have given the same diagnosis. The practical solution that Calchas recommends—the return of the daughter and a sacrifice to Apollo in the sanctuary of the offended priest—is only too self-evident.

Achilles conceivably already knew the real cause of the problem. The following considerations speak in favor of this view: by rejecting the priest's offer, Agamemnon finds himself in opposition to "all the rest of the Achaeans," who wanted "to respect the priest and accept the glorious ransom" (I 22–23). Immediately afterwards, the plague began, from which first the pack animals, then the dogs, and then the Achaeans themselves, died. Death stretched over nine long days, while Agamemnon as the affected king and also as supreme commander, sat it out in idleness together with the other kings. Eventually, Achilles reacted by summoning the meeting. Naturally, he traced the plague to the wrath of Apollo. That the anger of the Archer God "who strikes from afar" had to do with the treatment of his priest by Agamemnon must then really be conceded as a possibility. Why did Achilles avoid drawing the logical conclusion himself? He sought to avoid a direct confrontation with Agamemnon by summoning a *neutral* specialist, and thus opened up a means for Agamemnon to make good his fault without too much loss of face.[3] Had Achilles himself exposed the situation, Agamemnon, with his consciousness of honor and power, would have felt himself immediately challenged. Calchas, however, as an aristocrat of lower rank in the role of seer had a better chance, to Achilles' mind, of moving the king to cooperate. Achilles' question is then directed to Calchas. There were no priests in the Achaean camp, as priests were always bound to particular sanctuaries. The subsequently introduced interpretation of a dream, like the interpretation of bird flights, fell within the competence of the seer. In the *Iliad*, however, the only seer who is mentioned among the Achaean ranks is Calchas. It would thus appear that Achilles has planned the entry of Calchas.[4] The strategy was almost successful: Agamemnon agreed,

---

[3] This calculation is reflected in the formal way in which he addresses Agamemnon as supreme commander and in the tone, which confines itself to the matter at hand; see Latacz 2000:50; Kirk 1985:59.

[4] That Achilles assumes a θεοπρόπιον in his reply to Calchas' request for protection (I 85–87)

albeit reluctantly, with the advice of the seer. But Achilles had not reckoned with Agamemnon's demand for compensation, which then made a personal confrontation unavoidable.

Calchas is characterized (a) as son of Thestor,[5] that is, as the descendant of a noble house; (b) through the exceptional form and quality of his art (I 69); (c) through all-embracing knowledge (of past, present, and future), rather than knowledge confined to a specific area; (d) through an exemplary achievement (that is, guiding the fleet to Ilium); and (e) through his divine designation: the *mantosunē* was granted him by Apollo. This authentication vouches for the coming disclosure by Calchas, and thus serves to structure the audience's expectations (and the narrative itself).[6] The poet uses Calchas as a mouthpiece within the story. The etiological part of Calchas' speech (I 94–96) in fact corresponds, in abbreviated form, with the report which is given in the opening scene of the *Iliad* (I 8–52). The vertical relationship between the poet and the Muses finds its parallel on the narrative level in the relationship between Calchas and Apollo.[7] According to Achilles, when he is praying to Apollo, Calchas prophesies to the Achaeans (I 86–87). Calchas stands in a privileged relationship to Apollo, the giver of his ability as seer. Both Achilles and the poet himself legitimate Calchas' disclosure by making explicit his special relationship to Apollo, who is again the source of the Achaeans' misfortunes.

Calchas is characterized in his role less by a specific mantic competence than by his ability to make clear that the present circumstances of the army are being adversely affected by the selfish interests of their leader. This ability owes to his particular social status: he is a respected aristocrat, but he is not among the Achaean leaders and champions.[8] He is not a rival in the competition for status, power, and reputation as they are. At the same time, he therefore cannot act on his own initiative. Calchas must also have recognized the real cause of the plague himself, but he could only speak when the meeting had been summoned by Achilles and he had been asked to address

---

can be explained by his wish to emphasize the authority of the seer. See Lactacz 2000:51–52, with the conclusion: "*Achills Vorschlag läuft also (ob bewußt oder unbewußt, bleibt offen) auf Kalchas hinaus.*" Achilles realized immediately that the unnamed powerful figure was Agamemnon, whose anger Calchas feared (I 90); cf. Taplin 1992:54–55. Latacz 1989:122 even considers a secret collaboration between Achilles and Calchas.

[5] See Latacz 2000:14. The father's name, Thestor, which means 'one who prays', speaks for itself: Latacz 2000:53.

[6] Latacz 2000:54.

[7] Dickson 1992:331.

[8] Calchas justifies his fear of Agamemnon: "For a king is mightier when he is angry at a lesser man" (I 80).

the matter. Beyond this, Calchas does not appear to belong to the entourage of any of the leading nobles. He must bid Achilles *ad hoc* for his protection.[9] Because he is not bound in obedience to any of the kings, and specifically not to Agamemnon, the leader of the Achaeans, and because he has no personal ambitions to pursue, he can represent the interests of the army.[10] Calchas' position, though, is not invulnerable, as his fear of Agamemnon shows. The seer, then, does not stand outside of the community but rather is integrated within its hierarchical order.

Agamemnon responds to Calchas' diagnosis with a visible display of anger. By identifying the seer with his messages, which allegedly always strike to his, Agamemnon's, disadvantage, he thus places Calchas' impartiality in question. He also complains that Calchas gives his oracles in public.[11] Odysseus characterizes the behavior of Calchas in a very similar way at the beginning of the second book of the *Iliad*;[12] here, it also becomes clear that Calchas' activity serves the entire Achaean contingent and that he is not merely at the disposal of the king and the other leaders. Agamemnon's argument is then directed against Calchas' conduct in general,[13] and not against his position in this particular situation. Agamemnon does not claim that Calchas has made a false diagnosis of the cause of the plague; on the contrary, he accepts the interpretation and is prepared to draw the relevant consequences. He even implicitly acknowledges the basis of Calchas' argument by legitimating his own concession with an appeal on his side to the well-being of the army: "I would rather have the army safe than perishing" (I 117).[14]

2. Calchas at Aulis (*Iliad* II 299–353)

In the assembly, Odysseus seeks to persuade the war-weary Achaeans to continue the war by appealing to something which Calchas said as the ships

---

[9] Significantly the *Iliad* does not indicate from which city Calchas came.

[10] The poet introduces Calchas' first speech in this sense with the following words ὅ σφιν ἐϋφρονέων ἀγορήσατο καὶ μετέειπε (I 73). The poet defines Calchas' conduct as "well intentioned, i.e. having in mind what is appropriate to the situation," and if σφιν refers not only to μετέειπε but also, as Latacz takes it (Latacz 2000:56), to the immediately following ἐϋφρονέων, then the reference to the Achaeans as a whole is also brought out *expressis verbis*.

[11] καὶ νῦν ἐν Δαναοῖσι θεοπροπέων ἀγορεύεις (I 109). See Latacz 2000:67.

[12] *Iliad* II 322: Κάλχας δ' αὐτίκ' ἔπειτα θεοπροπέων ἀγόρευε.

[13] Certainly, Agamemnon is annoyed by the fact that he cannot control what Calchas says in public. Further, on the question whether the poet already alludes to the sacrifice of Iphigenia in Aulis here, see Taplin 1992:86.

[14] βούλομ' ἐγὼ λαὸν σῶν ἔμμεναι ἢ ἀπολέσθαι.

were gathering at Aulis before sailing for Ilium, when the army received a "great portent" at their sacrifice: a snake slithered out from beneath the altar and up a plane tree, devoured eight sparrow chicks as well as their mother, and subsequently turned to stone. Calchas saw this event as a sign from Zeus, and explained that the Achaeans would conduct the war for nine years before Ilium, but in the tenth year they would conquer the city. Following Odysseus, Nestor spoke in the same vein. He, too, appealed to a sign which occurred at their departure, when Zeus struck lightning on the right.

Calchas interpreted the great portent (*mega sēma*, II 308), which he himself called a great miracle (*teras mega*, II 324). Whether he spoke on his own initiative in this case, or whether, as a competent seer, he was questioned by the leading nobles, is not mentioned. His activity is here defined by Odysseus, as also earlier by Achilles (I 87) and Agamemnon (I 109), as the mediation of divine communication (*theopropeōn*, II 322). The sign, "late in coming, late in fulfillment, the fame of which shall never perish" (II 325), concerns the future and has the unusual term of ten years. Its meaning operates according to the pattern of figurative analogy, where only the number of victims is explicitly included in the interpretation—the birds eaten by the snake denote the number of years of the unsuccessful siege of Troy. The relationship between sign and meaning is similarly not immediately obvious, and Calchas did not attempt to explain it more clearly.[15]

Particularly significant is the moment in which the sign occurs: at the mustering of the troops in Aulis, during the sacrifice (that is, the communication with the gods), before the departure for Troy. This coincidence guarantees that this is an authentic sign from the gods. Its relationship to the common undertaking which the Achaeans have immediately before them is also clear. The snake ("blood-red on its back, terrible"), which slithers from under the altar and snatches the sparrows from the branch, disturbs the sacrifice and logically represents something hostile.[16] That it cannot enjoy its plunder or permanently interrupt the sacrifice but that it subsequently turns to stone speak for the eventual success of those performing the sacrifice. The fact that the number of devoured sparrows represents years rather than months is also scarcely surprising: the eventual success will be won at a high price, and will cost many victims. The mother of the sparrows evidently represents the

---

[15] See Kirk 1985:150, whose hypothetical consideration of the semantics of this sign nonetheless fails to improve our understanding.

[16] Although it may be logical to identify the snake with either the Trojans or the Achaeans, such an identification is not made in the text, where the primary significance is attached rather to the loss of nine years.

current, ninth year, which proves to be the most difficult for the Achaeans. This interpretation points almost automatically towards Zeus as the giver of the sign, as only he, and not, for example, Artemis as goddess of the sanctuary at Aulis, can decide the outcome of the war and reveal it so far in advance.[17] The sign is a simile which requires analysis. The interpretation follows no definite rule, but requires an ability to combine the figurative content of the sign with the actual situation, and in this way achieves the spontaneous conviction of the assembly. Calchas' interpretation is then based neither on a technical knowledge nor on immediate divine inspiration.

The sign, "the fame of which," in the words of Calchas, "shall never perish" (II 325), must be recalled completely by Odysseus: it acquires its power to persuade first from his rhetorical ability to apply it to the present. Odysseus uses the sign in order to offer the army, which is ready to sail home, the prospect of an imminent outcome in its favor, and thus to justify a longer stay before the walls of Troy. While the epic's audience already knows that the interpretation of Calchas in Aulis will prove to be correct, the Achaeans cannot be certain of this. Odysseus begins his speech on the sign with the words:

> Endure, my friends, and stay for a time, that we may know, whether
> the prophecies of Calchas are true or not. (II 299–300)

Odysseus himself is convinced that the prophecies are true, as he emphasizes again at the end of his speech (II 330), but obviously he cannot take this for granted. The enthusiasm with which the Achaeans react to his speech (II 333–335) speaks for the rhetorical skill of Odysseus.[18]

Nestor takes the same position, but he also reckons with divine deception. He challenges the army: do they want to sail home and thus accept defeat, "even before we have learned whether the promise of Zeus who bears the aegis is a lie or not" (II 348–349). Certainly, Nestor himself believes Zeus, and he justifies this by appealing to the day when they sailed from Aulis, when Zeus shot a bolt of lightening on the right, which can be construed as an encouraging sign: "for he lightened on our right and showed forth signs of good."[19]

Once again, it is the significance of the occasion itself that authenticates the sign. Lightning is the instrument of Zeus: when it appears on the right, it is always a lucky sign in epic. The assertion of a recent commentator: "Nestor's

---

[17] See Kirk 1985:149.
[18] See Latacz 2003:92–93, 100. Collins 2002:23–26.
[19] ἀστράπτων ἐπιδέξι᾽, ἐναίσιμα σήματα φαίνων. (II 353).

emphatic declaration that Zeus has given his approval shows the 'falsehood' idea in 349 to be ironical,"[20] is mistaken. Nestor also considered the possibility of divine deception in the case of Agamemnon's evil-omen dream, in order then—mistakenly!—to accept the truth of the dream message.[21] It is much more typical of his wisdom that when it comes to communication from the gods, he reckons with deception as a matter of principle. In this context, irony would certainly not be appropriate, even if Nestor is here convinced of the truth of the sign. The signs at Aulis, which occurred more than eight years earlier and therefore require a certain rhetorical art in order to make them present again, can only be proven when they are fulfilled.

3. Helenus (*Iliad* VI 73–102; VII 44–53)

Helenus, son of Priam and "by far the best interpreter of bird flight" among the Trojans, calls on Hector and Aeneas to halt the fleeing Trojans and bring them back to fight. Hector should then return to the city and order his mother to bring Athena a splendid sacrifice and pray the goddess to hold the advancing Diomedes back from Ilium's walls (VI 73-102). Athena and Apollo arrange a duel between Hector and an Achaean in order to end the hostilities for the day. Helenus hears the message and tells Hector to offer the Achaeans a duel (VII 44-53).

Helenus is no outsider. As a son of Priam, he belongs to the highest social class in Troy. He fights regularly in the Trojan ranks, as his appearance in the battle at this point as well as elsewhere shows.[22]

His advice to the Trojan leaders is not based on the evidence of bird flights, but rather on his estimation of the strategic position.[23] Nonetheless, it is not independent of his mantic qualification, which, as with Calchas (see above), also includes knowledge of ritual. Helenus demonstrates his awareness of the need to seek divine assistance in difficult situations by his concrete and detailed instructions for sacrifice and vows. The instructions for the ritual, however, reflect no objective and established knowledge, but are rather guided by the desire to present an impressive ceremony.

Athena does not accept the sacrifice and prayers of Hecabe (VI 311). As this situation shows, rituals cannot oblige the gods to act in a particular way

---

[20] Kirk 1985:152. Also unfounded is Latacz 2003:106.

[21] See Homer *Iliad* II 79–82.

[22] See Homer *Iliad* XII 94; XIII 576–600, 758–782. Here, Helenus is presented as a champion of the Trojans, while nothing is said of his augury.

[23] See Kirk 1990:237.

or ensure their favor. Helenus' attempt to reconcile the goddess thus fails, even though he had identified Athena, as the cause of Diomedes' aggression, as the proper recipient of the sacrifice.

Helenus seems to have a good ear for the gods. In the seventh book, he repeats the agreement between Apollo and Athena, and so functions as the intermediary between the gods' decision and the human realization of it. How he comes to know this remains unclear: "He intuits the divine plan, *suntheto thumō*, 'put it together for himself ... in his heart' (or mind)."[24] Helenus knows still more, because he justifies his advice to Hector in the following way:

> Not yet is it your fate to die and meet your doom; for thus have I heard the voice of the gods who are for ever. (VII 52–53)

The fate of Hector is not, however, discussed in the conversation between Athena and Apollo (VII 23–42).[25] In any case, the statement *op' akousa theōn* (VII 53) seems to imply that he literally heard what the gods said to one another.

> That kind of prophetic eavesdropping on divine plans is unparalleled in Homer; yet it is clear that in the present instance the gods could hardly resent it, indeed must have intended some device for putting their scheme into effect.[26]

In contrast to Calchas, the poet does not say that Helenus owes his ability to a god. Rather, the leading mantic specialist on the Trojan side is shown to have an instinctive ear, which proves equally well his own closeness to the gods.

4. Polydamas (*Iliad* XII 195–258)

While the Trojans consider how they can cross the trench and storm the wall around the Achaean ships, a bird sign appears: an eagle, which flies to the left, carries a large, blood-red snake in its talons, which viciously defends itself and wounds the eagle in the neck; it drops the snake among the Trojans and flies away with a scream. Polydamas, who interprets the sign in a negative sense and so calls on the Trojans to cancel their planned attack, experiences Hector's disdain. The latter appeals to his direct communication with Zeus and admits that he tends to ignore bird signs on principle. He accuses Polydamas of cowardice and compels him to remain silent if he values his life. Hector and

---

[24] See Kirk 1990:237.

[25] Either VII 52 is an interpolation, or the poet failed to repeat the entire conversation between Athena and Apollo; see Kirk 1990:238.

[26] Kirk 1990:238.

the Trojans take the battle further, and Zeus supports them by raising a whirl-wind against the Achaeans, blinding them with dust.

The sign occurs during a pause in the fighting, as the Trojans weigh their options. It is therefore clear that it refers directly to the planned attack on the wall around the ships. The sign is again constructed along the lines of a figurative analogy: the eagle, which cannot hold its prey, represents the Trojans. Thus Polydamas' interpretation: the Trojans will certainly break through into the Achaean camp, but they will then be forced to retreat with heavy losses. The direction of the eagle's flight—from right to left over the front lines of the armies—points to the same sense, although Polydamas does not comment on this. *Right* represents the advantageous side in epic, and subsequently always in Greek divination, while *left* represents the unfortunate side.[27] On another level, the eagle represents Zeus himself, who, after initially supporting the Trojans, will change sides.

Polydamas interprets the omen correctly, as the further unfolding of events shows (particularly in books XIV and XVI), although he is no *mantis* or *oiōnoskopos* or *theopropos*. In the *Iliad*, he appears much more in the role of a fighting hero and adviser,[28] although his advice always seems to reflect a greater concern with safety than with honor.[29] Here, too, he gives Hector cautious advice, and at the end of his speech claims for himself the authority of a *theopropos*:[30]

> This is the way a soothsayer would interpret, one who in his mind had clear knowledge of omens, and to whom people gave ear. (XII 228–229)

If Polydamas can play the seer without actually being one, then one quickly gains the impression that in general, no special or secret knowledge is neces-

---

[27] In Hector's speech (XII 239–240) there is a rare comment concerning the technical conditions for augury. The interpreter faces north, so that the East is to his right and the West to his left; see also *Odyssey* ix 26. In the event of unexpected, spontaneous or prayer-provoked bird flight, however, the direction always appears to be reckoned according to the position of the interpreter at the time.

[28] On Polydamas as hero, see *Iliad* XIV 449–464; XV 339, 453–457, 518; XVII 597–600. As adviser, see *Iliad* XII 60–80; XIII 725–748; XVIII 249–283. In all four cases, Polydamas advises Hector, and in their interaction, they always form the same archetypical constellation; see Stockinger 1959:35–36. In XVIII 250, the poet characterizes Polydamas with a formula which recalls the mantic qualification ascribed to Calchas: "for he alone saw both before and after." See further Collins 2002:36–37.

[29] Hainsworth 1993:325.

[30] See Roth 1982:94.

sary in order to interpret Homeric signs from the gods.[31] At the same time, perhaps Polydamas also fails because his advice lacks the authority of a specialist.

Hector rejects the advice of Polydamas with three arguments: (a) he appeals to his own direct communication with Zeus, who has already agreed to support his plans;[32] (b) he questions the relevance of augury:

> But you tell us to be obedient to birds long of wing, which I do not regard or take thought of, whether they go to the right toward the dawn and the sun, or to the left toward the murky darkness. Let us be obedient to the counsel of great Zeus, who is king over all mortals and immortals. One omen is best, to fight for one's country. (XII 237–243)

And (c) he attacks the integrity of the interpreter by suggesting that Polydamas' real motivation is cowardice. This assertion subsequently finds expression in his threatening Polydamas with death.

Although the poet declines to offer his own commentary (even if he allows the snake as *Dios teras* to fall among the Trojans in verse 209), the audience is left in no doubt that the sign is authentic and that Polydamas has understood it correctly. The scene has the narrative function of preparing the audience for the eventual failure of the Trojan attack on the ships. It also serves to characterize the important actors. Here, as at another point (XVIII 249–313), Polydamas is presented as the bearer of a warning ignored, while Hector is given the role of the heroic fighter, excessively proud and blind. Instead of calmly and carefully considering the situation, Hector allows himself to be led by his own wishful thinking to an inappropriate action.[33] He not only castigates the bearer for his message, he even expresses fundamental doubts about the most prominent form of divination.[34] It is remarkable that such criticism

---

[31] Hainsworth 1993:341.

[32] See *Iliad* XI 181–215.

[33] Struck 2003:175–178 emphasizes Hector's ability to master the crisis provoked by the omen. This aspect of Hector's behavior was indeed regarded as exemplary in Antiquity: see e.g. Epaminondas, cited by Diodorus Siculus 15.52.4. At the same time, Hector fails as an interpreter, while his reaction to Polydamas betrays a tendency to tyranny. To judge him from Struck's examples, he belongs rather beside Agamemnon and Oedipus than with Themistocles. Again, in the assembly scene in XVIII 249–311 Hector rejects the sensible advice of Polydamas with exaggerated self-consciousness, and so ironically prepares the way for his own death.

[34] According to Stockinger 1959:34 the "enlightened" attitude of Hector towards augury, in this sharpness, is exceptional in the *Iliad*. He further asserts that Priam's reply to Hecabe (*Iliad* XXIV 218ff) can scarcely be compared with it. On the contrary: like Hector, Priam also appeals

of a central element of religion can be articulated at all in epic. Even when the poet does not share Hector's doubts, and in the continuation of his story effectively rejects them, his account reflects the fact that such doubts were possible and defensible in the aristocratic circles of the Homeric period. The Trojans applaud their leader, whose superior power and higher prestige lend him credibility.[35]

The whirlwind with which Zeus lends new momentum to the Trojan attack follows directly after the unfavorable bird omen. Each of the interventions has a different perspective, and as such can be reconciled at the narrative level.[36] With respect to how the actors should conduct themselves, however, there is a lack of specificity: the contradictory valence of the signs makes it difficult to recognize the divine will.

5. Halitherses (*Odyssey* ii 1–259)

Telemachus complains about the erosion of his property by the suitors of his mother, Penelope, before an assembly of the people in Ithaca which he himself has summoned. In the name of the suitors, Antinous denies Telemachus' charge: he emphasizes that Penelope's behavior towards the suitors is contrary to custom, and challenges Telemachus to force his mother to marry again. Telemachus in turn rejects this suggestion and reminds them of the respect which should be shown to his mother; he requests again that the liberties taken in his house should stop, and he prays that Zeus may vindicate him. A bird sign appears: two eagles fly close together with extended wings from the heights of the mountains. As they fly over the middle of the assembly, "they wheeled about, flapping their wings rapidly, and down on the heads of all they looked, and death was in their glance. Then they tore with their talons their own cheeks [or one another's cheeks] and necks on either side, and darted away to the right across the houses and the city of those who stood there" (151–154). The old seer Halitherses interprets the omen as a warning to the suitors and the entire town, because he sees Odysseus as an angel of vengeance *ante portas*. The suitor Eurymachus answers him with harsh words:

---

to direct communication with the gods against divination. His doubts, however, are directed against mantic specialists generally, and so against every form of divination which is dependent upon human mediators and interpreters.

[35] See Collins 2002:36–39.

[36] Stockinger 1959:33 rightly sees here no contradiction for the poet and his audience. However, he overlooks the perspective of the protagonists, who must act without the poet's omniscience.

he deprives the interpretation of verity, asserts that Halitherses' interpretation is rather motivated by his own interests, and threatens him with heavy sanctions if Halitherses continues to encourage the young Telemachus against the suitors.

On the narrative level, the omen functions as guidance to the recipients. A conflict is brought into the open before the assembly, where it is not at all clear which side is justified.[37] The sign indicates the side that the gods have taken, and thus anticipates the subsequent development. Zeus sends the two eagles in order to show that he has accepted the prayer of Telemachus. By means of this mantic incident, which interrupts the speeches of the two parties in the assembly, the poet awakens in the audience the expectation that the apparently weaker cause of Telemachus will triumph in the end.

Once again, the sign is constructed according to the pattern of a figurative analogy. The relationship is clear: the behavior of the eagles—their appearance from the mountains, their wings flapping over the *agora*, and their departure over the houses of the town—is a commentary on what is happening in the assembly. The estimation of this episode is also clear, although here, the poet does not draw attention to the left-right polarization: the eagles are recognized by everybody as a bad omen. Verse 153, however, is problematic.[38] Its wider meaning is dependant on the question whether the participle *drupsamenō* here should be understood as reciprocal or reflexive. Do the eagles fight against each other, in which case they prophesy the civil war? Or do they represent Odysseus and Telemachus, who then do not wound one another, but rather themselves, as an act of mourning? The interpretation of Halitherses offers here no direct key, as it avoids an explanation of the analogy between the sign and the situation. The seer instead gives only a summary interpretation, in which he identifies Odysseus and the suitors as the opposing parties, without revealing the source of his understanding. It may be that Halitherses does not dare to speak openly because of the overwhelming strength of the suitors. If, as appears from the bird flight, the suitors and the entire community of the Ithacaeans are the addressees of the evil omen, then we may take the two eagles as symbolic representatives of the means of ruin. Odysseus would then be one of the eagles, while the other remains undistinguished. Halitherses behaves as if only one eagle appears, because he considers it inappropriate to bring Telemachus into the open as a protagonist.[39]

---

[37] See Flaig 1995.

[38] δρυψαμένω δ' ὀνύχεσσι παρειὰς ἀμφί τε δειράς (*Odyssey* ii 153).

[39] This interpretation follows Stockinger 1959:52n3; Thornton 1970:53 (and n7); West 1988:141–142; and de Jong 2001:53, who all take δρυψαμένω in verse 153 as reflexive. Cf., however, the

Halitherses is introduced as an old hero, prominent among his contemporaries because "he surpassed all men of his day in knowledge of birds and in uttering words of fate" (ii 158–159). He says of himself: "Not as one untried do I prophesy, but with sure knowledge."[40] Here, he refers to his prophecy concerning the Trojan campaign and Odysseus which, as he claims, has been partly fulfilled but which remains to be completely fulfilled.[41] Even Eurymachus admits that his opponent is wise in the wisdom of the old (ii 188: *palaia te polla te eidōs*). Like Calchas, Halitherses also receives authentication from the poet, who leaves the audience in no doubt that he discloses the truth. And like Calchas, he takes the stage with the aim of giving expression to the interests of the entire community. As an introduction to his speech, the poet uses the same words which were used with Calchas in the first book of the *Iliad*.[42] At the same time, this episode recalls the figure of Polydamas as a bearer of disregarded warnings. Halitherses is further associated with the two seers of the *Iliad* in that he, too, must tolerate insults from one more powerful than he.

Eurymachus threatens to take the seer's children and impose a painful penance on him. He expresses skepticism towards bird signs and their interpreters. "Many birds there are that pass to and fro under the rays of the sun, but not all are fateful."[43] Birds can have significance, but the ability and the authority to stipulate the criterion for their significance is in effect denied

---

reasonable objections of Roth 1982:113n29: "Aside from the implausible and ludicrous picture presented by the two eagles engaged in mournful self-mutilation in mid-air, the adoption of human characteristics by animals in Homer is unparalleled (though the reverse is, of course, common)." The same author (Roth 1982:92) defends understanding the verb as reciprocal: "The violence which the eagles inflict on each other foreshadows the internecine violence that will erupt in Ithaca when Odysseus returns home." West (see above) suggests textual corruption in verses 152–154, as Wilamowitz 1927:102n3 had earlier proposed.

[40] *Odyssey* ii 170: οὐ γὰρ ἀπείρητος μαντεύομαι, ἀλλ᾽ ἐὺ εἰδώς· He is presented in a very similar fashion in xxiv 451–462 when, after the death of the suitors, he again appears before an assembly and advises the fathers of the dead not to take revenge: ὁ γὰρ οἶος ὅρα πρόσσω καὶ ὀπίσσω (452). Cf. the commentary by Russo 1992:409: Halitherses "is not credited with supernatural mantic powers but with wisdom and clear understanding which enable him to draw conclusions about the future from the past."

[41] See West 1988:142: "Halitherses' argumentation is circular; he infers from his interpretation of the present omen that this prophecy twenty years before was correct, and hence that his interpretation of what has just happened is trustworthy. But the validity of his warning is not affected by this illogicality; the omen simply confirms the moral judgement of right-minded men." Yet the matter is not so simple, as Penelope's behavior also violates certain social conventions: see Flaig 1995.

[42] *Odyssey* ii 160 (see xxiv 453, and *Iliad* I 73): ὅ σφιν ἐυφρονέων ἀγορήσατο καὶ μετέειπε.

[43] *Odyssey* ii 181–182: ὄρνιθες δέ τε πολλοὶ ὑπ᾽αὐγὰς ἠελίοιο φοιτῶσ᾽, οὐδέ τε πάντες ἐναίσιμοι·

to Halitherses and his colleagues. This skepticism naturally characterizes the overweening pride of the suitors on the narrative level. At the same time, it is significant that such skepticism can be expressed in a public assembly, as we have already seen. Eurymachus does not seek the real explanation for Halitherses' interpretation in the domain of divination: he questions Halitherses' impartiality and incorruptibility, and he claims that the seer hopes to win a gift for his prophecy.[44] Of course, Halitherses was not entirely impartial: at xvii 69 he is listed among the *patrōioi hetairoi* of Telemachus. The speech of Eurymachus shows once again that in the Homeric world, a recognized seer, even when he is old, is assured neither immunity nor uncontested authority. When conflicts arise, signs, interpreters, and interpretations may reflect communal interests, but this is not sufficient to reestablish a consensus, as the *stasis* on Ithaca illustrates. Karen Piepenbrink in particular has observed the precarious function of divination in the social communication of Homeric society:

> Der Bezug auf Zeichen der Götter ist dabei um so erfolgreicher, je größer der Konsens in der Gesellschaft bereits ist; er wird also dann gut aufgenommen, wenn er nur unterstützende Funktion hat und zu anderen Argumenten hinzutritt.[45]

6. Theoclymenus (*Odyssey* xv 222–286, 508–546)

As Telemachus offers sacrifice in Pylus before his return to Ithaca, Theoclymenus, a seer from the family of Melampus, comes to him seeking asylum (he had killed a man in Argos); the seer asks to be taken along, and Telemachus agrees (xv 222–286). After their arrival in Ithaca, Theoclymenus asks Telemachus where he should go. The latter recommends the house of Eurymachus, "for he is by far the best man, and is the most eager to marry my mother and to have the honor of Odysseus." Telemachus concludes with the words: "Nevertheless, Olympian Zeus, who dwells in the sky, knows whether before the wedding he will bring upon them the day of reckoning." There

---

[44] In this way, the poet introduces into Greek literature, through the mouth of Eurymachus, a motif which would have a profound influence, above all in tragedy and comedy. It is formulated in an almost gnomic fashion by Creon in Sophocles' *Antigone* 1055: τὸ μαντικὸν γὰρ πᾶν φιλάργυρον γένος.

[45] Piepenbrink 2001:22–23 (and *passim*). The author convincingly traces "the comparably weak position of the seer" back to the weaknesses of the gods as norm-establishing authorities (22–23).

appears a bird sign: a hawk, "the swift messenger of Apollo," flies from the right with a dove in its talons and devours it, scattering feathers over the earth between the ship and Telemachus himself. Theoclymenus interprets this allegorically, rejecting the apparent ambitions of Eurymachus: "No other descent than yours in Ithaca is more kingly; you are supreme forever." Telemachus is pleased to hear this message, promises him many gifts in the event of success, and entrusts him to his companion Piraeus (xv 508–546).

The poet combines the appearance of Theoclymenus with a genealogical excursus (xv 222–255). He explains the story of the Melampodidae as the history of a *normal* aristocratic family. However, it is not *normal* that many members of this family, like Theoclymenus, are permanent wanderers or in flight. This fate is already ascribed to the founder of the family, Melampus, as well as to Amphiaraus and Polyphides. Not by chance, the latter two are the leading representatives of this family of seers, in terms of their mantic ability. While Amphiaraus enjoys the special favor of Zeus and Apollo (244–246), Apollo makes Polyphides "by far the best seer among mortals after the death of Amphiaraus" (252–253). The poet offers here no example of their mantic ability.[46] As Melampodid and son of Polyphides, Theoclymenus is thus introduced here in a way which leaves the audience in little doubt as to his mantic qualification.[47]

The sign appears in an ominous situation. Telemachus has just returned to Ithaca with his men from an unsuccessful journey. He was unable to obtain reliable information as to the fate of his father, and so has no reason to be optimistic. When Theoclymenus asks him where he should go, Telemachus directs him *contre cœur* to the most powerful noble, who is in a position to take over the wife and the position of honor (*geras*) of Odysseus. Finally, he directs this view of the future, which on the face of it is quite plausible, as a question to Zeus, who answers with the omen. As the bird flies from the right, the answer implies that it concerns the wishes of Telemachus. Further, the feathers of the victim confirm the connection: "The feathers, which are the symbol of the imminent destruction of Eurymachus, fall into the realm of power of Telemachus."[48] The hawk represents Odysseus,[49] while the dove symbolizes Eurymachus.

---

[46] But see *Odyssey* xi 291–297, where it is reported that Melampus is liberated from imprisonment after having proven his ability as a seer.

[47] See Thornton 1970:58–61; Dillery 2005:173–174.

[48] Thornton 1970:54.

[49] Irene de Jong 2001:383 gives two arguments for the fact that here the bird is a hawk (or falcon, as she has it): "(i) Apollo is the god of prophecy and this bird-sign is interpreted by a professional seer, and (ii) the Suitors will be killed during a festive day for Apollo."

In contrast to the poet's audience, Theoclymenus is not in a position to give a "complete" interpretation of the sign, because he does not know the situation in Ithaca; moreover, as a suppliant, he should display a certain reserve. He goes only so far as to identify the hawk with Telemachus' concerns because of the direction of flight. The superiority of the hawk then suggests the enduring primacy of Telemachus' family. Who precisely is denoted by the dove and by the hawk, and which confrontation is symbolized in the sky, Theoclymenus leaves open, in spite of the previous information which he has from Telemachus.

After he has learned more of the situation in Ithaca, Theoclymenus makes his interpretation more precise. On the basis of the sign which appeared at the moment of his arrival in Ithaca, he informs Penelope that Odysseus is already back in his homeland and is preparing trouble for the suitors.[50] The real art of the seer thus lies less in the technical deciphering of the sign than in the correct and convincing contextualization; that is, in the application of the sign to a specific situation, which takes into account the needs of the addressee. This in turn assumes good knowledge and sensitivity on the part of the seer.

7. Conclusions: The Seer in Homer—and Beyond

The Homeric seer represents a social type which is particularly characteristic of Greek culture. By this I mean first, that from the sixth century the historical figure of the Greek seer stands in a direct relationship of continuity with the situation described by Homer; second, that there are fundamental differences between the Greek seer and mantic specialists in other ancient cultures. By way of illustrating and substantiating these claims, I would like to make some general observations.

There is a contrast between, on the one hand, the authoritative statements by the poet about the seers and, on the other hand, the way in which the practice of the seers is described within the story. For example, although, as we have seen, the poet introduces the seer Calchas as a man who has knowledge of the past, the present, and the future, and who has received his mantic ability and extraordinary insight directly from Apollo, nonetheless, like other seers, he is not treated with respect by the powerful in every situation. While

---

[50] *Odyssey* xvii 151–165. Like Helen in *Odyssey* xv 177–178, Theoclymenus leaves a secondary aspect open: "whether he [Odysseus] now sits or wanders somewhere" (xvii 158). Penelope is pleased by this message, and promises rich rewards in the event of his return. Yet in spite of this positive reaction, she does not trust the prophecy, as her behavior shows.

the seers' advice and foresight can be seen to have been justified throughout the narrative level, in practice their advice cannot always be implemented and it is often received with a pervasive skepticism. How can this contrast be explained? I do not think we need to resort to the kind of theory which would argue that at some time before Homer, seers were generally accepted as *masters of truth* but that they had subsequently lost their credibility.[51] Rather, I believe that the poet invests seers with authority because they fulfill an important literary function. The epic seers, whose prophecies always prove to be right, represent the poet within the narrative. Their knowledge, which transcends ordinary temporal perception, characterizes the narrator and the seer in exactly the same way. Yet if one wishes to analyze the social standing and authority that the seer enjoys within Homeric society, it would be more useful to examine the seer in action. This is why I have concentrated on the most important and prominent performances of the seers in the *Iliad* and the *Odyssey* here.

In the first book of the *Iliad*, Calchas prevails with his proposals concerning the plague because the good sense of his judgment is perfectly obvious to everybody. Nonetheless, he needs the backing of Achilles, a powerful nobleman, in order to be able to stand up to Agamemnon, the commander of the Achaean army. Yet the interventions of Polydamas and Halitherses are easily dismissed by more powerful figures such as Hector and Eurymachus, who employ threats to force the seer to remain silent. Theoclymenus, who came as a stranger into the Ithacaean community, is treated with contempt and arrogance by the suitors. In public discourse, the seer must always respect the dominant status of the powerful. Although the character of the community assembly in the Archaic period changed, and differences in status have an increasingly limited significance, the mantic professionals did not gain in authority, as the famous debate over the oracle concerning the *wooden wall* in Athens shows.[52] Unlike other professionals, the mantic specialists could claim no particular authority in public debates, even in their own area of ostensible competence. This situation is also reflected in political institutions which, as

---

[51] Detienne 1967 regards the seer, the poet, and the king as prephilosophical "maîtres de vérité"; cf. 1967:6: "La préhistoire de l'*Alétheia* philosophique nous conduit vers le système de pensée du devin, du poète et du roi de justice, vers les trois secteurs où un certain type de parole se définit par l'*Alétheia*." These three archetypal figures cannot, however, be anchored in a specific historical reality, and already appear to be anachronistic in Homeric society, as Detienne himself admits (1967:81–103). For criticism of this approach and similar concepts in F. M. Crawford and J.-P. Vernant, see Leszl 1996:47–54.

[52] Herodotus 7.142–144. Another fine example is the debate over the succession of King Agis in Sparta, ca. 400 BC: Xenophon *Hellenica* 3.3.1–3.

far as we know, included no office of seer in any Greek *polis*, at least in Pre-Hellenistic times. Certainly, though, within the *polis*, the seer could exercise some informal influence on the formation of public opinion, while outside the city, on campaign, his influence depended on the personal confidence of the generals.

Already in the Homeric epics, skepticism towards signs and dreams as well as towards their professional interpreters is repeatedly expressed.[53] Admittedly, this skepticism is directed not towards divination as such, but rather always concerns the question of its appropriate interpretation. Moreover, the possibility of divine deception in mantic communication is often taken into account.[54] That contradictory signs are reported also leads, at least in the short term, to uncertainty.[55] The chronological context of signification—the time frame within which the message conveyed by the sign will be realized—is often unclear; this constitutes another important difference from Mesopotamian and Etruscan divination. Occasionally, direct communication is placed in opposition to the interpretation of signs.[56] Even positive signs often appear to have only an ephemeral capacity to persuade, insofar as they do not seem to influence the conduct of the actors to any degree, as is particularly clear in the cases of Telemachus and Penelope in the *Odyssey*. Signs only appear to important actors. The relevance can remain questionable for the people concerned, though not for the audience of the poetry. As is also common in later literature, the poet exposes such disrespect and skepticism through his narrative. It is clear that it is never the interpretation which is determined by particular interests, but rather the skepticism, which reveals itself as a futile refusal to recognize the will of the gods. Skepticism is also occasionally used as a pretext by actors who cannot allow their true faces to be seen. Nonetheless, it remains significant that an admitted disrespect and skepticism towards divination and its professional interpreters not only can make itself heard, but even be articulated in a serious manner. This aspect also binds Homer with the later literary tradition.[57]

---

[53] Disrespect and/or skepticism towards divination and its interpreters is expressed by Hector (*Iliad* XII 237–243), Priam (*Iliad* XXIV 219–222), Telemachus (*Odyssey* i 413–416), Eurymachus (*Odyssey* ii 180–186), and Penelope (*Odyssey* xix 560–569). See Collins 2002:39–40.

[54] See Schmitt 1990:259f (and n278).

[55] Homer, *Iliad* VIII 169–171, XII 200–258.

[56] Hector: *Iliad* XII 235–238; Priam: *Iliad* XXIV 220–224.

[57] E.g. Sophocles *Oedipus Tyrannus* 380–389, *Antigone* 1033–1061; Euripides *Helena* 744–760, *Bacchae* 255–258, fr. 795 (Nauck²); Aristophanes *Pax* 1043–1126; *Aves* 958–999; Thucydides 5.103.2, 8.1.1; Diodorus Siculus 15.52.3–7.

While the poet only reports appropriate diagnoses and prognoses of the seers,[58] some actors, without doubting their mantic qualifications, nevertheless certainly do question the seers' impartiality and incorruptibility, threatening them with sanctions or subjecting them to mockery. This occurs especially when individual seers stand in the way of the powerful and defend the concerns of the community against egoistic interests. The serious threats which such resistance repeatedly provokes are presented by the poet in changing constellations (Agamemnon—Calchas; Hector—Polydamas; Eurymachus—Halitherses; suitors—Theoclymenus). In such situations, a seer can even be killed, as the example of Leodes, who acts as a soothsayer at sacrifices among the suitors, shows. Although Leodes is characterized by the poet as a "good" (that is, reserved) suitor, Odysseus is explicitly unwilling to show him mercy because he had supposedly approved prayers against his return.[59] It is precisely his qualifications which work here to his disadvantage. Their capacity as seers ensured mantic specialists no unconditional respect and no *sacrosanctitas*.[60]

The activities of the seer are based more or less on older, traditional techniques. In addition to the specific arts which are already mentioned by Homer (above all the observation of bird flight, the interpretation of dreams, and the indications to be discerned in the burned sacrifice), there appeared in the sixth century the reading of entrails, which immediately established itself as the most important technique of the seers. However, neither Homer nor any later sources devote any particular attention to the technical principles of the seer.[61] Technical expertise was not considered especially important in the mantic culture of the Greeks, and it was not highly developed. Unlike the mantic professionals in Mesopotamia or Etruria, for example, the Greek seers were not scholars who were bound together by a *disciplina* and who based themselves on a fixed written canon.[62] It is then not surprising that at the level of their sophistication, the techniques of the Greek seers could not compete

---

[58] The recommendations of the seers, however, are not always represented by the poet as being successful: see Helenus in *Iliad* VI 311.

[59] *Odyssey* xxii 310–329; see also the murder of the seer Hegesistratus by the Spartans in Herodotus 9.37.

[60] See Kett 1966:113–114.

[61] On the augury see now Collins 2002; Baumbach and Trampedach 2004 (both with further references).

[62] In my opinion, it is therefore misleading to identify Greek seers with the mantic specialists of Mesopotamia, as do e.g. Pritchett 1979:77, Burkert 1992:43–53, and West 1997:46–51. It is not coincidental that in Greece, in contrast to Mesopotamia, the Levant, Anatolia, and Etruria, no clay or bronze liver models have been found.

with those of seers in the Near East or in Italy, and that a layperson such as Xenophon could claim that merely by watching, he learned the principles of reading entrails.[63]

In practice, the Homeric seer considered himself to be primarily a reader of signs. The signs are integrated into the narrative, as also in later texts, and thus refer directly to specific situations. In contrast to Mesopotamian and Etruscan traditions, there was no *objective* sign. Rather, the coincidence of an observation with an important human event decides the semantics of a sign, at least to the extent that it appears to be spontaneous and unsolicited. The typical pattern, which is reflected in Homer, is the principle of allegory.[64] The art of the seer displays itself in concrete terms: (1) in the recognition of signs as divine messages; (2) in the interpretation—above all in placing the sign in relation to a personal and situational context; (3) in taking account of the needs of the addressee.[65] The better the seer is informed about the situation of his client, the more precise will be his interpretation. The seer's epistemology involves both rational and nonrational elements which, however, do not result in a contradictory picture. On the one hand, the assumption of an eclectic intelligence on the basis of a rational evaluation of the situation is not sufficient to explain their activity; on the other hand, the way in which the attributed divine designation affected their activity remains unclear. Apart from one exception,[66] they display no exceptional spiritual nature, as in spirit possession or ecstasy. To suppose that they employed techniques of one sort or another, which would have been passed on within the families of seers, would seem to be indispensable if we are to understand this phenomenon at all, with its subcategories of augury, dream interpretation, and evaluation of burnt sacrifices. Such techniques are, however, never mentioned in epic and can at best be inferred; at least at the level of poetry, they obviously did not contribute to the authority of the seer. There remains, then, little more to say of seers in Homer than what Michel Casevitz has summarized:

---

[63] Xenophon *Anabasis* 5.6.29; cf. Xenophon *Cyropaedia* 1.6.2; Onasander *Strategicus* 10.25.

[64] All omen scenes in the Homeric epics are listed by de Jong 2001:52–53, who also describes their typical pattern. Configurations of animals on this pattern are to be found in later literature of various genres, too: see e.g. Herodotus 1.78, 3.76; Xenophon *Cyropaedia* 2.4.18f; Plutarch *Alexander* 73.1–3; Aeschylus *Agamemnon* 107–257, *Persians* 175–230, 518–526.

[65] See above: the varying emphases in the interpretation of the same sign by Theoclymenus, at *Odyssey* xv 525–534; xvii 151–165.

[66] In *Odyssey* xx 345–383, Theoclymenus announces their impending disaster to the suitors by a spontaneous visionary outburst. They react with laughter and regard the stranger as a madman. The reaction of the suitors demonstrates both their *hubris*, and the exceptional character of this prophecy. See Russo 1992:124.

> ... *mantis* désigne à l'origine un explicateur, un annonceur, un spécialiste des décryptages, un «décodeur.»[67]

The way in which seers observe and *read* and decipher such signs in reference to the situation demonstrates the competence of the seer, which, however, should not be regarded as exclusively his own. The art of the interpretation derives from a practical intelligence and is an individual power, not (as again, for example, in Mesopotamia and Etruria) a privilege of a particular group. Besides seers, other prominent figures appear as interpreters of signs; and because of their social position, these others are in a better position to impose their views.[68] We find the same constellation in later sources, in which the first recipients and interpreters of unsolicited signs are more often military commanders and politicians than seers. Yet if technical expertise is not conspicuously important, and if interpretative competence is not invested exclusively in them, then on what basis do seers acquire their reputation? I agree with Michael Flower's view that membership of certain families and, above all, a personal and reliable *charisma* proven by success, are deciding factors.[69]

If the Greek seer displays no typological resemblance to Mesopotamian and Etruscan technical experts, then do they display any greater resemblance to shamans or magicians? The answer is clear: definitely not. While in the *Iliad* and the *Odyssey* none of the more prominent kings is himself a seer, it is not uncommon for a famous exponent to be a descendant of a royal house, as, for example, the Priamide Helenus.[70] Already in the *Odyssey*, wandering belongs to the characteristic traits of seers, as is reflected above all in the story of Theoclymenus and his family, the Melampodidae. Wandering seers in other, lost epics as definite motifs are here relevant.[71] Admittedly, in the *Odyssey*, as

---

[67] Casevitz 1992:7; see Roth 1982:75–81; Chirassi Colombo 1985, esp.148–149. According to Casevitz 1989, tragedy mediates a similar picture. It is precisely the activity of Homeric seers which cannot be confined within the corset of the Platonic distinction between inspired and technical divination: see Trampedach 2003. The difficulty of employing this famous differentiation can be seen e.g. in the paper of Di Sacco Franco 2000, who fails to perceive the distinction between the normative speech of the seer and his real activity, and is consequently led to a grotesque overestimation of the importance of the seer for *Homeric society*.

[68] In addition to the mantic specialists (*Iliad*: Calchas, Helenus; *Odyssey*: Halitherses, Theoclymenus), other leading figures (*Iliad*: Agamemnon, Odysseus, Nestor, Hector, Polydamas; *Odyssey*: Helen, Odysseus, Penelope) are also active as interpreters.

[69] See above, in this volume.

[70] See Bremmer 1996a:100–101; Roth 1982:124–127.

[71] See Löffler 1963:30–58 (on the myths concerning seers in the *Melampodia*, the Theban legend cycle, and the *Nostoi*); and Scheer 1993:153–271.

in later literature, the seer appears as a wandering professional who offers his services as a stranger to different *employers*.[72] At the same time, he is not an outsider, but rather a typical product of the Greek aristocracy, which is particularly clear from his lifestyle. Without exception, the Homeric seers participate in aristocratic activities—warfare, competitive sports, courtship, theft, and so on. It is equally natural for their historical successors to see themselves as warriors. Apart from literary accounts, lists of the dead preserved as inscriptions testify to their often fatal exploits.[73] Evidence of the self-perception of the seers, such as victory songs and grave inscriptions, tend to emphasize their activities in war.[74] Seers are occasionally conspicuous in war for possessing levels of strategic ability and cleverness that make them comparable or even superior to their commanders.[75] Nor were other aristocratic pursuits foreign to them. Thus, we hear repeatedly of seers as winners in the Panhellenic games, who are honored in odes and the dedication of statues.[76] The aristocratic lifestyle was possible for seers because, unlike the mostly female mediums (for example, the Pythia), they were not expected to observe any bodily restraints. In their outward appearance, seers also displayed no specific characteristics, aside from the fact that in the fulfillment of their activities they seem to have assumed the marks of office of a priest, principally the wearing of the laurel wreath and the priest's headband.[77] Given these considerations, it seems to me to be rather misleading to associate Greek seers with shamanism or magic,[78] at least to the extent that they enjoyed public recognition. Neither asceti-

---

[72] *Odyssey* xvii 382–386. Citing this passage, Burkert 1992:42 declares the early Archaic seers to be "the mobile bearers of cross-cultural knowledge," but fails to give sufficient and convincing evidence for the "cross-cultural" aspect.

[73] *IG* I³ 1147.128; *SEG* 29, 1979, no. 361.3. Cases transmitted in literary sources: Herodotus 7.219–221; Xenophon *Hellenica* 2.4.18–19; Plutarch *Lysander* 28.5; Pausanias 4.21.10–11; see Bremmer 1993:153–154.

[74] Pindar *Olympian* 6.12–21; *SEG* 16, 1959, no. 193 (see Kett 1966:52–53); *SEG* 23, 1968, no. 161; *SEG* 41, 1991, no. 226; *IG* XII ix 291; Pausanias 3.12.8; see Flower, above, in this volume.

[75] Herodotus 8.27.3 (see also Pausanias 10.1.10–11); Thucydides 3.20.1–2; Pausanias 4.21.8–12; see Dillery 2005:200–209.

[76] Pindar *Olympian* 6 (see Flower, in this volume); Herodotus 9.33.2; Pausanias 3.11.6, 6.14.13, 6.4.5, 6.17.5–6. Even their mantic abilities could be represented as an *agōn*, as the famous story of seers' competition shows: Hesiod fr. 278–279 (Merkelbach/West); see Scheer 1993:162–173.

[77] Kett 1966:103–104; Roth 1982:141–142 In artistic representations, seers are not particularly prominent; on vases, they usually appear as gesticulating older men wearing an *himation*: van Straten 1995:156–157, 168. Portrayals of mythical seers similarly display no specific characteristics: V. Saladino, *LIMC* 5.1 (1990), 934–935, s.v. Kalchas; E. Simon, *LIMC* 6.1 (1992), 409, s.v. Melampous.

[78] As do e.g. Dodds 1951:140–156; Luck 1990:302; and Metzler 1990. The presentation of Burkert 1962 is more balanced and circumspect.

cism and seclusion nor spirit possession nor ecstasy nor psychological instability belong to the characteristics of Greek seers, even though some of these tendencies existed at the geographical and social periphery of Greece and found expression in individual figures such as Pythagoras and Empedocles.

Epilogue

Practitioners of the Divine
A Task with Many Prospects

Beate Dignas and Kai Trampedach

A LBERT HENRICHS WARNED US at the beginning of this volume. Did we even know what we were talking about when we invited scholars to a conference on Greek priests? To be sure, for practical reasons we were using the term *priest* in its broadest and most inclusive sense. The American anthropologist Melford Spiro defines religion convincingly as "an institution consisting of culturally patterned interaction with culturally postulated superhuman beings"; placing our subject within this framework, we may say that a priest is anyone who plays a prominent role in the described interaction. Applied to Greek culture, this definition of priesthood includes *hiereis* and *manteis* and all the other practitioners of the divine listed by Henrichs. Inevitably, our approach raises the following two questions. First, how do various types of Greek priests differ from one another? Second, what is specifically Greek about Greek priests? Individual chapters, as well as the volume as a whole, seek to address these questions.

Regardless of terminology, what mattered at first was to invite a group of scholars with wide-ranging expertise; with a variety of approaches toward Greek religion; and with interests ranging from the history of classical scholarship on the subject to social history, historiography, cult operation, and divination. We knew that Greek priests presented a challenging topic, at once central and neglected. Monographs on Greek priests are virtually nonexistent, and this for various reasons. During our symposium in Washington, DC, Walter Burkert's verdict that "Greek religion might almost be called a religion without priests" was quoted more than once. Yet, numerous priests appear in our sources, and they are by no means subsidiary figures. The new and welcome volume of the *Thesaurus Cultus et Rituum Antiquorum*, half of which is dedicated to the personnel of cults, illustrates not only how rich and diverse our evidence is but also the need for interpretation. In her introduction to the subject, V. Pirenne-Delforge raises two crucial points that should form the basis of any study of Greek priesthood.[1] First, it is essential to bring together literary, epigraphic, and visual sources in order to grasp the complexity of the phenomenon of priesthood. The priests who appear in Greek literature have to be congruent with priests in inscriptions or their visual representations. Discrepancies (which clearly emerge) deserve examination and should afford an incentive to reevaluate the relevant material.[2] Second, neither the lack of a sacerdotal class based on vocation nor the political face of Greek priesthood necessarily turns the Greek priest into a magistrate like any other.

As we are confronted with a complicated terminology of priestly office as well as with different images conveyed in different genres, aspects of definition are crucial. There is no doubt that Greek priests are different from our charged expectations of what a priest should be like, but what *are* their roles? Are they political figures, *sacred* personnel, administrators, volunteers, good citizens, mediators, representatives of any particular socio-economic group? Did individuals—the great men and women who used their role as priests or made priesthood special through charisma and exceptional achievements—shape the nature of priesthood? Are Greek priests of the Archaic period comparable to those of the late Hellenistic period? How did an Athenian priest compare to a priest in a small *polis* in Western Asia Minor? How did priestly families shape Greek religion?

It is impossible to give general answers to any of these questions or to make firm statements that describe *the* Greek priest. At the same time, it must be possible to identify criteria that shaped Greek priesthood—criteria which apply to many places and many points in time. To give but a few examples, these criteria could involve local contexts, specific political settings, special events, urban or rural settings, private or public contexts, gender roles, and ritual traditions. We hope that the fruits of our symposium will help to give *Greek priests* their due place (or places) in handbooks of Greek religion as well as in comparative works, specialized studies on ancient ritual, and general works on ancient Greece.

The eleven contributions to this volume illustrate the fact that priests and other religious officials—*practitioners of the divine* as we have chosen to call them—abound in Greek religion. We are trying to be more cautious than most

---

[1] *ThesCRA* 5:2–3.

[2] Examples of a comparison or integration of epigraphic and literary material can be found in Motte 2005, as well as in Pirenne-Delforge 2005.

scholars of Greek religion before us, some of whom did not hesitate to use the problematic word *priest* when talking about a variety of Greek phenomena. This term is employed for lack of a suitable modern alternative and denotes "one who concerns himself with *hiera*," although we know that we are being vague; hence, a subtitle that does come back to the *priest*, the *anachronistic misnomer*, but which does not neglect the variety of religious personnel with whom we are concerned. Most chapters address problems of definition and reflect the critical awareness that the introduction postulates.

From Homer to Heliodorus—the scope of this volume is immense. Yet rather than offer a chronological survey, these chapters present analyses of factors that shaped or even determined the role of sacred practitioners in general. The criteria that come into play are different in each case because some chapters focus on very specific points in time, on political premises, ritual peculiarities, or particular sites, whereas others address gender roles, the question of Greek- and non-Greek contexts, or ideals as opposed to a more general day-to-day reality. Nonetheless, all contributions ask about the status, background, expertise, and self-representation of the religious practitioners involved. We were struck by the degree to which the character of the evidence used for analysis is crucial when attempting to reconstruct profiles of Greek priests; we were equally impressed to see how instructive it can be to engage with unfamiliar textual genres—both experiences that we wish to share with our readers and that are, in part, reflected by the table of contents.

Angelos Chaniotis's survey of *priests as ritual experts*, a theme that draws primarily on epigraphic evidence, goes well beyond testing the long-standing view that the performance of ritual, above all animal sacrifice, is what defines a *hiereus*. Chaniotis distinguishes between priests as performers of ritual ("they certainly were") and priests as ritual experts ("in most cases not a requirement but there were many exceptions"), and then moves on to ask about the parameters that determined whether priests were not merely the former but also the latter. Priests could become ritual experts for various reasons: individual attitudes, most visible in acts of beneficence; family traditions; and an interest in ancient customs and local ritual particularities. References to Aristotle's *Politics* as well as to Plato's *Laws* are not rare when it comes to definitions of priesthood. The passages cited (most often *Politics* 1322b and *Laws* 909d–910e) are poignant and show one thing above all: priesthoods—imaginary or real—belonged to the context of the *polis* and can only be properly understood within this context. However, Chaniotis's seemingly banal observation that "not every priest received an honorary decree, [which] suggests that some of them were fulfilling their duties in a more successful manner than others" is crucial and invites us to look beyond a civic framework of Greek priesthood; to look, that is, at the potential rather than just the constraints of priestly office. Such an approach applies, for example, to those responsible for writing down sacred regulations: "we can be certain that in most cases they were holders of priesthoods." If this is true—and it must be—then who can claim that priests did not shape the religious life of a *polis*? The many examples of priests who were exceptionally involved in the cults they served illustrate the plurality of priesthood. The wide temporal scope of Chaniotis's survey and his frequent references to mystery cults may provoke objections as to the applicability of such general parameters to all times and all Greek cults. In fact, however, his examples do come from every period of Greek history and every possible cult setting. His findings correspond nicely with the survey's emphases on priestly ambitions in reviving traditional rites and customs, and on the close interaction between private and public rituals—two themes that are explored in their own right by Beate Dignas and Susan Cole in the following group of chapters.

Each essay in the section on *Variations of Priesthood* investigates either a particular religious site, or cults of a particular deity. Each of the four contributions examines settings that are in one way or another *out of the ordinary*—if this term applies to Greek religion at all. In contrast to Mary Beard and John North's *Pagan Priests* (1990), the emphasis here is on the *Greek* priest, rather than on comparisons with Roman, Near Eastern, or Egyptian priesthoods. At the same time, non-Greek elements in a Greek setting (or vice versa) can be an excellent and rewarding focus when trying to establish criteria that shaped Greek priesthood. The contributions by Jan Bremmer and by Beate Dignas highlight this element and make us aware of yet another caveat regarding priests: what may look Greek may not be Greek, and what may look un-Greek may well be Greek.

Jan Bremmer examines the characteristics of priestly functions in the Ephesian Artemision in light of the complex Persian, Anatolian, and Greek background and influences on the cult. In this case, terminology affords an avenue towards understanding the easily misunderstood meaning and function of priestly office. We also see, to give but one example, how the many versions of myth have been used by both ancient commentators and modern scholars to fill in the gaps in their knowledge. At the end of his chapter, Bremmer reminds us of the differences between important characteristics of Greek priesthoods and those of a monotheistic experience. This shift in focus assumes that Ephesian priests were *Greek* priests, in spite of the complex ethnic, geographical, and cultural origins discussed earlier. The analysis of the genesis and development of Ephesian priests reveals an almost unlimited ability to adapt to new circumstances and to integrate *alien* elements. Curiously, the non-Greek elements in the cult of Ephesian Artemis thus reveal a very Greek characteristic of the practitioners of the divine involved. Bremmer's observations dovetail with those made by Dignas on the priests of Sarapis in the Greek world.

Priests of Sarapis emerge in many places and contexts in the Greek world. Dignas's chapter addresses two common assumptions that do not stand up to scrutiny. First, we tend to explain unconventional aspects of priests of Sarapis by the foreign character of the cult they served, but the epigraphic record shows that a priestly profile was in fact very much shaped by local custom, by ways of administering and structuring the religious life of a particular city. Public documents describe the activities of priests of Sarapis in just the same way as they record the activities of priests in traditional shrines. Second, and closely linked to the first point, we often distinguish between a private and a public setting and assign a *Greek* status to the cults of the Egyptian gods when they were transformed from *private* into *public* cults. However, an examination of the sanctuaries of Sarapis on Delos shows that even in the official cult, which was administered by annual priests and representatives of the Athenian state, the Delians did not and could not do away with traditional structures and customs. In particular, the observation that on Delos, and in other places, many organized groups of devotees of Sarapis were active in both private and public settings makes the common polarization between private and public priests of Sarapis unhelpful. With regard to the characterization of priesthood, the chapter encourages us to pay attention instead to the origins and history of each cult and to examine its personnel and internal structures carefully.

Case studies form the substance of Ulrich Gotter's contribution, and these lead us away from the realm of the *polis*. The relationship between secular rule and sacred authority in Anatolia has often been presented as a counter-image to the world of Greek religion. This chapter demonstrates that the situation is complex and far from stereotypical. Gotter carefully analyzes Strabo's accounts of the so-called temple states and comes to the conclusion that in most cases their priests did not, as has often been suggested, replace secular rule but were "nothing other than particularly privileged administrators of temple possessions." (It is striking that this definition of priesthood is actually not so very different from one that applies to an urban Greek context.) Only in exceptional cases was priestly rule combined with secular rule. As Gotter shows, such instances were the result of the appropriation of important priesthoods by incoming secular rulers in order to consolidate their position. Accordingly, King Archelaus absorbed and phased out the traditional authority of the priest of Zeus at the Corycian Cave, whereas the outside successor to the priestly dynasty at the sanctuary of Zeus Olbius assumed his office with pride.

Susan Cole's contribution on the preservation of ritual tradition in the cult of Demeter adds an important dimension of Greek religion to the volume: female priesthood. As Henrichs puts it in the introduction, "gender discrimination was alien to Greek religion"; indeed, the fact that women priests played a role in Greek sanctuaries that was as important as that of their male counterparts has been and is still a puzzling one to scholars. If, as is often argued, Greek priesthoods were comparable to political magistracies, then the role of women in the ritual life of the city (women being excluded from political participation) must have been determined by different guidelines and models. The general rule that female deities required female priestesses may explain why a process of democratization could not entirely impose its principles on the religious sphere, but this factor does not throw light on the profile of these holders of priestly office. Cole concentrates on priestesses of Demeter in considering the broader question of how communities guaranteed the continued and correct observance of traditional rites. The reminder to perform rites *kata ta patria* often indicates that "some kind of a change or challenge is already underway." Sometimes, such an injunction reflects merely a practical necessity to provide part-time religious officials with basic guidelines on how to do their jobs, but in many cases (see Cole's fascinating example of the Andanian mysteries) the issuing of such regulations conveyed sanctity and authenticity to a cult and its rites. Were priests central to this process? This question is of special relevance with regard to female religious officials, whose terms of office were (at least officially) formulated by an exclusively male world. Cole's findings support a statement from Robert Garland's article on "Religious Authority in Archaic and Classical Athens" (1984) to the effect that the "authority of any priest or priestess did not reach outside the boundaries of the sanctuary." However, Chaniotis's more than plausible assumption that priests contributed to the formulation of sacred laws must be read in terms of their being represented in political institutions, where they made and argued for proposals with the help of their priestly authority and first-hand knowledge. One wonders whether and how women priests were consulted, and on the basis of Cole's famous accounts of "good and bad girls," we may speculate that the priestesses' input was actually considerable. A *koinon* of priestesses of Demeter at Mantinea, a collective oath sworn at the onset of office, and epiphanies of the goddess to her priestesses as a group suggest strong links between office holders, links which transcend the confines of individual sanctuaries. Looking at the institutions which were responsible for maintaining ritual tradition, such as *genē*, political groups within the citizen body, written records, or ritual conventions, it does not seem too far-fetched to see priests, both male and female, as the crucial link in this process. The so-called Lindian Chronicle to which Cole refers is the best example of priestly letters (if only we knew more about them) and an important source for reconstructing the history and status of a sanctuary.

There is no need to justify the fact that Ralf von den Hoff's analysis of the visual representation of cult personnel on the Athenian Acropolis stands on its own. A volume on Greek priests cannot neglect the archaeological evidence, not least because this is certainly an area where priests have received considerable scholarly attention. Yet as von den Hoff observes, this attention has been at once guided and limited by the notion that Greek priests did not enjoy prestige *qua office*. A synoptic survey of images of cult personnel on the Athenian Acropolis revises this assumption and looks at how prestige was articulated over time. In the first instance, the chapter reminds us that visual attributes of priests and priestesses, be it the long *khitōn*, the priestly wreath or *strophion*, the sacrificial knife, the temple key, or the *phialē*, are important symbols that would have contributed to the status and visibility of priests at any time. Von den Hoff's chapter also stimulates the discussion of gender distinctions as we see, for example, the *female character* of the cult of Athena emphasized through the statues of young girls serving the goddess. Again, the archaeological record is very suggestive of the socio-economic background of priests, or rather of priestly ambitions, and confirms an emphasis—especially during the Hellenistic period—on the financial support that office holders may provide for the cults. The reader finds here illustrations of many of the examples presented by Angelos Chaniotis in his essay. With regard to the Archaic and Classical periods, the contrast between Athens and other places where portraits of cult officials did exist cautions us against drawing hasty general conclusions and demonstrates the fact that we need further studies with a comparable focus. At Athens, the *signa* of civic *eusebeia* take precedence over the religious service of an individual. The changes that von den Hoff observes for the fourth century are difficult to account for, even if, as he shows, the growing prestige of holding cult offices is reflected mainly in the private sphere and is used by the traditional *genē* as a means of asserting their preeminence in religious affairs. This situation is taken to a new level by the family monuments of the late fourth and early third centuries.

The section *Ideal Concepts and their Transformation* presents priests who are rather different from those whom we have met in the preceding chapters. The constructed character of the *theios anēr* in Heliodorus and the *philos-*

opher and priest among the local elites in the Roman imperial East represent specific parameters and genres as well as new and different worlds of religion. Nevertheless, the two chapters here share fundamental insights in their approach to, and understanding of, Greek priesthood. With Matthias Haake's contribution, we are confronted with inconsistencies between concept, perception and practice. The analysis shows how ideas are transformed in the real world, and Haake's observations are striking. The clash between philosophical schools and *polis* religion is a commonplace and thus offers a suitable starting point for the chapter, which scans the epigraphic evidence for individuals who were both priests and philosophers. Social practice, as Haake labels the activities of individuals in their communities, was not influenced by philosophical ideas, at least not when it came to holding priesthoods. As both the study of philosophy and the holding of priestly office were part of a model code of behavior among the local elites, potential conflicts between the two activities must have been smoothed over in some way. Haake's focal point is the philosopher, not the priest. He questions our expectations with regard to the former but not the latter. The chapter does not ask if a priest who emphasized his identity as *pepaideumenos* engaged in the study of philosophical ideas was compromising his role as priest. Yet the reminder that the conversation between Epictetus and the man from Nicopolis may not have expressed public opinion makes us rethink our approach. As we take it for granted that priesthood was about service and status in the context of *polis* life, we easily forget that other charged identities fulfilled the same role—yet we should not deny the latter a theoretical discourse.

The theme *philosopher and priest* reappears in Manuel Baumbach's contribution. To begin with, we are reminded that an unexpected genre, the romantic novel, yields abundant opportunities to explore the notion of priesthood: in Heliodorus, the Egyptian priest Calasiris is *Greek* in many ways, but above all, he is a *priest*. Distinguished by both his outward appearance and his demeanor, he is perceived by the reader as a priest throughout the novel. This also applies to the other *priests* in the work, prominent among them the heroic couple, who are even proclaimed to be a perfect match because of their identity as high priest and consecrated priestess. It thus looks as if the priest of the third century AD—at least as a literary construct—was the counterimage of a priest in the Classical or the Hellenistic period. Baumbach's observations on the second aspect of Calasiris' identity, the persona of the wise man or philosopher, support this impression. Heliodorus' priest wants to be seen as a learned man. Interestingly, to some extent he promotes this image not because he is an Egyptian priest (in whom the union of priesthood and scholarship would be expected) but because the link between the two is a universally applicable link. This representation leads us in the direction of the pagan *theios anēr*, who emerges as a role model with the second or third century AD. Apparently, this significant transformation of priesthood calls for labels such as *divine, sacred,* and *absolute religious authority*, terms which we strictly avoid in the context of *polis* religion. With these two chapters back to back, one cannot help noticing that the theoretical clash between priest and philosopher that was the focus of Haake's chapter not only becomes irrelevant but is even transformed into its opposite in Baumbach's analysis of Heliodorus. Both chapters, however, may be placed within the same temporal framework, and both can serve as models for further studies that seek to account for the reasons why such a transformation is perceived or took place.

Our volume concludes with two chapters that raise the general question: Should there be a place for *manteis* in a volume on Greek priests? As Henrichs postulates in the introduction, finding an example of one person who was labeled both *mantis* and *hiereus* might strengthen the case, but such an example is certainly not a prerequisite for including the contributions by Kai Trampedach and Michael Flower. Sometimes a discussion of *otherness* explains the matter at issue, but in this case both differences and similarities exist between two groups of *practitioners of the divine*. It is almost ironic that Michael Flower's chapter is the only one in the volume that gives a confident definition of Greek priesthood (along the lines of our textbooks on Greek religion), which serves his purpose of showing what the seer *was not*. Inevitably, the exercise is characterized by a strong dichotomy between *mere performers of ritual* and *successful practitioners of a skill*, an *authority which depends on an office* rather than one based on *personal charisma*. However, seers were also employed in contexts where the distinction is blurred and where the seer performed additional duties that were characteristic of priests. The Iamid *mantis* employed at Olympia was responsible for the care of the great altar of Zeus and certain monthly sacrifices, and we know of other *manteis* who were involved in purification rites or the initiation ceremonies of mystery cults. It would appear that such cases distinguish themselves by the fact that the seer was based at one sanctuary. His handling of the sacrifice, which forms part of the divinatory act, brings the *mantis* close to the realm of the priest. Yet because Flower deals for the most part with itinerant diviners, his practitioners of the divine appear rather distinct from the priestly agents seen in all of the previous chapters. The analysis of self-promotion in the mantic family of the Iamidae is extremely fruitful. It seems that the *mantikē tekhnē* was drawn in two directions: it served as a justification for claims to aristocratic excellence, but it was also dependent on an aristocratic status. Martial valor (a theme that stems from the frequent use of seers in the army), a respected family tradition or even divine descent, and one's role as benefactor in a local or supraregional context were certainly ways of shaping one's own image to which every aristocrat could relate. When this strategy was successful, as in the case of Tisamenus I, it translated into substantial political authority; when it was not, as we may assume was the case with Tisamenus II, no professional skill could restore a lapsed status. The new fragments of Simonides' account of the battle of Plataea (*IEG Simonides Frr.* 11–14) illustrate this link impressively: assigning Tisamenus his own epic speech may be a narratological device of a poet commissioned to promote the image of a man; in Herodotus' account, the seer's role is directly translated into *history*.

Flower's observations illustrate precisely what Kai Trampedach, who focuses on the epic seer's political authority, wants to show. His examples from the *Iliad* and the *Odyssey* are respected aristocratic heroes just like the later, *historical* representatives of the mantic families discussed by Flower. Although the *manteis* function as welcome and needed neutral specialists—and are credited with divine inspiration, mantic knowledge, and wisdom—their impartiality can easily be questioned and their authority is frequently contested. Whereas the mantic techniques of the seer are not emphasized—and this is true in the epics as well as in the mantic culture of the Greeks in general—the sensitive application of the sign to the specific personal or situational context was crucial. In order to succeed, the seer needed practical intelligence, an acknowledged aristocratic background, and *kharisma*. Here we come back to the Iamidae, who modeled their image according to precisely these criteria. Trampedach suggests both a literary function of the epic seer and a Homeric paradigm for the historical transmission of the concept of the seer.

Interestingly, this final chapter likens priest to seer by claiming that the *mantis* did not enjoy more political authority than a priest, albeit, as Trampedach insists, for different reasons. It is also noteworthy that Trampedach's first example involves Achilles' proposal that "a seer or a priest or an interpreter of dreams" (the first classification of *practitioners of the divine* in Greek literature?) be consulted. It would appear that different groups who engaged with religious matters could be perceived as appropriate advisors with authority. Could it be that Calchas, a seer rather than a priest, stepped forward for the banal reason that there was no priest present in the Achaean camp?

Just as Flower and Trampedach have given us the criteria that *could* invest the seer with authority and renown (even if unstable), an epilogue is the place for a careful corresponding assessment of the Greek priest and of other religious officials. Our volume is obviously not a telephone book of priests, nor does it propose a general definition of Greek priesthood. In any case, we prefer a definition in the widest sense. Undoubtedly, it would be convenient to conclude with a glossary of the relevant terms and categories that appear in this volume, but such a glossary would by its very nature gloss over what has emerged from our discussions: different genres of text, local idiosyncrasies, inconsistencies in Greek terminology, and discrepancies in ancient and modern thought make clear-cut definitions impossible. Albert Henrichs has already hinted at what may be the most important conclusion of this volume: the uniformity associated with our concept *priest* is in sharp contrast with the diversity of Greek religion. Greek priests had many faces, and they were and still can be perceived in many ways. The factors that determined the roles and activities of every *practitioner of the divine* are political as well as historical, religious as well as economic, idealistic as well as pragmatic, personal as well as communal.

We are still convinced, then, that there is no one answer to the question, What is a Greek priest? But we have moved on from and responded to many of the *doxai* with which the introduction confronted us. Whereas we used to note or even complain about the *lack of a priestly caste*, here we have been encouraged to look at how in each case priests used a potential authority to promote themselves and their priesthood, at times even forming a *group identity* of priests. Whereas we used to see the limits and part-time character of priestly activities, we have been encouraged to examine the wide-ranging administrative duties of religious officials and the important role they played in conserving, shaping, and reviving cult activity. Whereas we used to see a lack of *religious authority*, we have been reminded of the inauguration of priests and of the fact that the idiosyncratic evolution of cults created its own *authorities*. Whereas we emphasized a lack of *political authority*, we are moving on to investigate the activities of priests behind the curtain of *polis* institutions. Whereas we used to deny priests any special access to the divine, we are now encouraged to see them as mediators between men and gods, as figures who were not only placed in that position by the *polis* but who in many cases placed themselves in that position.

Indeed, not every priest received a statue and a crown, not every priest was honored for having lived a life in a manner appropriate for a priest: priestly office *entitled* one only to *some*—and we may call these *modest*—privileges, but it opened doors to all of the above. May *Practitioners of the Divine* open even more doors by inspiring scholars of all ancient disciplines to continue exploring the topic without adhering to certain genres of text, periods in Greek history, or to an *a priori* dichotomy between an idea and the real world, or even, perhaps, between *us* and *them*.

Works Cited

Acosta-Hughes, B., Kosmetatou, E., and Baumbach, M., eds. 2004. *Labored in Papyrus Leaves: Perspectives on an Epigram Collection Attributed to Posidippus (P.Mil.Vogl. VIII 309)*. Cambridge, MA.

Ajootian, A. 1996. "Praxiteles." In Palagia 1996:91–129.

———. 2007. "Praxiteles and Fourth century Greek Portraiture." In Schultz and von den Hoff 2007.

Aland, B., Hahn, J., and Ronning C., eds. 2003. *Literarische Konstituierung von Identitätsfiguren in der Antike*. Tübingen.

Alcock, S., Cherry, J. E., and Elsner, J. 2001. *Pausanias: Travel and Memory in Roman Greece*. Oxford.

Alcock, S. E. 2001. "The Peculiar Book IV and the Problem of the Messenian Past." In Alcock, Cherry, and Elsner 2001:142–153.

Aleshire, S. B. 1989. *The Athenian Asklepieion*. Amsterdam.

———. 1991. *Asklepios at Athens: Epigraphic and Prosopographic Essays on the Athenian Healing Cults*. Amsterdam.

———. 1994. "The Demos and the Priests." In Osborne and Hornblower 1994:325–337.

Aleshire, S. B., and Lambert, S. D. 2003. "Making the *Peplos* for Athena: A New Edition of IG II^2 1060 + IG II^2 1036." *ZPE* 142:65–86.

Alföldy, G., and Panciera, S., eds. 2001. *Inschriftliche Denkmäler als Medien der Selbstdarstellung in der römischen Welt*. Stuttgart.

Altheim, F. 1942. *Helios und Heliodor von Emesa*. Amsterdam.

Alzinger, W. 1967. "Koressos." In Braun 1967:1–9.

Alzinger, W., and Neeb, G., eds. 1985. *Pro Arte Antiqua II*. Vienna.

Amato, E. 2005. *Favorinos d'Arles. Introduction générale—Témoignages—Discours aux Corinthiens—Sur la fortune*. Vol. 1 of *Œuvres*. Ed. and comm. E. Amato. Trans. Y. Julien. Paris.

Ameling, W. 1987. "Die Herkunft des Malers Zeuxis." *EA* 9:76.

Anderson, G. 1989. "The *pepaideumenos* in Action: Sophists and their Outlook in the Early Empire." In *ANRW* II 33.1:79–208.

Andreae, B. 2001. "Kephisodotos II." In Vollkommer 2001:410–411.

Andreou, V. 2000. "Remarques sur l'histoire des classes dirigeantes de Milet." In Mooren 2000:1–13.

Arafat, K. W. 1996. *Pausanias' Greece*. Cambridge.

Arndt, P., and Bruckmann, F., eds. 1891–1942. *Griechische und römische Porträts*. Munich.

Athanassiadi, P., and Frede, M., eds. 1999. *Pagan Monotheism in Late Antiquity*. Oxford.

Attridge, H. W. 1978. "The Philosophical Critique of Religion under the Early Empire." In *ANRW* II 16.1:45–78.

Avram, A., Barbulescu, M., and Georgescu, V. 1999. "Deux tables sacrées de Callatis." *Horos* 13:225–232.

Baillet, J. 1926. *Inscriptions grecques et latines des Tombeaux des Rois ou Syringes*. Cairo.

Balty, J. 1981. "L'oracle d'Apamée." *AC* 50:5–14.

———. 1997. "Le sanctuaire oraculaire de Zeus Bêlos à Apamée." *Topoi* 7:791–799.

Balty, J., Boardman, J., et al., eds. 2005. *Thesaurus cultus et rituum antiquorum [ThesCRA] 5: Personnel of Cult, Cult Instruments*. Los Angeles.

Barnes, J. 2002. "Ancient Philosophers." In Clark and Rajak 2002:293–306.

Barnes, S. J., and Melion, W. S., eds. 1989. *Cultural Differentiation and Cultural Identity in the Visual Arts*. Washington.

Barton, S. C., and Horsley, G. H. R. 1981. "A Hellenistic Cult Group and the New Testament Church." *JbAC* 24:7–41.

Baslez, M. F. 1977. *Recherches sur les conditions de pénétration et de diffusion des religions orientales à Délos*. Leiden.

Baudy, G. 1998. "Ackerbau und Initiation: Der Kult der Artemis Triklaria und des Dionysos Aisymnetes in Patrai." In Graf 1998:143–167.

Baumbach, M. 1997. "Die Meroe-Episode in Heliodors Aithiopika." *RhM* 140:333–341.

Baumbach, M., Köhler, H., and Ritter, A. M., eds. 1998. *Mousopolos Stephanos: Festschrift für Herwig Görgemanns*. Heidelberg.

Baumbach, M., and Trampedach, K. 2004. "'Winged Words': Poetry and Divination in Posidippus' Oiônoskopika." In Acosta-Hughes, Kosmetatou, and Baumbach 2004:123–160.

Beard, M. 1990. "Priesthood in the Roman Republic." In Beard and North 1990:41–48.

Beard, M., and North, J. 1990. *Pagan Priests: Religion and Power in the Ancient World*. London.

Bendlin, A. 2006. "Vom Nutzen und Nachteil der Mantik: Orakel im Medium von Handlung und Literatur in der Zeit der Zweiten Sophistik." In Elm von der Osten et al. 2006:159–207.

Bent, T. J., and Hicks, E. L. 1891. "A Journey in Cilicia Tracheia." *JRS* 12:206–273.

Benveniste, E. 1966. *Titres et noms propres en iranien ancient*. Paris.

Bergemann, J. 1997. *Demos und Thanatos*. Munich.

Berger, E., and Gisler-Huwiler, M. 1986. *Der Parthenon in Basel: Dokumentation zum Fries*. Mainz.

Berranger-Ausserve, D. 2000. *Paros II: Prosopographie générale et Étude historique du début de la période classique jusqu'à la fin de la période romaine*. Clermont-Ferrand.

Berthiaume, G. 1982. *Les roles du mágeiros: Étude sur la boucherie, la cuisine, et le sacrifice dans la Grèce ancienne*. Leiden.

Berve, H. 1967. *Die Tyrannis bei den Griechen*. Munich.

Beschi, L. 1984. "Il fregio del Partenone: Una proposta di lettura." *RendLinc* 39:173–194.

Bieber, M. 1923–24. "Die Söhne des Praxiteles." *JdI* 38/39:242–275.

Bieler, L. 1935. ΘΕΙΟΣ ANHP. *Das Bild des "göttlichen Menschen" in Spätantike und Frühchristentum*. Vienna.

Bielman, A. 2002. *Femmes en public dans le monde hellénistique*. Paris.

Billault, A., ed. 2001. ΟΠΩΡΑ: *La belle saison de l'hellénisme; Etudes de littérature antique offertes au Recteur Jacques Bompaire*. Paris.

Bishop, P., ed. 2004. *Nietzsche and Antiquity: His Reaction and Response to the Classical Tradition*. Rochester.

Blech, H. 1982. *Studien zum Kranz bei den Griechen*. Berlin.

Blum, H., Faist, B., Pfälzner, P., and Wittke, A., eds. 2002. *Brückenland Anatolien? Ursachen, Extensität und Modi des Kulturaustausches zwischen Anatolien und seinen Nachbarn*. Tübingen.

Blümel, W. 1994. "Two New Inscriptions from Cnidia." *EA* 23:155–159.

Boffo, L. 1985. *I re ellenistici e i centri religiosi dell' Asia Minore*. Florence.

Bordreuil, P., and Gatier, P.-L. 1990. "Le relief du prêtre Philôtas." *Syria* 67:329–338.

Borg, B. 2004. "Glamorous Intellectuals: Portraits of *pepaideumenoi* in the Second and Third Centuries AD." In Borg 2004a:157–178.

———, ed. 2004a. *Paideia: The World of the Second Sophistic*. Berlin.

Bosch, E. 1967. *Quellen zur Geschichte der Stadt Ankara im Altertum*. Ankara.

Bouché-Leclercq, A. 1979–1982. *Histoire de la divination dans l'antiquité.* 4 vols. Paris.

Bowden, H. 2003. "Oracles for Sale." In Derow and Parker 2003:256–274.

Bowersock, G. W. 1965. *Augustus and the Greek World.* Oxford.

———. 1969. *Greek Sophists in the Roman Empire.* Oxford.

———. 1973. "Greek Intellectuals and the Imperial Cult in the Second Century A.D." In Den Boer 1973:179–206.

———. 1997. *Fiction as History: From Nero to Julian.* Berkeley.

———. 2002. "Philosophy in the Second Sophistic." In Clark and Rajak 2002:157–170.

———. 2004. "Artemidorus and the Second Sophistic." In Borg 2004a: 53–63.

Bowie, E. L. 1994. "The Readership of Greek Novels in the Ancient World." In Tatum 1994:435–459.

———. 1997. "Hadrian, Favorinus, and Plutarch." In Mossman 1997:1–15.

———. 1999. "The Greek Novel." In Swain 1999:39–59.

———. 2002. "The Chronology of the Earlier Greek Novels since B. E. Perry: Revisions and Precisions." *Ancient Narrative* 2:47–63.

Bracht Branham, R., and Goulet-Cazé, M.-O., eds. 1996. *The Cynics: The Cynic Movement and Its Legacy.* Berkeley.

Bradford, A. S. 1977. *A Prosopography of Lacedaemonians from the Death of Alexander the Great, 323 B.C., to the Sack of Sparta by Alaric, A.D. 396.* Munich.

Brady, T. A. 1978. *Sarapis & Isis: Collected Essays.* Chicago.

Brandt, H. 1992. *Gesellschaft und Wirtschaft Pamphyliens und Pisidiens im Altertum.* Bonn.

Braun, E., ed. 1967. *Festschrift für Fritz Eichler zum achtzigsten Geburtstag.* Vienna.

Breidbach, W., and Huyse, Ph., eds. 2000. *Ruediger Schmitt: Selected Onomastic Writings.* New York.

Bremmer, J. N. 1992. "Mythe en rite in het oude Griekenland: Een overzicht van recente ontwikkelingen." *Nederlands Theologisch Tijdschrift* 46:265–276.

———. 1993. "Prophets, Seers and Politicians in Greece, Israel and Early Modern Europe." *Numen* 40:150–183.

———. 1994. *Greek Religion.* Oxford.

———. 1996. *Götter, Mythen und Heiligtümer im antiken Griechenland.* Darmstadt.

———. 1996a. "The Status and Symbolic Capital of the Seer." In P. Hägg 1996:97–109.

———. 1998. "'Religion,' 'Ritual' and the Opposition 'Sacred vs. Profane': Notes towards a Terminological 'Genealogy.'" In Graf 1998:9–32.

———. 1998a. "The Novel and the Apocryphal Acts: Place, Time and Readership." In Hofmann and Zimmerman 1998:157–180.

———. 1999. "Achilles Tatius and Heliodorus in Christian East Syria." In Vanstiphout 1999:21–29.

———. 1999a. *Greek Religion*. 2nd ed. Oxford.

———. 1999b. "Kassandra." *DNP* 6:316–18.

———. 1999c. "Transvestite Dionysos." *The Bucknell Review* 43:183–200.

———, ed. 2001. *The Apocryphal Acts of Thomas*. Louvain.

———. 2003. *Greek Religion*. 3rd ed. Oxford.

———. 2004. "Attis: A Greek God in Anatolian Pessinous and Catullan Rome." *Mnemosyne* 57.5:534–573.

———. 2004a. "The Spelling and Meaning of the Name Megabyxos." *ZPE* 147:9–10.

———. 2005. "Myth and Ritual in Ancient Greece: Observations on a Difficult Relationship." In von Haehling 2005:21–43.

Briant, P. 1996. *Histoire de l'empire perse de Cyrus à Alexandre*. 2 vols. Paris.

Bricault, L. 1996. "Les prêtres du Sarapieion C de Délos." *BCH* 120.2:597–616.

———. 2001. *Atlas de la diffusion des cultes isiaques (IVe s. av. J.-C.–IVe s. ap. J.-C.)*. Paris.

———, ed. 2005. *Recueil des inscriptions concernant des cultes isiaques (RICIS)*. 3 vols. Paris.

Brinkmann, V. 2003. *Die Polychromie der archaischen und frühklassischen Skulptur*. Munich.

Brodersen, K., ed. 2001. *Prognosis: Studien zur Funktion von Zukunftsvorhersagen in Literatur und Geschichte seit der Antike*. Münster.

Broneer, O. 1942. "The Thesmophorion in Athens." *Hesperia* 11:250–274.

Brown, P. 1992. *Power and Persuasion in Late Antiquity*. Madison.

Brulé, P. 1987. *La fille d'Athènes*. Paris.

Brulé, P. 1996. "La cité et ses composantes." *Kernos* 9:37–63.

Brun, J.-P., and Jockey, P., eds. 2001. *Technai: Techniques et sociétés en Méditerranée. Hommage à Marie-Claire Amouretti*. Paris.

Bruneau, Ph. 1970. *Recherches sur les cultes de Délos à l'époque hellénistique et à l'époque impériale*. Paris.

Bruneau Ph., and Ducat, J. 1983. *Guide de Délos*. 3rd ed. Paris.

Brunt, P. A. 1977. "From Epictetus to Arrian." *Athenaeum* 55:19–48.

Brumfield, A. 1997. "Cakes in the Liknon: Votives from the Sanctuary of Demeter and Kore on Acrocorinth." *Hesperia* 66:147–172.

Buchheim, H., 1960. *Die Orientpolitik des Triumvirn M. Antonius*. Heidelberg.

Budin, S. L. 2003. "Pallakai, Prostitutes, and Prophetesses." *CP* 98:148–159.

Burke, P. 1980. *Sociology and History*. London.

Burkert, W. 1962. "ΓΟΗΣ. Zum griechischen 'Schamanismus'." *RhM* 105: 36–55.

————. 1976. "Kekropidensage und Arrhephoria." *Hermes* 94:1–25.

————. 1977. *Griechische Religion der archaischen und klassischen Epoche*. Stuttgart.

————. 1979. *Structure and History in Greek Mythology and Ritual*. Berkeley.

————. 1985. *Greek Religion: Archaic and Classical*. Oxford.

————. 1990. "Herodot als Historiker fremder Religionen." In Nenci 1990:1–32.

————. 1992. *The Orientalizing Revolution: Near Eastern Influence on Greek Culture in the Early Archaic Age*. Cambridge, MA.

————. 1999. "Die Artemis der Epheser: Wirkungsmacht und Gestalt einer grossen Göttin." In Friesinger and Krinzinger 1999:59–70.

————. 2002. "Mythos und Ritual: Im Wechselwind der Moderne." In Horstmannshoff et al. 2002:1–22.

————. 2003. *Die Griechen und der Orient*. Munich.

————. 2004. *Babylon, Memphis, Persepolis*. Cambridge, MA.

Burnett, A. P. and Edmonson, C. E. 1961. "The Chabrias Monument in the Athenian Agora." *Hesperia* 30:74–91.

Burrell, B. 1993. "Two Inscribed Columns from Caesarea Maritima." *ZPE* 99:287–295.

Burschel, P., Distelrath, G., and Lembke, S., eds. 2000. *Das Quälen des Körpers: Eine historische Anthropologie der Folter*. Cologne.

Buschor, E. 1979. *Das hellenistische Bildnis*. 2nd ed. Munich.

Buxton, R., ed. 2000. *Oxford Readings in Greek Religion*. Oxford.

Byrne, S. G. 2003. *Roman Citizens of Athens*. Louvain.

Cabanes, P. 1996. "Le noms latins dans les inscriptions grecques d'Épidamne-Dyrrhachion, d'Apollonia et de Bouthrotos." In Rizakis 1996:89–104.

Cain, H. U., and Salzmann, D., eds. 1989. *Beiträge zu Ikonographie und Hermeneutik: Festschrift für N. Himmelmann*. Mainz.

Calame, C. 1977. *Choruses of Young Women in Ancient Greece*. Lanham.

Campanile, M. D. 1994. *I sacerdoti del Koinon d'Asia (I sec. a.C.-III sec. d.C.): Contributo allo studio della romanizzazione delle élites provinciali nell'Oriente greco*. Pisa.

Campanile, D. 2003. "Vivere e morire da sofista: Adriano di Tiro." In Virgilio 2003:245–273.

Cancik, H., Gladigow, B., and Kohl, K.-H., eds. 1998. *Handbuch religionswissenschaftlicher Grundbegriffe IV*. Stuttgart.

Cartledge, P. A., and Spawforth, A. 1989. *Hellenistic and Roman Sparta: A Tale of Two Cities*. London.

Cartledge, P., and Spawforth, A. 2002. *Hellenistic and Roman Sparta: A Tale of two Cities*. 2nd ed. London.

Carne-Ross, D. S. 1979. *Instaurations: Essays in and out of Literature; Pindar to Pound*. Berkeley.

———. 1979a. "Weaving with Points of Gold: Pindar's Sixth Olympian." In Carne Ross 1979:29–60.

Casadio, G. 1994. *Storia del culto di Dioniso in Argolide*. Rome.

Casevitz, M. 1989. "Les devins des tragiques." In Ghiron-Bistagne 1989:115–129

———. 1992. "Mantis: Le vrai sens." *REG* 105: 1–18.

Cauderlier, P., and Worp, K. A. 1982. "SB III 6012 = IBM IV 1076: Unrecognised Evidence for a Mysterious Philosopher." *Aegyptus* 62:72–79.

Cébeillac-Gervasoni, M., Lamoine, L., and Trément, F., eds. 2004. *Autocélébration des élites locales dans le monde romain: Contexte, textes, images (IIe s. av. J.-C.-IIIe s. ap. J.-C.)*. Clermont-Ferrand.

Ceccarelli, P. 1998. *La pirrica nell'antichità greco romana*. Pisa.

Chaniotis, A. 1988. *Historie und Historiker in den griechischen Inschriften: Epigraphische Beiträge zur griechischen Historiographie*. Stuttgart.

———. 2002. "Old Wine in a New Skin: Tradition and Innovation in the Cult Foundation of Alexander of Abonouteichos." In Dabrowa 2002:67–85.

———. 2003. "Negotiating Religion in the Cities of the Eastern Roman Empire." *Kernos* 16:177–190.

———. 2004. "Epigraphic Evidence for the Philosopher Alexander of Aphrodisias." *BICS* 47:79–81.

———. 2004a: "New Inscriptions from Aphrodisias (1995–2001)." *AJA* 108:377–416.

———. 2004b. "Under the Watchful Eyes of the Gods: Divine Justice in Hellenistic and Roman Asia Minor." In Colvin 2004:1–43.

———. 2008. "Ritual Performances of Divine Justice: The Epigraphy of Confession, Atonement, and Exaltation in Roman Asia Minor." In Cotton, Hoyland, Price, and Wasserstein 2008 (forthcoming).

Chastagnol, A., Demougin, S., and Lepelley, C., eds. 1996. *Splendidissima civitas: Études d'histoire romaine en hommage à F. Jacques*. Paris.

Chéhadeh, K., and Griesheimer, M. 1998. "Les reliefs funéraires du tombeau du prêtre Rapsônès (Babulin, Syrie du Nord)." *Syria* 75:171–192.

Chirassi Colombo, I. 1985. "Gli interventi mantici in Omero: Morfologia e funzione della divinazione come modalità di organizzazione del prestigio e del consenso nelle cultura greca arcaica e classica." In Fales and Grottanelli 1985:141–164.

Chirassi Colombo, I., and Seppilli, T., eds. 1998. *Sibille e linguaggi oracolari: Mito, storia, tradizione. Atti del convegno internazionale di studi. Macerata-Norcia 20-24 Settembre 1994*. Pisa and Rome.

Chuvin, P. 1981. "Apollon au trident et les dieux de Tarse." *JS* 305–326.

Clairmont, C. W. 1993. *Classical Attic Tombstones.* 8 vols. Kilchberg.

Clark, G., and Rajak, T., eds. 2002. *Philosophy and Power in the Graeco-Roman World: Essays in Honour of Miriam Griffin.* Oxford.

Clinton, C. 1992. *Myth and Cult.* Stockholm.

Clinton, K. 1974. *The Sacred Officials of the Eleusinian Mysteries.* Philadelphia.

Cole, S. G. 2004. *Landscapes, Gender, and Ritual Space: The Ancient Greek Experience.* Berkeley.

Collins, D. 2002. "Reading the Birds: *Oiônomanteia* in Early Epic." *ColbyQ* 38:17–41.

Collins, J. J. 1978. *Primitive Religion.* Ottowa.

Colloquio Internazionale su Epigrafia e ordine senatoria 1982. *Atti del Colloquio Internazionale AIEGL su Epigrafia e ordine senatorio. Roma, 14-20 maggio 1982.* Vol. 2.5. Rome.

Colvin, S., ed. 2004. *The Greco-Roman East: Politics, Culture, Society.* Cambridge.

Connelly, J. B. 1988. *Votive Sculpture of Hellenistic Cyprus.* Nicosia.

Corso, A. 1988. *Prassitele: Fonti epigrafici e litterarie.* Vol. 1. Rome.

Cotton, H. M., Hoyland, R. G., Price, J. J., and Wasserstein, D. J., eds. 2008. *From Hellenism to Islam: Cultural and Linguistic Change in the Roman Near East.* Cambridge.

Crahay, R. 1956. *La littérature oraculaire chez Hérodote.* Paris.

Dabrowa, E., ed. 1997. *Donum Amicitiae: Studies in Ancient History Published on Occasion of the 75th Anniversary of Foundation of the Department of Ancient History of the Jagiellonian University.* Cracow.

———, ed. 2002. *Tradition and Innovation in the Ancient World.* Cracow.

Dasen, V., and Piérart, M., eds. 2005. *Idia kai demosia. Les cadres "privés" et "publics" de la religion grecque antique.* Liège.

Daux, G. 1958. "Notes de Lecture: Le devin Cléoboulos." *BCH* 82:364–366.

———. 1959. "Inscriptions de Delphes." *BCH* 83:466–495.

———. 1978. "Notes de lecture." *BCH* 102:591–627.

Davies, J. K. 1971. *Athenian Propertied Families 600-300 B.C.* Oxford.

de Jong, I. J. F. 2001. *A Narratological Commentary on the Odyssey.* Cambridge.

Demougin, S. 2006. "*Archiereus Alexandriae et totius Aegypti*: Un office profane." In Vigourt et al. 2006:513–519.

Den Boer, W., ed. 1973. *Le culte des souverains dans l'Émpire Romain.* Geneva.

Derow, P., and Parker, R., eds. 2003. *Herodotus and His World.* Oxford.

Detienne, M. 1967. *Les maîtres de vérité dans la grèce archaïque.* Paris.

Dickie, M. W. 1999. "The Learned Magician and the Collection and Transmission of Magical Lore." In Jordan, Montgomery, and Thomassen 1999:163–193.

————. 2001. *Magic and Magicians in the Greco-Roman World*. London.

Dickson, K. 1992. "Kalkhas and Nestor: Two Narrative Strategies in *Iliad* 1." *Arethusa* 25:327–358.

Diefenbach, S. 2000. "Jenseits der 'Sorge um sich': Zur Folter von Philosophen und Märtyrern in der römischen Kaiserzeit." In Burschel et al. 2000:99–131.

Dignas, B. 2002. *Economy of the Sacred in Hellenistic and Roman Asia Minor*. Oxford.

————. 2002a. "Priestly Authority in the Cult of the Corybantes at Erythrae." *EA* 33:29–40.

————. 2003. "Rhodian Priests after the Synoecism." *AncSoc* 33:35–52.

Dillery, J. 2005. "Chresmologues and Manteis: Independent Diviners and the Problem of Authority." In Johnston and Struck 2005:167–231.

Dillon, J. 2002. "The Social Role of the Philosopher in the Second Century C.E.: Some Remarks." In Stadter and Van der Stockt 2002:29–40.

Dillon, M., ed. 1996. *Religion in the Ancient World: New Themes and Approaches*. Amsterdam.

————. 2002. *Girls and Women in Classical Greek Religion*. London.

Di Sacco Franco, M. T. 2000. "Les devins chez Homère: Essai d'analyse." *Kernos* 13:35–46.

Dodds, E. R. 1951 *The Greeks and the Irrational*. Berkeley.

Dobbin, R. F. 1998. *Epictetus: Discourses Book I. Translated with an introduction and commentary*. Oxford.

Donohue, A. A. 1988. *Xoana and the Origins of Greek Sculpture*. Atlanta.

Donnay, G. 1997. "L'Arrhéphorie: Initiation ou rite civique?" *Kernos* 10:177–205.

D'Orbeliani, R. 1924. "Inscriptions and Monuments from Galatia." *JHS* 44:24–44.

Dörpfeld, W. 1911. "Zu den Bauwerken Athens." *MDAI(A)* 36:39–72.

Dow, S. 1937. "The Egyptian Cults in Athens." *HThR* 30:183–232.

Dowden, K. 1989. *Death and the Maiden*. London.

Drake, H. A. 2000. *Constantine and the Bishops*. Baltimore.

Dreizehnter, A. 1975. "Pompeius als Städtegründer." *Chiron* 5:213–245.

Duemmler, F. 1886. "Inschriften von Amorgos und Melos." *MDAI(A)* 11:97–119.

Dunand, F. 1973. *Le culte d'Isis dans le basin oriental de la Méditerranée*. 3 vols. Leiden.

Durugönül, S. 1998. *Türme und Siedlungen im Rauhen Kilikien: Eine Untersuchung zu den archäologischen Hinterlassenschaften im Olbischen Territorium*. Bonn.

Du Toit, D. S. 1997. *THEIOS ANTHROPOS*. Tübingen.

Eck, W. 1992–1993. "Urbs Salvia und seine führenden Familien in der römischen Zeit." *Picus* 12–13:79–108.

Eck, W., and Heil, M., eds. 2005. *Senatores popoli Romani: Realität und mediale*

Repräsentation einer Führungsschicht. Kolloquium der Prosopographia Imperii Romani vom 11-13. Juni 2004. Stuttgart.

Edelmann, M. 1999. *Menschen auf griechischen Weihreliefs*. Munich.

Edsall, M. 1996. *The Role and Characterization of the Priest in the Ancient Novel*. New York.

Edwards, M. J., et al., eds. 1999. *Apologetics in the Roman Empire: Pagans, Jews and Christians*. Oxford.

Elm von der Osten, D. 2006. "Die Inszenierung des Betruges und seiner Entlarvung: Divination und ihre Kritiker in Lukians Schrift 'Alexandros oder der Lügenprophet'." In Elm von der Osten et al. 2006:141–157.

Elm von der Osten, D., Rüpke, J., and Waldner, K., eds. 2006. *Texte als Medium und Reflexion von Religion im römischen Reich*. Stuttgart.

Elsner, J. 1997. "Hagiographic Geography: Travel and Allegory in the *Life of Apollonius of Tyana*." *JHS* 117:22–37.

Empereur, J.-Y., and Simossi, A. 1994. "Inscriptions du port de Thasos." *BCH* 118:407–415.

Engelmann, H. 1964. *Die delische Sarapisaretalogie*. Meisenheim.

———. 1975. *The Delian Aretalogy of Sarapis*. Leiden.

———. 2000. "Neue Inschriften aus Ephesos XIII." *JÖAI* 69:77–93.

Erler, G., ed. 2000. *Epikureismus in der späten Republik und der Kaiserzeit: Akten der 2. Tagung der Karl-und-Gertrud-Abel-Stiftung vom 30. September–3. Oktober 1998 in Würzburg*. Stuttgart.

Eule, C. 2001. *Hellenistische Bürgerinnen aus Kleinasien*. Istanbul.

———. 2002. "Die statuarische Darstellung von Frauen in Athen im 4. und frühen 3. Jh. v. Chr." In Blum and Faist 2002:205–229.

Faber, R., and Seidensticker, B., eds. 1996. *Wörter, Bilder, Töne: Studien zur Antike und Antikerezeption*. Würzburg.

Fales M., and Grottanelli, C., eds. 1985. *Sopranaturale e potere nel mondo antico e nelle società tradizionali*. Milan.

Faraone, C. A., and Obbink, D., eds. 1991. *Magika Hiera: Ancient Greek Magic and Religion*. New York.

Feaver, D. D. 1957. "Historical Development in the Priesthoods of Athens." *YClS* 15:123–158.

Fein, S. 1994. *Die Beziehungen der Kaiser Trajan und Hadrian zu den litterati*. Beiträge zur Altertumskunde 26. Stuttgart.

Feld, O., and Weber, H. 1967. "Tempel und Kirche über der Korykischen Grotte (Cennet Cehennem) in Kilikien." *MDAI(I)* 17:254–278.

Feldmeier, R. 1998. "Philosoph und Priester: Plutarch als Theologe." In Baumbach et al. 1998:412–425.

Ferguson, W. S. 1938. "The Salaminioi of Heptaphylai and Sounion." *Hesperia* 7:1–74.

Fernoux, H.-L. 2004. *Notables et élites des cités de Bithynie aux époques hellénistiques et romaine (IIIe siècle av. J.C.-IIIe siècle ap. J.C.): Essai d'histoire sociale.* Lyon.

Festugière, A. J. 1949. "A propos des arétalogies d'Isis." *HThR* 42:209–234.

Fick, S. M. E. "Heliodors Heldin Chariklea und die Vorstellungswelt der Priesterdynastie von Emesa." In Ulf and Rollinger 2002:515–524.

Figueira, T. J. 1986. "Population Patterns in Late Archaic and Classical Sparta." *TAPA* 116:165–213.

Fisher, R. S. 1985. "A New Priest of Sarapis on Delos." *ZPE* 58:117–118.

Fittschen, K. 1977. *Katalog der antiken Skulpturen in Schloß Erbach.* Berlin.

———, ed. 1988. *Griechische Portraits.* Darmstadt.

Flaig, E. 1995. "Tödliches Freien: Penelopes Ruhm, Telemachs Status und die sozialen Normen." *Historische Anthropologie* 3:364–388.

———. 2002. "Bildung als Feindin der Philosophie: Wie Habitusformen in der hohen Kaiserzeit kollidierten." In Goltz et al. 2002:121–136.

Flamand, J.-M. 1989. "Apulée de Madaure (A 294)." In Goulet 1989:298–317.

Flinterman, J.-J. 1995. *Power, Paideia & Pythagoreanism: Greek Identity, Conceptions of the Relationship between Philosophers and Monarchs, and Political Ideas in Philostratus' Life of Apollonius.* Amsterdam.

Flower, M. A. 2000. "From Simonides to Isocrates: The Fifth-Century Origins of Fourth-Century Panhellenism." *ClAnt* 19:65–101.

———. 2008. *The Seer in Ancient Greece.* Los Angeles.

———, M. A., and Marincola, J., eds. 2002. *Herodotus: Histories, Book IX.* Cambridge.

Follet, S. 1976. *Athènes au IIe et au IIIe siècle: Études chronologiques et prosopographiques.* Paris.

———. 1989. "Arrien de Nicomédie (A 425)." In Goulet 1989:597–604.

———. 1989a. "Athénodore de Tarse *dit* Cordylion (A 498)." In Goulet 1989: 658–659.

———. 2000. "Favorinus d'Arles (F 10)." In Goulet 2000:418–422.

———. 2001. "Un ami de Plutarque, l'orateur athénien Glaukias." In Billault 2001:85–96.

———. 2003. "Ctèsiphon, fils de Némônios, de Thasos (C 225a)." In Goulet 2003:86–87.

Fontenrose, J. 1988. *Didyma: Apollo's Oracle, Cult and Companions.* Berkeley.

Fossey, J. M., ed. 1994. *Boeotia Antiqua IV: Proceedings of the 7th International Congress on Boiotian Antiquities.* Amsterdam.

Fowden, G. 1982. "The Pagan Holy Man in Late Antique Society." *JHS* 102:33–59.

Frankfurter, D. 2001. "Dynamics of Ritual Expertise in Antiquity and Beyond:

Towards a New Taxonomy of 'Magicians'." In Mirecki and Meyer 2001:159–178.

Fraser, P. M. 1960. "Two Studies on the Cult of Sarapis in the Hellenistic World." *OA* 3:1–54.

Frede, M. 1997. "Euphrates of Tyre." In Sorabji 1997:1–12.

———. 1999. "Monotheism and Pagan Philosophy in Later Antiquity." In Athannassiadi and Frede 1999:41–67.

French, D. H. 1996. "The Site of Barata and Routes in the Konya Plain." *EA* 27:93–114.

French, D. H., and Merkelbach, R. 1997. "Eine Priesterin der Leukothea in Sinope." *EA* 29:67.

Freyer-Schauenburg, B. 1974. *Bildwerke der archaischen Zeit und des Strengen Stils.* Berlin.

Friesinger, H., ed. 2000. *Die Ägäis und das westliche Mittelmeer.* Vienna.

Friesinger, H., and Krinzinger, F., eds. 1999. *100 Jahre österreichische Forschungen in Ephesos: Akten des Symposions 1995.* Vienna.

Fuentes González, P. P. 2000. "Épictète." In Goulet 2000:106–151.

Furley, W. D. 1988. *Studies in the Use of Fire in Ancient Greek Religion.* Salem.

———. 1993. "Besprechung und Behandlung: Zur Form und Funktion von Epodai in der griechischen Zaubermedizin." In Most, Petersmann, and Ritter 1993:80–104.

Furley, W. D., and Bremer, J. M. 2001. *Greek Hymns.* 2 vols. Tübingen.

Furnée, E. J. 1972. *Die wichtigsten konsonantischen Erscheinungen des Vorgriechischen.* The Hague.

Furtwängler, A. 1907. "Das Mädchen von Antium." *Münchner Jahrbuch der Bildenden Kunst* 2.2:1–11.

Galli, M. 2001. "*Pepaideumenoi* am 'Ort des Heiligen': Euergetische Initiativen und Kommunikationsformen in griechischen Heiligtümern zur Zeit der Zweiten Sophistik." In Reusser 2001:43–70.

Garland, R. 1982. "A First Catalogue of the Attic Peribolos Tombs." *ABSA* 77:125–176

———. 1984. "Religious Authority in Archaic and Classical Athens." *ABSA* 79:75–123.

———. 1996. "Strategies of religious Intimidation and Coercion in Classical Athens." In R. Hägg 1996:91–99.

Geagan, D. J. 1983. "Greek Inscriptions from the Athenian Agora." *Hesperia* 52:155–172.

———. 1991. "The Sarapion Monument and the Quest for Status in Roman Athens." *ZPE* 85:145–165.

———. 1994. "Children in Athenian Dedicatory Monuments." In Fossey 1994:163–173.

———. 1996. "Who was Athena?" In Dillon 1996:145–164.

Gebauer, J. 2002. *Pompe und Thysia*. Münster.

Geerard, M., ed. 1990. *Opes Atticae: Festschrift R. Bogaert, H. Van Looy*. The Hague.

Gehrke, H.-J. 1982. "Der siegreiche König: Überlegungen zur hellenistischen Monarchie." *AKG* 64:247–277.

Geominy, W. 1989. "Eleusinische Priester." In Cain and Salzmann 1989:253–264.

Georgoudi, S. 1993. "Lisimaca, la sacerdotessa." In Loraux 1993:157–196.

———. 1998. "Les porte-paroles des dieux: réflexions sur le personnel des oracles grecs." In Chirassi Colombo and Seppilli 1998:315–365.

Gernet, L. 1932. "Le culte." In Gernet and Boulanger 1932:191–232.

Gernet, L., and Boulanger, A. 1932. *Le génie grec dans la religion*. Paris.

Ghiron-Bistagne, P., ed. *Transe et théâtre*. Lyon.

Ginouvès, R., et al., eds. 1994. *L'eau, la santé et la maladie dans le monde grec: Actes du colloque organisé à Paris du 25 au 27 novembre 1992*. Paris.

Gleason, M. W. 1995. *Making Men: Sophists and Self-Presentation in Ancient Rome*. Princeton.

Godley, A. D. 1920 *Herodotus*. Vol. 1. London.

Goette, H. 1989. "Römische Kinderbildnisse mit Jugend-Locken." *MDAI(A)* 104:203–217.

Goldhill, S. 1991. *The Poet's Voice: Essays on Poetics and Greek Literature*. Cambridge.

Goltz, A., Luther, A., and Schlange-Schöningen, H., eds. 2002. *Gelehrte in der Antike: Alexander Demandt zum 65. Geburtstag*. Cologne.

Gordon, P. 1996. *Epicurus in Lycia: The Second-Century World of Diogenes of Oenoanda*. Ann Arbor.

Gordon, R. 2004. "Raising a Sceptre: Confession-Narratives from Lydia and Phrygia." *JRA* 17:177–196.

Gotter, U. 2001. "Tempel und Großmacht: Olba und das Imperium Romanum." In Jean 2001:289–325.

———. 2003. "Ontologie versus exemplum: Griechische Philosophie als politisches Argument in der späten römischen Republik." In Piepenbrink 2003:165–185.

Goulet, R., ed. 1989. *Dictionnaire des philosophes antiques*. Vol. 1. Paris.

———. 1989a. "Athénodore de Tarse *dit* Calvus (A 497)." In Goulet 1989:654–657.

———, ed. 1994. *Dictionnaire des philosophes antiques*. Vol 2. Paris.

———, ed. 2000. *Dictionnaire des philosophes antiques*. Vol. 3. Paris.

————, ed. 2003. *Dictionnaire des philosophes antiques Supplément*. Paris.

————, ed. 2005. *Dictionnaire des philosophes antiques*. Vol. 4. Paris.

————. 2005a. "Lépidus d'Amastrée (L 47)." In Goulet 2005:95–96.

————. 2005b. "Lysias de Tarse (L 95)." In Goulet 2005:214.

————. 2005c. "Nestor de Tarse (N 26)." In Goulet 2005:660–661.

————. 2005d. "Nicostratos d'Athènes (Claudius) (N 55)." In Goulet 2005:699–701.

Goulet, R., and Aouad, M. 1989. "Alexandros d'Aphrodisias (A 112)." In Goulet 1989:125–139.

Goulet-Cazé, M.-O. 1996. "A Comprehensive Catalogue of Known Cynic Philosophers." In Bracht Branham and Goulet-Cazé 1996:389–413.

————. 2005. "Ouranios Kynikos (O 49)." In Goulet 2005:862.

Graf, F. 1985. *Nordionische Kulte: Religionsgeschichtliche und epigraphische Untersuchungen zu den Kulten von Chios, Erythrai, Klazomenai und Phokaia*. Rome.

————. 1997. "Griechische Religion." In Nesselrath 1997:457–504.

————, ed. 1998. *Ansichten griechischer Rituale: Geburtstags-Symposium für Walter Burkert*. Stuttgart.

————. 1999. "Ephesische und andere Kureten." In Friesinger and Krinzinger 1999:255–262.

Graf, F. 2000. "The Locrian Maidens." In Buxton 2000:250–270.

Graindor, P. 1938. "Parthénon et corés." *RA*:193–211.

Gregory, J., ed. 2005. *A Companion to Greek Tragedy*. Oxford.

Gregory, T. E. 1979. "Roman Inscriptions from Aidespos." *GRBS* 20:255–277.

Grélois, J.-P. 1998. *Dr John Covel: Voyages en Turquie 1675–1677. Edited text, annotated and translated*. Paris.

Groag, E. 1902. "Cn. Claudius Severus und der Sophist Hadrian." *WSt* 24:261–264.

Grossardt, P. 2001. *Die Erzählung von Meleagros*. Leiden.

Gschnitzer, F. 1989. "Bemerkungen zum Zusammenwirken von Magistraten und Priestern in der griechischen Welt." *Ktèma* 14:31–38.

Gschwantler, K. 1975. *Zeuxis und Parrhasios*. Vienna.

Günther, W. 1971. *Das Orakel von Didyma in hellenistischer Zeit: Eine Interpretation von Stein-Urkunden*. Tübingen.

————. 2003. "'Unsterbliche Kränze': Zur Selbstdarstellung milesischer Propheten in den didymeischen Inschriftendenkmälern." *Chiron* 33:447–457.

Haake, M. 2003. "Warum und zu welchem Ende schreibt man *peri basileias*? Überlegungen zum historischen Kontext einer literarischen Gattung im

Hellenismus." In Piepenbrink 2003:83–138.

———. 2006. "Der Philosoph im Heiligtum: Überlegungen zum Auftreten von Philosophen in den panhellenischen Heiligtümern von Olympia, Delphi und Delos im Hellenismus und in der Kaiserzeit." In Naso 2006:523–544.

———. 2007. *Der Philosoph in der Stadt: Untersuchungen zur öffentlichen Rede über Philosophen und Philosophie in den hellenistischen Poleis.* Munich.

Hagel, S., and Tomaschitz, K. 1998. *Repertorium der westkilikischen Inschriften.* Vienna.

Hägg, P., ed. 1996. *The Role of Religion in the Early Greek Polis.* Stockholm.

Hägg, R., ed. 1994. *Ancient Greek Cult Practice from the Epigraphical Evidence.* Stockholm.

———, ed. 1996. *Religion and Power in the Greek World.* Uppsala.

Hägg, T. 1983. *The Novel in Antiquity.* Berkeley.

Hahn, J. 1989. *Der Philosoph und die Gesellschaft: Selbstverständnis, öffentliches Auftreten und populäre Erwartungen in der hohen Kaiserzeit.* Stuttgart.

———. 2003. "Weiser, göttlicher Mensch oder Scharlatan? Das Bild des Apollonius von Tyana bei Heiden und Christen." In Aland, Hahn, and Ronning 2003:87–109.

Hainsworth, B. 1993. *The Iliad: A Commentary.* Vol. 3 (Books 9–12). Cambridge.

Halfmann, H. 1982. "Die Senatoren aus den kleinasiatischen Provinzen des Römischen Reiches vom 1. bis 3. Jahrhundert (Asia, Pontus-Bithynia, Lycia-Pamphylia, Galatia, Cappadocia, Cilicia)." In *Colloquio Internazionale su Epigrafia e ordine senatoria* 1982:603–650.

Hamilton, R. 1985. "Euripidean Priests." *HSCP* 89:53–73.

———. 2000. *Treasure Map: A Guide to the Delian Inventories.* Ann Arbor.

Hansen, P. A. 1983. *Carmina Epigraphica Graeca Saeculorum VIII–V a. Chr. n.* Berlin.

———. 1989. *Carmina Epigraphica Graeca Saeculi IV a. Chr. n.* Berlin.

Hanson, V. D., ed. 1991. *Hoplites: The Classical Greek Battle Experience.* London.

Harper, R. P. 1968. "Tituli Comanorum Cappadociae." *AS* 18:93–147.

Harris, D. 1995. *The Treasures of the Parthenon and Erechtheion.* Oxford.

Harris, E. M. 1995. *Aeschines and Athenian Politics.* New York.

Harrison, E. B. 1953. *Portrait Sculpture: The Athenian Agora.* Vol. 1. Princeton.

———. 1977. "The Shoulder-cord of Themis." In Höckmann 1977:155–161.

———. 1988. "Sculpture in Stone." In Sweeney 1988:50–54.

———. 1989. "Hellenic Identity and Athenian Identity in the Fifth Century B.C." In Barnes and Melion 1989:41–61.

Harrison, S. J. 2000. *Apuleius: A Latin Sophist.* Oxford.

Hartog, F. 1988. *The Mirror of Herodotus: The Representation of the Other in the Writing of History.* Berkeley.

Hartswick, K. J., ed. 1998. ΣΤΕΦΑΝΟΣ: *Studies in Honor of B. S. Ridgway*. Philadelphia.

Harvey, F. D. 1991. "Herodotus 1.78 and 84: Which Telmessos?" *Kernos* 4:245–258.

Hatzopoulos, M. B. 1994. *Cultes et rites de passage en Macédoine*. Athens.

———. 1996. *Macedonian Institutions under the Kings: A Historical and Epigraphic Study*. 2 vols. Athens.

Heberdey R. 1899. "Das Weihrelief des Lakrateides." In Masner 1899:111–116.

———. 1904. "Ein Beitrag zum ephesischen Artemiskult." *JÖAI* 7:210–215.

Heberdey, R., and Wilhelm, A. 1896. *Reisen in Kilikien*. Vienna.

Hedrick, C. W., Jr. 1990. *The Decrees of the Demotionidai*. Atlanta.

Hellström, P., and Alroth, B., eds. 1996. *Religion and Power in the Ancient Greek World: Proceedings of the Uppsala Symposium 1993*. Uppsala.

Henrichs, A. 1984. "The Sophists and Hellenistic Religion: Prodicus as the Spiritual Father of the Isis Aretalogies." *HSCP* 88:139–158.

———. 2002. "Writing Religion Inscribed Texts, Ritual Authority, and the Religious Discourse of the Polis." In Yunis 2002:38–58.

———. 2003. "*Hieroi Logoi* and *Hierai Bibloi*: The (Unwritten) Margins of the Sacred in Ancient Greece." *HSCP* 101:207–266.

———. 2004. "'Full of Gods': Nietzsche on Greek Polytheism and Culture." In Bishop 2004:114–137.

———. 2005. "Nietzsche on Greek Tragedy and the Tragic." In Gregory 2005: 444–458.

Hermann, K. F. 1858. *Lehrbuch der gottesdienstlichen Alterthümer der Griechen*. Vol. 2. Heidelberg.

Herrmann, P. 2002. "Eine 'pierre errante' in Samos: Kultgesetz der Korybanten." *Chiron* 32:157–172.

Heubeck, A., West, S., and Hainsworth J. B., eds. 1988. *A Commentary on Homer's Odyssey*. Vol. 1 (Introduction and Books 1–8). Oxford.

Heyob, S. K. 1975. *The Cult of Isis among Women in the Graeco-Roman World*. Leiden.

Higbie, C. 2003. *The Lindian Chronicle and the Greek Creation of their Past*. Oxford.

Hiller, F. 1965. "Mädchenstatue der Glyptothek Munich Nr. 478." *AntP* 4:43–46.

Hilton, J. L. 1996. "Theagenes, Chariklea and the *enagismós* of Neoptolemos in Delphi." In Faber and Seidensticker 1996:187–195.

Himmelmann, N. 1997. "Die Priesterschaft der Kyrbantes in Erythrai." *EA* 29:117–121.

———. 2001. *Die private Bildnisweihung bei den Griechen*. Düsseldorf.

Hintzen-Bohlen, B. 1990. "Die Familiengruppe: Ein Mittel zur Selbstdarstellung hellenistischer Herrscher." *JDAI* 105:129–154.

Hoben, W. 1969. *Untersuchungen zur Stellung kleinasiatischer Dynasten in den Machtkämpfen der ausgehenden römischen Republik.* Mainz.

Höckmann, U., ed. 1977. *Festschrift für Frank Brommer.* Mainz.

———. 1996. "Die Sitzstatue des 'Propheten' aus Didyma." *MDAI(I)* 46:93–102.

Hoff, C., ed. 1987. *The Romanization of Athens.* Oxford.

Holderman, E. S. 1913. *A Study of the Greek Priestess.* Chicago.

Hölkeskamp, K.-J., Rüsen, J., Stein-Hölkeskamp, E., and Grütter, H. T., eds. 2003. *Sinn (in) der Antike: Orientierungssysteme, Leitbilder und Wertkonzepte im Altertum.* Mainz.

Holloway, R. R. 1992. "Why Korai?" *OJA* 11:267–274.

Hölscher, T. 1977. "Die Aufstellung des Perikles-Bildnisses und ihre Bedeutung." Reprinted in Fittschen 1988:377–391.

Holtheide, B. 1983. *Römische Bürgerrechtspolitik und römische Neubürger in der Provinz Asia.* Freiburg.

Holtzmann, B. 2003. *L'Acropole d'Athènes.* Paris.

Hofmann, H., ed. 1991. *Groningen Colloquia on the Novel.* Vol. 4. Groningen.

Hofmann, H., and Zimmerman, M., eds. 1998. *Groningen Colloquia on the Novel.* Vol. 9. Groningen.

Hornblower, S. 2004. *Thucydides and Pindar: Historical Narrative and the World of Epinikian Poetry.* Oxford.

Hornbostel, W. 1973. *Sarapis: Studien zur Überlieferungsgeschichte, den Erscheinungsformen und Wandlungen der Gestalt eines Gottes.* Leiden.

Horsley, G. H. R. 1992. "The Mysteries of Artemis Ephesia in Pisidia: A New Inscribed Relief." *AS* 42:119–150.

Horstmannshoff, F. J., et al., eds. 2002. *Kykeon: Studies in honor of H. S. Versnel.* Leiden.

Hunter, R., ed. 1998. *Studies in Heliodorus.* Cambridge.

Hurwit, J. 1998. *The Athenian Acropolis.* Cambridge.

Hutchinson, G. O. 2001. *Greek Lyric Poetry: A Commentary on Selected Larger Pieces.* Oxford.

Immerwahr, H. R. 1942. "Five Dedicatory Inscriptions from the North Wall of the Acropolis." *Hesperia* 11:338–348.

Jacquemin, A., and Morant, M.-J. 1999. "Inscriptions de Kadyanda." *Ktèma* 24:283–288.

Jahn, O., and Michaelis, A. 1931. *Arx Athenarum a Pausania descripta.* 3rd ed. Bonn.

Jameson, M. H. 1991. "Sacrifice before Battle." In Hanson 1991:197–228.

Jean, E., ed. 2001. *La Cilicie: Espaces et pouvoirs locaux (2ème millénaire av. J.-C.-4ème siècle ap. J.-C.).* Paris.

Jenkins, I. 1994. *The Parthenon Frieze.* London.

Jeppensen, K. 1979. "Where Was the So-called Erechtheion?" *AJA* 83:381–394.

Johnston, S. I. and Struck, P. T., eds. 2005. *Mantikê: Studies in Ancient Divination.* Leiden 2005.

Jones, C. P. 1970. "A Leading Family of Roman Thespiae." *HSCP* 74:223–25.

———. 1971. *Plutarch and Rome.* Oxford.

———. 1978. *The Roman World of Dio Chrysostom.* Cambridge, MA.

———. 1978a. "Three Foreigners in Attica." *Phoenix* 32:222–234.

———. 1980. "Prosopographical Notes on the Second Sophistic." *GRBS* 21:373–380.

———. 1982. "A Family of Pisidian Antioch." *Phoenix* 36:264–271.

———. 1986. *Culture and Society in Lucian.* Cambridge, MA.

———. 2002. "Epigraphica II: Two Consular Philosophers." *ZPE* 139:111–114.

———. 2003. "Epigraphica IV: Philosophers and Sophists at Phocaea." *ZPE* 142:127–130.

———. 2003a. "Epigraphica VII: Euphrates of Tyre." *ZPE* 144:160–163.

———. 2004. "Multiple Identities in the Age of the Second Sophistic." In Borg 2004a:13–21.

———. 2005. "Culture in the Careers of Eastern Senators." In Eck and Heil 2005:263–270.

Jordan, B. 1979. *Servants of the Gods.* Göttingen.

Jordan, D. R., Montgomery, H., and Thomassen, E., eds. 1999. *The World of Ancient Magic: Papers from the First International Samson Eitrem Seminar at the Norwegian Institute at Athens, 4-8 May 1997.* Bergen.

Jost, M. 1996. "Évergétisme et tradition religieuse à Mantinée au Ier siècle avant J.-C." In Chastagnol, Demougin, and Lepelley 1996:193–200.

———. 1998. "Sanctuaires publics et sanctuaries privés." *Ktèma* 23:301–306.

Kaltsas, N. 2002. *Sculpture in the National Archaeological Museum Athens.* Los Angeles.

Känel, R. 1989. "Drei hellenistische Grabreliefs aus Smyrna in Basel." *AK* 32:50–58.

Kapetanopoulos, E. 1994. "The Sarapion Monument at Athens." *Prometheus* 20:234–242.

Karageorghis, V. 2000. *Ancient Art from Cyprus: The Cesnola Collection.* New York.

Karakasi, K. 2001. *Archaische Koren.* Munich.

Karwiese, S. 1985. "Koressos—ein fast vergessener Stadtteil von Ephesos." In Alzinger and Neeb 1985: 214–225.

———. 1995. *Die Münzprägung von Ephesos.* Vienna.

Kearns, E. 1994. "Cakes in Greek Sacrificial Regulations." In R. Hägg 1994:65–70.

Keesling, C. M. 2003. *The Votive Statues of the Athenian Acropolis.* Cambridge.

Keil, J., and Wilhelm, A. 1931. *Denkmäler aus dem Rauhen Kilikien*. Manchester.

Kern, O. 1926. *Die Religion der Griechen*. Vol. 1. Berlin.

Kett, P. 1966. *Prosopographie der historischen griechischen Manteis bis auf die Zeit Alexanders des Großen*. Erlangen.

Kienast, D. 1999. *Augustus: Prinzeps und Monarch*. 3rd ed. Darmstadt.

Kirk, G. S. 1985. *The Iliad: A Commentary*. Vol. 1 (Books 1–4). Cambridge.

———. 1990. *The Iliad: A Commentary*. Vol. 2 (Books 5–8). Cambridge.

Klaffenbach, G. 1948. "Epigraphische Studien 3." *Philologus* 97:376–379.

Klinger, E., and Böhm, S., eds. 2003. *Geschlechterdifferenz, Ritual und Religion*. Würzburg.

Klinkott, H., ed. 2001. *Anatolien im Lichte kultureller Wechselbeziehungen*. Tübingen.

Kloppenborg, J. S., and Wilson, S. G., eds. 1996. *Voluntary Associations in the Graeco-Roman World*. London.

Kluge, F. 1975. *Etymologisches Wörterbuch der deutschen Sprache*. 21st ed. Berlin.

Knibbe, D. 1981. *Der Staatsmarkt: Die Inschriften des Prytaneions*. Vienna.

———. 2002. "Topographica Ephesiaca." *JÖAI* 71:207–219.

Knibbe, D., Engelmann, H., and Iplikçioğlu, B. 1993. "Neue Inschriften aus Ephesos XII." *JÖAI* 62:113–150.

Knibbe, D., et al. 1979. "Der Grundbesitz der ephesischen Artemis im Kaystrostal." *ZPE* 33:139–147.

Koch Piettre, R. 2005. "Des Épicuriens entre la vie retirée et les honneurs publics." In Dasen and Piérart 2005:259–272.

Koester, H., ed. 1995. *Ephesos: Metropolis of Asia*. Valley Forge.

Kopanias, K. 2001. "Der ägyptische Branchide aus Didyma." In Klinkott 2001:149–166.

Kortum, H.-H. 1997. "Zur Typologie der Herrscheranekdote in der mittelalterlichen Geschichtsschreibung." *MIöG* 105:1–29.

Kosmopoulou, A. 2001. "Working Women." *BSA* 96:281–319.

Kraemer, R. S. 1992. *Her Share of the Blessings: Women's Religions among Pagans, Jews, and Christians in the Greco-Roman World*. New York.

Kretschmer, E. 1930. "Beiträge zur Wortgeographie der altgriechischen Dialekte." *Glotta* 18:67–100.

Kron, U. 1992. "Frauenfeste in Demeterheiligtümern." *AA*:611–650.

———. 1996. "Priesthoods, Dedications and Euergetism: What Part Did Religion Play in the Political and Social Status of Greek Women?" In Hellström and Alroth 1996:139–182.

Krumeich, R. 1997. *Bildnisse griechischer Herrscher und Staatsmänner*. Munich.

Kuhn, G. 2003. Review of Muss and Bammer 2001. *Gött. Gel. Anz.* 255:197–226.

Kyrieleis, H. 1980. "Archaische Holzfunde aus Samos." *AM* 95:87–147.

———. 1995. "Eine neue Kore des Cheramyes." *AntP* 24:7–36.

Laffineur, R., and Hägg, R., eds. 2001. *Potnia*. Liège.

LaGamma, A. 2000. *Art and Oracle: African Art and Rituals of Divination*. New York.

Lakmann, M.-L. 1995. *Der Platoniker Tauros in der Darstellung des Aulus Gellius*. Leiden.

Lambert, S. D. 1994. *The Phratries of Attica*. Ann Arbor.

———. 1997. "The Attic Genos Salaminioi and the Island of Salamis." *ZPE* 119:85–106.

———. 1999. "IG II^2 2345, Thiasoi of Herakles and the Salaminioi Again." *ZPE* 125:93–130.

Lampe, G. W. H. 1961. *A Patristic Greek Lexicon*. Oxford.

Langlotz, E. 1939. "Die Koren." In Schrader 1939:3–184.

Lane, E. N., ed. 1996. *Cybele, Attis, and Related Cults*. Leiden.

Lane Fox, R. 1986. *Pagans and Christians*. New York.

La Rocca, A. 2005. *Il filosofo e la città: Commento storico ai Florida di Apuleio*. Rome.

Latacz, J. 1989. *Homer: Der erste Dichter des Abendlands*. 2nd ed. Munich.

———. 2000. *Homers Ilias: Gesamtkommentar*. Vol. 1.2 (Book 1). Munich.

———. 2003. *Homers Ilias: Gesamtkommentar*. Vol. 2.2 (Book 2). Munich.

Lawton, C. L. 1995. *Attic Document Reliefs*. Oxford.

Lechat, H. 1891. "Terres cuites de Corcyre." *BCH* 15:1–111.

———. 1903. *Au musée de l'Acropole*. Paris.

Lefkowitz, M. R. 1996. "Women in the Panathenaic and Other Festivals." In Neils 1996:78–91. Madison.

Legras, B. 1993. "Mallokouria et mallocourètes: Un rite de passage dans l'Égypte romaine." *CCG* 4:113–127.

Lendon, J. E. 1997. *Empire of Honour: The Art of Government in the Roman World*. Oxford.

Leschhorn, W., Miron, A. V. B., and Miron, A., eds. 1996. *Hellas und der griechische Osten: Studien zur Geschichte und Numismatik der griechischen Welt; Festschrift für Peter Robert Franke zum 70. Geburtstag*. Saarbrücken.

Leszl, W. 1996. "I messaggi degli dei e i segni della natura." In Manetti 1996:43–85.

Levick, B. 2002. "Women, Power, and Philosophy at Rome and Beyond." In Clark and Rajak 2002:133–155.

Lewis, D. M. 1955. "Notes on Attic Inscriptions." *ABSA* 50:1–36.

LiDonnici, L. 1999. "The Ephesian Megabyzos. Priesthood and Religious Diplomacy at the End of the Classical Period." *Religion* 29:201–214.

Liesenfelt, A.-M., and Le Bohec, Y. 1974–1975. "À propos d'une inscription de Timgad: Notes sur les Crétois en Afrique." *BCTH*:123–134.

Lindholm, C. 1990. *Charisma*. Oxford.

Lindner, R. 2003. "Priesterinnen." In Klinger and Böhm 2003:53–77.

Linnemann, J. 2001. "Eubulides (I)," "Eubulides (II)," and "Eucheir (III)." In Vollkommer 2001:219–221. Munich.

Lippold, G. 1916. "Ismenias." *RE* IX:2141.

———. 1921. "Kephisodotos 9." *RE* XI:236.

Lippolis, E. 1988–1989. "Il santuario di Athana a Lindos." *ASAA* 66–67:97–157.

Llewellyn-Jones, L. 2002 "Eunuchs and the Royal Harem in Achaemenid Persia (559–331 BC)." In Tougher 2002:19–49.

Lobeck, C. A. 1829. *Aglaophamus sive de theologiae mysticae Graecorum causis libri tres*. Königsberg.

Loewe, M., and Blacker, C., eds. 1981. *Oracles and Divination*. Boulder.

Löffler, I. 1963. *Die Melampodie: Versuch einer Rekonstruktion des Inhalts*. Meisenheim am Glan.

Lohmann, H., and Schäfer, H. 2000. "Wo lag das Herakleion der Salaminioi ἐπὶ πορθμῷ?" *ZPE* 133:91–102.

Löhr, C. 2000. *Griechische Familienweihungen*. Rahden.

Lo Monaco, A. 2004. "L'*élite* elea ad Olimpia nel I secolo a.C." In Cébeillac-Gervasoni et al. 2004:287–305.

Long, A. A. 2002. *Epictetus: A Stoic and Socratic Guide to Life*. Oxford.

Lonis, R. 1979. *Guerre et religion en Grèce à l'époque classique*. Paris.

Loraux, N., ed. 1993. *Grecia al femminile*. Rome.

Lorenz, B. 1999. "Zum Lob des Arztes in griechischen Inschriften." In *XI Congresso Internazionale di Epigrafia Greca e Latina I* 1999:761–767.

Luck, G. 1990. *Magie und andere Geheimlehren in der Antike*. Stuttgart.

Luraghi, N. 1997. "Il carnevale macabro, ovvero, morire da tiranno." *AASA* 4:53–67.

———. 1997a. "Un *mantis* eleo nella Siracusa di Ierone: Agesia di Siracusa, Iamide di Stinfalo." *Klio* 79:69–86.

———, ed. 2001. *The Historian's Craft in the Age of Herodotus*. Oxford.

Ma, J., and Tracy, S. 2004. "Notes on Attic Statue Bases." *ZPE* 150:121–126.

MacKay, Th. S. 1990. "The Major Sanctuaries of Pamphylia and Cilicia." In *ANRW II* 18:2045–2129.

Magie, D. 1953. "Egyptian Deities in Asia Minor in Inscriptions and on Coins." *AJA* 57:163–187.

Malay, H. 1999. *Researches in Lydia, Mysia and Aiolis*. Vienna.

Malkin, I. 1987. *Religion and Colonization in Ancient Greece*. Leiden.

Manetti, G., ed. 1996. *Knowledge through Signs: Ancient Semiotic Theories and Practice*. Bologna.

Mansfield, J. M. 1985. *The Robe of Athena and the Panathenaic Peplos*. Ann Arbor.

Mantis, A. 1990. *Problemata tes eikonografias ton iereion kai ton iereon sten archaia ellenike techne*. Athens.

Marcadé, J. 1948. "Parthénoklès d'Athènes." *RA* 688–699.

Marek, C. 1984. *Die Proxenie*. Frankfurt.

———. 1993. *Stadt, Ära und Territorium in Pontus-Bithynia und Nord-Galatia*. Tübingen.

Martini, W. 1990. *Die archaische Plastik der Griechen*. Darmstadt.

Masner, K., ed. 1899. *Festschrift für O. Benndorf zu seinem 60. Geburtstag*. Vienna.

Masson, O. 1962. "Recherches sur le vocabulaire d'Hipponax." *RPh* 36:46–50.

Mastrokostas, E. I. 1966. "Epistêmata ek Myrrinountos." In Orlandos 1966:281–299.

Matthaiou, A. P. 1987. "*Erion Lukourgou Lukophronos Boutadou*." *Horos* 5:31–44.

———. 1992–1998. "Νεο θαύσμα τῆς IG II² 689." *Horos* 10–12:29–48.

———. 1994. "Two New Attic Inscriptions." In Osborne and Hornblower 1994:175–188.

Mayrhofer M. 1979. "Megabyxos." *Iranisches Personennamenbuch* 1.2:16. Vienna.

McK. Camp, J. 1989. "The Philosophical Schools of Roman Athens." In Walker and Cameron 1989:50–55.

Meritt, B. D. 1933. "The Inscriptions." *Hesperia* 2:149–169.

———. 1946. "Greek Inscriptions." *Hesperia* 15:169–253.

Merkelbach, R. 1962. *Roman und Mysterium in der Antike*. Munich.

———. 1985. "Eine Inschrift des Weltverbandes der dionysischen Technitai." *ZPE* 58:136–138.

———. 1995. *Isis Regina Zeus Serapis: Die griechisch-ägyptische Religion nach den Quellen dargestellt*. Stuttgart.

Merkelbach, R., and Stauber, J. 1988. *Steinepigramme aus dem griechischen Osten*. Vol. 1. Stuttgart.

Merker, I. L. 1986. "Habron the Son of Lykourgos of Boutadai." *AncW* 14:41–50.

Meritt, B. D. 1961. "Greek Inscriptions." *Hesperia* 30:205–292.

Metzler, D. 1990. "Der Seher Mopsos auf den Münzen der Stadt Mallos." *Kernos* 3:235–250.

Meyer, M. 1989. *Die griechischen Urkundenreliefs*. Mainz.

Meyer-Zwiffelhoffer, E. 2003. "Bürger sein in den griechischen Städten des römischen Kaiserreiches." In Hölkeskamp et al. 2003:375–402.

Mikalson, J. D. 1998. *Religion in Hellenistic Athens*. Berkeley.

———. 2004. *Ancient Greek Religion*. London.

Millar, F. 1965. "Epictetus and the Imperial Court." *JHS* 55:141–148.

———. 1993. "The Greek City in the Roman Period." In Hansen 1993:232–260.

———. 1993a. *The Roman Near East. 31 BC–AD 337*. Cambridge, MA.

Miller, D. G. 1968. "Megabyxos." *Language* 44:846.

Miller, M. C. 1989. "The Ependytes in Classical Athens." *Hesperia* 58:313–329.

Mirecki, P., and Meyer, M., eds. 2001. *Magic and Ritual in the Ancient World*. Leiden.

Miron, A. V. B. 1996. "Alexander von Abonuteichos: Zur Geschichte des Orakels des Neos Asklepios Glykon." In Leschhorn et al. 1996:153–188.

Mitchell, St., and Waelkens, M. 1998. *Pisidian Antioch: The Site and Its Monuments*. London.

Mitford, T. B. 1980. "Roman Cyprus." In *ANRW* II 7.2:1285–1384.

———. 1990. "The Cults of Roman Cyprus." In *ANRW* II 18.3. Berlin, 2176–2211.

Möbius, H. 1967. "Diotima." In Möbius 1967a:33–46.

———. 1967a. *Studia Varia: Aufsätze zur Kunst und Kultur der Antike*. Ed. W. Schiering. Wiesbaden.

Montserrat, D. 1997. "Heron 'Bearer of Philosophia' and Hermione *grammatike*." *JEA* 83:223–226.

Mooren, L., ed. 2000. *Politics, Administration and Society in the Hellenistic and Roman World: Proceedings of the International Colloquium, Bertinoro 19–24 July 1997*. Louvain.

Mordtmann, J. 1874. *Marmora Ancyrana*. Berlin.

Moretti, L. 1976. "*Epigraphica* 16: Un successore di Posidonio d'Apamea." *RFIC* 104:191–194.

Morgan, J. R. 1979. *A Commentary on the Ninth and Tenth Books of Heliodorus' Aethiopica*. Oxford.

———. 1989. "Heliodorus: An Ethiopian Story." In Reardon 1989:349–588.

———. 1991. "Reader and audiences in the Aithiopika of Heliodoros." In Hofmann 1991:84–103.

———. 1999. "The Story of Knemon in Heliodoros' Aithiopika." In Swain 1999:259–285.

Morricone, M. L. 1991. "Due teste femminili dall'Asklepieion di Coo." In Stucchi 1991:181–207.

Morris, I., ed. 1994. *Classical Greece*. Cambridge.

Morris, S. P. 2001. "The Prehistoric Background of Artemis Ephesia: A Solution to the Enigma of her 'Breasts'?" In Muss 2001:135–151.

———. 2001a. "Potnia Aswiya: Anatolian Contributions to Greek Religion." In Laffineur and Hägg 2001:423–434.

Morrison, J. S. 1981. "The Classical World." In Loewe and Blacker 1981:87–114.

Mossman, J., ed. 1997. *Plutarch and his Intellectual World: Essays on Plutarch.* London.

Most, G. W., Petersmann, H., and Ritter, A. M., eds. 1993. *Philanthropeia kai Eusebeia: Festschrift für Albrecht Dihle zum 70. Geburtstag.* Göttingen.

———. 2003. "Philosophy and Religion." In Sedley 2003:300–322.

Motte, A. 2005. "Figures de prêtre dans la literature grecque." In Motte and Marchetti 2005: 1–31.

Motte, A., and Marchetti, P., eds. 2005. *La figure du prêtre dans les grandes traditions religieuses.* Louvain.

Mouterde, R. 1963. *Mélanges offerts au Père René Mouterde pour son 80e anniversaire.* Vol. 2. Beirut.

Müller, H. 1968. "Marcus Aurelius Olympiodorus, *ekgonos Hippodromou.*" ZPE 3:197–220.

Müller, K. O. 1825. *Prolegomena zu einer wissenschaftlichen Mythologie.* Göttingen.

Munson, R. V. 2001. *Telling Wonders: Ethnographic and Political Discourse in the Work of Herodotus.* Ann Arbor.

Murray, O. 2001. "Herodotus and Oral History Reconsidered." In Luraghi 2001:314–325.

Muss, U. 2000. "Das Artemision von Ephesus—Wege von und nach Westen." In Friesinger 2000:149–155.

———, ed. 2001. *Der Kosmos der Artemis von Ephesos.* Vienna.

Muss U., and Bammer, A. 2001. *Der Altar des Artemisions von Ephesos.* Vienna.

Musurillo, H. A. 1954. *The Acts of the Pagan Martyrs: Acta Alexandrinorum. Ed. with commentary.* Oxford.

Mylonas, G. E 1961. *Eleusis.* Athens.

Nagy, H. 1998. "Divinity, Exaltation and Heroization: Thoughts on the Seated Posture in Early Archaic Greek Sculpture." In Hartswick 1998:181–191.

Naso, A., ed. 2006. *Stranieri e non cittadini nei santuari greci: Atti del convegno internazionale.* Grassina.

Nauck, A. 1848. *Aristophanis Byzantii grammatici Alexandrini fragmenta.* Halle.

Neils, J., ed. 1996. *Worshipping Athena. Panathenaia and Parthenon.* Madison.

———. 2001. *The Parthenon Frieze.* Cambridge.

Neils, J., and Oakley, J. H., eds. 2003. *Coming of Age in Ancient Greece.* Exhibition catalogue. Hanover.

Nemes, Z., and Németh, G., eds. 1997. *Heorte: Studia in honorem Johannis Sarkady septuagenarii.* Debrecen.

Nenci, G., ed. 1990. *Hérodote et les peuples non grecs.* Vandœuvres and Geneva.

Nesselrath, H.-G., ed. 1997. *Einleitung in die griechische Philologie.* Stuttgart.

Neumann, J. 1998. "Priester." In Cancik, Gladigow, and Kohl 1998:342–344.

Nietzsche, F. 1872–1874. "Die Geburt der Tragödie." In Nietzsche 1967-, 3.1:17–152.

———. 1875–1876. "Der Gottesdienst der Griechen." In Nietzsche 1967-, 2.5:355–520.

———. 1967-. *Werke: Kritische Gesamtausgabe*. Ed. G. Colli and M. Montinari. Berlin.

Nilsson, M. P. 1955. *Geschichte der griechischen Religion*. Vol. 1. 2nd ed. Munich.

———. 1967. *Geschichte der griechischen Religion*. Vol. 1. 3rd ed. Munich.

North, J. A. 1996. "Priests (Greek and Roman)." *OCD* 3:1245–1246.

Nutton, V. 1977. "Archiatroi and the Medical Profession in Antiquity." *PBSR* 45:191–226.

Ober, J. 1989. *Mass and Elite in Democratic Athens*. Princeton.

———. 2000. Review of P. Wilson 2000. *BMCR* 2000.10.02.

Oelmann, F. 1957. "Homerische Tempel und nordeurasische Opfermahlhäuser." *BJ* 157:11–52.

Oliver, J. H. 1975. "The Empress Plotina and the Sacred Thymelic Synod." *Historia* 24:125–128.

———. 1979. "Flavius Pontaenus, Priest of the Philosophical Muses." *HThR* 72:157–160.

———. 1982. "Arrian in two Roles." *Studies in Attic Epigraphy*:122–129.

Olshausen, E. 1987. "Der König und die Priester: Die Mithradatiden im Kampf um die Anerkennung ihrer Herrschaft im Pontos." In Olshausen1987:187–212.

———, ed. 1987a. *Stuttgarter Kolloquium zur Historischen Geographie des Altertums 1 (1980)*. Bonn.

———. 1991. "Zum Organisationskonzept des Pompeius in Pontos—ein historisch-geographisches Argument." In Olshausen and Sonnabend 1991:443–455.

Olshausen, E., and Sonnabend, H., eds. 1991. *Stuttgarter Kolloquium zur Historischen Geographie des Altertums 2 (1984) und 3 (1987)*. Bonn.

Oppenheim, A. L. 1977. *Ancient Mesopotamia: Portrait of a Dead Civilization*. Chicago.

Orlandos, A. K. 1966. *Charistêrion eis Anastasion K. Orlandon III*. Athens.

Osborne, M. J. 1970. "Honours for Sthorys (*IG* ii². 17)." *BSA* 65:151–174.

Osborne, R. 1993. "Women and Sacrifice in Classical Greece." *CQ* 43:392–405.

———. 1994. "Looking on—Greek Style?" In Morris 1994:81–96.

Osborne, R., and Hornblower, S., eds. 1994. *Ritual, Finance, Politics: An Account of Athenian Democracy*. Oxford.

Özgan, R. 1978. *Untersuchungen zur archaischen Plastik Ioniens*. Bonn.

Pakkanen, P. 1996. *Interpreting Early Hellenistic Religion*. Helsinki.

Palagia, O. 1980. *Euphranor*. Leiden.

―――. 1987. "Classical Encounters: Attic Sculpture after Sulla." In Hoff 1987:81–95.

―――. 1990. "A new relief of the Graces and the Charites of Socrates." In Geerard 1990:347–56.

―――, ed. 1996. *Personal Styles in Greek Sculpture*. Cambridge.

―――, ed. 2003. *The Macedonians in Athens 323-229 B.C.* Oxford.

Palagia, O., and Coulson, W., eds. 1993. *Sculpture from Arcadia and Laconia: Proceedings of an International Conference Held at the American School of Classical Studies at Athens, April 10-14, 1992*. Oxford.

Panayotakis, S. 2002. "The Temple and the Brothel: Mothers and Daughters in Apollonius of Tyre." *Ancient Narrative* Supplement 1:98–117. Groningen.

Pani, M. 1970. "Archelao II e la fine della dinastia dei Teucridi di Olba." *Athenaeum* 48:327–334.

Papangeli, K. 2002. *Eleusina: O archaiologikos choros kai to mouseio*. Athens.

Papenfuß, D., and Strocka, V. M., eds. 2001. *Gab es das griechische Wunder?* Mainz.

Park, G. K. 1963 "Divination and Its Social Contexts." *JRAI* 93:195–209.

Parke, H. W. 1967. *The Oracles of Zeus*. Oxford.

Parker, R. 1983. *Miasma. Pollution and Purification in Early Greek Religion*. Oxford.

―――. 1988. "Spartan Religion." In Powell 1988:142–172.

―――. 1991. "Potamon of Mytilene and his Family." *ZPE* 85:115–129.

―――. 1996. *Athenian Religion: A History*. Oxford.

―――. 1999. "Mantis." *DNP* 7:834–836.

―――. 2000. "Sacrifice and Battle." In van Wees 2000:299–314.

Parker, R., and Obbink, D. 2000. "Aus der Arbeit der Inscriptiones Graecae. VI. Sales of Priesthoods on Cos I." *Chiron* 30:415–449.

Parsons, A. W. 1949. "A Family of Philosophers at Athens and Alexandria." In Shear 1949:268–272.

Payne, H., and Young, G. M. 1936. *Archaic Marble Sculpture from the Acropolis*. London.

Peachin, M., ed. 2001. *Aspects of Friendship in the Graeco-Roman World: Proceedings of a Conference Held at the Seminar für Alte Geschichte Heidelberg, on 10-11 June, 2000*. Portsmouth, RI.

Peek, P. M., ed. 1991. *African Divination Systems: Ways of Knowing*. Bloomington.

Peek, W. 1960. *Griechische Grabgedichte*. Berlin.

―――. 1978. "Zu griechischen Epigrammen." *ZPE* 31:247–264.

Pemberton, J., III, ed. 2000. *Insight and Artistry in African Divination*. Washington.

Peppas-Delmousou, D. 1970. "*Basis andriantos tou Arrianou*." *AAA* 3:377–380.

Perry, B. E. 1964. *Secundus the Silent Philosopher: The Greek Life of Secundus*. Ithaca.

Petrakos, B. C. 1999. *Ho demos tou Rhamnountos*. Athens.

Petzl, G. 1994. *Die Beichtinschriften Westkleinasiens*. Bonn.

Pfisterer-Haas, S. 1989. *Darstellungen alter Frauen in der griechischen Kunst*. Frankfurt.

Pfuhl, E., and Möbius, H. 1977. *Die ostgriechischen Grabreliefs*. Mainz.

Picard, C. 1922. *Ephèse et Claros*. Paris.

Piepenbrink, K., 2001. "Prophetie und soziale Kommunikation in der homerischen Gesellschaft." In Brodersen 2001:9–24.

———, ed. 2003. *Philosophie und Lebenswelt in der Antike*. Darmstadt.

Piolot, L. 1999. "Pausanias et les Mystères d'Andanie: Histoire d'une aporie." In Renard 1999:196–228.

Pirenne-Delforge, V. 1994. "La loutrophorie et la 'prêtresse-loutrophore' de Sicyone." In Ginouvès et al. 1994:147–155.

———. 2005. "La cité, les *dèmotelè hiera* et les prêtres." In Dasen and Piérart 2005:55–68.

Piettre, R. 2002. "Un buste parlant d'Épicure, un passage de Lucien (*Alexandre le faux prophète*, 26): La philosophie au péril des religions." *Kernos* 15:131–144.

Pleket, H. W. 1969. *Texts on the Social History of the Greek World*. Vol. 2 of *Epigraphica*. Leiden.

———. 1998. "Political Culture and Political Practice in the Cities of Asia Minor in the Roman Empire." In Schuller 1998:204–216.

Poralla, P. 1913. *Prosopographie der Lakedaimonier bis auf die Zeit Alexanders des Grossen*. Breslau. 2nd ed. Ed. A. S. Bradford. Chicago, 1985.

Powell, A., ed. 1988. *Classical Sparta: Techniques behind her Success*. London.

Price, S. 1999. *Religions of the Ancient Greeks*. Cambridge.

Pritchett, W. K. 1971. *The Greek State at War*. Vol. 1. Berkeley.

———. 1979. *The Greek State at War*. Vol. 3. Berkeley.

———. 1999. *Pausanias Periegetes*. Vol. 2. Amsterdam.

Puech, B. 1989. "Ailianos de Milet (Aelius) (A 61)." In Goulet 1989:78.

———. 1989a. "Apollonios (A 262)." In Goulet 1989:280.

———. 1989b. "Aurelianus de Smyrne (Sextus Claudius) (A 510)." In Goulet 1989:687.

———. 1989c. "Autoboulos de Chéronée (Sextus Claudius) (A 512)." In Goulet 1989:688.

———. 1992. "Prosopographie des amis de Plutarque." In *ANRW* II 33.6:4831–4893.

———. 1994. "Bacchios de Paphos (B 6)." In Goulet 1994:47–48.

———. 1994a. "Callisthène d'Olbia (C 35)." In Goulet 1994:182–183.

———. 1994b. "Charilampianè Olympias (Aurelia) (C 98)." In Goulet 1994:294.

———. 1994c. "Démétrios Tullianos (D 63)." In Goulet 1994:642.

———. 1994d. "Dionysodoros (Flavius Maecius Se[veros]) (D 190)." In Goulet 1994:874.

———. 1994e. "Diogène d'Oinoanda (D 141)." In Goulet 1994:803–806.

———. 1998. "Prosopographie et chronologie delphique sous le Haut-Empire: L'apport de Plutarque et de l'histoire littéraire." *Topoi* 8:261–266.

———. 2000. "Eucratidas de Rhodes (E 85)." In Goulet 2000:278.

———. 2000a. "Flavianus Sulpicius (G. Aelius) (F 14)." In Goulet 2000:426.

———. 2000b. "Héraclite de Rhodiapolis (H 65)." In Goulet 2000:627.

———. 2000c. "Isidore de Thmouis (I 35)." In Goulet 2000:890.

———. 2002. *Orateurs et sophistes grecs dans les inscriptions d'époque impériale.* Paris.

———. 2005. "Leitè (Aurelia) (L 27)." In Goulet 2005:84–85.

———. 2005a. "Nicétès (Iulius) de Bithynion (N 37)." In Goulet 2005:666.

———. 2005b. "Maxime de Gortyne (T. Flavius) (M 65)." In Goulet 2005:323.

———. 2005c. "Maximus (T. Flavius) (M 73)." In Goulet 2005:366.

———. 2005d. "Matinianus de Nicomédie (M 48)." In Goulet 2005:303.

———. 2005e. "Magnilla d'Apollonia (M 11)." In Goulet 2005:244.

———. 2005f. "Magnus d'Apollonia (M 12)." In Goulet 2005:244.

———. 2005g. "Mènios d'Apollonia (M 128)." In Goulet 2005:467.

———. 2005h. "Maxime d'Antioche (M. Atilius) (M 61)." In Goulet 2005:312–313.

———. 2005i. "Lupus (P. Cornelius) de Nicopolis (L 77)." In Goulet 2005:195.

———. 2005j. "Macedo (C. Calpurnius Collega) (M 4)." In Goulet 2005:225.

———. 2005k. "Léon de Stratonicée (L 38)." In Goulet 2005:91.

———. 2005l. "Léon (P. Memmius) de Nicopolis (L 35)." In Goulet 2005:90.

———. 2005m. "Maximus (Quinctilius) (M 72)." In Goulet 2005:365–366.

Quass, F. 1993. *Die Honoratiorenschicht in den Städten des griechischen Ostens: Untersuchungen zur politischen und sozialen Entwicklung in hellenistischer und römischer Zeit.* Stuttgart.

Rahn, P. J. 1986. "Funeral Memorials of the First Priestess of Athena Nike." *BSA* 81:195–207.

Ramsay, W. M. 1919. "A Noble Anatolian Family of the Fourth Century." *ClR* 33:1–5.

Raubitschek, A. E. 1945. "The Priestess of Pandrosos." *AJA* 49:434–435.

Reardon, B. P., ed. 1989. *Collected Ancient Greek Novels*. Berkeley.

Reeder, E. D., ed. 1996. *Pandora: Frauen im klassischen Griechenland; Ausstellungskatalog Antikensammlung Basel und Sammlung Ludwig*. Baltimore.

Reisch, E. 1919. "Die Tempeldienerin des Nikomachos." *ÖJh* 19/20:299–316.

Renard, J., ed. 1999. *Le Péloponnèse: Archéologie et Histoire*. Rennes.

Reusser, C., ed. 2001. *Griechenland in der Kaiserzeit: Neue Funde und Forschungen zu Skulptur, Architektur und Topographie; Kolloquium zum sechzigsten Geburtstag von Prof. Dietrich Willers. Bern, 12–13 Juni 1998*. Bern.

Rey-Coquais, J.-P. 1973. "Inscriptions grecques d'Apamée." *AArchSyr* 23:39–84.

———. 1997. "La culture en Syrie à l'époque romaine." In Dabrowa 1997:139–160.

Rhodes, P. J. 1997. "Deceleans and Demotionidae Again." *CQ* 47:109–120.

Richardson, N. J. 1974. *The Homeric Hymn to Demeter*. Oxford.

Richer, N. 1999. "La recherche des appuis surnaturels topiques par les Spartiates en guerre." In Renard 1999:135–148.

Richter, G. M. A. 1968. *Korai*. London.

Ridgway, B. S. 1977. *Archaic Style in Greek Sculpture*. Princeton.

———. 1982. "Of Kouroi and Korai Attic Variety." In Thompson 1982:118–127.

———. 1990. "Birds, Meniskoi, and Head Attributes in Archaic Greece." *AJA* 94:583–612

Riemann, O. 1877. "Inscriptions grecques provenant du recueil de Cyriaque d'Ancone." *BCH* 1:286–294.

Riess, W. 2001. "Stadtrömische Lehrer zwischen Anpassung und Nonkonformismus: Überlegungen zu einer epigraphischen Ambivalenz." In Alföldy and Panciera 2001:163–207.

Rigsby, K. J. 1996. *Asylia: Territorial Inviolability in the Hellenistic World*. Berkeley.

———. 2001. "Founding a Sarapeum." *GRBS* 42:117–124.

Rives, J. B. 1994. "The Priesthood of Apuleius." *AJP* 115:273–290.

Rizakis, A. D., ed. 1996. *Roman Onomastics in the Greek East—Social and Political Aspects: Proceedings of the International Colloquium Organized by the Finnish Institute and the Centre for Greek and Roman Antiquity, Athens 7-9 September 1993*. Meletemata 21. Athens.

Rizakis, A. D., and Zoumbaki, S. 2001. *Roman Personal Names in their Social Context (Achaia, Arcadia, Argolis, Corinthia and Eleia)*. Vol. 1 of *Roman Peloponnese*. Meletemata 31. Athens.

Rizakis, A.D., Zoumbaki, S., and Lepenioti, C. 2004. *Roman Personal Names in their Social Context (Laconia and Messenia)*. Vol. 2 of *Roman Peloponnese*. Athens.

Robert, C. 1895. *Die Marathonschlacht in der Poikile*. Halle.

Robert, J., and Robert, L. 1954. *La Carie II*. Paris.

Robert, L. 1962. "Apparitions divines à Milet." *Hellenica* 11–12:545–546.

———. 1937. *Études anatoliennes: Recherches sur les inscription grecques de l'Asie Mineure.* Paris.

———. 1978. "Documents d'Asie Mineure V. Stèle funéraire de Nicomédie et séismes dans les inscriptions." *BCH* 102:395–408.

———. 1980. *À travers l'Asie Mineure: Poètes et prosateurs, monnaies grecques, voyageurs et géographie.* Paris.

———. 1983. "Documents d'Asie Mineure." *BCH* 107:497–599.

———. 1990. "Deux poètes grecs à l'époque impériale." *OMS* VII:569–598.

Robertson, N. 1988. "Melanthus, Codrus, Neleus, Caucon: Ritual Myth as Athenian History." *GRBS* 29:201–261.

———. 1996. "New Light on Demeter's Mysteries: The Festival Proerosia." *GRBS* 37:319–380.

———. 1999. "Splanchnoptes." *ZPE* 127:175–179.

Robiano, P. 2000. "Euphratès (Mestrius) (E 132)." In Goulet 2000:337–342.

Roccos, L. J. 1995. "The Kanephoros and Her Festival Mantle." *AJA* 99:641–666.

———. 2000. "Back-mantle and Peplos." *Hesperia* 69:235–265.

Rogers, G. M. 1991. *The Sacred Identity of Ephesos: Foundation Myths of a Roman City.* London.

Rohde, E. 1894. "Die Religion der Griechen." In Rohde 1901:314–339.

———. 1901. *Kleine Schriften.* Vol. 2. Tübingen.

———. 1914. *Der griechischen Roman und seine Vorläufer.* Leipzig.

Romano, I. B. 1980. *Early Greek Cult Images.* Ann Arbor.

Rosen, R. M., and Sluiter, I., eds. 2003. *ANDREIA: Studies in Manliness and Courage in Classical Antiquity.* Leiden.

Roth, P. A. 1982. *Mantis: The Nature, Function and Status of a Greek Prophetic Type.* Bryn Mawr.

Roussel, P. 1916. *Les cultes égyptiens à Délos du IIIe au 1er siècle ac. J.-C.* Paris.

———. 1987. *Délos Colonie Athénienne.* Repr. Ed. Ph. Bruneau, M.-Th. Couilloud-Ledinahet, and R. Etienne. Paris.

Rozenbeek, H. 1993. "Another Archiatros from Ephesos?" *EA* 21:103–105.

Rudhardt, J. 1958. *Notions fondamentales de la pensée religieuse et actes constitutifs du culte dans la Grèce classique.* Geneva.

Ruge, W. 1932. "Tarsos (2)". *RE* II 8:2413–2439.

Rumscheid, J. 2000. *Kranz und Krone.* Tübingen.

Runia, D. T. 1988. "Philosophical Heresiography: Evidence in Two Ephesian Inscriptions." *ZPE* 72:241–243.

Rüpke, J. 1996. "Controllers and Professionals: Analyzing Religious Specialists." *Numen* 43:241–262.

Russo, J. 1992. *A Commentary on Homer's Odyssey.* Vol. 3 (Books 17–24). Oxford.

Şahin, M. Ç. 1997. "New Inscriptions from Lagina." *EA* 29:83–105.

Şahin, S. 1977. "Ein Stein aus Hadrianoi in Mysien in Bursa." *ZPE* 24:257–258.

Şahin, S., Schwertheim, E., and Wagner, J., eds. 1978. *Studien zur Religion und Kultur Kleinasiens.* Leiden.

Saller, R. P. 1980. "Anecdotes as Historical Evidence for the Principate." *G&R* 27:69–83.

Salomies, O. 2001. "Roman Nomina in the Greek East: Observations on Some Recently Published Inscriptions." *Arctos* 35:139–174.

Salviat, F. 2001. "Les Nyktophylaxia, l'enfermement de la truie et les Thesmophories de Délos d'après ID 440+456." In Brun and Jockey 2001:735–747.

Samana, É. 2003. *Les médecins dans le monde grec: Sources épigraphiques sur la naissance d'un corps médical.* Geneva.

Sanders, J. M. 1993. "The Dioscuri in Post-Classical Sparta." In Palagia and Coulson 1993:217–224.

Sarikakis, Th. Ch. 1965: "Aktia ta en Nikopolei." *AE*:145–162.

Sayar, M. H. 1999: "Kilikien und die Seleukiden." In *Studien zum antiken Kleinasien* 4:125–136.

Sayar, M. H., Siewert, P., and Taeuber, H. 1994. "Asylieerklärungen des Sulla und des Lucullus für das Isis- und Sarapisheiligtum von Mopsuhestia (Ostkilikien)." *Tyche* 9:113–130.

Schachter, A. 1999. "The Nyktophylaxia of Delos." *JHS* 119:172–174.

———. 2000. "The Seer Tisamenos and the Klytiadai." *CQ* 50:292–295.

Schäfer, T. 1987. "Diphroi und Peplos auf dem Ostfries des Parthenon." *MDAI(A)* 102:185–212.

Scheer, T. S. 1993. *Mythische Vorväter Zur Bedeutung griechischer Heroenmythen im Selbstverständnis kleinasiatischer Städte.* Munich.

———. 2000. *Die Gottheit und ihr Bild.* Munich.

Schmidt, S. 1991. *Hellenistische Grabreliefs.* Cologne.

Schmitt, A. 1990. *Selbständigkeit und Abhängigkeit menschlichen Handelns bei Homer: Hermeneutische Untersuchungen zur Psychologie Homers.* Mainz.

Schmitt, R. 2000. *Selected Onomastic Writings.* New York.

———. 2002. *Die iranischen und Iranier-Namen in den Schriften Xenophons.* Vienna.

Schmitz, T. 1997. *Bildung und Macht: Zur sozialen und politischen Funktion der zweiten Sophistik in der griechischen Welt der Kaiserzeit.* Munich.

Schneider, L. A. 1975. *Zur sozialen Bedeutung der archaischen Korenstatuen.* Hamburg.

Scholl, A. 1996. *Die attischen Bildfeldstelen des 4. Jhs. v. Chr.* Berlin.

———. 2002. "Kult im klassischen Athen." In *Die griechische Klassik* (exhibition catalogue Berlin/Bonn):190–195. Mainz

Schönborn, H. B. 1976. *Die Pastophoren im Kult der ägyptischen Götter.* Meisenheim.

Schörner, G. 2003. *Votive im römischen Griechenland: Untersuchungen zur späthellenistischen und kaiserzeitlichen Kunst- und Religionsgeschichte.* Stuttgart.

Scholz, P. 2003. "Ein römischer Epikureer in der Provinz: Der Adressatenkreis der Inschrift des Diogenes von Oinoanda. Bemerkungen zur Verbreitung von Literalität und Bildung im kaiserzeitlichen Kleinasien." In Piepenbrink 2003:208–227.

Schrader, P., ed. 1939. *Die archaischen Marmorbildwerke der Akropolis.* Frankfurt.

Schuller, W., ed. 1998. *Politische Theorie und Praxis im Altertum.* Darmstadt.

Schultz, P. 2003. "Kephisodotos the Younger." In Palagia 2003:186–193.

Schultz, P. and R. von den Hoff, eds. 2007. *Early Hellenistic Portraiture: Image, Style, Context.* Cambridge.

Schulze, H. 1998. *Ammen und Pädagogen.* Mainz.

Schwabl, H. 1999 "Nachrichten über Ephesos im Traumbuch des Artemidor." In Friesinger and Krinzinger 1999:283–287.

Sebillotte, V. 1997. "Les Labyades: Une phratrie à Delphes?" *CCG* 8:39–49.

Sedley, D., ed. 2003. *The Cambridge Companion to Greek and Roman Philosophy.* Cambridge.

Senff, R. 1993. *Das Apollonheiligtum von Idalion.* Jonsered.

Shapiro, H. A. 2001. "Atene prima e dopo le guerre persiane." *ArchClass* 52:1–14.

———. 2001a. "Zum Wandel der attischen Gesellschaft nach den Perserkriegen." In Papenfuß and Strocka 2001:91–98.

Shear, Th. L. 1949. *Commemorative Studies in Honor of T. L. Shear.* Princeton.

Sherk, R. 1992. "The Eponymous Officials of Greek Cities IV. The Register—Part III: Thrace, Black Sea Area, Asia Minor (Continued)." *ZPE* 93:223–272.

Siard, H. 1998. "La crypte du Sarapieion A de Délos et le process d'Apollonios." *BCH* 122:469–486.

Simms, R. 1989. "Isis in Classical Athens." *CJ* 84:216–221.

Simms, R. M. 1998. "The Phrearrhian *lex sacra*: An Interpretation." *Hesperia* 67:91–107.

Smith, J. O. 1996. "The High Priest of the Temple of Artemis at Ephesus." In Lane 1996:323–335.

Smith, M. F., ed. 1993. *Diogenes of Oinoanda: The Epicurean Inscription.* Naples.

———. 1996. "An Epicurean Priest from Apamea in Syria." *ZPE* 112:120–130.

———. 2003. *Supplement to Diogenes of Oinoanda, The Epicurean Inscription.* Naples.

Smith, N. D. 1989. "Diviners and Divination in Aristophanic Comedy." *ClAnt* 8:140–58.

Smith, R. R. R. 1991. *Hellenistic Sculpture*. Oxford.

Solin, H. 2002. "Analecta Epigraphica CIC–CCVI." *Arctos* 36:107–142.

Solin, H. 2003. *Die griechischen Personennamen in Rom*. Vol. 1 of *Ein Namenbuch*. 2nd ed. Berlin.

Solmsen, F. 1979. *Isis among the Greeks and Romans*. Cambridge, MA.

Sorabji, R., ed. 1997. *Aristotle and After*. London.

Sosin, J. 2005. "Unwelcome Dedications: Public Law and Private Religion in Hellenistic Laodicea by the Sea." *CQ* 55.1:130–139.

Sourvinou-Inwood, C. 1988. "Further Aspects of Polis Religion." *AASA* 10:259–274. Reprinted in Buxton 2000:38–55.

———. 1988a. *Studies in Girls' Transitions*. Athens.

Spiro, M. E. 1987. *Culture and Human Nature: Theoretical Papers of Melford E. Spiro*. Chicago.

Sporn, K. 2002. *Heiligtümer und Kulte Kretas in klassischer und hellenistischer Zeit*. Heidelberg.

Stadter, P. A., and Van der Stockt, L., eds. 2002. *Sage and Emperor: Plutarch, Greek Intellectuals, and Roman Power in the Time of Trajan (98–117 A.D.)*. Louvain.

Staffieri, G. 1978. *La monetazione di Olba nella Cilicia Trachea*. Lugano.

Stambaugh, J. E. 1972. *Sarapis under the Ptolemies*. Leiden.

Steinhart, M. 1997. "Die Darstellung der Praxiergidai im Ostfries des Parthenon." *AA*:475–478.

Stengel, P. 1910. *Opferbräuche der Griechen*. Leipzig.

———. 1920. *Die griechischen Kultusaltertümer*. 3rd ed. Munich.

Stephan, E. 2002. *Honoratioren, Griechen, Polisbürger: Kollektive Identitäten innerhalb der Oberschicht des kaiserzeitlichen Kleinasien*. Göttingen.

Stephens, S. A. 1994. "Who Read Ancient Novels?" In Tatum 1994:405–418.

Stewart, A. 1979. *Attika*. London.

———. 1990. *Greek Sculpture*. New Haven.

Stieber, M. 2004. *The Poetics of Appearance in the Attic Korai*. Austin.

Stier, H. E. 1929. "Stephanephoria." *RE* III A 2:2343–2347.

Stockinger, H. 1959. *Die Vorzeichen im homerischen Epos*. Munich.

Straten, F. T. 1995. *Hiera kala: Images of Animal Sacrifice in Archaic and Classical Greece*. Leiden.

Stravrianopoulou, E. 2006. *"Gruppenbild mit Dame": Untersuchungen zur rechtlichen und sozialen Stellung der Frau auf den Kykladen im Hellenismus und in der römischen Kaiserzeit*. Stuttgart.

Strelan, R. 1996. *Paul, Artemis, and the Jews in Ephesus*. Berlin.

Strubbe, J. H. M. 1991. "Cursed Be He That Moves My Bones." In Faraone and Obbink 1991:33–59.

Strubbe, J. 1997. APAI ΕΠΙΤΥΜΒΙΟΙ. *Imprecations against Desecrators of the Grave in the Greek Epitaphs of Asia Minor: A Catalogue*. Bonn.

Struck, P. T. 2003. "The Ordeal of Divine Sign: Divination and Manliness in Archaic and Classical Greece." In Rosen and Sluiter 2003:167–186.

Stucchi, S., ed. 1991. *Giornate in onore di A. Adriani*. Rome.

Suarez de la Torre, E. 1992. "Les Pouvoirs des devins et les récits mythique: L'example de Melampos." *Les Études Classiques* 60:3–21.

Sullivan, R. D. 1978. "Priesthoods of the Eastern Dynastic Aristocracy." In Şahin, Schwertheim, and Wagner 1978:914–939.

———. 1980. "The Dynasty of Cappadocia." In ANRW II 7.2:1125–1168.

Susemihl, F. 1891. *Geschichte der griechischen Litteratur in der Alexandrinerzeit*. Vol. 1. Leipzig.

Suys, V. 1998. "Déméter et le prytanée d'Éphèse." *Kernos* 11:173–188.

Swain, S. 1989. "Favorinus and Hadrian." *ZPE* 79:150–158.

———, ed. 1999. *Oxford Readings in the Greek Novel*. Oxford.

———. 1999a. "Defending Hellenism: Philostratus, *In Honour of Apollonius*." In Edwards et al. 1999:157–196.

Sweeney, J., ed. 1988. *The Human Figure in Early Greek Art, Ausstellungskatalog Washington D. C.* Athens.

Syme, R. 1968. "The Ummidii." *Historia* 17:72–105.

———. 1979. *Roman Papers*. Vol. 2. Oxford.

———. 1982. "The Career of Arrian." *HSCP* 86:181–211.

Szymanski, T. 1908. *Sacrificia Graecorum in bellis militaria*. Marburg.

Taeuber, H. 1992. "Eine Priesterin der Perasia in Mopsuhestia." *EA* 19:19–24.

Talamo, C. 1984. "Sull' Artemision di Efeso." *PP* 39:197–216.

Taplin, O. 1992. *Homeric Soundings: The Shaping of the Iliad*. Oxford.

Tatum, J., ed. 1994. *The Search for the Ancient Novel*. Baltimore.

Taylor, M. C. 1997. *Salamis and the Salaminioi: The History of an Unofficial Athenian Demos*. Amsterdam.

Teja, R. 1980. "Die römische Provinz Kappadokien in der Prinzipatszeit." In ANRW II 7.2:1083–1124.

Thomas, C. M. 1995. "At Home in the City of Artemis: Religion in the Literary Imagination of the Roman Period." In Koester 1995:82–117.

Thomas, R. 1989. *Oral Tradition and Written Record in Classical Athens*. Cambridge.

Thompson, D. 1990. "The High Priests of Memphis under Ptolemaic Rule." In Beard and North 1990:95–116.

Thompson, H. A. 1982. *Studies in Athenian Architecture, Sculpture and Topography presented to H. A. Thompson*. Princeton.

Thornton, A. 1970. *Peoples and Themes in Homer's Odyssey*. Dunedin.

Threatte, L. 1980. *Morphology*. Vol. 1 of *The Grammar of Attic Inscriptions*. Berlin.

Timpe, D. 2000. "Der Epikureismus in der römischen Gesellschaft der Kaiserzeit." In Erler 2000:42–63.

Tloka, J. 2003. "… dieser göttliche Mensch!" In Aland, Hahn, and Ronning 2003:71–85.

Todd Lee, B. 2005. *Apuleius' Florida: A Commentary*. Berlin.

Todisco, L. 1993. *Scultura greca des IV secolo*. Milan.

———. 1997. "L'immagine di Sye[ris]." *PP* 293:121–123.

Totti, M. 1985. *Ausgewählte Texte der Isis- und Sarapis-Religion*. Hildesheim.

Tougher, S., ed. 2002. *Eunuchs in Antiquity and Beyond*. London.

Tracy, S. V. 1990. *Attic Letter-Cutters of 229 to 86 B. C.* Berkeley.

———. 2003. *Athens and Macedon: Attic Letter-cutters of 300 to 229 B. C.* Berkeley.

Trampedach, K. 1999: "Teukros und die Teukriden: Zu Gründungslegende des Zeus-Olbios Heiligtums in Kilikien." *Olba* 2.1:94–110.

———. 2001. "Tempel und Großmacht: Olba in hellenistischer Zeit." In Jean 2001:269–288.

———. 2003. "Platons Unterscheidung der Mantik." In Piepenbrink 2003:52–66.

———. 2003a. *Politische Mantik: Studien zur Kommunikation über Götterzeichen und Orakel im klassischen Griechenland*. Unpublished Habilitationsschrift. Konstanz.

Trianti, I. 1998. "La statue 629 de l'Acropole et la tête Ma 2718 du Musée du Louvre." *MonPiot* 76:1–33.

Trombley, F. R. 1993. *Hellenic Religion and Christianization c. 370-529*. Vol. 1. Leiden.

Turcan, R. 2000. "Une Artémis d'Éphèse trouvée sur l'Aventin." *CRAI*:657–669.

Turner, J. A. 1983. *Hiereiai: Acquisition of Feminine Priesthoods in Ancient Greece*. Ann Arbor.

Ulf, C., and Rollinger, R., eds. 2002. *Geschlechter—Frauen—Fremde Ethnien in antiker Ethnographie, Theorie und Realität*. Innsbruck.

Ustinova, Y. 1992-1998. "Corybantism: The Nature and Role of an Ecstatic Cult in the Greek Polis." *Horos* 10–12:503–520.

van Berchem, D. 1980. "La gérousie d'Éphèse." *MH* 37:25–40.

van Bremen, R. 1996. *The Limits of Participation: Women and Civic Life in the Greek East in the Hellenistic and Roman Periods*. Amsterdam.

Vanderpool, E. 1982. *Studies in Attic Epigraphy, History and Topography Presented to Eugene Vanderpool*. Princeton.

Vansina, J. 1985. *Oral Tradition as History*. Madison.

Vanstiphout, H., ed. 1999. *All those Nations ...: Cultural Encounters within and with the Near East*. Groningen.

van Straten, F. T. 1976. "Daikates' Dream: A Votive Relief from Kos, and some other Kat'onar Dedications." *BABesch* 51:1–38.

———. 1995. *Hierà kalá: Images of Animal Sacrifice in Archaic and Classical Greece*. Leiden.

van Wees, Hans, ed. 2000. *War and Violence in Ancient Greece*. London.

Várhelyi, Z. 1997. "Representation of the 'Other': The Religion of the Egyptians in the Greek Novel." In Nemes and Németh 1997:89–114.

Varinlioğlu, E. 1989. "Eine Gruppe von Sühneinschriften aus dem Museum von Uşak." *EA* 13:37–50.

Vatin, C. 1970. "Notes d'épigraphie delphique." *BCH* 94:675–697.

Veligianni, C. 2001. "*Philos* und *philos*-Komposita in den griechischen Inschriften der Kaiserzeit." In Peachin 2001:63–80.

Verilhac, A. M., and Dagron, G. 1974. "Une nouvelle inscription du temple de Zeus à Diocésarée Uzuncaburç (Cilicie)." *REA* 76:237–242.

Versnel, H. S. 1990. *Ter Unus: Isis, Dionysos, Hermes. Three Studies in Henotheism*. Leiden.

———. 1991. "Beyond Cursing: The Appeal to Justice in Judicial Prayers." In Faraone and Obbink 1991: 60–106.

———. 1994. Πεπρημένος: The Cnidian Curse Tablets and Ordeal by Fire." In R. Hägg 1994:145–154.

Victor, U., ed. 1997. *Lukian von Samosata: Alexandros oder der Lügenprophet*. Religions in the Graeco-Roman World 132. Leiden.

Vidman, L. 1968. "Sarapispriester in Lindos." *LF* 91:31–38.

———. 1969. *Sylloge inscriptionum religionis Isiacae et Sarapiacae*. Berlin.

———. 1970. *Isis und Sarapis bei den Griechen und Römern: Epigraphische Studien zur Verbreitung und zu den Trägern des ägyptischen Kultes*. Berlin.

Vigourt, A., Loriot, X., Bérenger-Badel, A., and Klein, B., eds. 2006. *Pouvoir et religion dans le monde romain*. Paris.

Villanueva-Puig, M.-C. 1998. "Le cas du thias dionysiaque." *Ktèma* 23:365–374.

Virgilio, B. 1981. *Il 'Tempio Stato' di Pessinunte fra Pergamo e Roma nel II–I Secolo A.C.* Pisa.

———. 2003. *Studi ellenistici XV*. Pisa.

Vollkommer, R., ed. 2001. *Künstlerlexikon der Antike*. Vol 1. Munich.

von den Hoff, R. 2003. "Tradition and Innovation: Monuments and Images on the Early Hellenistic Acropolis." In Palagia 2003:173–185.

von Haehling, R., ed. 2005. *Griechische Mythologie und Frühchristentum.* Darmstadt.

von Heintze, H. 1993. "Athena Polias am Parthenon als Ergane, Hippia, Parthenos." *Gymnasium* 100:385–418.

von Wilamowitz-Moellendorff, U. 1886. *Isyllos von Epidauros.* Berlin.

———. 1927. *Das homerische Epos.* Berlin.

———. 1931. *Der Glaube der Hellenen.* Vol. 1. Berlin.

Vorster, C. 1983. *Griechische Kinderstatuen.* Cologne.

Voutiras, E. 1996. "Un culte domestique des Corybantes." *Kernos* 9:243–256.

———. 2005. "Sanctuaire privé—culte public? Le cas du Sarapieion de Thessalonique." In Dasen and Piérart 2005:273–288.

Wachsmuth, D. 1967. *POMPIMOS O DAIMON: Untersuchung zu den antiken Sakralhandlungen bei Seereisen.* Berlin.

Wachter, R. 2001. *Non-Attic Greek Vase Inscriptions.* Oxford.

Walker, S., and Cameron, A., eds. 1989. *The Greek Renaissance in the Roman Empire: Papers from the 10th British Museum Classical Colloquium.* London.

———. 1989. "Two Spartan Women and the Eleusinion." In Walker and Cameron 1989:130–141.

Warren, J. 2000. "Diogenes *Epikoureios*: Keep Taking the Tablets." *JHS* 120:144–148.

Weber, M. 1978. *Economy and Society: An Outline of Interpretative Sociology.* Ed. G. Roth and C. Wittich. Berkeley. (Translation of *Wirtschaft und Gesellschaft.*)

Wehner, B. 2000. *Die Funktion der Dialogstruktur in Epiktets Diatriben.* Stuttgart.

Weinreich, O. 1962. "Zum Verständnis des Werkes." In Heliodororus, *Aithiopika: Die Abenteuer der schönen Chariklea,* ed. R. Reymer, 219–259. Zurich.

Weir, R. 2004. *Roman Delphi and its Pythian Games.* Oxford.

Weiss, P. 1996. "Ein Priester im lydischen Philadelphia: Noch einmal zu einer Münzlegende." *EA* 26:145–148.

Welles, C. B. 1934. *Royal Correspondence in the Hellenistic Age.* New Haven.

———. 1963. "Hellenistic Tarsus." In Mouterde 1963:43–75.

Weniger, L. 1915. "Die Seher von Olympia." *Archiv für Religionswissenschaft* 18:53–115.

Wesenberg, B. 1995. "Panathenäische Peplosdedikation und Arrhephorie." *JDAI* 110:149–178.

West, M. L. 1997. *The East Face of Helikon: West Asiatic Elements in Greek Poetry and Myth.* Oxford.

Whitehead, D. 1986. *The Demes of Attica.* Princeton.

Whitmarsh, T. 1998. "The Birth of a Prodigy: Heliodorus and the Genealogy of Hellenism." In Hunter 1998:93–124.

Whittaker, J. 2000. "Gaius (G 2)." In Goulet 2000:437–440.

Wiemer, H.-U. 2003. "Käufliche Priestertümer im hellenistischen Kos." *Chiron* 33:263–310.

Wilson, P. 2000. *The Athenian Institution of Khoregia.* Cambridge.

Winkler, J. J. 1999. "The Mendacity of Kalasiris in the Aithiopika." In Swain 1999:286–350.

Witt, R. E. 1971. *Isis in the Graeco-Roman World.* London.

Woodhead, G. 1997. *Inscriptions: The Decrees; The Athenian Agora 16.* Princeton.

Woodward, A. M. 1927–1928. "Excavations at Sparta, 1924–28. II: The Inscriptions, Part I." *ABSA* 29:2–56.

Wörrle, M. 1988. *Stadt und Fest im kaiserzeitlichen Kleinasien: Studien zu einer agonistischen Stiftung aus Oinoanda.* Munich.

———. 1990. "Inschriften von Herakleia am Latmos II." *Chiron* 20:19–58.

Wörrle, M., and Zanker, P., eds., 1995. *Stadtbild und Bürgerbild im Hellenismus.* Munich.

Wright, D. P. 1987. *The Disposal of Impurity: Elimination Rites in the Bible and in Hittite and Mesopotamian Literature.* Atlanta.

Yunis, H. 2002. *Written Texts and the Rise of Literate Culture in Ancient Greece.* Cambridge.

Zevi, F. 1969/70. "Tre iscrizioni con firme di artisti greci." *RPAA* 42:95–116.

Ziegler, R. 2002. "Aspekte der Entwicklung tarsischer Kulte in hellenistischer und römischer Zeit." In Blum et al. 2002:363–379.

Ziehen, L. 1913. "Hiereis." *RE* VIII 2:1411–1424.

Zoumbaki, S. 1996. "Die Verbreitung der römischen Namen in Eleia." In Rizakis 1996:191–206.

Zwierlein, O. 1992. *Bacchides.* Vol. 4 of *Zur Kritik und Exegese des Plautus.* Mainz.

Index

This book was composed by Ivy Livingston
and manufactured by Edwards Brothers, Lillington, NC.

The typeface is Gentium, designed by Victor Gaultney
and distributed by SIL International.